We're Far Fae Hame Now!

Aberdeen and the North East's experience of military service abroad

The Great War to the Gulf

● Palestine: photo Walter Watt

Aberdeen and the North East's
experience of military service abroad

The Great War to the Gulf

● Spanish Civil War – Bob Cooney, centre.

Sunny Africa

Land of sunshine, glorious, gold,
Mosquitoes, flies and pests untold.
Moonlit skies jewelled by God's hand,
Dirt and dust, and burning sand.
City boulevards and shows,
Splendour hides the backs street's woes,
Of Arab hovels, ragged clothes,
And smells, that sully heaven high,
A smiling face, a living lie.

Fiction tells of Arab steeds,
Dark eyed-beauties, stirring deeds,
Arab sheiks, with fearsome mein,
Camels laden, desert train.
Nought is said of mules o'er-loaded,
Donkeys beaten, cursed and goaded,
Staggering in with piled up pack,
And lazy driver on his back.

Pictures bright show troops on leave,
In shorts so cool, and rolled-up sleeve,
With smiling maids, and ice cold drink,
In paradise, so one would think.
But what of men gone mad with wine,
Or packed in cattle trucks like swine.
Of bodies found all hacked and torn,
Their clothing now by Arabs worn.

Midst sham and lies, one thing is true,
The sea that glorious azure blue,
It washes off the dust and sweat,
And one emerges dripping wet,
Body clean, refreshed of mind,
All cares and troubles left behind,
Forgotten, like some dusty tome,
One's thoughts and love, go winging home.

C. Dewar,
CQMS, "HQ" Coy.
6 Gordons, B.N.A.F.

● Press and Journal headline
referring to the retreat of the BEF in
1940 and featuring Lord Forbes

● Hr.Ms. Maurits von Nassau (see B. Procee)

● The Fish troop in 1944

Dedication.

To those who fought,
To those who fell.

Introduction

On the 11th day and the 11th hour of the 11th month we commemorate those who lost their lives fighting for their country. This book marks this day by not only honouring those in the North East who made that sacrifice but also those who fought in any of the conflicts since 1914.

On this day of Armistice, we pay tribute to them with the publication of this book. Here remembered, are their dangerous adventures in the form of reminiscences, letters, photographs and writings. All are borne with that North East stoicism and humour epitomized in our title.

We're Far Fae Hame Now!

We salute them.

A Note on the Transcripts

The reminiscences within this publication have been transcribed as faithfully as possible with only minor alterations being made to retain the narrative flow.

To the best of our knowledge, all the relevant copyrights have been checked and permissions granted pertaining to the information and images contained in this book. Should any be outstanding, we apologise and corrections will be made in future editions.

● Bert Procee

● The Fish Troop
in 1990's

Contributors

David Adam	Jack Kilgour	Alec Ross
Miss Allan	Frank Ledingham	Ms Mackie
Bill Bain	George Leiper	George Martin
Lawrence Baldwin	John Londragon	Alexander Moir
Robbie Bremner	Charlie Low	Dougal Milne
Malcolm Chisholm	Albert MacIntosh	Ted Munro
George J Duguid	William J McHardy	Ernie Mundie
Colin Duncan	Major William	Bert Procee
Joyce Everill	MacHardy	Bill Proven
Mr Finlayson	Sandy McKenzie	K.F. Thomson
John Fowler	Alex McLeod	William Simpson
Lord Forbes	Gordon McRae	Sinclair Slater
Billy Henderson	Sammy Robertson	Walter Watt

● Jimmy Davidson - front right - at an airfield in Keil. The plane is a Blohm und Voss Bv 138 flying-boat, which has had its propellers removed apparently to prevent it from absconding

We're Far Fae Hame Now!

● contents

●1

First World War

"to the shouts
of "Raus! Raus!"
the survivors
were rounded up"

First World War

1914-18

*T*HE GREAT WAR BETWEEN THE ALLIED POWERS – *including the British Empire, France, Russia, Japan, Italy and America – and the Central Powers – including Germany, Austria-Hungary and Turkey, was fought in response to the fear of Germany's colonial ambitions after the defeat of France in the Franco-Prussian war. Sparked off by the assassination of Archduke Ferdinand, the heir to the Austro-Hungarian throne, on the 28th June 1914, Britain joined the fray upon Germany's invasion of Belgium at midnight on 4th August.*

The story of Pte. J W Forbes.
A Company 1/7th Gordon Highlanders.

William J McHardy: "Would you like to see my treasures?" my father-in-law would ask his children with a bit of a chuckle. "Oh yes!" they would reply and a well worn pocket book would be produced containing a note book, a few post cards, religious texts and assorted tattered and yellowing bits of paper. The interest was not so much in the items themselves but in the stories and anecdotes they stimulated. The pocket book and its contents were the 'souvenirs' of his experiences on the Western Front in the First World War. I knew I had been accepted into the family when I too, was asked if I'd like to see his treasures. I was fascinated by his tales and used to encourage them at every opportunity, whether the treasures were produced or not. His stories were not of heroics and glory which made them all the more credible and I often used to think that this material ought to be written down. I did nothing about it at the time apart from my noting a few names in an old diary. Now that I have started to put my recollections of his reminiscences on paper some 10 years after his death, I find myself with a long list of questions I wish I had asked.

When the war started, John (John Willum to his family) was 16 and employed as office boy to Alexander Ross at the Crombie woollen mill where his father was a Foreman in the Raising Department. Exactly when he joined the Gordon Highlanders I'm not sure but both he and his pal Heb Scott lied about their age when they enlisted. Heb would lose an arm in the conflict but survived

to run a well known sweetie shop in Woodside.

Basic training was at Ripon where his initiation into life in the army was a long march from the station to the camp in heavy snow. He remembered one chap being very distressed but being forced to carry on; he very nearly died. There was little sympathy from the authorities for those who were not equipped physically and mentally for the rigours of army life. Although access to live ammunition was strictly controlled, suicides were not uncommon. After basic training, John went on a course on signalling and as a result found himself posted to the front sooner than he should have been because of a shortage of signallers.

He remembered arriving in France at Letreport where he was assigned as batman to a Captain Merriless, who he described as a very nice man. Letreport had some sort of cable car or railway system to transport men and stores from the harbour area to the top of the cliffs where they proceeded to march towards the front along endless sunken roads. During this march to the front he was given a Lewis gun to carry. Being a small man he began to struggle with this thing when a fellow soldier, (a man called Clark I think) a stronger man with a lighter load, swapped loads with him, a memorable act of kindness.

As a signaller, his function was to follow behind advancing troops playing out wire from a reel. As such, he would have been protected to some extent from the worst of the defending machine gun fire but would have been a prime target for enemy snipers. He recalled casualties being very high among the 'rougher elements' of the Battalion

● Left: Courtesy S. Coppock

who were often chosen for no man's land patrols. When such patrols were out, his duty was to stand by the fire step awaiting their return or signal. On one occasion, a returning patrol, by way of a joke crept up on him and thrust round the corner at him the head of a German soldier, complete with helmet, stuck on the end of a bayonet. "What a scare I got!" he would say - something of an understatement I should think. Such is the brutalising effect of war.

Another incident that stuck in his mind occurred at an allied machine gun post under attack from three determined German soldiers. They were big strong men, seemingly seven feet tall and in spite of being hit many times still they came on. At last they fell some yards short of their objective but for a few moments it had seemed they were indestructible. It was not all brutality. He remembered during one of their rest periods Andy Stopper sitting on a box in the middle of a hut playing a wistful tune of home on his chanter. Soon the men had gathered round and spontaneously began to sing along, many with tears in their eyes. Andy's two brothers had already been killed and Andy himself was killed in action on 20th of November 1917.

He witnessed the arrival of the first tanks on the battlefield and their subsequent floundering in the mud and shell craters. At one point where a German position had been over-run he marvelled at how much better engineered the German trenches were - deeper, drier, roomier, almost luxurious in comparison with what he had been used to. The larders were also very well stocked but unfortunately they were not allowed to touch any of it in case of booby traps.

One of his 'treasures' is a small tatty piece of card with the simple hand written message, 'With best wishes for a merry Christmas. H Williams.' This is a memento of some time he spent in hospital in

● Courtesy S.Coppock

CAMPAGNE 1914-1917

'ALBERT (Somme). — Fabrique en ruines.
The ruins of a factory.

France after tearing his leg badly on barbed wire. Which Christmas it was I'm not sure. I think 1917 although it might have been 1916. H. Williams was an American nurse at the hospital, who was very popular with the patients. Every man got a card and a small gift. (I forget if it was money or chocolate.) It was very much appreciated and a great morale booster.

Many of his most vivid memories are of the last six months, which he spent as a prisoner of war. His group had been pulled out of the line for a rest period where they had the comparative luxury of sleeping in huts. They had passed on the way a detachment of the Black Watch who were moving up to take their place. Banter was exchanged, the Black Watch telling them how lucky they were because a German attack was widely expected. Sure enough, the German artillery opened up in the early hours of next morning but concentrating initially on the rear positions which included the huts housing John's company. There was great panic and confusion as shrapnel ripped through the wooden huts. Some men fled completely naked. John and another, also called Forbes, leapt into a crater just as another shell burst. John found himself covered with blood but it was that of his companion who had been mortally wounded. When the barrage died down they could see columns of German troops passing by in the distance. Eventual capture was inevitable.

Eventually, to the shouts of "Raus! Raus!" the survivors were rounded up and taken to a camp at Denain in northern France. I'd read that the Germans took about 90,000 prisoners during their offensive of 21st - 28th of March 1918 so it is not surprising that food for the prisoners was going to be scarce. The daily diet seemed to consist of one plate of watery soup, which the men referred to as 'Soor Krap', probably a corruption of sauerkraut. Dysentery was also a great problem.

Life as a prisoner became very much a battle for survival. On the whole, the younger men adapted better to the conditions and maintained the will to live which was important. Some of the older men gave up hope, despaired and just faded away. He was fortunate in that his closest friend during the period of captivity turned out to be a real expert at scavenging, eyes always looking down searching for possible tit-bits. The pair attempted an escape once by mingling with some refugees. Fortunately, they were picked up before getting too far. They had been walking towards Germany! Working parties were formed from the prisoners and they were set to repairing roads and drains. Initially, there was some advantage in these work parties

> " one of the older friendlier guards they called 'Papa' obliged with a light and the bits of putrid mule were duly boiled "

● German prisoner
courtesy S.Coppock

because local women would secrete bits of food for them under their dust-bin lids. However, the guards quickly cottoned on to this practice and put a stop to it. One day, while on such a work detail, the whiff of decaying flesh was detected. One of the party, who had been a butcher in Aberdeen, (his name might have been Knowles) watched his chance and managed to slip away unnoticed and locate the source of the smell which was a dead mule. With his knife he cut out a sizeable chunk of meat. Slipping back into the working party the piece of flesh was further cut up so that individuals could smuggle it back into camp under their tunics. On their way back to camp the guards were obviously puzzled by the terrible smell that their charges seemed to have acquired but probably thought it was too revolting to investigate too closely. Once back in the camp one of the older friendlier guards they called 'Papa' obliged with a light and the bits of putrid mule were duly boiled. In spite of its condition and the fact that it was incredibly tough there was much clamouring for a share. Some of the men who took part became even more ill and were taken away, presumably to hospital, and were never seen again.

The attitudes of the guards varied. Some of the older men, like 'Papa', were quite kindly while the younger men tended to be less sympathetic and could be quite vicious. On one occasion when John presented himself to what passed for a medical station within the camp with a badly poisoned finger the reaction of the guard on duty was to bang it as hard as he could with his

knuckles. The pain was excruciating but John was excused work detail for a few days. On another work party occasion one of these younger guards began to rain blows on a prisoner who had incurred his displeasure. Open flew the door of a nearby hut and out charged a German Officer with half his face covered in shaving soap. He had seen what was happening and was outraged at this barbarous treatment of a prisoner of war. He tongue lashed the guard in no uncertain terms and then told the prisoners that he had a brother who was a prisoner in Scotland and that he had heard that he was being very well treated. He would see to it personally that that particular guard was sent back to the front. The Guard was never seen again.

They were moved several times during their captivity. Initially they were at Denain in the North of France close to the Belgian border. Then he spoke of 'Proovie' (the spelling maybe wrong but that's how it sounded) and one fellow prisoner, Frank Steven, who he used to meet in the street from time to time long after the war always greeted him with the remark, "Do you ever wish you were back in Proovie?"

At one time they were housed in what had been a school where they slept on tiered bunks. The dilemma was whether it was better to be on the upper or lower level. In the lower bunk you had easier access to the toilet, important if suffering from dysentery. However, the danger was that the man above you might lose control before he could get down. The guards at this location became very annoyed at the filthy state the latrines got into but there was nothing the men could do about it and eventually they were moved.

When armistice came there was no liberation as such. Although there had been rumours that war was about to end there was no official announcement made to the prisoners. Suddenly, the guards had all disappeared and the gates of the camp were open. Some French prisoners from a nearby camp walked past and shouted to them, "Come on Tommy, the war is over!"

They set off in groups following the French, John his pal and a third man making up a group of three. Soon word was passed back to keep away from the railway line because returning German soldiers were sitting on top of the carriages taking pot shots at anything that moved. Whether this was true or not he didn't know but they kept well away from the railway just in case.

Eventually, John and his two companions came to a small village. I once asked him how long this trek had taken but he was a bit vague. In any event they must have looked terrible, vermin ridden, dirty and clothes all tattered. On one foot John wore the remains of an army boot, on the other, a Dutch clog. They paused at the window of a little shop where some cakes were on display. They were gazing longingly at these things when a girl came out of the shop and gave them the cakes. Then she took them across the road to an innkeeper who let them sleep in an outhouse and then directed them next morning to the next town where he assured them arrangements had been made to receive returning prisoners of war.

When they arrived at this town - a mining town where the shower facilities had been made available to the men - they thought they had happened on a fancy dress party. The good citizens of the town had been told that if they would provide food, clothing and lodging to these men until such time as transport could be arranged then they would be generously compensated by the allied authorities. Accordingly they had raked out their old clothes - a selection of fashions from the previous century! Some men were kitted out with top hats and frock coats. John and his two companions were taken in by a Mr Andre Mathelot, 74 Rue Alphonse, Dargent, Flemalle Haute, a town near Liege. This gentleman and his family treated their lodgers kindly except that he would insist on locking them into their attic bedroom at night. (He had three daughters). This was rather inconvenient considering the state of their health. The third member of the group solved the problem by using the tin dish they had all been issued with, opening the skylight and tipping the contents down the roof. However, it was not long before Mr Mathelot noticed the brown stain on his roof and was not at all amused. He insisted the offender be removed from his house and billeted elsewhere. John and his pal never saw him again. How long they stayed at Flemalle Haute, he couldn't really remember. It may have been a couple of weeks.

Eventually, a train was laid on and they began the journey home. His first meal back in the tender care of the British army was a boiled egg, which turned out to be rotten! Back in Britain he was hospitalised in the King George Hospital in London. One of the fragile pieces of paper in his pocket book indicated that he was released from hospital on the 16th of December 1918 on a two month furlough. He was supposed to report back before tattoo at the 16th of February 1918 to the 4th Battalion Dreghorn camp Colinton and also among his papers is a railway warrant for the journey. He never did go back, Alexander Ross interceding on his behalf apparently.

When he arrived at Aberdeen station it seemed that every returning soldier had relatives to greet them - except him. Apparently, his family had been meeting every train for several days, but this one they had missed. He caught the tram to Woodside and on his way up Pirie's Lane he met a boy coming in the opposite direction. "Ernest?" he asked. "John Willum." his brother replied and promptly burst into tears.

Early on in their captivity while still at Denain, they were informed that they could write home and were given instructions as to how to go about it. In his notebook are the faded notes and diagrams of how the envelope should be addressed. The notes state that, 'no man can make a statement as to where he is. One parcel weighing 10 pounds per month. Money to the value of 800 Marks monthly. Information as to forwarding will be obtained from the Post Office. The notepapers must be headed as on the front of the envelope and end as on the envelope with senders name and Company' etc. Presumably the German authorities were hoping these letters home would result in food parcels being sent. John didn't write, perhaps being suspicious of the German motives but many of the men did, often using family photographs printed on post-cards to do so. The post-cards and letters were duly collected but whether by accident or design they were never dispatched. Some time later when preparing to move camp, the prisoners came across a heap of them where they had been unceremoni-ously dumped among some rubbish behind a hut. Rummaging through the pile John retrieved two of local interest and stuck them into his pocket book, where they still remain - perhaps the most poignant of his 'treasures'.

MONEY FOR NOWT.

● Courtesy S.Coppock

He didn't know the men who had written the cards and I remember asking him why he hadn't delivered them once he got home. He had obviously given the matter a lot of thought at the time and concluded that if the men had got home safely, then all was well - the letters were redundant. If the men hadn't come back, then introducing these cards would only have added to the misery of the grieving families.

The difference in tone between the messages is quite remarkable. The one from William Freeland wastes no time with pleasantries but launches straight into a shopping list. He makes no attempt to hide the fact that he is not at all happy with the situation he finds himself in. On the other hand George Murdoch's message to his mother in Stonehaven is one of re-assurance that he is keeping well and getting on fine - almost as though he was on holiday. He asks for nothing.

Photograph portrait of a child approximately six months, propped up in the corner of a settee. The photograph is embossed with the photographers stamp: Ledingham, Rosemount, Aberdeen.

Mrs Freeland c/o Murison
17, Bannermill Road
Aberdeen, Scotland

Mrs.Freeland,

Dear Mary,
Kindly ask Elsie and Maggie to help you make up a parcel. Any kind of tinned meat, mealy puddings, oatcakes, chocolate, cheese, writing pad, soap, hankies, all are sorely needed. Take card over to 139 and show them, for you will all understand how much we now depend on the dear folks at home. Don't forget the cigs Mary, as we can't get a smoke. Willie Collie will give you a box to send. Hope you are all well.

From Will.
201,749, 4th Gordons,
Kriegsgefangenen,
Sammellager,
Denain.

Photograph of two girls, 3 – 4 years old, sisters and possibly twins.

Mrs Murdoch
Stonehaven
Kincardineshire
Scotland
15/4/18

Dear Mother,
Just a P.C. to let you know that I am always keeping well and getting on fine. I hope father and you are both well and not worrying about me. Don't write to me yet as this is only a temporary address. I will write and give you the correct address when once I am settled down, but don't be surprised if this takes some time yet.

Love George.
1134 L/C Geo. Murdoch.
1/7th Gordon Highlanders,
Kriegegefangenan - Komp,
Sammellager,
Denain.

● (top of page) The two postcards that John Forbes found and kept in his pocket book.

Spanish Civil War

"any man who has ever been in war an' who sez he's never been afraid is either an ignoramus or an idiot"

Spanish Civil War 1936

OPPOSITION TO THE ELECTED REPUBLICAN GOVERNMENT *spread throughout the garrisons of Spain and on the 19th of July 1936 a state of war was declared by a group of conspirators. The Republic sought a compromise but failed and violence erupted. In places where the security forces sided with the Government and in towns where the proletarian forces were strong, the rising was defeated – in Madrid, Barcelona and in the Basque Provinces - the Nationalists retained Navarre. This initial reaction to the uprising accelerated into a spontaneous revolution. By the end of September the Nationalists elevated General Franco to the position of their supreme commander and thus began the civil war.*

Both sides were short of arms and each appealed to foreign allies for support with varying degrees of success. In its confusion, the war emerged as a conflict between the Church, the Military and the Spanish bourgeois on the one hand, and the working class on the other. Consequently, the Soviet Union aided the Republicans organisationally and materially. Whilst the Germans and Italians supported Franco with equipment and an expeditionary force. The Soviet brokered International Brigades first went into action in November, 1936.

John Londragon left Aberdeen with 18 others to fight a war against Fascism and for the rights of the under-class.

John Londragon: This flag here was used t' bury three o' we comrades from Aberdeen, in Spain. All that dirty marks, - see the marks here an' that - it's not been washed, that's blood. That's the blood off the casualties. We wrapped it up and sent it back here and the Anti Fascist Committee in Aberdeen got it and sewed that banner on to it across here (indicating). It disappeared for 40 years until 1985. We were moving premises and it had fallen doon the back o' the cupboard.

Bill Tinto: Where were the premises?

● The flag used to bury International Brigade volunteers from Aberdeen

John: Urquhart Road. It was found behind a cupboard there and we found it after all those years.

David: Which group had it?

John: The Communist Party.

David: How many people went across t' Spain? (From Aberdeen.)

John: Nineteen. Five were killed.

David: Why did you go?

John: Well things got so bad with unemployment, housin' an' all the rest o' it and people had reached a point where they couldn't go back any further an' they started commin' forward but in their effort t' fight back against unemployment, bad housin' they became more politically conscious of events that were takin' place. Simultaneously we had the threat of the rise of Fascism in Germany. It was there already in Italy but it wasn't seen as such a danger. But in Germany in 1931 after Hitler became the Führer in Germany they started head huntin'. Now the first concentration camps in Germany were not for the Jewish people they were for the political leaders of any form of opposition that existed in Germany. They were the first inmates of the concentration camps. Many of them were murdered in these camps there. Fascism got such a name, it got through in the form of newsreels and the newspapers at that particular time and was educating the people as to what was happening in Germany. The people had a distaste for it, what was happening in Germany but it wasn't on their doorstep and it wasn't until 1932 the emergence of the British Union of Fascists in this country here. That was a different kettle o' fish altogether when Fascism actually came into this country here and people had to face up to the fact that there was a Fascist party in this country here.

The first thing that Oswald Mosely did was to take advantage of the unemployment situation, of the bad housin' and of all the bad conditions an' the fact that the people were so dispirited in many things, he wanted to bring them out on his side and he tried to use the Jewish people even in this country here for pogrom purposes in trying to blame them for all these conditions which was absolute rubbish of course. To do this he started marches through the Jewish quarters in London. A similar thing happened here in Aberdeen although the Jewish question didn't come intil it in Aberdeen but nevertheless, the mere fact that their party was tainted with this was enough for the people in Aberdeen to fight against them. So prior t' the Spanish Civil War, the people already had almost four years of fightin' against Fascism in this country. We had three very hectic years here in Aberdeen from 1933 to 1936 in particular and on to 1937 in which we fought Fascism here in Aberdeen. Our reaction to fascism was shown in two ways. There was the active participation of the political parties trying to stamp out Fascism. The party who was giving the lead

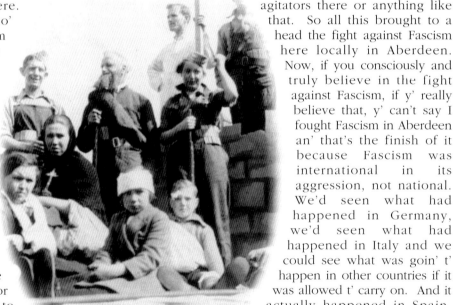

● © Imperial War Museum

was the Communist party at that particular time but the people themselves were becoming involved. In these days we didn't have the buses we have today we had tramcars, a conductor and a driver on a tramcar. And all the tramcars with the exception of one in the Woodside area all came to the Castlegate, t' the roundabout to start on their journey again. This was a tremendous benefit to us because it was a form of communication that we ourselves couldna put into operation. It happened accidentally but it was taken advantage of. There was a meetin' taking place out in Woodside and a conductor saw this Fascist meetin' taking place and he phoned back t' the Castlegate and told them that the Fascists were startin' a meetin' at Woodside there and everybody piled on to the tramcars there, went out t' Woodside an' broke up the meetin'. Now this happened many times all over Aberdeen, and the people got involved in it. It wasn't just the Communist Party or the Independent Labour Party, the ordinary people themselves got involved in it. Even when there were no political agitators there or anything like that. So all this brought to a head the fight against Fascism here locally in Aberdeen. Now, if you consciously and truly believe in the fight against Fascism, if y' really believe that, y' can't say I fought Fascism in Aberdeen an' that's the finish of it because Fascism was international in its aggression, not national. We'd seen what had happened in Germany, we'd seen what had happened in Italy and we could see what was goin' t' happen in other countries if it was allowed t' carry on. And it actually happened in Spain. When the fight started in Spain there was only one thing that we could do. It was an individual choice, it was either stop here and say, right I'm doing my bit here, well and good they were doin' their bit in this country here and they did stop Fascism in this country here but some of us thought there was a danger in not helping the Spanish people to fight Fascism there otherwise it woulda meant that France which at that particular time was a democracy, (although it had certain Fascist elements in it as we found out in the Second World War) but nevertheless it was a democracy there and there was always the chance that Germany on one side and a fascist Spain on the other would be able to stifle any democratic procedures comin' from France itself. There was a tremendous danger here that the whole of Europe could go fascist even without a war takin' place. This was the political outlook of it. And this is the reason we went to Spain.

In June 1936, wir first intimation of what was happenin' came in the form of a boat which arrived here in Aberdeen. It was a Spanish cargo boat. *'Eola'* was the name of it. There was about 16 sailors o' a crew on it and they went on strike because the Republican government which was elected in Spain in February 1936 had promised an increase in wages. This increase had not been paid and the crew had said that they werena goin' any further until such time that we get wer increase in wages.

So they were stuck here for nearly 10 days. In the process o' doin' so we, as members o' the Communist Party, along with the members of the Seamen's Union went doon to see if we could help the Spanish seamen. They were gettin' no money, very little food so we used t' take them oot in groups and take 'em round in Aberdeen, entertain them and keep 'em occupied and so forth. But before the war started they got an agreement from the skipper that the owners would pay them their increase in wages. So the ship sailed away. This was the first contact we had with Spain. It wasn't long after this that the war broke out in Spain. My contact with the sailors down there and the conditions they had, plus the fact that I knew what was happening in Germany and what was happening with the British Union of Fascists in wer own country here. To me there was only one choice, the choice was to go t' Spain an' do something about it. Try and stop it at the root because if Germany could have been defeated in Spain, the Second World War might never have taken place. He might have drawn back from the fact because now there was an alliance taking place between France and Britain; we tried t' stop him before the war actually started, instead of which, what happened was, instead o' doing that they pandered to Hitler and to Mussolini and handed out territories they had no control over, that didn't even belong to them; Poland and so forth.

One day talkin' t' Bob Cooney who was the local party organiser in Aberdeen here and I mentioned that I would like t' go t' Spain and asked him to make enquiries. So he came back two or three days later an' he sez, "I've got word from Glasgow an' it's OK y' can go." He got the sanction of the Party t' let me go. Some of the comrades in the

> ❝ **if Germany could have been defeated in Spain, the Second World War might never have taken place** ❞

party were very active here and were needed for the work takin' place here in Aberdeen. But anyhow, I was cleared as regards that. Bob sez, "Not only that, I'm commin' with y' as well". We set off the two of us down t' Glasgow there an' Bob sez, "One thing t' do before we carry on. I'll have to go and report up to party headquarters." So he went up to party headquarters and I went along with him. Peter Kerrigen and some other comrades who were within the executive were there and when Bob said he was on his way t' Spain they said, "No, y' can't go". They wouldn't let him go because he was far too valuable here. So poor Bob was turned back. He was broken hearted about it but eventually they did allow him over. I carried on down t' London and when I arrived in London I made my way to the Spanish aid committee and I told 'em what I wanted t' do and they agreed to help me because they had taken up collections and money and all the rest o' it and they were the ones who would give us the money not the Communist Party or anybody else but the Spanish Aid Committee. They gave me four pounds t' get to the ferry at Dover and over to France there. I'll always remember that 'cause it was a stormy sorta evenin' when we left and I was seasick just goin' over on the ferry, not that I was much of a sailor anyhow. Included with me were 11 young lads who were goin' to join the International Brigades also. So we made a group of about 11 or 12 of us with me bein' the only one from Aberdeen. I was the first one over as a matter of fact.

We arrived in France, took a train t' Paris and we were told t' make our way to the trades union head quarters. I had an address an' that and I had a glance at the map before I left to find out where the trades union headquarters were. Anyhow, we managed t' get lost as usual so we wondered about for half an hour and not being able t' speak French it was very difficult an' that. I said t' the lads at the finish, "Well there is only one thing to do, sit doon there an' I'll go out and have a look round about and try and pin-point where we were. So, they sat down at the café an' that there and away I goes. Coincidence again; I'm walkin' along one street and there was a figure walkin' down the other side and I said t' m'self, I recognise that figure, it was a woman and it was Charlotte Haldane. Professor Haldane's wife, she was the chairman of the Spanish Aid Committee for Britain and I'd seen her up here. I never new her personally but I'd seen her an' so forth. So I give her a shout an' she come over and she apologised 'cause she was the one that was supposed to meet us but she had been delayed at the French T.U.C headquarters. So, we were taken up there to the French T.U.C. Headquarters and we stayed there in Paris for about eight days. Be this time brigaders from all over the world were pourin' in. There musta been nearly a thousand and we were all billeted in what was known as the 'Red Quarter'. Now the Red Quarter in Paris was a Communist area. It was like a small city within a city. All the families living there were Communists and they put us up an' that, food, sleepin' accommodation and so forth while we were there. Then we had t' report back at a certain time, the different groups and my group reported back and they told us that we would be on a train that night t' go down t' Lyon. That evening we got word to go and we were on the way to Lyon. We were told that French men don't act in the same way that we do. When they meet each other in the street they always shake hands. This was completely foreign to us 'cause we would normally say, "Hello Jock" or as the case maybe but to stand up and shake hands as though y' hadn't seen them for about 20 years was absolutely foreign an' that. The more we tried to become foreign the more obvious we became! We were told to walk in groups of two and three but in these groups we looked like a small army marchin' down the street. It just got ridiculous! In France at that particular time there were those who were pro Franco and those who were anti Fascist. It applied to the police and everything else. If you were lucky you'd bump into the right policeman and he'd close his eyes and let things go but the next one might stop y'. This happened to a number of comrades who went over to France. Anyhow, we arrived in Lyon and we got off the train and we were met there by a Frenchman and he told us that the next thing that we were going t' do was to go down to Perpignan right down in the South. So, onto the lorries from Lyon, I don't know why we didn't get a train all the way down, I always wondered about that but anyhow there were about 30 of us by this time. There was my group and another group that joined us and we went on t' Perpignan. Then they said, "We are going to take you down to the border and we are going to hand you over to a Spanish guide and he'll take you over the Pyrenees. Now at this particular time the border was closed. They closed the border two or three times but they finally closed the border at the end a March, April. But sometimes the border was open and you could g' right through but at this time the border was closed so we couldna get through unless we went over the mountains. So when we arrived at Perpignan of all the things that came t' meet us in the form o' transport was a fleet of taxis! They packed us into taxis and down to

> ## "There musta been four, five hundred o' us at least on the train"

the border there. The French guide who was with us told us that before we get to the border proper there were some small bridges to cross and it was dangerous. He advised us t' take off our shoes so there wouldn't be any noise. We all wore boots at that time there was none o' the fancy shoes they have nowadays. We just wore boots, a thin jacket, a cap and so forth. So, some of us took off our boots to go over this wooden bridge an that so as not to make a noise 'cause there were French republican police an' that patrolling the area. There was no sense in makin' it obvious, they may not have been friendly. Anyhow we crossed over and the thing was that one or two of them had lost their shoes in the process of doing that. Now there were bloody mountains in front of us and it would obviously be a problem. Anyway, we arrived at the bottom of the Pyrenees and the Spanish guide emerged. He didn't speak a word of English but the French guide told us in English to do what the Spanish guide told us. Anyway, the Spanish guide inspects us and spots two of the boys without boots. He made them take off their jackets rip them up and wrap them round their feet. When we were ready our guide points the way. He leads and we were to follow. If you don't keep up it's just too bad he doesn't stop he just carries on mile after mile after mile over the Pyrenees. Believe me when y' climb the Pyrenees y' don't just climb a mountain y' climb a mountain then a mountain and a mountain! Because every one y' climb there's another bugger in front o' it! Most of us were young and fit, I was fit enough so it didn't bother me much but one or two o' them were very bad, as a matter of fact one or two of them died. They weren't in my group but in other groups that I heard about later. They died in the Pyrenees from exposure an' that and were particularly unfit for the job. As in any tense situation you come across, it'll always stay in my mind, comin' over that last hill at about six in the morning with the sun coming up behind us. Down we go down to the farmyard there an' got a cuppa coffee and a piece o' crusty bread. We were there for about two hours, they musta sent word down t' the garrison. It was an old Spanish Napoleonic fortress. The walls were about 18 feet thick. When we left Britain it was Spring, it was still cold, rainy and miserable. Here in Spain it was such a contrast that the sweat started pouring off us. Well, we arrive down t' this fortress and the contrast was that when you were outside you were sweatin', it was so hot but in the fort it was as cool as anything. We stayed for two days where we had a Captain of the International Brigade who belonged to the 11th brigade which was the Czechoslovakians and the Romanians. Now he was a tremendous lad this

Captain. He spoke six or seven languages. There were Americans with us, Germans and all the rest o' it and we used t' get up in the mornin' and he asked us to parade in the different divisions. That is the British Battalion on one side along with the Americans and the Germans, Czechoslovakians and the Polish an' all the rest o' it. All these different groups were there and he'd speak to them in their own language. He was really good telling them the events of that particular day and what they were going to do and what was going to happen in the near future. I saw him on the first day I landed in Spain and I saw him on the day I left Spain 'cause he was in charge of the transport. So he took us in an' he took us out. He told us that we would be leavin' for Albacete which was the headquarters for recordin' all the International Brigaders comin' in. He explained in all the different languages, "Anybody with any military service step forward." And I, along with some of the others stepped forward. He said, "I'm relyin' on you t' give the others a bit o' military discipline. I want you t' get them into columns o' three, (The Spanish marched in columns of three) and march 'em backwards and forwards and try t' get some discipline into them." So we did this for half the day then we had a rest. Well that's by the way, the next day we got on to a train to go down to Albacete.

There musta been four, five hundred o' us at least on the train, a special military train, so, the first stop we come to was Barcelona and we arrived in time for an air raid. Now this was the first time I'd seen an air-raid and it was the first time that an air-raid was seen t' be a deliberate act of warfare on a civilian population. It was the first time that it was seen by us. There were people runnin' about the streets they didna know what the hell was happenin' with the bombs rainin' down an' that. We wanted t' help an' that but they wouldn't let us. They told us that we had a job t' do, so, back on the trains an' away. So we left the poor devils in Barcelona t' clean up the mess that was left there. So we arrived at Albacete and they took us t' the bullring. There was no such thing as bullfightin' durin' the war but the bullring was used as a parade ground. They marched us in there and allocated us to the different groups, British, American and the other different groups. They checked up on all the names and addresses and so forth. From that point onwards, there were four International Brigades. There were the 11th, 12th, 13th, 14th at that time and this was the first time that they had created a new brigade, the 15th International Brigade. This was to include all the English speaking people there. The British

● Bomb damage to Barcelona © Imperial War Museum

speakin' brigaders were already there and were what was known as 'Centurias'. Centurias was an old Roman column y' know and they were spread throughout the other four brigades but the difficulty was language, always language, difficulty gettin' enough interpreters with so few people speakin' different languages so they decided to create an English speakin' brigade. And that was the 15th International Brigade. That included the British, the Americans, all the South Americans who had a smattering of English. They were a great help to us because they could speak Spanish as well, as interpreters an' so forth. They allocated different trainin' areas. The Americans, they went up to a place called Tarazona up north and we went to Madrigueras about eight miles outside Albacete as a trainin' area. When we arrived there the first one t' meet us was Lieutenant Dunbar. He'd been wounded at Jarama in the very early fights. He was just out of hospital so they had sent him down t' Madrigueras t' take charge of the new groups comin' in.

———————

We didna know at this particular time we thought we were goin to the British Battalion which was newly formed but no, what happened was that unknown to us the Russian anti-tank guns were arrivin' in Barcelona and they decided to make up an anti-tank crew from the recruits that they had from that day. My group was called on and they were formed into the anti-tank battery under Lieutenant Dunbar. The next thing was that we did a bit o' trainin' out there of an elementary kind because as it was we only had about two rifles. The one rifle was French and the other was a British 303 rifle. Even the ammunition was mixed it was really terrible the condition they were in. Well, we did the trainin' and then they called three of us t' go down t' Barcelona and pick up the guns. So we set off with the lorries and into Barcelona there and this is where I first met 'Potato Jones'. Potato Jones was a sea fairin' Captain and he had a tremendous knowledge of the Mediterranean because he got his name by ferryin' potatoes from Spain up to Italy and then from Italy back to Spain! Economically, I don't know how it worked, but he got his name 'Potato Jones' because he always seemed to be carryin' potatoes. He was very sympathetic to the Spanish Republican government maybe for business reasons but nevertheless he was one of those who continually bust the blockade all the time. He was taking the guns in and we got three anti-tank guns, hitched 'em on to the back of the lorries and back t' Madrigueras where we had set up our unit. Then we started trainin' an' the first obstacle that we'd never foreseen. When we were usin' the sights we came across the fact that the sights were calibrated in metres. We didna understand a thing about metres so we spent a considerable amount o' time, - an' luckily, one o' the members o' the battery was a student, an undergraduate so he started a conversion an' that convertin' them back into yards an' so forth.

———————

So, we started trainin' on the guns for a while. Dummy runs an that. No live ammunition or anything, just dummy runs. Then we got our first supply of live ammunition. I always remember the lorry that arrived with all the ammunition. The shells an that were all in shell case boxes - wooden boxes - we took 'em doon. The detonators were separate; the detonators were in small black boxes an' y' needed a tin opener t' open 'em. The instructions in Russian, said that it was important t' watch the heat, the temperature for the detonators - y' screwed the detonators on t' the nose o' the shell. So, we were lucky, we were careless, we got away without any damage an' that y' know. So we put on the

● British volunteers in the International Brigade: middle row, far left is Archie Dewar from Aberdeen

● British International Brigade volunteers stringing up an effigy of Franco. © Imperial War Museum

detonators an' started firin' an' so forth. An' after that, we got on not too bad. So after about a week o' practicin' an that there a few o' that we started. My job was t' sight the gun an' fire it. Well they said, "We are goin' t' tek y' up t' the test firin' range against targets." So up we goes to the test firin' range. They had great big cardboard cut-outs o' tanks on a rope and they travelled from one end o' the valley and travelled right across t' the other end o' the valley. There was maybe 40 or 50 feet between the cut-outs and our job was to fire on these cut-outs. Of the four tanks that we were allocated we got three o' them. I don't know what happened to the fourth one, I haven't got a clue at all. But any how we got three o' em an' that, a tank's not a small thing particularly when you're lookin' through the sight but it's a different thing lookin' through the barrel o' the gun it self.

One of the people that was there was a French revolutionary. He was the Political Commissar of the International Brigades. I forget his name now but he was a great revolutionary. Perhaps I should tell you a bit about the Political Commissars of the different units. A Political Commissar was exactly the same as a Welfare Officer in the British army and they had them in all the units - a Welfare Officer. The difference was this, that his job was not only to look after his men, that they received their letters or parcels but he also was t' give us a talk on what was happenin' because all we ever saw when we were at war was the little bit at the front that you were fightin' in. Y' didn't see the rest; the rest could just be rumours y' know. But his job was t' tell us exactly what was happenin' at other parts of the front and so forth and how the Republican Army as a whole was gettin' on. An' this was his job. Also though, the military commander of the unit, Lieutenant Dunbar for example, would never go into action until he had consulted the Political Commissar as regards the condition that the men were in both mentally an' physically. On that depended the success or failure of the mission. This applied to all the units so he played a very important part in working with the military commander by expressin' the feelin' and thoughts of the men. Sometimes y' got one hell of a hidin' over there an' that an' yer nae feelin' like goin back in again. Anyhow, we went up to the ranges an' that and we passed our training - at least we were told that we had passed and that was the finish o' that.

We pulled the guns out and went away for a rest for a couple o' days. Then they sez, "Alright, this is y' first test o' it. Up t' Jarama." That was our first battle. Now the early battles of Jarama were horrendous and the British Battalion got a hell o' a beatin' that day. When we went up there we got a hidin' also but not quite as bad as in the early days. Anyhow, Jarama consisted of small hills in which it looked like a landscape of the First World War. There were throwbacks from the First World War which still existed in the early days of the Spanish

● Fighting in the Spanish Civil War
© Imperial War Museum

Civil War, - trench warfare, bomb craters, shell craters and everything all round about half filled with water and the rest o' it. Luckily enough, where we were it was very sandy ground so that any water that was there used t' drain away very quickly so we weren't too bad as regards that. So we stayed in Jarama for about a fortnight fightin' an that and we got our first casualty there, George Murray from Edinburgh who was the first one that got wounded. He got wounded in the chest, he wasna killed, in fact he was still alive in 1992.

The first thing that I fired at was, an enemy trench - the trenches were built at an angle, in a steep line so that incomin' fire could be controlled. And I used t' tek the apex where the trenches intersected because this was the obvious point and they had the machine gun nest set up there. Malcolm Dunbar said t' me, "Hey Jock there seems t' be something movin' over there." I looked through the binoculars and sure enough there was a small machine gun nest there and I could see small movements. So, we let go at that an' we blew the thing apart. Oh yes, these actions were every day actions they were nothing in particular. Perhaps the next day lookin' farther up the hill an' y' see

maybe even here for that matter the motor or a lorry at the back of the hill givin' the supplies t' the Fascists and that there, and you'd let off one or two rounds over the top of the hill t' see if we could do any damage, pick 'em off an that. Anyhow, it was good trainin' for us' because it wasn't too bad but there was enough action to teach us what war was about. We pulled out, but before we did, a runner come up from down below an' he said, "You're wanted down below." So I goes down t' see what had happened - the night before there was a tremendous thunderstorm. When there was a thunderstorm it was black, totally black and you couldn't see anything an' this is the time when fear comes to the surface. Any man who has ever been in war an' who sez he's never been afraid is either an ignoramus or an idiot. Everybody feels fear in certain conditions - the point is, if you're fightin' back against it, it takes the fear away, y' don't feel it the same. Well, that's by the way - this particular night it was thunder an' lightnin' an' that and every little sound seemed magnified, every little sound. Somebody was sayin', "Is that tank tracks up there?" an' things like that. Nobody got any sleep that night so in the mornin' I was gey tired when the boy comes along an sez, "You're wanted down below." So down I goes and who was it down below? Harry Pollitt, Bill Rust and quite a number of members of the Communist Party were visitin'. I didn't know at the time but the reason for the visit became obvious later. He said that he wanted t' see Malcolm Dunbar so I said "OK. The headquarters are farther down the valley." So, I took 'em doon the valley an' gave Malcolm a shout and down he comes. They introduce themselves and I go back up the valley t' my unit. But we found out later what the reason was for it. The next battle was goin' t' be the first offensive by the Spanish Republican Government against the Fascists. Up until then it had always been on the defensive. Now the Spanish Government thought that they had enough arms and everything to be able t' mount an offensive against Franco. Point o' fact they made a mistake they didn't have but they thought they had anyhow. So, the next battle is goin' t' be Brunete. So that was the reason why Harry Pollitt an' them were there was t' see what condition the Battalion was in before the first battle took place because everything and everybody was being thrown intil't.

So, in early July 1937 we packed up our guns an' everything and took them down t' the lorries an' away we went. On the way to Brunete we had t' take two or three villages. The very first village we took there was an incident happened. It was very distasteful from a moral point of view. The Battalion was in the fields surrounding the village and there was a look-out on top of the church tower viewing everything that was happenin' then the doors opened, all the villages had big gates an' that and a crowd o' young women, children and old men come out. They were wavin' white flags. We wondered what was happenin', whether the

Fascists were puttin' them out so they wouldna be involved in the fightin'. I was a bit further back with the anti-tank gun but a lot o' the Battalion were at the front then the women an' that dropped t' the ground and the Fascists fired over the top of them and cut down quite a number of the Republican Army. Another incident, I wasn't there - Frank Ryan; I don't know if anyone remembers him, he was commander of the Irish contingent in Jarama in the early days just before I arrived. The Moors who were opposite, the Fascists comin' wavin' their rifles and shoutin' "Vive la Republic!" an' all the rest o' it. As they came forward t' give themselves up and when Frank Ryan and his section stood up the Moors mowed 'em down. This was all the tricks o' the trade that we learned durin' the war. Anyhow, we finally took this village and then we come t' the hard part because every village we took, every step y' take towards the Fascists an' that there, you lengthened your lines of communication but you shortened theirs. Unless you are heavily armed and capable of carrying on the offensive, you've got to get round about them and cut off their lines of communication. We were

> " **the battle for Mosquito Ridge was the finish of the Brunete battle as far as the British Battalion was concerned** "

unable t' do this and the result was that we landed outside Brunete on what was known as Mosquito Ridge. It was a high hill and it overlooked the country for miles round about. And we had t' get Mosquito Ridge it was impossible for us t' go any further because they would be able t' see what was happenin' and cut us down on the roads and so forth. So, the battle for Mosquito Ridge was the finish of the Brunete battle as far as the British Battalion was concerned. We were right in the centre and we fought there for nearly a month without any rest periods or anything. I remember lying on top of a small hill - it's funny how things come t' mind, lying on top of this mound at night. At night unlike here there's no gloaming, we were up near Madrid and darkness jist comes down like a curtain. And through the curtain comes this moon a great big moon in the sky. And I always remember lookin' at the moon there thinkin' back to Aberdeen. It was about the only time I looked back to Aberdeen, normally you have t' clear your mind of all these things. I used t' have arguments with the boys up in the Castlegate and at two or three in the mornin' we'd go away home down

● Troops and Russian tanks at the battle of
Brunete: © Imperial War Museum

17

King Street with Alex Shepherd an' old Dodd Shepherd and then past the fire station. I'd leave them there and come through St. Clare Street down t' West North Street where I lived. Lookin' back an' wavin' t' the boys there an' the moon up in the sky. Silly things like that comes t' mind. Anyhow, we were up there as I say, we had run out of ammunition and communications were chaotic with only one telephone line from the company headquarters to the brigade but there were no lines o' communication t' the different companies that was spread out alongside you. They had t' use runners. By the time one runner had run from one point to another point the military situation could change in five minutes. This was the sort o' thing that was against us, we'd no equipment we'd no guns. There were only two armament factories in Spain, one in Madrid and one in Barcelona. They were very small because they never had a big army in Spain. They thought they could do it with this one blow. Get round Brunete and cut off the Fascist that were besiegin' Madrid. They were shellin' Madrid from University city. That was the idea but it actually failed because of a lack of ammunition and so forth. So on the last day, the 25th o' July the last day of the battle I got wounded. I was carted away about 300 yards to a small dressin' station that was set up there. About an hour later an old van came along. Not an ambulance but a van converted for the purpose. There were two places either side. It would carry four altogether and when the boy comes across an sez, "Who's the next?" Some o' them were very badly wounded and he already had four in so he could only take someone who was lightly wounded to lie in the aisle on the bottom there. So they chose me, I'd been wounded in the leg, the head and the hand. It was lucky for me lyin' down at the bottom. So, the van starts off across the ploughed field. Y' can imagine the state of the wounded and some o' them were very, very bad. We got onto the road makin' for the hospital just outside Madrid. I don't know what happened, I think that the driver fell asleep but he went off the road down an embankment and the van turned over and over. My luck was that I was lying on the floor an' I got a grip o' the beds an' steadied me up but the other boys, they were thrown all over the place. When they opened the doors two o' them were dead. The other two were in very bad condition, I don't know what happened to them. Then they got me out an' stopped a lorry that was commin' along the road. They threw us onto the lorry and it drove us to an hospital well, a small hospital at any rate. The doctor had a look at us an' that and

Headline in the Aberdeen Journals referring to the Eola

he said, "As far as I'm concerned we'll get you to hospital in the morning." So the next mornin' I arrived at a hospital in Madrid. It was a Spanish hospital and my Spanish - I wasn't that long in Spain so it was not that bloody good. There were only one or two words that I knew, usually 'yes' and 'no'! The Spanish doctor came along and I'm sure he sez t' me, "What's happened t' you?" Or something like that. I was too dumbfounded to answer 'cause I thought it was his job! Anyhow, he got round to proddin' me an' so forth then he made a decision to send me to another hospital.

I arrived at a beautiful hospital, an American hospital. Look, I'm one who criticises Americans at times but I'm usually criticisin' the adminis-tration. Now this was an American hospital and oh boy! It was a beautiful hospital, doctors, nurses and beds with white sheets and everything. The doctor come along an' looked at me and as a matter of fact the head sister came along also. The two of them married later on. Anyhow, they had a look at me and the doctor sez, "OK, I'll try to do something for you, I'll be back tomorrow." So, I lay there in bed recovering just glad t' get some rest and a meal. It was quite good food an' that an' everything. Before that it was jist beans, beans an' more beans! By the way there's a lotta bulls in Spain, if y' don't know that for the bullrings. But there's bloody few cows, there's no meat. The only meat we had was horse meat and donkey meat this wis all we had an' that. You'd a thought with all these bloody bulls about there would a been a lotta cattle but there wasn't! Anyhow, it was beans we had and it was good meals we had here in the American hospital. So the next day the doctor comes along and examined m' wounds. He picks out the shrapnel outa m' leg but he sez, "Y' hands a different matter it's quite critical." My hand was as stiff as a board, I coudna move a finger, a muscle or anything an' it was cold an' that. He said, "The first thing to do is t' get the shrapnel oot an' see if we can get it workin' later on, see how much damage is done later on." Even the Americans, as good as they were, they couldn't get all the drugs that they wanted. He said, "We haven't got all the drugs we require but we'll see what we can do about it." So, the next day he arranged for me t' come down t' the surgery. Now he sez, "Put your hand on the table." I put my hand on the table. The head nurse came along and he cut a strip right along here (Indicating his hand) and a strip recht along here, cut all the blood vessels but before he did it, there was no anaesthetic, well he had an anaesthetic but he could only use it on certain patients. The nurse was at one side with tweezers holdin' the skin back and I was at this side holdin' the skin back here and he had the pincers tekin' the bits oot. He was tekin' the shrapnel out and droppin' it into a tumbler. When y' come in here, the dangerous part, the bones an that you'd t' push the bones apart and y' wouldn't want t' do too much damage in the process and he had t' cut the artery along there and he sez, "I've cut your artery, can't do any thing aboot 'at but the artery will start developin' new veins for t' feed the parts." I still feel the coldness and that but anyhow it cleared up. This was the sort o' thing that happened not only to me but t' practically everybody y' know.

I was in Madrigueras and I'd got the toothache and I was in agony. I'd have done anything to stop it. Malcolm Dunbar said to me, "You'd better go down to Albacete and get something done about it." So the next day I caught a lorry and went down t' Albecete and reported into the local barracks there. The dentist was a big German woman about six foot two both ways! With a stern face like a block o' granite. "Open your mouth." She had a sma' steel rod an' she was tappin' the teeth and then she hit the wrong one and I almost took off! No anaesthetic again, that's why I mention it, she just got the bloody nippers fer tekin' it oot an' took a hod o' it there. "Open y' mouth now." An' she twisted, an' out it come and the relief was fantastic. She said, "How do you feel now?" An' I sez, "Fine." And her face lit up with a beam o' light! The contrast between the two, I'll always remember that.

Anyhow, I was passed on from the American hospital to another hospital where I was given a thing like an old mangle. Y' put y' fingers intil it an' that, an' it went up an' doon t' move your hand - manipulation an things like that. They tried that for a while but it was a long job. They knew they couldn't do much about it so I suffered for about six weeks there and they passed me on to another hospital but it was jist a waste o' time. So, I got fed up so I said, "I'm not goin t' stick this." It's a funny and peculiar thing about war, y' leave your relationships behind; family and friends and so forth but y' build another one wherever you are. The people you're livin' with, the unit you're in become your adopted family an' y' wanted t' get back t' them. So I sez, "T' hell with this I'm going t' get back t' the unit, I'm not goin' t' sit here any longer." So, I said to the doctor, "I'm goin' down to Albacete I can't stay here any longer and I want to see the senior administrator of the British Battalion in Albacete." He was later to become the president of the South Wales Miners Federation. Anyway, I arrives at Albacete and I see this individual responsible for the brigade administration. I told him what the position was as regards the hospital. He sez, "I haven't the right to send you back up until you are discharged from hospital." "But," he said, "I'll tell y' what y' can do in the mean time till your papers come through and I'll give y' clearance, you can act as a message boy for me. That is goin' down and meetin' new brigaders commin' in." So, for a couple o' month I was doin' that sorta job an' that there. Time came when things were gettin' that bad that the battle at Belchite in the winter of 1937/38, all of the Battalions got a hell o' a hidin'. So they went to their defensive positions and rested for a while and the Spanish army, which had been built up numerically although not militarily as regards guns an' that. So the first big push by the Fascists was at Gandesa. This was in 1938 and as a matter of fact one of our boys was killed there. Davidson, Tommy Davidson was

> **" I'd been wounded in the leg, the head and the hand. "**

killed there and things got so bad that a call went out to stop brigaders comin' in because of the way thing were goin' an that. So, my job more or less became redundant. The call went out from brigade headquarters that all unessential personnel had to join a Battalion. Cooks, the whole lot, had t' get up there t' make up the numbers and I was one o' them that went along anar. The first battles of the Ebro started tekin' place then. There were two battles o' the Ebro and the first battle started at this time. The Battalion didna do too bad, they pushed the Fascists back nearly 22 miles, but it was a limited success in the sense that we were pushin' them back but the problem of extendin' the lines of communication as against the fact that you were shortenin' the lines of communication on the other side for the Fascists. So, it was a partial success. I must say that. Then the Fascists started a counter attack and when they started they usin' a blitzkrieg as it should be used as theorized by panzer General Guderian. They used it in the first battle of the Ebro. The result was, they chased

● Bob Cooney

us right back right across the river to the other bank and this is where the incident happened involving Bob Cooney who was the Political Commissar of the Battalion. The men were very down hearted, they had lost so many comrades about them and they were very weak numerically and at the same time they had been asked t' go back across the river to attack again. So Bob did a wonderful job there rallying them all an' getting them back across. They had a partial success in the sense that there were isolated groups on the wrong bank and it was a chance for them t' get back so it was successful in that sense. Just as this battle was closin' as a battle, the government announced the withdrawal of the International Brigades because in July the Spanish government had already approached the United Nations and said that they wanted t' withdraw all the International Brigades from Spain if Franco would withdraw all the international forces that he had which meant the Moors the Germans and the Italians which made up 80 percent of his army. So it was proposed and to emphasise this proposal he actually took action and did it and withdrew the International Brigades hopin' that the United Nations would say that they (the Fascists) would do the same but of course it never happened. The result was from September onwards they started withdrawin' the International Brigades from Spain altogether.

There were many incidents which happened in Spain. One was about Juan the seaman who was off the ship 'Eola'. I met him in June 1936 before the war started and it so happened that when I was wounded one of the hospitals I was in. I was walkin' through a village with an American there passin' one of the shop windows and in the window was a lot of postcards and one of them automatically caught my eye. It was a postcard from Aberdeen it was with other post cards of different ports from Europe and so forth. So we went in to inquire where they got the postcard from. He said his son was a seaman and he had sent them from the different ports that he had arrived from. It so happened that he had a photograph there of his son there also; being a photographer. And I recognised Juan right away. I told his father the circumstances which happened in Aberdeen. His father was delighted and it so happened that Juan's wife and two daughters were living with him because they had been living in Bilbao which was his home port but they were being heavily bombed at that particular time so they decided that they would come and live with the grandparents rather than stay up there. So we got some photographs of the old man and his grand children. These girls were about five or six but they'd be pensioners now if they are still alive.

David: When you were in the anti-tank unit did you ever shoot at a tank?

● Two Spanish children with John Londragon and comrade.

John: At a tank? Oh yes, Christ yes, that was our job.

David: Well could you tell us when you first fired at a tank? It must have been terrifying.

John: No not really it was goin' side on. It wasn't commin' towards us. It was makin' it's way possibly to a fortified point but it didn't know where we were that's the point. The first one was in Jarama. They were light tanks that they had at that time. Y' can never really tell at a distance whether you've damaged a tank, knocked it out or whether you've missed it out altogether because there's so much dust is thrown up by the explosion and y' don't want to expose yourself at the same time because as soon as you've fired your gun you pull out y' gun and go to a new position. Y' never remain in the same position because they have got their lookouts also. They could pinpoint it, you sittin' there with an anti-tank gun we wouldn't last very long. All it takes is two tanks t' knock you out. One t' draw your fire and the other t' knock you out.

When we came outa Spain it was the same Czechoslovakian Captain who took us into Spain. Well, we arrived in Paris and the first thing they did was they tried t' give us clothes because we were in rat soled shoes, khaki trousers, shirts that's all I had. So they took us along to a place which was like one

of those demob centres after the Second World War. They took us into an outfitters in the main street t' give us a suit. Well, you could imagine two years outa my life as it were and outa fashion. I hadn't a clue what people were wearin' or anything like that so I finished up with a herrin' bone suit. Black and white checks, the sort y' go shootin' in y' know. It was a bit tight but the worst thing for me was ma feet. I had been wearing zapatoes, aye the rat soled shoes, for two years an' ma feet had spread and I couldna get 'em inta shoes. I knew m' size was size eight but gettin' my feet in was another matter. I squeezed 'em in an' I took 'em off when we got on the train t' go t' London. It was pure torture! Well when I got back in London we got a tremendous reception and a fella was with me we were very pally. He went over with me and he came back with me. Mike White, a Jewish boy from London. And he sez, "Are y' goin right home?" Well, I didn't feel like it, there seemed something wrong, I didn't feel right. I said, "No, not yet. I'll settle down first." So I stayed a week in London and I stayed with Mike and his Jewish family. The Jewish Sunday is on a Friday and they used t' get me t' pit on a' the lights an' that they wouldn't touch anything, I had t' do it all. Anyhow, I got m' fare, I think I got about 10 pounds altogether from the Spanish aid committee when we arrived back there in London. It was for my fare back t' Aberdeen plus ma food an' I sez, "T' hell, I'm not goin' back." So, I spent m' 10 pound instead. I bought a suit, shirt, socks, a pair o' shoes, underwear. I felt outa place till I got dressed. It was a beautiful suit, hand made, on the spot. I ordered it one day and got it the next from Mike's uncle. I arrived back in Aberdeen. I got off the train and I had a little bundle under my arm and there was a crowd waitin' for me 'cause they had got word that I was commin' back. There was 100s in the station waitin'. Duncan Robertson (the party secretary) sez t' me, "Jesus I was expectin' y' t' come back like a tramp an' you're back all done up!"

A big highlight for me was about three weeks after that when Bob an' the rest o' them came home, we took 'em up to the hotel in Market Street an' gave 'em a civic do. A week after that we got a call t' go back down t' London. So we went down t' London to a big parade held at the Albert Hall and they took all the British Battalions in and we were all formed up with our banners an that. Malcolm Dunbar who had been my Battery Commander, he was now Chief of Staff and he took a salute. Well, it was a tremendous parade in Albert Hall with all the banners flyin', thousands inside and 100s o' thousands outside. It's difficult to express the feelin' o' the people at that particular time and the enthusiasm because when we came back, Fascism was being beaten not only on the continent but here at home also, the British Fascists were being defeated.

Second World War

A British Crusader II making speed in the desert. Courtesy the Tank Museum

" **you could hardly breath for the stench o' dead bodies**"

Second World War
1939-45

*ITLER HAD ALREADY TRIED OUT HIS NEW WEAPONS AND TACTICS **against the Republicans in the Spanish Civil War. Mussolini also supported the Nationalists in Spain whilst previously (1935/36) he had seized Ethiopia. This collaboration, formalised by treaties (which included Japan in 1943) formed the Rome-Berlin-Tokyo Axis.***

Hitler annexed Austria in an act of expansion in 1938 and Britain and France side-stepped the issue by accepting Hitler's claim that Austria was an internal affair. The Sudetenland quickly became Hitler's next target. 3.5 million ethnic Germans populated this area, regarded as part of Czechoslovakia. The British and French persuaded the Czechs to accede Germany's demand whilst Hitler agreed not to take more Czech territory. This became known as the Munich Pact. Retrospect was to see this 'Peace in our Time' as appeasement to a well armed aggressor and within six months, in March 1939, the rest of Czechoslovakia had been taken by the Germans. Hitler then began to threaten Poland and an exasperated Britain pledged aid to Poland if Germany invaded. On the 1st of September, 1939, Germany invaded Poland. On the 3rd of September, both Britain and France declared war on Germany.

In Aberdeen and the North East young men and women were quickly absorbed by, or pressed into, war service. This included joining the local regiment, the Gordon Highlanders, joining a particular skill-based regiment, e.g. the Royal Corps of Signals or a different arm of the services, e.g. the RAF or Royal Artillery.

The Early Years:
Joining up and Training

Frank Ledingham: I became a Territorial in 1938 by joining the 51st Highland Divisional Signals. War broke out and I was called up on the 1st of September 1939. I packed up from Henderson's and walked out in the afternoon. M' lodgings were in King Street jist over from the works and I was there till jist after Christmas and the Army paid me my subsistence allowance because I wasna at home, so I thought I was quite

well off then. Then we took off and went to Crieff, to the Hydro.

A truck came up, brand new and the first one in the section. The Sergeant said to me, "You can drive can't you?" and I said, "Well, I got tuition in Crief." He says, "Oh aye you're down as that, having had driving tuition." That was once round a field! I was never on the road but I was able to drive. When I was a boy I used to drive. Anyway, he took me down the road in the lorry then he said, "OK you're going off to Fort George with a dispatch, you'll manage it." It took me about six hours to get from Strathpeffer to Fort George, I'd never given on the road before! After about a month of that, they wanted an electrician for the signals which was repairing telephones land lines that sort of thing. So I went to Bradford Technical College for six weeks on a crash course for electrics. Then I came back here and I got a good job as an electrician in the Signals. It was pretty good and I was interested in the radio. Before the war, I couldn't tell negative from positive or anything electrical. I learned the whole lot in the army. I was with the 5th Seaforth for a while putting up big aerials and things like that so they could get through to headquarters.

Eventually, they got another operator and when we got out of the area everything was plain sailing and then I just charged batteries for the three Battalions - and that's all I did for years and

● Frank Ledingham with Andy Steele and battery charging plant, Cuxhaven. Note the 'HD' (Highland Division) symbol on the rear of the trailer.

years. From 1940, all through the desert charging batteries till 1945. Of course when the batteries were being charged I was repairing number 18 sets and putting coils into the number 39 sets when we got them. We started off with 11 wireless sets and we ended up with 164 sets and there were only the two of us, Andy Steel and me. In the desert we had 20 sets. Nine of them using two six volt accumulators at a time and two on charge. The other 11 No. 18's had dry batteries. We had a generator on a trailer pulled by a five ton truck.

Then we were workin' steady and during the Battle of Alamein, the last week of it, the engines were absolutely finished. They were just wee Norman engines. We decoked this wee engine every night, took the head off and ground the valves, put the head back on and charged the batteries. Then I got a sleep while they were charging. I delivered them in the mornin'. That was not difficult because despatch drivers with Jeeps, they would come in and pick 'em up and take 'em to whatever Battalion they were going to. They were used for communication between the Battalion, HQ, back to brigade HQ, then Brigade HQ back to divisional HQ. They were big things. We started off with number 11 sets and then they

changed them to number 19 sets in the desert.

When Dunkirk was on I was shifted up to John O'Groats. In a bell tent there was a wireless set and I was there all by myself. I had to get a regimental signaller up to come and listen to it when I was having my meals. The 5th Seaforth Highlanders' regimental headquarters was only a quarter of a mile away and it was to them that I had to relay messages. But it was only for emergencies. The Bird Man came on everyday at 12 o' clock, on the BBC normal programme before the news.

Trevor: 'Bird Man', what's that?

Frank: Well, the Bird Man would come on and say, "The Bird Man today has nothing to report." I just wrote that down and related it to headquarters. After a couple of days, "The Bird Man has seen a Yellow Hammer but there's nothing to report." This message was something to do with an invasion. That was the only message that came through today. I had a wireless for other communications but this was a normal domestic set separate from that which I had for this BBC bit.

We were working mainly on short wave. From there I went down and got this wireless truck. Then I got sorta sacked out of the signal office for not spelling Brigadier right! That got me on the road to becoming an electrician in the Signals.

At Strathpeffer a motorbike dispatch rider told me that he'd a spare bike and he asked me if I'd like to go a run around the hill. Well, I did that and got seven days CB for usin' the bike! I was never on a bike again until we went t' Normandy and they said that I could ride a motorbike. The bike was in between the cab and the body. The trailer was inside for landin' on the beaches. I went through Caen with that motor bike, oh boy, it wasna a road it was jist bomb craters all over. The truck got drowned in the D-Day landin's but it was pulled out nine days later. We got everything replaced new. It was parachuted out in containers.

After Strathpeffer I went to Banchory then from there to Bellahousten Park and then on t' Bolton. From there, in transit again to Reading, Fleet and Church Cookham. We then got kitted out with tropical kit and pith helmets so we thought we'd be

> " they taught us how to live off the land in the desert "

goin' to somewhere in the East. From here we went up to Liverpool to board the liner the *Duchess of Richmond* the 22,000 ton Canadian Pacific liner. We were right up forard in the focsle. There were tables which were two feet wide and they packed y' in like that. At the back of us were pigeon holes with hammocks rolled up in them. So, that was us. We got so many hours on deck, we got a hose down and things like that. We counted them up and there was about 400 in the focsle and there was about 2,000 on the boat altogether. When you went up on deck and then come back, the stench was terrible.

This was the second run that this boat had done and being built for the North Atlantic and the cold weather, there was no provision for the hot tropical weather. The wiring started to boil out, the insulation that is and the nine electricians on board were asking for help. So me and Andy, we went up to help. We asked if there was any other place we could sleep. We were told t' take our pick so we went intil a cupboard and took all the electrical equipment off the top shelf and we slept on the top shelf! It was about 10 feet long but it was a lot better than the focsle with folk sleepin' in the hammocks and two lyin' on each table.

Goin' round the Cape it took us about six weeks. We zig-zagged all the way down keeping well clear o' Dakar because that's where we suspected the Germans had submarines. The cruiser HMS *Warrior* went up and down the line of ships. It was one of the biggest convoys that went out with about 14 liners. We were standing at action stations and I was standing at a lifeboat station and I thought if we've to abandon ship I'll be in a good position to get off. It was a fast convoy and so we

only had about three hours of that because the Germans couldn't keep up with us so there were no ships lost. We dropped depth charges here and there and that was ok.

We got into Cape Town and had three days there. A woman asked us out to dinner one night but because we went early she took us round Cecil Rhodes' house and showed us his gold mine maps. We left there and went up to Aden and took in oil and then on to Port Taufiq in Egypt.

Major William MacHardy: At 18, I was a gamekeeper with Lady Davidson at Huntly Lodge in Huntly, Aberdeenshire. Previously I had worked on a farm and was used to shooting 12 bore. With the head gamekeeper I had the opportunity with a .22 to shoot Red Deer, Roe Deer and then there were the pheasants, partridges and the grouse.

David: What skills did you develop as a gamekeeper which you found useful in the war?

William: Moving about the countryside; we had a lot of poachers from time to time so we had to be extremely careful. The river Deveron was a famous river and at that time there was an abundance of sea trout and salmon and because of that you got

● The Gordon Highlanders recruit platoon, March 1940: "You will see from this picture how desperate we were for experienced troops; beside the SM in the Glen Garry is a Lance-corporal, the only other NCO in the squad! I am to the left of the SM". (Maj. W. MacHardy).

● British 'Covenanter' cruiser tanks training (somewhere in England), showing the correct way of moving through a built-up area. Courtesy the Tank Museum

poaching. From that point of view you learnt to be careful moving through the country and especially at night-time if you were going down to the river just to see if everything was alright so you had to move very cautiously. So that helped together with camouflage. When it came to field craft in the army it became second nature in the infantry. I then came to Aberdeen to join the Gordons at the barracks Bridge of Don. I set off early in the morning and got there about 8 o'clock and lined up at the main gate. The Sergeant was a very wild looking character. Then we proceeded into a room where we had to give all our particulars. Well the most amazing thing that I remember was the chap in front of me was an assistant bank manager, the chap behind me named Macphee, was a tinker. So there was an assistant bank manager, a poacher, and me!

I was only three weeks in and I was promoted to what they called 'Provisional Lance Corporal'. That was just a start. The Sergeant must have noticed me as a potential person to go on. You had to hold that position for three weeks then you became a Lance Corporal and you got paid. This is where the schoolmaster and the army came together again. One of the first things I had to do was to go out as a right marker, which I had done at school but it was under different circumstances. On that huge barracks square where perhaps 800 men were lined up and you were right marker for say 30 men. You had to march out to the Regimental Sergeant Major. We had to stop at a certain time and keep in line behind and then from there get ready to move and then the drill would be ready to begin. It was an experience that I will always remember because you would be terrified that you would drop your rifle or something would go wrong and get a shout from the RSM but he was a good fella and would comment. He knew the ones who had been in service before but the like of myself with no previous army service he would always help and instruct us. That was the kind of thing he did, which was good. It stopped you making mistakes.

David: When did you realise that you were there to kill people. In other words when was the first time that you did something aggressive?

William: Bayonet practice. The dummies were lined up and you had to fix bayonets and charge into the dummy, out and pass on. It was a peculiar feeling because you were up against a straw thing but at the same time I thought this could be a human being and of course it was drummed into you that it was either you, or them. We became proficient at that, for example firing whilst you run even though you might want to bayonet it. If someone was dodging left or right fire at them if they fell and then finished them with the bayonet. Then I went to the commando training. It was advanced training and was different altogether.

R S M Gordon was a very bright character, very, very smart. On one occasion, I'll never forget it, when I went to get my tape on at the tailors shop, I came out of the tailors shop, feeling very good having this stripe on and walking round the corner I bumped into the R S M. Of course he wore the tunic and the Sam Brown just like an Officer you see. Well, I thought he was an Officer and quickly saluted him. He called me up and said, "I am not an Officer, I'm a Regimental Sergeant Major you don't salute me!" Well, this RSM wanted to push on and get people trained quickly. He would hold a training group and from that group you would be promoted. It was three weeks training and he was very, very hard on that sort of thing but at the end of three weeks I was promoted to Corporal. That was in 1941. I went in 1940 and by 1941 I was a full Corporal. After that I went on various courses.

The whole idea of putting you on a course was that - they always tried to send someone who would do well so the regiment would get a good report back, this was someone that had done well rather than someone who had failed and so forth. I did quite a lot of courses in my first year and second year and then six months later I was promoted to Sergeant. I was the youngest Sergeant in the Sergeant's mess. The first course I went on was down in Kent. There, I learned to drive army vehicles, particularly the 15 hundredweight, it was known as the P.U. It was a small thing and it was pretty useless. Then I trained for the three tonner. The second course I went on was in the winter of 1940/41 and I went to York for training. That was an awful winter and we were trained on a lake that was frozen. We had to move across this lake in these stupid canvas boats and they got burst with the ice and we were marooned hanging on to the boats in freezing conditions in the water. Quite a lot went down with colds and flu.

Digging trenches was another part of the training and we dug a lot of trenches in Aberdeen. We did a lot of that on the beaches.

David: What vehicles did you use?

William: Well you could only get vehicles on roads. On the Gothic Line vehicles were completely useless. You might get a jeep to go a certain distance up a hill but that is as far as it got. It became so bad due to the conditions in Italy in 1944 that the tanks and the guns were out of action due to flooded pits and the fact that the tanks couldn't get a grip.

David: To get back to your training in Scotland, what did the special training consist of?

William: Well I was selected for special training. I was sent for by the C/O and said, I'm sending you to Lochailort on the West Coast and its in conjunction with Achnagarry. It was called something like the Special Services Centre and Lord Lovat was there as the head of the field craft. It was a bit of a shock right from the very beginning. You weren't allowed to cross a bridge you had to go through the water! Everyone had a toggle rope of course but it meant that you needed a strong chap if the water was deep to swim across and belay for the rest coming across, but they wouldn't allow you to cross a bridge! That was the first thing that happened to us. We came off the train at Lochailort station, it was two miles to the camp and we had to carry our kit all the way. There was no transport laid on so I knew we were in for a tough time.

Each one of us had a commando knife and we were taught how to use it, where to hide it and have it ready for use. It was often strapped on to your leg. It was a good thing if something happened to you, perhaps you were stuck and you couldn't handle your machine-gun or rifles you could always use your knife. We learned about the tying of knots - very important for things like abseiling and how to jump from heights and land on your feet with a full pack. That was a jarring experience. One very important thing with regards to learning field craft was how to live off the land. Learning to live off fruits and berries so that you could exist with perhaps the killing of a rabbit, skinning and gutting it and so forth and the fact that you could have a very small fire with just a couple of sticks and cook without pots and pans. That was very useful in Italy.

David: What different weapons did you learn to use?

William: Well, I didn't see a Tommy gun because there weren't any at the time. The Americans were issued with them but we weren't for a start. But the commandos had them and they also had all the German weapons, the Spandaus, the Schmieser and the Lugers and we were taught to use them all. Then when we went on patrol you weren't worried about which weapon you were handed because you knew how to use them.

David: And you'd be taught demolition presumably?

William: Yes, it was Mad Mike Calvert he was some character. The type of training you had to do made it so that you were always tired, you were always at the full gallop and then suddenly they would say, "Right, into the Nissen hut for a lecture." Well, of course it was very difficult to keep awake. What he had done was he had these little fuses which he put under some of the seats and around the wall. You couldn't see them and you'd be sitting there and they'd go off! He taught us the different weapons. He showed us the Italian

● Gordon Highlanders training WAAF's in rifle shooting at Dyce airfield
The woman in the foreground is Sgt. Cecile Wheat

maps but we also studied Italian, French and German maps. The maps we were issued with in Italy were so bad that the artillery couldn't range on them. Then we got aerial photography and eventually new maps were issued to us and then our artillery could fire on them. A lot of maps were very, very poor indeed.

After training, I got two options, I was sent for by the CO and he said t' me "MacHardy, two things here for you, they want you back at Lochailort as a Sergeant Major and instructor and also you have been put forward for a Commission. Which one do you want?" George Anderson who was my CO at the time, took me into the office and said, "Go for your Commission." So that's what I did. So I went off after that to Morecambe and passed my Commission there as a Second Lieutenant. Then I went back. They didn't usually post you back as an Officer to your old unit but then we were so short of instructors that I was sent back to Gordon barracks.

mines, we saw how they worked and what they looked like. We also looked at our own mines and then the different types of ammunition. There was BSA ammunition, Italian ammunition - we were taught how to use it and recognise it. The other main thing was showing you what our other weapons were capable of doing, which was very good. I saw links there that I had never seen before. We had a Lieutenant Colonel of the Scots Guards who came and gave us a demonstration on the Lee Enfield rifles. He would stand there and fire nine rounds in as many seconds using the middle finger of the hand, dead on target every time. I never saw that before and he showed us the accuracy of the rifles at 1000 yards firing up in the hillside. He showed us that the Lee Enfield rifle was one of the best weapons ever produced. We always had Lee Enfields and I never went anywhere without it because you didn't know what orders, plans and situations you might be involved with in clandestine operations. For example in 1942 there was a Colonel who got a posthumous VC. He got killed trying to capture Rommel in the desert. A few of them got killed there. It was things like that which we did. Like the SAS but at that time we called it the Long Range Desert Group. We were shown how they worked in the desert and the type of things that they did. It was very useful because they taught us how to live off the land in the desert. We also studied map reading. We used Ordnance Survey

> "this was the first time at the Bridge O' Don barracks they had seen live ammunition"

Miss Allan: I started my training in 1932 so I was quite an experienced nurse by the time I went away in 1940. I had been staffing up at the infirmary and I'd been in maternity as well. When we finished our general training the matron sent for us and she said, "In the event of war will you go abroad? Will you take this home and get your parents to sign it?" So home I went and I produced the papers for my father to sign. He said, "You are not going into the army. No no, none of my folk are going in to the army." So he wouldn't sign it. So back I went and told the matron and she said, "Oh yes, but you're sitting comfortably at home and the folks are fighting for you." So I took the thing back and said, "Put your name down there father, there's not going to be a war." He put down his name reluctantly but he still said, "You're not going." I said, "No, I know I'm not going." But all the time I'd got everything arranged. And eventually we went away.

We were going to this place then that place then there would be a delay and all the rest of it. One night we were wakened up and we were told to get out of bed and take a case. We were out at

Cruden Bay and there used to be a big hotel. It was where the golf course is now and we were mobilised from there. So we were told to get down to the golf course and lie down because the Germans were attacking the ships in the North Sea. One of the girls who I shared a bedroom with said, "Oh no, we've had enough of this Germans if you think I'm going to sit out here all night they've had it. Come on down and get a cup of coffee and we'll go back to our beds." The next day we went into various hotels.

I was in the George Hotel and we waited there until we went away abroad and in June 1940, we set off from Aberdeen and went down to Liverpool.

Ernie Mundie: In 1939 I joined the Territorial Army based in Inverurie. By joining the Territorial Army I was able to decide more the service I would serve with than if I was conscripted. In peacetime, when you joined the Gordon Highlanders you stayed as a Gordon Highlander but when hostilities began you could be split up.

The first night that we were signed up, it was a case of going down, signing your papers being medically examined. You were then given a lecture by the Company Sergeant Major and that was about doin' what you were told and learin'

what they had taught you and to instil in you to obey orders regardless. These Sergeant Majors were always regular class one or class two NCO's.

In 1940 I volunteered (you should never volunteer but I did!) to go to a special unit. Once we got there we discovered that we were all volunteers and all joined to serve special units and these became known as Independent Companies who were responsible only to the War Office and then to the Commandos. That was the start of the Commandos with the Special Service units. Well, I finished up in hospital in 1940 down in Johnson Castle. At that time we'd been on route to Norway and we'd been taken off the boats because Norway was finished and we came back to Johnson Castle where I got appendicitis. I was in hospital for two weeks and then I went back to Bridge o' Don. By this time the 6th Independent Company had moved from Johnson and as a result I was sent to the Ninth Battalion which was a holdin' Battalion for the Gordon Highlanders. This was for any Gordon Highlander who had come out of hospital. They found out who your unit was and they posted y' back to your unit. They couldn't get information on me because the information had come from the War Office it was secret and nobody was to know that it was a special service unit.

David: What did you learn in the special unit?

● The Fish Troop cleaning gear at Spenny Moor, Durham. Far right is Gunner Reid from Aberdeen; next to him is Sergeant Bridges from Leith

● Beside an early model AEC 'Matador' gun tractor, l to r: Sergeant Johnstone Duguid, Carnegie, Angus McDougal, unknown, Worthington, Bill Card and Sergeant Cardno

Ernie: You learned stalking, firing, you learned machine weapons, all infantry weapons and you learned to live off the land and operate independently. On exercise down in the Trossachs you were given a knife, walkin' boots and specialised clothes. We were never cold.

You signed on for six months in the Special Service. There was Blackwatch, Seaforth Highlanders, Gordons and Argyll & Sutherland Highlanders. These were the infantry sections within the company. There was an Argyll & Sutherland Major, an Argyll & Sutherland second in command and an Argyll & Sutherland Regimental Sergeant Major. We all thought that we would be used by the Argylls so most of us refused to sign on after six months. It was the clan system, it definitely was. We were returned to the Bridge O' Don barracks in Aberdeen. This was the first time at the Bridge O' Don barracks they had seen live ammunition. This was November 1940. We came back with two bandoliers of 50 rounds each from the Special Service. At the first kit inspection when the Officer saw the 100 rounds of ammunition and the Tommy guns that some of us had he took them away from us and the next time we saw them was on the firing range down in England. I fired for the Battalion team for about four years with a .303 as a marksman.

Anyway, from the Bridge O' Don I went down to Lincolnshire where we did field exercises with different strengths of unit. On Special Service exercises you did individual cross country marches and you had to find your own way also river crossings and canal crossings. Then we boarded the *Duchess of York* and eventually landed in Algiers.

Dougal Milne: I was born in Aberdeen in 1924 and I have lived here all my life apart from being away during the war. In 1952 I started up on my own as a painter. All my five brothers were painters, my father also and they were all in the forces as well. My father was in the First World War naturally. Before the war I worked as a painter for Edward Copland who was well known in Aberdeen at the time. Then of course the war came along and I went away. As soon as I was old enough I joined the Home Guard and I was on what they called 'Z' guns which had twin barrels and they fired rockets and they were positioned just on The Links just below Pittodrie stadium. There were 48 cannons and with twin barrels you could fire ninety six rockets all in one go. When they were fired masses of wires came out of them which were supposed to tangle round the props and whatnot.

Hall Russell's? Well, it was lunch time. My father and my eldest brother who was out o' the Air Force by this time were going back t' work at the school in Urquhart Road when the plane came along right from the University, dropped bombs on King Street all the way in. On Urquhart Road then on and dropped bombs on the Neptune Bar and on Hall Russell's boiler room where they were having their meal. My brother in law had an argument with his father walked out and up on to the prom. Looked around and saw Hall Russell's bein' bombed. My second eldest brother, he didn't go into the forces until 1941, he was actually down in that area 'cause he belonged t' Fittie and he actually went into the Neptune Bar and helped to take a lot of the bodies out.

I joined the Home Guard as soon as I was 17 in

1941. I was then called up but with all my brothers bein' in the forces and my sister a nurse in Woodend Hospital, I got a deferment until February '43. I then went to the Bridge of Don barracks. I was there six weeks and we all did tests and I found that I was goin' into the Royal Armoured Corps at Barnard Castle. I was in as a driver's mechanic which meant I did about seven months vehicle training, gunnery, learning to fire the two pounder and the 7.92 BSA and to learn to use the wireless which had a range of about 15 miles. So you were trained to be either a driver operator, a driver mec. Or an armoured car driver. If you were a 'gunner up', you'd be in an armoured car as a gunner operator. We trained on Humbers which had a crash gearbox and had a 37 milli gun on it. The Daimler was an entirely different thing. They were so simple because you had a pre selected gearbox. In a troop y' had two armoured cars and two scout cars and there was a complement of 10 men, two in the scout cars and three in the armoured cars. Then there was an infantry troop which was about 21 men. Well we were

"it was a cold night and we were pinchin' each others blankets"

static so often in Italy that we were put in with this infantry. Then there was the troop with two half tracks with French 75mm guns. This was our artillery. They were old fashioned things but they were dashed good.

After our training we left for Algeria.

Robbie Bremner: I jined the 65th Medium Regiment. We were told if we jined the 'Terriers' we wouldna get called up and we'd do our trainin' at home in Foggie Loan. I was quite keen t' do that 'cause I was courtin' a girl from Banff. I used t' get 9 pence to make the journey up and down on my bicycle so the more parades I got the more money I got paid. I used t' go round the village selling goods so this day that the war startit up it came through the radio and said, "Every Territorial report to their unit." And I'm sittin' in this house and I said, "Hip, hip hooray!" She looked at me and said, "Laddie little div y' ken." So

● Royal Engineers marching down Union Street on their way to the station, 8th October 1939. © Aberdeen Journals

that wis us away and we went doon t' Banff and we got signed up and got wer blankets and this and that and we settled down in the hall for the first night. It was a cold night and we were pinchin' each others blankets. I was the first man t' be wounded because I'd held on t' my blanket and I was pulled across the floor and I got splinters in my backside! I was about a week attemptin' t' get these splinters oot.

We then went up to the school on the hill and we were on guard with a Lewis gun but we used t' get wer girls up there – it was great bein' a soldier! Then we were posted t' Peterhead where we all got inoculated and my god, he wis doin' 20 or 30 with the same needle! Two days after 'at we were out for the count! After Peterhead we went inta Aberdeen. It was Golden Square, Ruby Lane where we were, it's the Boys Brigade now. We used t' march to Fonthill for wer meals. We weren't awfa pleased wi wer food there and we so we had a sit in strike there and they took up the Gordon Highlanders. They'd got machine guns to shoot the lot o' us!

Eventually we went awar doon south and landed up in Wickwar and after three or four days we were sent doon t' Charfield where we got intil a brickworks and we slept in the kilns! My biggest memory was; I was getting married at New Year and I got my pass out but they gave it me for Christmas instead. I met one o' the old reservists and he said, "Don't mess about, go and see the Colonel." Well, I waited for two or three nights but I couldna get the Colonel in but on night that I went I was told that he was in his bed. So I knocked the Colonel up and I sez, "Hey sir, I'm getting' married in the New Year y' know." And he sez to me, "I know that Bremner, I know that. What d' y' want me to do about it, get the hell outa here and get somebody t' change your pass!" The next day efter I'd seen the Colonel he asked how I'd got on and I said, "Nae problem." He said, "He didna put you on a charge nor nothin'?" Anyway, eventually I went back and got married but the wife said t' me, "If y' g' back right away y' don't love me." So I had t' go to the doctor and get a line! That was great!

After Dunkirk we went up to Salisbury Plain. We were getting' treated for sores, it was like impetigo which we had got off the straw which we'd slept on in a picture house. It landed up in m' groin and I could have got a discharge and I had it for years efter. It was terrible that itch. We then moved up to Wales where I had a crackin' billet. There wis this lady and her daughter and I was oot playin' tennis and life was great. However, we were always tryin' t' get home and eventually I got home on leave. I knew that

● Dod Martin (left) and Bob Jeffries, from Edinburgh, practising for the real thing.

later we were all goin' t' the Isle O' Man but fen I got home the wife gave me the same old story sayin' that I couldna go back yet and, "No, no you'll have t' bide at hame." So I got three weeks off from the Banff doctor and he told me that was all he could give me so then I went up to the Foggie Loan doctor. I told him that I'd been really ill and I wis nae recht at ar and he sez, "Och well I'll gi 'y a fortnight." Well, in the end I never got t' the Isle O' Man like the rest o' the Regiment instead I went to Seahouses in Northumberland. When I come back, what wis the boys name, Darkie Nichol, that's him, he came back and his heed wis shaved y' see and he sez, "Oh Bingo you're away this time, they are goin' t' have ya, they ken you've been scroungin'. You'll jist end up like me wi yer hair ar shaved off!" Well, I'll tek ma chance. I had all m' doctor's tickets and I jist gid 'em 'at and I was ok. Then I went doon t' Eyemouth and I got hold of a ferret an' I wis oot all day catchin' rabbits an' tekin' 'em inta the cookhoose. I got a job wi a cook and he went roond ar the gun emplacements wi the rations. We did about 20 in a day. Then we got moved to Newcastle and we were a training Battalion, we were auld soldiers and we were trainin' up this guys and showin'

> " fen the bottle was empty I jist filled it o' water and pit it back inta the case again "

them how t' fold the blankets and make their beds. However, the wives wis commin' down so there was Johnny Donald's wife, my wife and Warwick's wife. We get this house by St. James' Park and this woman took in all the theatrical folk. We had a great time. The first night we were there, she showed us our room an' there was a bed and a shackey doon. So Johnny sez t' me, "Now Bingo, you hae the bed 'cause were nae hain nae femly till efter the war." But Johnny landed up wi twins wi that shakey doon! When we got up in the mornin' at 6.30 t' get t' the barracks there was not a soul, the regiment had moved durin' the night! Johnny sez t' me, "Oh Bingo, this is the end of our army career, we're finished! It's the glesshoose for us!" Well, I started thinking There was a big verandha and I got up on to it and I was waitin' to see what was goin' t' happen. In aboot come es PU truck and the RSM and his driver so down I went. He sez, "What the hell are y' doin' here Bremner." and I said, "I've been sent back sir to prepare a meal for the boys commin' back and to look for rations and things like that." "All right, carry on." Ha, ha!

Then I went t' Spennymoor. Well, I was at RHQ and I was a batman at this time to Lieutenant Sterling. A hell o' a fine chap. Then t' Bishop Auckland where they tried t' train us as drivers and I mind Jim Beattie trainin' me to drive this lorry and

I had a hell of a job t' drive y' ken. Then up t' Reidsdale (sic) Camp and then on to Ponteland and I was in the Sergeant's Mess be this time. I wasna promoted though, I was jist one o' the boys. There was Bill Lorrimer, M'sel, there wis wee Davey an' somebody else. I made a deal with the landlord's wife. I sez, "Look I'll jist gi you all the rations and you jist serve it all up an' do yer job then you'll get yours and we'll get oors. They'd ar the drinks stored up in this loft far we slept. I didn't drink at the time but these three boys drunk a bottle every night so that fen the bottle was empty I jist filled it o' water and pit it back inta the case again. When that case wis drunk I wrapped it up so that fen we moved arthing wis alright, the weight was right and it looked all right. Then the cat wis oota the bag an' I said, "I dinna ken far did 'at, no idea at all!" So, that wis Ponteland. We went to Bishop efter 'at and that takes us up t' the time that we went to North Africa.

David Adam: I was in the 5/7th Gordons. It was 1940 and I was jist 20 and I went to the Don Barracks and did my trainin' and what I remember was it was at the same time as the Heinkel 111

● The Gordon Highlanders loading up, 1939.
© Aberdeen Journals

● Aldershot, August 1939. 3rd Battalion Grenadier Guards provide the Guard of Honour for a visit by King Carol of Romania. Ensign the Lord Forbes is carrying the Colour on the right.

came down into the icerink. That day I happened to be on ack-ack duty. We gets the red alert and we had t' go over to the golf links where there was an ack-ack position and we had a Bren gun and no ammunition, Ha! So we got there and we were standing and lookin' up and this plane's coming in from Peterhead way.

I was lookin' up and I said, "That's funny," you could see the markings on the wing no bother and we couldn't do a thing about and we watched it fly in to Aberdeen. Down at the beach the ack-ack had rockets but they were pointin' in towards the town in the wrong direction. The Spitfires were wanting them to stop so they could put him out t' sea t' shoot him down but oh no, they kept firing away and the German was commin' down and down. My father he worked in the shipyards and he was lucky he came home on his bike. We stayed in Seaton Road and he was on his way back to work down the Golf Road and the plane was straffin' the road and ma Father, he flew for his life into a bunker! He was lucky again 'cause they bombed Hall Russell's and a few people were killed there.

I got in with two or three Glasgow chaps, oh what a bunch they were. Anyway they'd just got back from Dunkirk and they said t' me, "We've volunteered to go to Singapore." and I sez, "Well I'd like to go." so I went t' jine up. But when I gid over to enlist, luckily, they'd got their full complement. I was lucky because they'd all got torpedoed. I don't know how the Glasgow boys got on but I never heard from them again.

I went up to the Orkneys with the 7th, gee, what a place, y' couldn't have lights there and you wern't supposed t' take off y' clothes because you were on alert all the time. Every time the siren went y' had t' go down to Scapa Flow for fear of an invasion. We were buildin' Nissen huts and the mud was up to y' knees and we were sleepin in duggies and there was 100 mile (mile per hour) gales so we were buildin' these huts. I was 13 weeks there and we came down on a boat to Aberdeen and then on to *Abergeldie Castle* with B Company. I remember, as a part of the trainin', we had to walk up Lochnagar with full pack.

Then to Minalty House where I was on mortars and then onto some other house where I was on signals training and from there to a camp in Hayton. One time on trainin', we had t' go up Brimmond Hill and my chum and I were wantin' cigarettes and we were lookin' down onto the Skene Road and we saw this farm house. Tommy sez, "Come on, away down and we'll see if we can get cigarettes." The next thing we knew the folk, each one o' them, was playing an instrument. One was playing a fiddle and another was on the piano. We were sittin' away there and we were supposed t' be there till next day. So eventually we decided to go and look for the rest of the platoon and we looked up but they had vanished. So, we started walkin' up hill then down and up again we didn't know which way they'd gone but finally we caught up wi them! I got 14 days confined to barracks for that. The next place we went to was Gordonstoun for more trainin'. It was a non event as far as I was concerned. Then it was Alamein and Sicily.

Sandy McKenzie: I was conscripted into the 5/7th Gordon Highlanders. We went up to Gordonstoun for wer trainin'. We were in R Company, that is the reserve company. The trainin' was mainly marchin' and drill. Takin' y' webbin' out and doing y' blancoin'. Things like that. There's a big assault course at Gordonstoun where we did FSMO. That was, Full Service Marching Order, y' big pack yer small pack, y rifle, respirator, gas cape, y' tin hat and we had t' fly over this assault course. We then trained t' go to the desert. We went down to Comberley in Surrey then we were put to different companies and I was put to C Company. Then we got a spot o' leave and after that we came back and was posted to your company where we did more trainin'. On the shootin' range, target practice and all that sorta thing.

Eventually we went up to Glasgow by train and saw our big boat was lyin' out in the bay and I said, "This is it now boy, we're awa fae hame now!" that took a few days to get all loaded up on the *Bergensfiord* which was a Norwegian vessel. The journey was a bit miserable because of the very cramped conditions and we were on that boat from about mid June to sometime in mid August. It was very hot as well. We eventually arrived in North Africa.

> **"beautiful larries wi six inch howitzers but they could only dae five mile an hour"**

Alec Ross: I never thought aboot war but early in 1939 the rumours started. Somebody hid t' go, I niver thought onything aboot it, an' I said t' m'sel, "I'm glad I'm in an Aberdeen regiment 'cause I know all the boys." Then when September come we wis goin' awar to Boddam for oor first camp. We wis goin' awar fer a wik. Well, I worked on the milk an' I startit at five o'clock in the mornin an' I finished at aboot ten - half past ten - in the mornin'. But onywye, on September the first, I wis tekin ma kit up t' Fonthill fen

the guys cam roond wi the conscription papers. That's when we got transferred into the 65th. We didn't leave Aiberdeen till October

We went doon t' Wickwar doon t' England. Well neen o' us had been t' England. It wis magic, we a' said, "This is the life!" Wickwar was about 20 miles away frae Bristol. We got motors an' a' thing when we got t' this place. Some o' them took motors doon from Aiberdeen but we got issued wi new motors when we arrived doon. I got a little 15 hundredweight Bedford but we didna get wi big Scammells till we left. That wis fa guns, beautiful larries wi six inch howitzers but they could only dae five mile an hour. I went home in December and I was in France in January 1940.

Billy Henderson: I joined the Territorials in 1937 mostly because my mates had joined but also there was a scare on with Germany. I didn't want to join the infantry and the Royal Corps of Signals were in Fonthill Barracks. We lived in Willowbank Road, which is just off Holborn Street, so that was the nearest place that we could join. Then war was declared and we were called up. We did a few months at the barracks then we went off to Crieff as reinforcements for the 51st Highland Division and as such we were picked out for the 9th Highland Division. So, after training in Crieff, 20 of us were picked out and sent down to Aldershot. We got our jabs there and then we went to France.

● Albert (Wag) Birch and Angus McDougal training in Britain in 1941. Their Matador is towing a 6-inch howitzer

"I thought that Dunkirk, at the finish, t' be quite honest, it wis every man for himself"

Dunkirk

*S*OON AFTER THE GERMANS INVADED THE LOW COUNTRIES, *the Allies sent troops to support the armies of Belgium and the Netherlands. Luxembourg was occupied by the Germans without resistance. In May 1940, the Belgian Army had to give up the fight and the Netherlands, quickly occupied by the Germans, ceded to their rule. With the Belgian surrender on the 28th of May, and the resulting holes in their lines of defence, the Allies were forced to make an evacuation across the English Channel. The 360,000 troops – British and French - waiting patiently and under continuous attack, were evacuated from Dunkirk by hundreds of boats of all sizes and returned to the shores of England.*
However, the Battle Of France did not end at Dunkirk, others fought on and with them the 51st Highland Division at St.Valery.

Dod Martin: I was a larry driver for William Wisely; Gordon Hutcheon was a farm servant at Bourtiebush oot at Portlethen, another chap Duthie he worked in the quarries at Rubislaw. We were a cross section of Aberdeen but the majority who were in the Fish Troop at that time had been in the fish.

Alec Ross: We sailed fae Southampton in the mornin' an' we landed in Cherbourg at night. We was pit intil a big camp an' reorganised an' a' the rest o' it y' know. Neen o' us was allowed oot.

David: You'd had training with the guns by then?

Alec: No, not a lot, we hidna fired em or onything.

David: So, you were a medium artillery regiment, sent to France in 1939 to fight the Germans and you hadn't fired the guns?

Alec: No! We'd plenty o' practice but when we went to France we went till a place up at Lille and we fired the guns there but as I said, the boys were raw. Firin' the guns wis a bitty scary kind bit we didna really think nothin' o it till we went into action. We were one o' the luckiest regiments' oot 'cause we never lost a man.

David: That must have been miraculous.

Dod Martin: Every day we had t' set oor sights. Now this chappie he wis a bombardier, Frankie Wiper - he come frae Montrose - he set his sights up t' fire but the night before they'd bin practisin' an' somebody had left the shell in the thing. Somebody fired the gun an' put the shell right through the (village) clock!

David: Didn't you have an opportunity to fire your guns before y' had to spike them?

Dod: Yes, my friend who was a bombardier, he wis in charge o' this gun. They took all the cream oot t' get back 't England if they could and left so much men t' blow the guns up. They went into a big area t' fire on the Germans but the Germans come roond the back o' us. Jock ma pal wis told t' blow the guns up but he wis told by an Officer Lieutenant Middleton he sez, "You'll fire every round at the Germans and we'll carry the breaches awar frae the guns." Well, the breech was over a hundredweight so this t' me was ridiculous. Well they walkit aboot three mile and then dug it, they buried 'em. Whether they are still there nobody could ever tell me. What we was told was a round down the muzzle and a round up, a big lanyard, then pull it and blow the guns up so the Germans would get no satisfaction oota them. We took them down to another place, where it was - I'm not right sure where it was. Anyway there was 100s o' vehicles an' Jerry never touched 'em. They were 'a supposed t' be smashed up but half of our blokes never touched 'em. Left 'em, jist walked awar from 'em. I was drivin' a Bedford at 'at time and I mind I got a spanner an' let the ile oot and left the engine runnin'. But some o' them they got

> ❝they were gettin' bombed t' hell as well. I thought I was a lucky man❞

● The Navy
rescuing
soldiers:
courtesy
J. Pelella

hemmers and bashed the engines but they were not doin' any real damage t' my mind but the stuff that was left for the Germans was ridiculous. Even the RAF didna come owra an' bomb 'em. So, we walkit 30 mile to Dunkirk fae there. It took us about five days 'cause we were gettin' hassle from the German aircraft. Then I wis a couple o' days in Dunkirk helpin' wounded on to the boat jist fer somthin' t' dee 'cause we couldna do onything on the beaches. There wis guys stannin' there, they didn't ken fit they were doin'. There wis this Officer there an' he sez, "Wid y' like t' gie us a hand?" an' I said, "Well I'm nae doin' nothin' else onyway."

David: You must have seen a lot of horror?

Dod Martin: The first time I saw a dead body was

at Lille. Efter we left the guns we drove back through Lille and t' let y' understand we had been in Lille for two or three wiks (I'd met a bit o' stuff there y' know her father had a jewellers shop). We stopped to have a look but there wis nobody there. The whole street wis deserted but there was a few bodies lyin', - civilians - they had been bombed. I went into the jewellers shop an' took hame some jewellery but fen I come on the boat at Dunkirk this chap Alex Pirie an' me - I wis soakin' weet an' I wis clarted wi bleed and I'd a change o' underwear wi me. On the boat, I couldna get a wash or ony thing. I changed m' clothes an' walked across an' threw this stuff (used clothes) in the Channel - fen I come back I never noticed this bag had disappeared with the jewellery. I left a little watchie, an' that had disappeared as well. After I went back to France, we went up through

They came through Dunkirk—Group of sergeants belonging to a battery of the Aberdeen Medium Artillery's second line.

N.-E. Medium Artillery in France

Happy Days on the Eve of the Blitz

By G. E. Ley Smith

ABERDEEN GUNNERS IN FRANCE

'SUICIDE SQUAD' BREAKS THROUGH NAZI ADVANCE

IN 2 BIG BATTLES—BUT UNSCATHED

Ley Smith

ABERDEEN ARTILLERY IN FLANDERS

Gunners' Ordeal Under Bombs

By G. E. Ley Smith

R.A.F. Pilot Freed

● Press cuttings following the fortunes of the 'Fish Troop' © Aberdeen Journals

Belgium an' when the war wis finished I went back t' Lille but it wis a' changed. The folk that was there didna like us onywye, the French didn't have much time for us.

Anyway, when we got t' Dunkirk I tossed away ma rifle. It wis nae good onyway it wis mair o' a hinderance. Actually fen we left we motors there happened t' be a NAFFI van lyin' there, the doors were wide open so the boys helped themselves. I got a lotta fags oota it and mind fen we were gettin' nearer Dunkirk there was this young Gordons commin' up, it was a young regiment jist come up fae England. I wis standin' there an' this roond tins o' fags, I was handin' them roond t' the boys who were goin' up there cause they were goin' t' save ma life. I thought it was terrible us gettin' awar doon an' them goin' up, 'cause this boys had never been in action, they'd never seen onythin'. They'd landed at Cherbourg and had been driven towards St. Valery but this wis nae the boys 'at wis caught prisoners. They hid come back oot t' Dunkirk an 'a but they'd been the last line o' defence for us gettin' off at Dunkirk because the boys at St. Valery they were trapped, they were surrounded they'd nae other option but t' gie in but they fought hard an' that was one o' the reasons why us artillery boys got outa there. We got telt that if we carried all es wounded doon we would get a lift in this Red Cross ship. It wis two days we humphed these chappies that wis wounded an' fen the boat was full we wis telt t' get aff the boat y' see. Fit could we dee? We got aff the boat. We went along the pier, the boat was lyin' alongside the pier an' we jist walked into the queue. Some o' the chappies they were nae affa happy bit they didna know the score but bein' messed wi the blood they thought we wis wounded. When we come to the middle o' the pier there was a big hole and to get t' the other side, there was some boats commin' in. We went onto an old tramp boat they got a mile fa Dunkirk an' they about turn an' took 'em back t' Cherbourg t' fight. So, they got ashore an' they leapt back onto the boat an' got landed in Britain. We were lucky we got on til es destroyer. We wis walkin' along the beach I seen this 20 French soldiers, they were havin' a feed, they'd plenty o' grub an' I went doon an' asked 'em if I could buy some bread from them an' they told us t' "F'- off". Anyway, I bartered an' I got two loaves they were like that table there (tapping the table) an' they were green inside. We'd had nothing to eat for five days an' we were gled t' eat this stuff that an' water. They didna hae pills either t' purify the water we got 'at fen we went back. We hid t' drink fit water we could get back because the water bottles were empty be this time. As I say we got intae Dunkirk an' we saw a lotta bodies lyin' there, horses an' people an' that's where the Major asked us t' tek these bodies in. If weeda stayed there we'd probably a landed on the beach in the water an' we dinna ken fit wida happened there 'cause most o' the boys that were picked up in the water were deid! The rowin' boats and the small lighters that went in aboot t' pick 'em up an' tek 'em oot t' the bigger boats - they were gettin' bombed t' hell as well. I thought I was a lucky man.

David: If you got on to a destroyer what happened to the others in your regiment?

Dod: As I said, a lot of 'em were on es boat but they were all in different places. Anyway, when we went back ere we landed in Margate. They put us up t' the pulich(sic) I'll never forget this, it's the funniest thing you've ever heard. This boy, Alex Pirie an' me walked through the gates. There were a' different kindsa regiments see an' a Sergeant sez t' me, "Here's a shovel, start diggin'." I said, "What d' y' mean start diggin'? I could do wi a feed." We had a sandwich on the boat and on the train we had a cup o' tea. "Get diggin'." he said, "cause Jerries gonna bomb us." Well, Jerry niver come near us that night. He wis more interested in blowin' up Dunkirk. Well, I stuck it for an hour an' I said t' the boy, "There's naebody aboot, lets get oot." We went oota there an' went doon t' the nearest station an' we got t' London an' we took the train hame t' Aberdeen. That's the funniest thing in the world man! Nobody took ony notice o' it, we still had our tunics wi the brass buttons shot up. Y' could see them from the pier, they didna seem t' be shootin' up the pier, jist the people on it. We landed hame in Aiberdeen an' we had aboot 48 'oors in Aiberdeen then we went back an' we landed in a place called Swindon. There wis still boys left doon in England doon at the ports but they didna ken far their regiments were but unknown t' me there wis heaps o' oor boys at hame. Well as I said, I landed in Swindon an' the Kings Royal Regiment wis ere an' I sez, "There's no way am I goin' t' march wi them. Have y' ever seen them Gorkies (Gurkhas) march at a 165 steps til a minute or something like 'at. Very very fast it's jist like runnin' this boys wis trainin'. I wis sore f' this boys but y' wouldna believe es, we reported in, we got intae the barracks, the boy come up an' he said, "If y' come doon the stairs I can gie y' a change o' underclothes. We canna gie y' tunics or onythin' like 'at but maybe we'll manage y' a pair o' trousers an' boots. Come doon the stairs an' get 'em." So we went doon the stairs an' we a' got handed a fiver each. Fiver! I hadna had that much in ma life! So, onywye, the boy said. "Would y' like t' go intae Swindon it's aboot twa three mile doon the road? Awar y' go doon the road an' come back at night." We'd still got these tunics on an' es boy Eric Blakeman, he wis jist walkin' doon the street an' a big car pulls up and took us in. They didna half treat us well, this people but onywise we wis 'ere four days an' every day we got a fiver. We never sent f' 'em, it musta been a benefactor or somthin'! We jined the regiment at Larkhill. From there we went t' the Isle O' Man guardin' Italian internees. They were very, very strict wi these guys. The whole O' the Isle O' Man was like Blackpool wi hotels up an' doon an' there was a fence aboot 15 feet high and about nine feet across and there was a fence behind an' we were behind. These boys could easily batter y' doon. There wis nae bullets in y' rifle. Y' had four in yer pocket in case they

broke oot. We met some o' the boys fae Aberdeen. There was a little wooden huttie doon by the links that used t' sell ice-cream an' they were taen oot an' locked up. Y' see, nane o' 'em had teen oot papers fen they come oot efter the First World War. That wis my experience of Dunkirk.

Charlie Low: I joined up 'cause we didna want the Germans comin' t' Britain, we didn't want that at all. I wanted t' get into the 'gunners'. Now a lot of the school pals they were called up they got the flannel the blazer and the beret, they got six month trainin' at the Brige O' Don and they thought they were getting' a choice but they didn't. Most of them ended up at St. Valery at Dunkirk, as we were retreating, the military police were there and they put the people t' the left with the Gordon Highlanders in the infantry for the defence of St. Valery. We were sent t' the beaches. A lot o' these boys that didna volunteer along with m'self landed in the infantry and they were taken at St. Valery.

If they weren't killed they spent five and a half years as prisoners o'war in Germany. That was my reason for joinin' up, I got ma choice.

On the beaches at Dunkirk I couldna see us getting' to the beach 'cause there were thousands o' soldiers in front o' us. We were just told t' stay there and the bombin' and the shellin' wis comin' in and we had t' take cover, scatter a wee bit then regroup again. This Captain Waller, he said, "I'm going to have a recce." Well, it wis the only Officer that I've ever seen in our regiment along with us. I thought he was goin' t' disappear, but no, he came back and he'd been t' the jetty maybe half a mile away and he said, "Y' can please y' self but we can go t' the jetty an' see if we can get off there." So, we moved t' the jetty and we queued up and queued up. The jetty wis getting' shelled. They were puttin' planks across and I got about 50 yards from the end and I could see that some o' them were jumpin' in the water so I said, "I'm not movin' from here I'm takin' my chance." Sure enough HMS *Jaguar* came in and the Navy boys were pullin' us aboard and handin' us cups of cocoa. Great! So that wis my vivid memory of Dunkirk.

(?) I thought that Dunkirk, at the finish, t' be quite honest, it wis every man for himself.

(?) When I come off at Dunkirk I come off at the harbour. I jumped onto this boat and it was pulled out (having had) two shells through it. The hold was open and a few men panicked (as shells hit it) an' fell doon in the hold. We then went t' Southampton an' they got winched off and then we went t' Cherbourg because there were a few important French folk (to get) on then we got another boat later. We were 10 days without food. There wis a big boat an' the propeller was half outa the water so it was movin' and no more.

● Lord Forbes

Lord Forbes: The Household Troops have always had strong family connections - the same surnames being found generation after generation. Field Marshall Lord Gort wrote to his new born grandson, Philip Sidney, who later followed in his grandfather's and father's footsteps by serving in the Grenadier or First Regiment of Foot Guards:

> *'Some day you also may be a Grenadier and, if so, I know you will never fail to be impressed by the fine sense of comradeship and loyalty which binds all ranks together imbued with one thought and one thought only - the honour of the Regiment. Never must its name be tarnished'.*

I was not the first of our family to serve in the Foot Guards. Our family service as Guardsmen with the Household Troops began with James Ochoncar, then Master of Forbes, who became an Ensign in the Coldstream Regiment of Foot Guards in 1765 aged 16. He served with the Regiment for 26 years during which time he took part in many campaigns including battles fought by the Duke of York in Flanders. He commanded the Grenadier Company of the Regiment and became a Lieutenant Colonel, later a brevet Colonel. At the age of 37 he was made a Major General and when aged 43 he became second-in-command of our Forces in the Mediterranean Army. Afterwards, he commanded first the Cork District and later the Eastern Districts in Ireland. He was promoted full General at the age of 54. His eldest son James was also a Coldstreamer and became a Lieutenant Colonel. Unfortunately, however, he died of apoplexy whilst attending a ball at the Pitti Palace in Florence. Ochoncar's second son Walter was also a Coldstreamer. Both brothers served with their Regiment at Waterloo. Walter had only just joined the Coldstream Guards and must have been one of the youngest - if not the youngest - Officer on the field of battle, as he was only aged 17. During the battle he took over command of a Company at Hougoumont.

My father, Atholl, served in the Grenadier Guards from 1905 till 1919, and during his service he was Adjutant of the 3rd Battalion, and later Regimental Adjutant. He also was on active service in North West Europe, but eventually had to retire through ill health. Jonathan, our second son, following in his ancestors' footsteps served with the Grenadier Guards from 1968 to 1977. He became Adjutant of the 1st Battalion and did several tours of duty in Northern Ireland with his Regiment before being seconded to the Sultan's Forces in Oman, where he was engaged in active service on the Yemen Frontier. He retired with the rank of Captain.

The Army today is very much smaller than it was when I did my military service. However, in an age when standards and moral values are falling, the Armed Services are still a haven of order and civilised values in the country. I can recommend service in the Household Troops to any future generation of my family. The profession of Arms is an honourable one where material reward is meagre but satisfaction immense, and the experience invaluable.

On the morning of 3rd September, whilst the Battalion was engaged in constructing air-raid trenches, we were told that a special announcement was due to be broadcast on the radio at 11.15. All the Officers foregathered in the Officers' Mess and we heard the Prime Minister, Neville Chamberlain, announcing to the nation that we were at war with Germany. This is what we had all expected to hear. Chamberlain had tried to play for time knowing that the British needed more time to get their forces onto a war footing and also he knew there were some influential dissident Germans who wished to see the end of Hitler. However there was now no alternative. The chips were down.

Immediately upon the outbreak, the Expeditionary Army began to move to France. The main movement of troops was through Cherbourg, with vehicles and stores going through Brest and Nantes. Assembly points were at Le Mans and Laval, and by mid-October four British Divisions were positioned south of Lille, along the Franco-Belgian border.

Two weeks after the declaration of war, Dick Crompton Roberts led a small advance party from the Battalion to France, and a week later a Detachment under the command of Captain Peter Clifton sailed during the night from Spithead to Brest. This Detachment consisted of all the transport under my command, Bren gun carriers commanded by Tommy Reynell-Packe, and Fred Turner the Quartermaster with the Battalion stores. We wore life-jackets for the whole voyage, which was uneventful, except for one moment when we suddenly altered course, because it was thought that a German submarine was tracking us. From Brest we went by road to Le Mans where we joined up with the remainder of the Battalion.

The 3rd Battalion, along with the 2nd Battalion Coldstream Guards, and the 2nd Battalion Hampshire Regiment, were the fighting troops of the 1st Guards Brigade, which made up the spearhead of the British Expeditionary Force. The Brigade was commanded by Brigadier 'Beckie' Beckwith-Smith, a charming and very efficient Coldstreamer, and formed part of 1st Division under the command of Major General Alexander, an Irish Guardsman.

On 30th October the whole Battalion moved by train to Arras. For this move the vehicles were loaded onto flat wagons. Officers were in 3rd class carriages, and the Guardsmen were in the famous First World War wagons which had '40 hommes 8 chevaux' marked on them. On arrival at Arras the Battalion took up positions near the villages of Bachy and Genech, close to the Belgian frontier, and I set up 'B' Echelon with Fred Turner in a farming area near Douai. Fred was billeted in a farmhouse with some of his stores in its outbuildings, and the remainder in the vehicles. I had a tiny room in a farm worker's house just across the road, and we had meals together in Fred's house. He was a marvellous congenial companion. We really enjoyed each other's company under conditions which were far from ideal. Our meals were monotonous to a degree, as they were army rations. It was not possible to buy food as we did not have French ration cards. There was a small issue of coal, so it was just possible to get the temperature above freezing when the weather was very cold. It was here that we spent a miserable winter with a particularly unpleasant mixture of wet or very cold weather, or snow.

During January the weather was especially severe with snow, followed by bitterly cold winds with hard frost both day and night. At times the roads were sheets of ice, with the old-fashioned cobbled ones being the most hazardous. Even with antifreeze in the radiators, some of the vehicles froze up, making life very difficult for me as Transport Officer. It was said to be the coldest winter in the north east of France for 100 years. We could all believe it!

Life was one of considerable boredom. The long dreary winter evenings were trying and many of the Guardsmen saved up their pay to buy radios in an effort to relieve the monotony. The Belgian frontier was closed to troops and the only relaxation was when a few Officers at a time were allowed to visit the flesh pots of Lille. Tommy Reynell-Packe and I usually managed to go there together. Here in Lille we discovered an excellent restaurant, which also had a good floor show. Once at the end of January when visiting Lille one evening, we each had a most welcome bath in a hotel. This was our first one since landing in France, and although we paid through the nose for it, it was well worth it. Then, after a good meal, we struggled back to the Battalion, hampered by many stops to free the frozen pedal controls of my vehicle.

Letters and parcels were always a great joy to receive, and I remember one in particular which Anne Chamberlain, wife of the Prime Minister, sent to me. It contained a suede waistcoat which gave marvellous protection from the icy winds. Such thoughtfulness and kindness was in complete contrast to the unfriendly and uncooperative nature of the French people around us. It was difficult to believe that they were our allies.

During November Stucs gave up being Adjutant of the Battalion on being posted to the 2nd Battalion, part of the 7th Guards Brigade, which was also in the British Expeditionary Force. Stucs had been a model Adjutant and as such was hard to follow. His successor was Charles Earle.

The winter months gave a breathing space to the army which was used to good account. The ready-prepared defences which the BEF had occupied, consisting of an anti-tank ditch with pill-boxes and wire entanglement, were extended and greatly improved to make a kind of Siegfried Line. To vary the experiences of the troops, they were moved by Brigades in rotation to a Sector of the French front which was in contact with the enemy. Our turn for this came in February 1940, and the Battalion moved by train at night, from Arras to Metz and then on to the Maginot Line, where we took up positions on what was called the Ligne de Contact. Brigade 'B' Echelon Officers were all billeted in an old abandoned farmhouse where, at night, it sounded as if an army was on the move. In actual fact it was the prowling rats on the move in the loft.

> "it was said to be the coldest winter in the north east of France for 100 years"

Here the country, with its hills and forests, was far more interesting and pleasant than in the flat windswept country of our main location, near the Belgian frontier in the north. One afternoon a French Officer invited me to do a tour of one of the big mainly underground fortresses of the Maginot Line, which he claimed was impregnable. I must say that it was very impressive with its steel doors which could be locked to isolate various sections. Ammunition could be brought up in little wagons, drawn by electric-powered units, from the cellars deep under the fort. Of course, what the French had not appreciated was the possibility of the line being outflanked or being broken at some spot, thus enabling the enemy to encircle it and attack it from the rear. At the time the Allies had not comprehended the potential of German armour, or the speed at which their forces could move.

At times the Germans, from their lines about 1,500 yards away, would fire a few shells at the Battalion positions. This resulted in two Guardsmen suffering minor wounds. Between us and the Germans there was a little village with a church, and it was thought that they might be using its tower as an observation post. So one morning Captain 'Cuckoo' Starkey led a patrol to the village while the Battalion waited eagerly and anxiously. Not a shot was heard, and then suddenly the silence was broken as the clear-toned bell in the church-tower began to ring. It was 'Cuckoo' ringing the bell. There were no Germans in or near the tower at the time. Cuckoo had gained control on the Battalion front of no-man's land.

During March I was sent on a nine day sniper's course at Hythe. Many of the sniper's skills were much the same as those which I was used to when stalking deer in Scotland, and proved of considerable interest to me. Some of the instructors were from the Lovat Scouts whose main recruiting area was around Inverness. I was fairly proficient with a rifle and remember one day, to the surprise of my instructor, putting an inch group of five shots in the bull's-eye at 200 yards. At the end of the course, my report stated: '....a really excellent Officer who should prove to be exceptional. Would make a good Intelligence Officer' - what a contrast to the educational reports I had been given whilst at school!

The course was followed by nine days' leave at home, where I was joined by my great friend Stucs who was now in the 2nd Battalion and, like me, on leave from France. On my return to the Battalion I found that I had been posted to No.2 Company as Platoon Commander. The Company was commanded by Roderick (Napoleon) Brinckman, a

very brave Officer, whose turnout was always immaculate. One evening 'Naps', as he was called, went to have a meal with our 1st Battalion who were not far away. He was obviously entertained very well, with the result that after dinner he fell down some stairs, and had to have five stitches put in his head by the Battalion Medical Officer. He was granted a week's leave following this, which he spent in Paris where, to the delight of our Company, he stocked up with a supply of pate de foie gras, strawberries, and cream. When he brought this treat back to the Officers' Mess, the Company Commander's misfortune was much appreciated by all the other Officers of the Company.

It was by now obvious that what had been called the 'phoney war' was at an end, imminently to be replaced by the real thing. Already the German Air Force was becoming active, and crossed the Belgian frontier from time to time to drop a bomb here and there. Any such bombers were soon sent scurrying away by our fighters or by ground fire. I remember one occasion when the Adjutant and I were standing talking and suddenly a German aircraft came over, making us dive rather smartly into what turned out to be a somewhat smelly ditch. During these later weeks we did dawn patrols to ensure that no Germans had reached the frontier.

By this time the people of France were being severely rationed, like everyone at home. The French could seldom obtain meat, and sugar was scarce. Coal, except for a limited amount for the forces, was almost non-existent, making cooking extremely difficult.

On the 10th of May the Germans invaded the Low Countries, and it so happened that the Battalion was in the awkward position of not having a Commanding Officer. Jack Aird had returned to be a courtier with the Royal Family. He was much better suited to this than to leading us in battle, but his successor, Alan Adair, had not yet arrived. After dark on 11th May the Battalion marched into Belgium through Tournai, and on to Velaines where our new CO joined us. Alan Adair was a man of great charm and esteem who later distinguished himself as Commander of the Guards Armoured Division.

After marching most of the night as well as during the daytime, we covered 21 miles. This was quite a long march under difficult conditions as, with there being much military traffic on the road, we were forced onto the dusty edges. This was the first such march of the war, and many of the Guardsmen's feet were not hardened by then, with the result that a number developed blisters. By 13th May the Battalion reached the area of the River Dyle. Here the 1st Guards Brigade was to

> " we blew the bridges just ahead of the advancing Germans "

take up a defensive position, with the Grenadier Battalion in reserve, near the junction of the Rivers Dyle and Lasne on the reverse slope of some high ground near Huldenburg. Here we dug in. The High Command plan was that the BEF should hold the line of the Dyle. Consisting of nine Divisions the BEF, together with Belgian and French Armies, was defending a front which extended from the coast at Antwerp southwards past Sedan to Montmedy and the Maginot Line. Right up to the time of the German invasion, Belgium had been neutral, thus precluding our entry to reconnoitre this forward position. In the event, the German advance began to our south.

During all the time that we had been in Belgium, fifth-columnists had been active. Now that we were in position overlooking the River Dyle, we experienced such activities twice. On two nights a man ran through our lines shouting: 'Gas!' We all put on our gas-masks, but it turned to be a hoax on both occasions. As it transpired, these were the only times during the whole war that I had to wear my mask. I was glad of that, as gas warfare is truly bestial. Except for the occasional German bomb, the only action seen here by the Battalion was when a parachute was observed floating to the ground. Several Bren gunners opened fire on it. Only when it reached the ground was it found to be supporting the pilot of a British Hurricane, who was unharmed by the bullets, but who broke his ankle on landing and altogether was in a very bad temper.

On 15th May the Brigade was ordered to prepare to withdraw to the Escaut Canal, because the BEF was in danger of being caught in a pincer movement, the Dutch having surrendered in the north, and the Germans having advanced through Luxembourg and the Ardennes. They had broken through the Allied lines to the south between Sedan and Meziere, thus outflanking the River Dyle line. As we rather expected after our time on the Magi not Line, the French troops were of doubtful quality.

The withdrawal began on the next day soon after dark, and we were faced with a sixty mile footslog. As we headed for Brussels, German aircraft constantly flew over us dropping flares to keep track of us, and whenever they came over, we could see lights flashing from houses. This was once again the fifth-columnists at work, signalling to the pilots. Then, as we went through the Forest of Soignes, to the east of Brussels, we found some relief as nightingales were joyfully singing, being oblivious of the war. tension was eased for a time.

On entering Brussels in darkness it seemed strangely deserted, and there were only a few silent figures about. It was in the city that at one stage the Battalion lost its way, and for a short time we were heading east. This led the Belgians to speculate that we were returning to counter-attack the Germans. Once on the west side of Brussels, we took up a defensive position before moving on the next night towards the River Dendre. Here we again took up a defensive position, covering the two main bridges leading over the river to Ninove. It was not until the following night that we blew the bridges just ahead of the advancing Germans.

Soon after the blowing of the bridges we received orders to withdraw still further to what was to become our main defensive position on the Escaut Canal. We hardly knew what rest was during the withdrawal for, on arrival at each new position, it was a case of getting down to digging slit-trenches. We had even worse exertion to face us, when on 20th May the Battalion began its long march to the canal. This was the worst day of the withdrawal. It was a terrible march.

The roads were jammed with refugees all moving westwards like ourselves. Some were trudging disconsolately, carrying large bundles of blankets and personal treasures. Others were pulling little carts piled high with possessions, or were leading horses, ponies, or donkeys pulling wagons containing as many belongings as possible. The many varied forms of transport included anything from cars to prams. It had obviously been a case of people using anything possible to help them carry what they could grab of their precious worldly goods.

We marched on and on in spite of the chaotic and somewhat bizarre situation. All the time we were becoming more and more foots ore and weary. The monotony of the march was broken at one stage when the whole Battalion was lifted for a few miles in army lorries. Apart from this welcome interlude, we had a number of very unwelcome visits from Stuka dive-bombers. When we heard the shrieks of the diving planes we would break ranks and hurl ourselves into the nearest ditch for cover. Some individuals would shoot at the German planes, but to no avail. The Germans had air supremacy, and we hardly saw a British fighter in the skies. To make matters worse, we were on the receiving end of sporadic shelling, and we had been told that a German column was advancing along a road within range and virtually parallel to our own, but miraculously we suffered no casualties. Tragically the refugees, many of whom could not take cover quickly enough, did fall victim to the strafing. During this time it became obvious that some were not refugees, but fifth-column

> " it became obvious that some were not refugees, but fifth-column people dressed as nuns "

A British Matilda mk.II knocked out during the battle of Arras. This tank was impervious to all anti-tank guns at the time but the Germans, with their typical ingenuity, used their 88mm anti-aircraft gun against them - with devastating effect. Courtesy the Tank Museum

people dressed as nuns. We did not stop to deal with them as we had to press on to the Escaut Canal as quickly as possible. We passed human bodies and dead animals amongst the debris of the various types of transport.

At a later date our Commanding Officer wrote of the withdrawal:

'I have never seen men more exhausted; it was only by sheer will power they reached their positions on the Escaut Canal late afternoon 20th May'.

Eventually on reaching the canal, the Battalion dug in on its banks, just south of Pecq. We really were a 'thin red line' along the canal, with Mont-St-Aubert on the other side overlooking our positions. Apart from this hill, there was flat ground on either side of the canal. The countryside consisted of small farms, with lines of poplars and willows along the farm roads and, in places, along the far side of the canal. Otherwise there were no dykes or hedges to be seen. In most places the canal banks rose four or five feet above the surrounding land, so that they provided a little cover. By the time darkness fell we were fairly well organised

but, due to the shortage of daylight, our trenches were little more than shallow scratches in the ground.

Just before first light on 21st May, after what seemed a long night, the whole Battalion stood-to. We were at the ready. There was an air of tension and we could see nothing in front of us, as a heavy early morning mist hung like a blanket all along the canal. At times we could just hear what sounded like the breaking of the odd twig or a little rustling noise on the other side of the waterway, which was about 20 yards wide. We did not know whether these confusing noises were made by animals or by humans.

At 0730 it was light, but the mist was still hanging around in patches when the Germans attacked with a violent mortar and machine gun barrage. They had not been observed forming up. Not only had the mist hidden their preparations, but also there was high corn in the fields, and there were clumps of trees and bushes on the far side of the canal. At the time the water level was exceptionally low in the waterway. The Germans crossed the canal between the Battalion's left flank held by 4 Company and the adjoining Coldstream Battalion, and then overran some of 4 Company's positions. Major Reggie Alston-Roberts-West, commanding 4

Company, at once formed a defensive flank in an effort to try to stop the Germans from cutting off the forward units of 2 Company, my Company, from its headquarters. By now the Germans were attacking all along our front with mortars and small arms fire. At times we could see them on the far side of the canal and we would open fire. Since the attack had started, I had been lying near the lip of the canal-bank trying to locate any movement on the far side. Our artillery was replying and there was considerable noise of battle.

Suddenly, I felt a thud on my left leg. My immediate reaction was to get lower down the bank for some extra cover. I tried to move, but my left leg would not respond. When I looked at it, I saw a tear in my battledress trouser by my knee. There was also blood. I looked behind me and saw one of my Platoon close to me. He had been hit in the arm and was receiving assistance from another Guardsman. I guessed that we had both been hit by the same mortar bomb. Then Guardsman Evans in my Platoon saw my plight, and dragged me down from the lip of the canal bank. Mortar bombs were bursting all around by now, and the larger German Artillery barrage continued to separate us from Battalion HQ which was located near our reserve Company, a mile to the rear of our front line.

The next moment their Commander, Reggie West, appeared, followed by George, Duke of Northumberland, I could hear heavy rifle and machine-gun fire around 4 Company to the left. Reggie told me he wanted to try to make contact with Battalion HQ so as to organise a counter-attack aimed at pushing the Germans back over the canal. He then asked me if I would like to be left where I was and taken prisoner, or whether I would prefer to risk being pulled back towards the Regimental Aide Post. Without any hesitation I opted for the latter. Next moment Reggie and George, crouching down to avoid being an obvious target, were pulling me along the ground by my shoulder straps, rather like a dead stag is pulled off the hill by its antlers. We had not gone far when I passed out.

When I came to I found myself being loaded into the front of a pick-up vehicle. I had probably not been dragged very far, because I recognised the driver as being Platoon Sergeant-Major Cassford from my Company. We were soon on the move but had not gone much more than about half a mile when the vehicle suddenly veered off the road, and ended up on its side in the ditch. I could just make out that PSM Cassford had been hit in the arm. I passed out again. On coming to again I found myself being laid on a stretcher in a

tiny brick shed with a pitched roof and concrete floor. I guessed that it was part of a farm building which was being used as a Regimental Aide Post. I could just hear voices as I took stock of my surroundings. Shortly a Medical Orderly, crouching down to enter the shed, attached a medical card to my battledress before giving me a shot of morphia.

From that moment I was oblivious to what was going on until there was a crash and I found myself covered in rubble. A German shell or mortar bomb must have hit the shed roof. At first I could see very little as there was so much thick dust, both on me and in the air. Gradually, as the dust cleared, I was able to make out that most of the timbered roof and a small part of one wall had collapsed. Luckily, all the bits and pieces that fell on top of me were not heavy, and I was none the worse for this incident. I never knew the full extent of the damage, and in no time at all Orderlies were extricating me from the rubble and putting me in an ambulance with other wounded. As I passed out again immediately after this, I remember nothing of the ambulance trip.

> "in no time at all Orderlies were extricating me from the rubble and putting me in an ambulance"

The next thing which I remember is being carried on the ambulance stretcher up some stairs, and being transferred to another stretcher on the floor of a very large room. This Casualty Clearing Station looked as if it might have been a school in normal times. There must have been between 70 and 100 wounded lying on stretchers on the floor. We were practically touching one another. Again I was given a jab of morphia and promptly passed out or went to sleep, as I remember nothing until sometime during the night, when I was taken on my stretcher to a little room where a Medical Officer told me he was going to operate, to remove some bits and pieces from my knee.

I next remember being given a blood transfusion back in the big room. From that moment I slept practically the whole time, except for being woken occasionally to be given a drink of water or a cup of tea. At some time during the evening of the next day I was put into an ambulance with others, to be taken a short distance to a hospital train. There were tiers of stretchers, one above the other down the side of the coach, and I was thankful that I was on the top tier. After dark the blacked-out train set off. At one stage during the night we stopped for some considerable time and there was much talk in French. Then, as so often happens on the continental railways, there was much blowing of whistles and eventually we set off again, but at what seemed little more than walking pace. One of the Medical Orderlies said that it was thought

● "Aye, I remember many scenes like this at Dunkirk". (Dod Martin). Courtesy J. Pelella

that the line ahead of us had been bombed, or otherwise cut, and that we were taking an alternative route on a single track line.

As dawn broke, we arrived at Dunkirk and were shunted to the quayside where we could see a ship tied up. We all thought that shortly we would be transferred on board to cross The Channel, but this proved to be wishful thinking. The train just remained on the quayside and nothing happened, except that during the space of about two hours we were dive-bombed three times by German planes. Each time we heard the Stukas screeching down, followed by the port and ships' antiaircraft guns going into action, and then the dreaded whine of the released bombs. As the bombs hit the ground, the whole train would shake. It was a

miracle that we did not receive a direct hit.

This was a frightening experience, as by now I was fully conscious. There was absolutely nothing one could do. We were incapable of moving and were sitting ducks, as we lay on our stretchers, listening and praying. Eventually, after enduring this ordeal three times, myself and some of the others in my coach asked one of the Medical Orderlies to request the Embarkation Officer to have the train moved into a nearby tunnel, which we remembered coming through. Thankfully, this was done, and we were all able to relax. I shall never understand why the train was left on the quayside in the first instance. After a while we moved back there and, to our great relief, embarkation soon began.

I was taken up the gangway of the hospital ship on a stretcher, and then put into a hammock bed. There were rows of these little wooden beds, which were suspended, and swung like hammocks. When all the pendant beds were occupied, more wounded were left on stretchers on the floor. An Officer with a chest wound was put down practically under my bed, and I was greatly surprised to discover that I knew him. He was none other than Major Dunn, now a Lieutenant Colonel, my first Company Commander at Sandhurst.

Shortly after setting sail, there was a muffled explosion, possibly caused by a mine, or by a bomb. The ship quickly changed course, and after that there were no other incidents. We berthed in Folkestone harbour and, as we were taken off the ship on stretchers, there were masses of ladies on the quayside dishing out cups of tea, which were most welcome. We were transferred to a train, and as I drank my cup of tea I noticed that Peter 'Piego' Radford-Norcop, my Company Second-in-Command, was in the same coach. He too had been hit in the leg.

The hospital train took us by a lengthy round about route to St Albans. Luckily, the rail system around London was fully linked, so we were spared having to change stations. On arrival at St Albans station, we were taken by ambulance to Hillend Hospital which, before being commandeered, had been a lunatic asylum. In the ward I found myself in the next bed to Piego. Now, nearly 60 hours after being wounded, my battledress was taken off. As a nurse was helping me into a pair of pyjamas, I noticed for the first time that my right arm was bandaged, and that I had also been wounded in the wrist. I am sure that this must have happened at the same time as I was hit in the leg, but it proved to be a minor wound, and no bones had been broken.

Jack Kilgour: If I'd have been in this country and not in France I wouldn't be here today. My mate and I were travelling back with a motorbike each from Luc St. Mere where we'd been down to a cinema. We were riding back on the right hand

● Courtesy J. Pelella

side of the road and we heard this woosh and we threw the bikes in the middle of the road and we dived into the ditch. When the stones and everything settled we got up and the crater was on the other side of the road. Nine inches of the road was away at the lip of the crater so we'd have been nicely in the crater if we'd been on the left. Cost me £27 to do that. Well, with shrapnel and stones they broke the glass of the speedometer, twisted the footrest because I threw it down, - that's what I had to pay for, that wasn't enemy action. There was a hole in the petrol tank, but that was all right. I got a new tank because that was considered enemy action but what I did by throwing the bike down, that was not enemy action so I had to pay for it. That was wilful damage to His Majesty's property!

Billy Henderson: We were at a place called La Baule and were stationed there as reinforcements for the 51st. We had what they called ENSA girls who came to entertain us. Being an electrician and I was picked out to look after the lightin' and the stage in general. So we scuttered aboot doin' that for a wee while. When Jerry broke through we had t' shift so we went down t' St. Malo.

Robbie Bremner: We eventually got shipped away in the winter down t' Southampton. It was so cold and the roads were like glass. We then got across the Channel and got wer lectures about the procedures if we got taken prisoner an' that. We landed in Cherbourg and that was a different story. From there we were in a lota different places and the other place I remember was being in charge of the canteen and I was in this byre and there was a lota mice and they'd nibbled the corners o' the boxes. This was the best thing that happened to me so efter 'at I started packin' everything awar in boxes but I ae kept the charge stump. When the Officer came round and said, "How y' getting' on?" I said, "Oh that mice sir, they're terrible and I'll have t' get this replaced and that replaced." And he said, "That's all right, jist tek it off yer book it's no problem." I always kept a book on these goods and when we landed at Dunkirk one o' the boys sez t' me, "I hope y' threw away that book!"

When we landed, Jerry started t' bomb us in this wood an' I said, "God all mighty, deed bodies!"

> " I said, "God all mighty, deed bodies!" an' it wis pigs, the Jerries had bombed these pigs "

an' it wis pigs, the Jerries had bombed these pigs, I keen 'at fine. Well, we was tekin' oot the shells and layin' them doon but they said, "Come on lets get outa here." Then we landed up in a place called Anapees (sic) and es wis when the Jerries where commin' and the civilians were commin'. We were defendin' this village and with an anti tank rifle. I can always remember this night, it was wi Robbie Campbell and they had this Piat gun (in 1940 it would have been a Boys anti-tank rifle). We lay doon in this brushwood and this night we hears the tanks commin'. Robbies lookin' at me an' I'm lookin' at him and I sez, "Dinna worry we'll easy knock 'em oot, jist wait." Wi good luck they didna come near us but the next mornin' the folks come in to express thanks. This woman come along wi her daughter and she sez, "Would you make love t' my daughter because we don't want the Germans to—"Well, I sez, "No, no I'm a married man." and I turned to Robbie and said, "Robbie you can get goin'!" Oh God, well that was it! Then when the thing started t' happen, we were in Belgium at the battle for Tournay and the Albert canal. We were with a brigade o' Guards they were really smart and I said, "This is great, we're in ahind them, we'll be alright." But it wasna long before the Belgian soldiers came through wi their tassels an' ar this. We had t' get crackin' and we come back t' Tournay. Johnny Walker, he'd awfa black rotten teeth, well him an' me we went inta Lille wi this PU track and we loaded up wi tinned ham, drink an' arthing and we gid awar wi ar this down t' the boys. We dished ar this out til 'em and had quite a party but the next day we were down to this big echelon where they spiked all the guns. I wisna on the guns I was a canteen man and we were lookin' fer rations an' things fit we could get. We loaded up from a place that we found all this food and we were bombed twice commin' along in this truck goin' t' meet up wi the boys. So after that we set off for the road t' Dunkirk. There was a chappie Reid, M'sel and Warwicks (sic) and I think it wis Stanley Falconer fae Banff and we were on the beaches for a couple o' days an' I sez t' the boys, "Na, we're nae gonna get off here, come on lets ging recht inta Dunkirk." In the harbour there was HMS *Greyhound* but the quay had been bombed but we got onto this ship by walkin' roond the holes in the pier. Not only was there soldiers goin' on, there were civilians an' ar commin' on. I think that we were one o' the most fortunate regiments because we only lost about five from our squad. We landed and went up t' Salisbury Plain.

" as far as dishin' out
rations were concerned we
would have trusted the
Germans before we would
have trusted our
own Sergeant "

St. Valery

'*T*HE FATE OF THE HIGHLAND DIVISION, *caught in the web of circumstance, can always be remembered by Scotland not only with sorrow but with pride. Officers and men fought the good fight: it was not theirs to determine how they should finish their course*'

Page 84. Volume 5. The History of the Gordon Highlanders.

Sammy Robertson: In January I went t' France in 1939. As a piper I did very little training, then we went t' Bremlin Woods and that was the first action we had. We lost a company there. They were captured. We'd a lot o' casualties and they were captured. I was a prisoner mainly in West Prussia. Where we were captured was just outside of St. Valery and it was a sorta ditch an' we were goin' along ere creepin' along keepin' oor heads down looked up an' there was a line o' tanks just lookin' down on us - and that was it. The 12th of June the whole division wis caught. The 51st division. We then walked through France t' Germany and we went up the Rhine in barges for three days. We then went into cattle trucks for another three t' four days. We eventually landed in Poland. Torun wis the name o' the place and that was the Polish equivalent of our Aldershot. We were there for a while then we were broken up in t' parties goin' oot doin' different jobs and then after that we were moved inta Germany - this was all in 1940.

David: What were the conditions like?

Sammy: There was one or two huge tents and it was jist like sand on the beach and we had no water we couldna get washed or nothing. Y' had y' hair shaved an' y' was as lousy as coots. They'd come out wi big dixies an' you'd get a bowl o' soup. It worked out at a litre o' soup a day. That's all y' got plus a bit o' bread. Apart fae that it was ersatz coffee. We went back intae Poland and they were buildin' ice-breakers on the river Weichsel as the Germans called it, we called it the Vistula. The bridges were all blown up an' we were stayin' in an old schloss. There was a party o' us; oh that was a dreadful place that, ice used t' be on the

inside o' the walls - and we went across in a boat like a trawler an' that took you across t' the place where the ice-breakers were. This was because when the thaw came the blocks of ice would come past the bridge.

David: So you were building ice-breakers on bridges?

Sammy: Well, we were just labourin' on them. Then one day we walked across. The river fell about 15 feet in one night and it froze up and what they had t' do was they had bored holes and then they put the explosives in t' break the ice so the could get the pile drivers in. Then when the woodwork was done it was sheathed in iron, which must have been about half an inch thick.

When we got de-loused which was about every two month y' just bundled everything t'gether an' put them in to the laundry but nine times outa 10 they come out worse than when they went in! Fut we found was efter we started gettin' Red Cross parcels then the lice disappeared. That woulda been about 1942. Up until then we weren't in very good shape at all - the Red Cross did a magnificent job.

We then went back t' West Prussia and I was workin' on a farm there. We didna live in the farmhouse but there was a house where some of us lived in one half and the others lived in the other and from there we went out t' work in the individual farms. There were huge state farms where they lived on the farm but we came back to the village and we went out every day an' worked there. We were entitled t' hard labour food so we got a bit more and on the whole that wasna too bad. It was long hours, six in the mornin' till eight at night.

In addition to walkin' to East Prussia we had t' walk back out. That was because of the Russian advance that started in 1945. We used t' get

> **"**We got a Red Cross parcel before we started oot and that was the last food we had for 19 days**"**

● Left: British prisoners in East Germany

snippets of information from a fella on one of the state farms an' he was pretty good wi wireless an' that. One o' the things we did hear about was when the Japs came into the war and a course the Germans made a great play on that. We were gonna be obliterated an' arthing, then when the Americans come in that was our chance. I got on well enough with the farmer but I didna like the farm. There was the farmer, a young lassie and meself. The farmer, he had two daughters but they workit in the fields. When the Russians started t' come we were moved out, in fact they were evacuating Germany, they were all movin' out. We were goin' across a river which was frozen and the refugees were too close together and the ice broke and there was a horse cart and everything just went in t' the lake. They jist detoured roond aboot, couldn't stop, no hope. We got a Red Cross parcel before we started oot and that was the last food we had for 19 days. Then y' just had t' scrounge, stop in places and maybe get a crust but they were as bad off as us. Y' jist scrounged as y' went along. One o' the things which was a great solace was if y' could get a smoke. If y' could scrape some bark off a beech tree or some off an oak tree rub it up an' roll it in a page o' the Bible. Everybody had a New Testament y' know and if y' sucked too hard y' went up in flames! If you were inhalin' smoke it killed the pangs o' hunger. I canna think o' many people that didna smoke.

David: Did you lose many friends on the march?

Sammy: Oh yes! There was Alec Murray, he played fitba before the war, he died on the march. Jim McDonald, he didna die on the march he developed tuberculosis, he spent a year and some months in hospital here. He was in Woodend first then he was doon in Inverurie. I was seven stone when I got home. I landed up in Hanover an' I got home on the 18th o' April. We were waitin' aboot t' get bathed an' get new kit. I was wanderin' about an' sez, "I'm nae queuing'." And there wis a fella an' he shouted, mind you y' could hardly totter aboot, "The first 20 people over here will go straight home t' Blighty." I was second! It wis a Sterlin' bomber an' we sat on crates an' I come right home and we landed at Horsham and oh my word when we went in there were trestles laid oot an' the table were groanin' under the food! Y' went through at the end o' that an' y' dropped all y' clothes then y' had a bath. Then y' got rubbed wi powder all over, then into a Nissen hut then intae bed then in the mornin y' repeated the process an' come back an' then y' got issued wi clothes. That wis it, I wis clear!

This contribution was taken from the then top secret document regarding the escape of Company Sergeant Major Alexander Moir from the Germans. Company Sergeant Major Alexander Moir went with the BEF to France with the Gordons. He was one of the first soldiers to meet the Nazis in front of the Maginot Line when patrols went out to probe the enemy defences. He was captured at St Valery. This is a diary of events of Company Sergeant Major Moir from the 9th of June 1940 until being taken prisoner on the 12th of June and the subsequent adventures of his first escape.

June the 9th. Forest of Eu. The position is becoming grave the line on our right has been broken once again and Jerry is moving fast. We've orders to withdraw in an attempt to form a new line; every dawn finds us nearer the coast. It appears to me that this will be a minor Dunkirk. We are withdrawing tonight, destination not known but believed to be about 20 kilometres distant.

June the 10th. South of the Forest of Eu. We withdrew during the night. A devil of a mix up, transports everywhere, jam packed solid vehicles and a pitch black night which did not help matters. Shells are coming over close by, too close in fact, the bombardment is continual. All kit not absolutely essential has been dumped and destroyed. We are almost entirely cut off and

" we are entirely cut off with the sea at our backs and only one small coastal village of St Valery "

the chance of getting away are getting more remote daily. Fighting, marching, riding and working 24 hours a day is a heavy strain on everyone.

June the 11th. Nr. St. Valery-En-Caux. Another withdrawal last night taking over seven hours to complete, our destination is in the hands of the enemy which means that we are entirely cut off with the sea at our backs and only one small coastal village of St Valery. There is still a chance that the Navy can save the day but in the opinion of most of us it is a very slender chance indeed. All vehicles except those carrying food or ammunition have been smashed and rendered useless to the enemy. At this time I was

● Corporal Alexander Moir (seated), circa 1939

C.S.M. of B company 1st Gordons. During the night withdrawal, myself with about one platoon of B and one platoon of C got separated from the remainder of the battalion. However, we reached our destination at about 04.30 hours. I saw the Brigade Commander at about this time and were ordered to take up a position guarding a crossroads about six kilometres inland from St Valery. The scene of the French retreating in one endless column with all types of transport and guns was not very encouraging. About midday the French seemed to rally and began to form up facing the enemy again. We were then ordered to withdraw and rejoin the Battalion which had taken up a defensive position but where, no one seemed to know. After marching hither and thither I eventually located the area held by my Battalion. At about 15.00 hours, I joined up with my Battalion and then all hell broke loose. Almost immediately, a tank attack supported by everything they had including aircraft. This attack was directed against the main St.Valery road part of which the battalion held and the tanks did not break through but our casualties were numerous, mostly from shell fire. There was a lull at about 5 o'clock and I took this opportunity of getting my men out to my Company which was hard to reach. No food had been got to them this day, although it had been sent out but was left some distance behind unknown to us at the time. There was a Chateau near the Battalion Headquarters full of wounded now and more to come in yet. The Regimental Quartermasters Sergeant - C went away some time ago and has not been heard of since. The position is getting hopeless so I asked the Company Commander what his orders was in case of all our officers becoming casualties and I am informed, "Last man and last round", unless told otherwise. I just say, "OK" but our only hope is a withdrawal tonight. The men are dead beat through lack of food and

sleep. The ammunition is also running low and they say the Gordons have been continually in action since their first taste of the Ligne De Contact in front of the Maginot line. They have not had one day's rest for about a month except for two days journey from Lorraine to the Somme. Shells are coming over thick and fast, big ones too. Nearly all our casualties are from shell fire or mortar. I think things might happen during the night to cause us to withdraw near St Valery.

June the 12th. Orders had apparently been issued this morning to withdraw but the runners never reached my Company B. About 8.00 hours the Company Commander decided to withdraw one platoon first, then myself with Company Headquarters in the direction of where Battalion Headquarters was situated. I knew the position of the Battalion Headquarters clearly as I'd been there the day previous but on reaching this point all I saw were the killed lying around and no one else to be seen. This was a cold wet rainy morning and visibility bad. The Company Commander who stayed with the last two platoons was wounded about this time so sent the stretcher bearers to attend to him. He was subsequently placed on a truck which was near and a driver detailed to try to get him to St Valery. We continued with our withdrawal but did not get very far when the Jerry opened fire from all sides and the heaviest from the direction of St Valery. It was obvious that they had surrounded us and was in possession of the village. However we attempted to fight our way in the direction of the village but soon about 16 German tanks came upon the scene and we were completely surrounded at point blank range. With nothing heavier than a Bren gun there was nothing for it but to surrender as further resistance was useless. We received the order to lay down arms. Even though there was nothing to be gained by continuing the fight the thought of surrender was very hard to bear. German troops came pouring in; tanks, armoured cars, motorcycles and on foot. Also most certainly we would have been up against some of the heavy stuff, Panzer divisions to say the least. We soon gathered that two brigades of the Highland Division plus attached troops had been captured in the fields, on the cliffs and everywhere. Some tried to depart in boats but they were sunk. There still appeared to be some activity North of St Valery but I don't think many got away. About this time I learned from P,S,M, D—- that the Colonel along with 8 others had been taken prisoner in an attempt to reach A and B companies with orders this very morning. All the prisoners were rounded up and taken into the grounds of a big Chateau. The Gordons have more or less got together as I called on them to fall in under me and there appears to be about 200 of us. The officers had been separated from us before leaving the field. Altogether there seems to be about 5000 French and British mixed up. They gave us a small piece of bread each and I got Sergeant F— to cook some food with any scraps which could be found near. There was just about a spoon full each. We soon got to know that we would be doing some marching tomorrow. They intend to march us each day right to the prison camps in Germany.

● Their captors employed British prisoners as manual labour. Here Bill Reaper (left) from Aberdeen tends horses on a farm

June the 13th. St Valery, Rouen road. A hell of a march today on no food. Some of us received sandwiches from the villagers on the way but they, poor devils had little enough for themselves. Myself, I managed to get a few raw carrots at one of the halts which I ate as I went along. We get a halt of 10 minutes in every three hours marching. Some of the men are looking none too good having been short of food for several days. Fortunately, they gave us some dried fish this evening and a small piece of brown bread. That and a drink of water will suffice and goes a long way to cheer us up. We are asleep now in this field, (well guarded naturally). Some have got a coat or a blanket but like myself the majority have only got a ground sheet. I hope it will keep fine and warm as at present.

June the 14th. Near Rouen. We were brought to the outskirts of Rouen today by lorry and also received a little food, biscuits and coffee. The biscuits are our own army biscuits which the enemy have found somewhere. Six of us are trying to stick together now W, McP, D, T and myself. Tiffy and I have been discussing the possibilities of an escape but if they intend to take us North by daily marches there's no hurry. We might have an opportunity once we wear near Boulogne or Calais. Our troops which are ill or have very bad feet, are taken by lorry to the next halt. This seems to indicate a march tomorrow. All the officers have been taken on by lorry and will probably be taken straight back to Germany.

June the 15th. Near St Valery again. I've returned to St Valery with the gang, quite a number of us (farmers in preference). The German Officer in charge asked for men with farming experience to step forward this morning. I decided to be a farmer if it meant staying in France as my mind was made up to escape and whatever happened I'd no intention of ever going to Germany. Therefore I wanted time in France to make plans. It was not for farming that we are required. We had been brought back to the battlefield of St Valery to round up stray French army horses. This has taken us all day. There are about 300 of us here to manage 900

horses, mules included. The procedure has been to collect all the bridles that can be found, then catch a horse or a mule, take it up to a German officer, trot it up and down and if he gives it the OK, then put it in a prepared, compound. If the horse doesn't pass, take off the bridal and let it go again. However, by evening we had caught about 900 which did pass. We were then given a demonstration of how to tie three together, informed through a French interpreter that Reveille would be at 4.00, coffee at 4.15 and each man would go and catch three horses and line up in groups of 150. I, being the only CSM, was sort of in charge and passed on all the orders to the men putting the senior PSMs or Sergeants in charge of the groups who looked after their own party. We were then to march off as soon as possible. It appears that we have to take the horses to some place four days journey from here. Today whilst rounding up horses, I managed to pick up a great coat and a blanket also a Balmoral cap and so have the others. Mac H who was taken to do some burying, came back with some tins of food, beans etc and this evening we had a fairly good meal. We start off tomorrow and those in charge are responsible for keeping order on the road. The guards are very alert and they are doing escort on bicycles. We set off bright and early tomorrow.

June the 16th. Near Totes. What a devil of a day, over 40 kilos, I finish up stiff and tired. Many of the men are worse and some of them had obviously never handled horses in their life. It must also be remembered that these horses have been used to French men speaking to them which makes matters worse. Myself, I had only one horse but I had to constantly dismount to help chaps who had three to manage and sometimes one got away which had to be caught again. They gave us a fairly good meal tonight, French army bread, boiled potatoes and coffee but this is hard work and the little we had saved from the last night's meal soon went. I am as tired as I have ever been and ready for sleep in an orchard this evening.

June the 17th. Near Neufchatel. That is our second day over. Not so far today and I am becoming quite a horse man. I rode the better part of the way. Some of the troops won't make attempt to mount so have a very hard time half walking half running all day. The country around here is familiar. I was in this sector a short time ago. Today, there were very few exceptions in that every village we passed had been bombed at sometime, little country villages of no importance whatsoever. The local remaining inhabitants are trying to be cheerful but it's easy to see how hopeless they feel about it all. Some of them were good enough to hand us a sandwich or a piece of bread as we passed I was lucky enough to receive a loaf of bead and a few lumps of sugar. Tonight when the six of us pooled our resources we managed to make a good meal of it. They don't give us much food, coffee and bread at about 04.15 hours and a little soup and bread when the day is finished, not a great deal to man handle horses about, but we've managed somehow. Several of the horses have become lame and have had to be shot. The guards are quite matter of fact about it, simply leading the horse in to the nearest field and putting a bullet to its head. Altogether we have lost about 100 in this way by the time the journey ended.

June the 18th. Abbeville. It rained last night and being in the open we all became very wet but the sun today has dried us a little. Passed through Blangy today, absolutely bombed flat and not an undamaged building to be seen. A few weeks ago it was a active little place, now the local people would not recognise it. Abbeville has also had its share, the Church especially. There are plenty of German troops in all the towns and villages, they must have a big army of occupation here. With our bread (which is now green and as hard as a brick) we had some stewed meat, the first meat for a longer time. I strongly suspect that it was one of our horses but did not stop to think about it, anything cooked is a luxury now.

June the 19th. Doullens. At last, we've got rid of the horses. Today we bought the whole train of them to a large field several miles from here and turned them loose among hundreds of others. Afterwards, we were brought along here by lorry and have now joined up with a batch of prisoners who have been marching from St Valery them. Some of them look pretty well all in. They faced even worse than us for food. Jerry has done one thing for me, that is to cure my nervousness where horses are concerned. This night's abode is in the moat of the fort and there is not enough room for everyone to stretch but we'll manage.

June the 20th. St.Pol. Arrived here about 17.00 hours after a march of about 30 Kilos. What a column, several of the troops are weak and several had to be taken on by lorry. Most of the boys are damned hungry and the sight of a kind old lady standing at the roadside with a few sandwiches makes everyone dive from the ranks to get something. The guards are getting very annoyed about it, someone will be fired upon soon and several warning shots have been fired over our heads but they will not always fire high. The food this morning was terrible, a small piece of ancient bread and a mouth full of coffee I think made with chicory beans as it has practically no taste at all. This is at 05.00 hours and the next meal will be another small piece of bread and a cup of what looks like soup but there, the resemblance ends. There are rumours that France has asked for an armistice, I suspect there is some truth in it but I'm sure we will not throw in the sponge.

June the 21st. Bethune. The troops are a lot happier today thanks to the French Red Cross who informed us we were to pass through. Hundreds of people were lining the roadsides in the village of Bruay which extends for miles with food and hot drinks for us. I'm certain that everyone left that halting place happier than for days. I gave my name and number and my home address to two different ladies in the hope that my people will be informed of my capture. (As it turned out that was not to be the case, but no doubts lie Allemande was to blame.) I discovered that all the larger towns were plastered with anti-British propaganda but Jerry is a master at that sort of thing. The most common thing is a grave with a wooden cross upon it. On the cross rests a French steel helmet with the inscription 'Pour qui? Pour les Anglais.' or 'L Angleterre' with loads of statistics to prove it. Tiffy and I have decided to go as soon as possible and are now marching North East towards Lille and each step takes us away from our goal and must be retraced. I therefore told him to keep alongside me in the column and we are continually on the look out for a chance to slip out as we will never be any nearer the coast. We had several halts today but there was very little cover of any sort in which to hide until dark.

June the 22nd. Near La Bassec. The opportunity occurred today and we managed to slip out of the column. We got out this morning when the column halted for 10 minutes on the main road near a small wood when the attention of the guards was directed elsewhere. We handed our coats to the others but kept our blanket and ground sheets. We also have a pack each containing some biscuits, (army) and tea. Also, our emergency ration and a few odds and ends. Everything is ready for the start now. All that is necessary is darkness and we are still in uniform. Our intention is to move due West avoiding all towns, villages and coal mining areas etc, moving by night only. We still have the very valuable asset of a compass which Tiffy has concealed on each search. (We had been previously warned by the enemy that if we were found with knives, razors, maps, arms, or compasses, we would be shot.) However the compass will hardly be necessary as long as the night's are clear and the stars can be seen. Travelling time will be limited because it is not really dark until about 23.00 hours and dawn breaks about 4.30 hours. It has just commenced raining to make matters worse and we're waiting patiently among some ferns till 23.00 hours. Start wet about 23.15 hours.

June the 23rd. South of Bethune. It rained heavily during the night which makes it more uncomfortable. This is also a coal mining area with villages everywhere. Each has allotments with barbed wire and netting wire fences in the vicinity which are very difficult to negotiate in the dark. Also, the mines with huge slag heaps, we thought they would probably be guarded and tried our very best to get round them but this made for many large detours. Also objects which loom up in the dark make one very cautious. To get one coal mining area, we had a detour of about four miles. Crops are another snag as they are all about waist high and soaking wet. The results of this night's marching is very poor progress Westwards. Very difficult to find a hideout this morning though eventually we came to rest under a large bush between two fields of wheat. We are very cold and very wet. I make some tea with a tommy cooker and ate one biscuit. Food is going to be difficult and it is quite tiring walking through tall crops all night. We then lie down and go to sleep. Although we have money, it doesn't look as though we will be able to spend it as we can't appear anywhere by daylight. On waking I studied the ground as far as I could see and progress is going to be difficult again tonight. Right in our path lie many huge slag heaps and houses etc which denotes difficulties once more and they are all likely to be occupied by the enemy.

June the 24th near Bruay. This was a most difficult place to get clear of as the village extended for some Kilos. along the main road and we were forced to go through the village in the middle of the night. Although we tried to creep along quietly the army boots seemed to make a terrible noise in the quietness of the night. In addition during several attempts to get out of the village we landed up in cul de sacs which meant we were tracing our steps. Dogs also kept barking, they are a curse. The village was also patrolled by German troops and we had a very narrow escape from one of these. However, we must have heard them first and disappeared up a side street keeping as quiet as mice. The patrol passed and did not spot us. I may mention that I had no difficulty keeping direction

wherever I went. It took us about three hours to clear Bruay and again we got mixed up in the plots etc. We helped ourselves to some carrots, leaks, potatoes but the potatoes were very small and far from being ready. However, anything will do to eat at the moment. So we just put them in our packs and some in our pockets which we eat raw as we go along. When dawn broke we had difficulty in finding a place to hide out but was eventually resolved and we came to rest between two hedgerows on the path which did not appear to be used much. We must go to ground now. I made a small fire with some twigs and got some tea made, never wasting more than one match. Also we have to be very careful as regards smoke. There is a village quite near occupied by the enemy. However, and about 1800 hrs I crept up to the nearest house to get some food. I managed to get half a loaf and we ate the lot. Our hide out is situated between two roads running Northwards. During the afternoon there has been considerable movement of German artillery going North along both roads. I've been studying a house all afternoon in the distance for any signs of the enemy entering or leaving and if they don't, I'm going to knock them up to ask for food after dark. It appears to be OK so we moved off and carry out our intention which was very successful. Although we made every effort to pay for it the peoples would not accept payments.

> **"all we could say or do would not induce this woman to accept one sou in payment for the food she gave us"**

June the 25th. Having moved off at about 23 hundred hours on the 24th we made very good progress in spite of some scares. Once again we bumped into a German patrol in a village but just managed to slip aside in a sort of alleyway keeping very quiet. This happened twice this night but we were lucky because it was a dark night. Dogs again kept barking but we eventually got clear and here and now I decide that under no circumstances will I go through the villages. So we strike off the road again but get mixed up amongst small fields surrounded by hedgerows and barbed wire fences. In addition it is most difficult to get through on account of their thickness. Later we passed a German fighter plane in a field which did not appear to be damaged much also did not know what the object was at first in the dark so we approached it very cautiously. There was no one near the machine so we passed on. We ate most of the food.

June the 26th. I estimate that we are about four days march from the coast. Best night, fairly easy going and we have got clear of the mines etc therefore few detours to be made and not many

● Warrant Officer, RSM Alexander Moir
leading a march of the Gordon
Highlanders in Elgin, 1941.

villages lying in our path. There are now German troops almost everywhere and I study them all within sight by day I can see their vehicles. We had a great spot of luck today (we got plenty of food). This morning chose a ditch to hide in near a farm (isolated) and go to sleep. About two hours later I awake and am amazed to see a couple of men standing over us on the bank equally amazed. They must have just arrived when I woke up. Anyway, they were certainly staring at us. I suppose that the shock of seeing two British Tommys. However, they were French farmers and they go and tell the farmers wife. A short while afterwards, she comes to see us with loads of food and also some rum. This kind woman carried on feeding us all day until we could just not eat any more. She also brought me a small map of the district and on finding my position I think that three more days will take us to the coast. Hardelot Plage about 15 ks south of Bolougne. I may say here that all we could say or do would not induce this woman to accept one sou in payment for the food she gave us.

June the 27th. Good progress. In the darkness I fell in to a very deep ditch early on during the move; the water took me up to the waist when stood up. This immersion made me rather cool during the night. We can now see many search lights in action around Bolougne. Got a good hide-out in a ward this morning and a good sleep until about midday. During the afternoon there were more Germans to be seen every day now as we approach the coast. We can see many German positions. The ground in front of us looks fairly easy, hedgerows etc. We've not been shaved now since we started and our clothes are muddy, boots soddened, so we look rather nice!

June the 28th. Make good progress although wet and uncomfortable again also find some difficulty finding cover and dawn. Eventually, hide amongst trees near a farm. Watched the farm carefully to make sure it's not occupied by the enemy then Tiffy tries to get food if possible. We are now preparing a store for the sea journey also collecting bottles of water. We've got about 7 wine bottles filled. The food quest was successful and we've now enough to last us for nine to ten days with care. I cook some potatoes and eggs, hard boiled then put them in small tins which we have collected. I must say that we are not that particular and can almost eat anything now.

June the 29th. Quiet night but we are compelled to make many detours round villages. Replenish water supply and hope to reach coast. I make no plans as it all depends on getting to the coast at an early hour and finding a boat in time with the tide in our favour and to be able to row far enough out from land westwards then northwest then with luck to be picked up and not machine gunned. Many German planes have been flying overhead and in the vicinity all day and the day previous. Our own planes have been active and were bombing Bolougne this evening.

June the 30th near Hardelot Plage. Our present position is about one and a half miles from the coast on high ground overlooking the sandy stretch between us and the sea. We can see the village of Hardelot Plage at the edge of the sea. Daylight is just breaking I decide to halt here all day and view the ground from some bushes trying to find out all the German positions. We will then attempt to get through after dark. There are many posts to be seen right to the edge of the sea. I can locate them by watching carefully from the movements of the enemy. The village is also occupied and must be evacuated of civilians as I've not seen any for days also there does not appear to be any boats about either, in fact I have not seen one anywhere in the Channel today. We each have about seven pints of water. During the afternoon some Germans passed us within a few yards but didn't see us. I'm sure I didn't breathe for some time. This happened twice during the day, the second time we were actually out in the open as I wanted to have a better look around but owing to them talking I heard them approaching and threw myself down behind a small sand hillock. The enemy actually passed the other side of it, a matter of a few yards.

July the 1st. Alas prisoners again. We succeeded in reaching the coast but we could not find any boats, this was about half mile south of the village. We commenced sneaking along the beach towards the village passing some machine gun posts and hoping to find a boat in this area. When we were in front of the village it was just an open promenade with a large Chateau - a sort of bathing beach - with no harbour. There was no cover of any sort and suddenly as we crawled along a challenge rang out. Not more than a few yards away on the edge of the promenade we could see four Germans pointing their rifles at us, and they were looking rather like business. The challenge was repeated as I had not yet answered but as nothing more could be done with the sea at our backs I stood up and surrendered again. The Jerry called to us to come to them and the first thing I noticed when I got up to them was that they were very very nervous. They first searched us for arms also the beach where we'd been. In the meantime our hands were still above our heads and the three sentries with fixed bayonets and rifles at the ready looking after us, whilst an NCO searched the beach with a torch. We then marched along the promenade for nearly a mile with our escorts still very business like and with our hands still above our heads. The NCO occasionally flourishing his automatic at our heads when we let our hands drop a little. However, I could not hold mine up any longer so I clasped them on the top of my head as a support and Tiffy did likewise. So the journey was completed in this fashion. I may mention that this took place at about 01.30 hours. Eventually we halted at a house on the outskirts of the village and were brought before a young German officer. Also, we were thoroughly searched again and everything was taken from us except our blanket and the spare food which we had saved up. This officer had obviously been doing himself well on wine at the expense of France and was very sarcastic accordingly about the British and the British army. This naturally got our blood up so we would not speak to him any more. He soon went away and a British 15 hundredweight duly arrived in which we were taken to see the Commandant. I also observed that we had made quite a stir among the Germans guarding the beach. They were definitely getting it in the neck for failing to see two British soldiers wandering through all their posts. The Commandant was very curious to know how we had managed to roam about the country in uniform and whether we had been prisoners before. Anyway, we did not tell one word of the truth as we had plans for all emergencies long before. For the remainder of this night we were put in a small stable where there were two chargers with German grooms over us as guards. Again very many threats with an automatic by the NCO, then off we go to sleep on some straw.

July the 2nd and 3rd. Montreuil-sur-Mer: We work hard all day. Good food free of charge as far as the enemy is concerned. We are asked a lot of questions which bore no fruit. The Commandant told us that we would not be prisoners long, Hitler had said so, and

whatever he said, the German believed. By August the 15th he reckoned that the war would be finished.

July the 4th. Taken to Hesdin. Some of the Jerries are good friends of ours. One of them had lived most of his life in Newcastle and his girl was still there. He hopes to get back soon. We work here cleaning barracks. There are also wounded French who have mostly recovered. Many British army vehicles in top condition, certainly someone did not scuttle as ordered. Informed that we go to Lille tomorrow.

July the 5th. Now at Caserne-St-Ruth. Barracks being used as a hospital. Quite a few British and French wounded here. French very kind, 7.30 each evening some food over the wall by string. All staff French. Guards Austrians, not like the Nazi from fanatics type. We've decided on another bid.

Alexander Moir did eventually escape, travelling South through France over into Spain but tragically after finding his way back to Britain, he was later killed at El Alamein.

ESCAPED FROM THE NAZIS, KILLED

THE Gordon's warrant officer, C.S.M. Alexander Moir, who escaped from the Nazis after being captured at St Valery was killed in the Battle of Egypt.

News of his death in action has been received by his wife, whose home is at 40 Skene Terrace, Aberdeen. They were married in Aberdeen in April a few months before he left for the Middle East.

Hail of Bullets

Before his death C.S.M. Moir figured prominently in one of the many dramatic incidents in the desert when the 51st Division went through the minefields to smash the enemy defences.

As recounted in yesterday's "Press and Journal" he was with his company under the command of Capt. M'Intosh in attacks on machine-gun posts. They attacked through fire from the flanks and amid bursting mortar bombs.

Digging in in the middle of a minefield they held their ground through the night. Every move they made brought a hail of bullets.

The Seaforths, attacking with tanks, came to the help of the sorely pressed Gordons company and smashed the enemy posts.

Twice Escaped

"The lads put up a terrific show," said Capt. M'Intosh.

C.S.M. Moir, who w[...] thirty - eight, joined t[...] Regular Army twenty ye[...]

BUCKINGHAM PALACE

The Queen and I offer you our heartfelt sympathy in your great sorrow.

We pray that your country's gratitude for a life so nobly given in its service may bring you some measure of consolation.

George R.I.

David Kilgour: You were a prisoner of war in Poland with my father Alex Kilgour, could you give us a background to how you got there?

Alex McLeod: Well, I was called up first in 1939 and at that time I was an apprentice painter. Everyone was being called up but if you were a Territorial, as I was, you were left at home where I could have finished my apprenticeship. A chap I knew was a guard on the railways and all railway guards had t' become nurses, because of their supposed skills in first aid, and he was in the Territorials. He asked me to go with him so I joined the RAMC. We were the 153 Field Ambulance stationed in Woolmanhill. We had t' report on the 3rd of September at Woolmanhill where we listened to Chamberlain speaking and as soon as he said that war was declared we were told to get our home things sorted out because we might be going away. We then had to report to the Grammar School playground and the Sergeant Major informed us of our instructions. There was about 320 in that playground and we had the option to take the day off to get things sorted. Well, Alex Kilgour and myself were the only two to walk off. That was 1939 and we were still chums till he died.

David Kilgour: I remember him telling me about the time he met you, so what was the next stage?

Alex: We did marches, evening marches with a lantern because of the blackout. We used t' go along the beach come up beside the Bridge of Don and up King Street then back to Woolmanhill.

David Kilgour : How old were you at this point?

Alex: I was just 19 in the December of '39 and I think I was the youngest in the unit and I missed being kept at home by about a week.

● Mr. A. McLeod (right) and Alex Kilgour as POW's at Fort 15, near Thorn

> " these tanks were like a double decker bus with a guard rail around it "

David Kilgour: What was the general atmosphere of going to war?

Alex: The atmosphere in the town was, "Are y' no awar yet!" everybody was wantin' t' see you going y' see. It didn't matter who you saw they always asked when you were goin' and of course you were desperate to get away yourself. In the middle of January we went down to the barracks and then marched to the station and we finished up down in Aldershot. I was there for about three months.

Before we went away we met the Queen Mother who was the Queen at the time. We had a parade there. We stood there from 9 o'clock in the morning till 2 o'clock in the afternoon when the Queen and the King walked past y'. When the King walked past the Scots he looked like a poof he'd got rouged cheeks, lipstick and mascara on. There was a hubbub got up about it, so the word was passed round that it was for photographers. Whether that was the case or no I don't know but that was the impression that we Gordon's got!

David Kilgour: When did you get to France then?

Alex: That would have been about April when we landed in Calais. We were put into woods and they gave us big axes to give us some exercise. After we left the woods we were fined 15.000 Francs because some o' the boys had been choppin' down little trees instead of the big trunks that were lyin' down on the ground!

It was on the 10th of June when I was captured. There was a farm which was a casualty clearing station which was then mortared and we all scattered and took cover. The main Officer put two Corporals outside to surrender the whole troop as medical corps. However, nobody came that night so we marched on again the next morning and we landed right on top of the cliffs at St

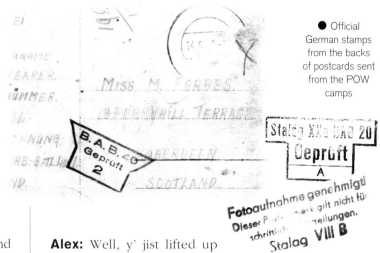

Valery. Previous to that we were told that the German tanks were only made of cardboard and were just imitations. Later we got up from the long grass to surrender because the Germans were coming in tanks. Well, these tanks were like a double decker bus with a guard rail around it and the Germans with their blond hair and their tommy guns slung on their arms tellin' y' to get your hands up and that. Those tanks looked no more like cardboard than anything I can think of!

The Germans told us t' put down our packs and take out anything we wanted t' keep, like photographs and cigarettes. We left the kit bags behind and started to march. We got onto the road and we were told to run. Every time we came to a German unit they got their guns and fired at you to make y' run. Y' ran half a mile every time y' passed a German unit! Every day they turned y' intil a park just before it got dark and there'd be about 300 men altogether but when you looked at the whole march, as far as you could see in front and behind there were soldiers, just solid. There was one night that the Germans turned cattle into the field that we were in and I remember my chum Alex Kilgour and myself finding hoof marks just besides where our heads had been. That was a bit of German sport that!

David Kilgour: What did you do for food on the march?

Alex: Well, y' jist lifted up what y' could; rhubarb, turnip or just whatever y' could find. The strange bit to me was that young girls would come in and take your money from y' and go and get biscuits or something like that for y'. If you can imagine a square in a town which we had just entered and got up t' the first corner y' dad and I gave this girl money to get us something to eat but before she could get back we had to go along to the other side o' the square so I was the other side from where the girl had taken the money. I could see the other soldiers saying to her, "It was me, it was me, it was me." as she was coming along looking for us. She was lookin' for us all the way round and eventually she did find us. Sometimes we were put into factory buildings and if you lowered down a bag with some money on the end of a rope someone would put stuff in it and y' pulled it back up again. If you were goin' through a town you might have a chance to knock on a door and someone would open it. The boys

● Alex McLeod, front row, fifth right. Alex Kilgour, same row, sixth right

always put me forward because I looked the youngest and the women would come out wi stuff and cry all the time they were givin' it! There was one woman in Belgium who gave us what we called coconut biscuits. She'd a big box o' these but we had t' cross the street for them and I kept going over to get them. I had this yellow bandage thing on and I realised that I was spotted so I ran back into the crowd and instead o' runnin' forward I ran backwards. I came out again and waved t' the woman as I passed her a second time so they all got a laugh there. The women were good to y' for that sort o' stuff.

I've seen us catching rain coming out of gutters and drinking it because we were so thirsty. We came to a river one time and a lot of prisoners ran down the bank to get water. For the Germans this was taboo because it would start a fever through the camp. It was here where I saw the only cruel thing all the time I was there. This German guard ran down to the river's edge and all the prisoners jumped up and ran but there was one who was a bit slow rising and the German guard took the butt of his rifle and knocked him right into the river. I only once saw that sort o' thing.

We walked as far as Holland where we were put on a wee train for some reason or other and we went as far as Essen in Germany. That's where we went onto barges and went down the Rhine and there were Germans on yachts sailing on the Rhine with girls and that sort o' thing. The barges were aboot 60 or 70 yards long and consisted of huge empty holds.

David Kilgour: Did you know where y' were going?

Alex: We'd no idea and you rarely saw a German to ask y' seemed t' be doing it all yourself. Eventually they took us to a big camp in Germany. There were Moroccan soldiers there as well and they used t' sell us their soup because they believed it was the wrong sort of meat for them. From there we went onto coal trucks, black coal trucks and when y' came out you were completely black. We arrived at Thorn and when we climbed out, there was a ring of steel. I was only a painter and y' dad was only a granite man and here we were coming out to a ring of steel because this was the Highland Division the most dangerous troops in the world! Ha! Ha! We could hardly see for hunger! The German soldiers were all there with their bayonets. Then we marched for about a mile

● LEFT - Bill Reaper, 18934, 1 KGFBAB 20, Heydebreck, o/s 5, Germany. ABOVE - Bill's camp watching a boxing match with the German guards

to a balloon hangar, it was a huge building. We were in there and the first thing was to dig toilets and they dug them down about six feet deep and they put these dry toilet things on the top for about 20 people. Ten either side and that was your toilets. If you were misbehaving you had to go into the toilets and empty them. They gave y' a six foot pole and a small pail for the end of the pole and y' had t' throw it into these tanks and empty it that way. When it got too low to reach you had to strip naked, stood in it and y' threw it up. I managed to avoid that one! We were there for a few months and we then finished up in a fort called Fort 15. There was a moat round about it but no water in it. That was the first time y' got fed properly with soup and bread. The loaves did five prisoners, two ends and three middles. If y' cut off an end and cut it into two pieces, that was enough for two men. Somebody had to cut it but the one that cut it was the last t' pick so there wis never a crumb o' difference in any o' the bits. Y' Dad and I were walking down the corridor one day and one o' the British cooks asked us t' give him a hand with a box with two handles and to go out with this German to get coal, take it down to the kitchens and empty it then come back for another one. When we did the second one the cooks gave us a ticket with a German eagle stamped on it which allowed us to get an extra bowl of soup. At night we used to wait until the workers outside used t' come in because that was when the soup was thickest. When y' got your soup at dinner time you got the top of the thin stuff but if you waited till the workers come in you got the top of the thick stuff. We would go down with this ticket and then we used t' bring up the dixie and sold the soup for cigarettes and tobacco. We made our own cigarettes and I always remember the name of the tobacco, it was 'Fumona'. You made them up and then you would say, "Three for 10 pfennigs!" The cry was as you went round the barracks was, "Three for 10 Fumona, three for 10 Fumona!"

In that camp they were building brick cook houses and the only place that we could get the bricks was from ruined houses about half a mile from the camp which had probably been bombed by the Russians or perhaps the Germans. We went there with a box about two feet deep and a bit like a sawn off sedan with handles for both of you. We walked down the street with that, through a lane and into a back yard and you put bricks in so that you could lift 'em but we discovered that with the strength we had, we could only lift six bricks. We used t' stagger along the street with it and as we went through this lane on the way back the guard would stand out in the street. In the lane there was a woman standin' wi a long loaf on her chest cutting us slices o' bread and as you walked past, you just took one.

David Kilgour: These were Poles then?

Alex: Yes, they were Poles. When you started t' walk back with this box over the cobble stones in all the dry cobbles that you could see there was a cigarette lyin'. We would do this sometime all day which would be about 10 or 12 trips and we did need all our strength to lift this box with six bricks in. We used t' look at these six bricks and feel ashamed that the two of you could only manage that amount! The guard knew that the cigarettes were there because he was leadin' you but he just ignored them. Your box was always goin' down and up again as we picked up the cigarettes. They'd be standin' on the pavements watching you and pointing to let you know there are cigarettes there. This would go on the whole day.

One time I had a boil in my groin and I had to go to another camp to get it treated. The camp was a little fort with a moat around it, fort 14 it was called. I was in there in the winter and when the moat was frozen over the soldiers came in with saws and cut out blocks of ice and took them away. They cut out the square and screwed a ring sorta thing into the ice and let it freeze. Then they pulled them out. In that camp there were two British doctors and medical corps men like myself. Y' got what they called invalid parcels which consisted of two tins of Ovaltine and two tins of Nestles tins of condensed milk and that sort o' thing. There was a library in each camp and you'd lie on the top o' your bunk wi a punctured tin o' condensed milk and smoking your tin of 50 cigarettes and you'd wonder if you were hard done til or not! This was out of this world and we got tinned chicken till we were sick of it! As a patient, things were really quite good.

David Kilgour: Did the Germans generally treat you not too bad?

Alex: They treated y' fairly and as far as dishin' out rations were concerned we would have trusted the Germans before we would have trusted our own Sergeant because there were cliques so they all helped themselves to wee bits here and there but the Germans didn't. The Germans were very honest and they would come round on a Sunday and speak to you through the wires. The guards left them because it was German soldiers that were speakin' to you. They'd ask if you'd got coffee or soap and things like that to sell. If you gave it to them and told them how much it was – perhaps a pullover might be two loafs and five eggs or something like that. The Germans would take the goods and tell you they would come back and give the necessary exchange. They always came back on Sunday with the stuff. They never ever let you down. I got a job in a Polish laundry doing the camp clothes. It was about 150 yards from 13A camp itself. 10 of us used t' work there. There were big boilers and we kept the water heated for the 15 or 20 girls and women who worked there.

> **"the 10 of us were called the 'Vasherie Party', the laundry party"**

The 10 of us were called the 'Vasherie Party', the laundry party. The women there would give us stuff and we would give them coffee and things like that from our Red Cross parcels. This one woman that we had a pet name for, I canna mind her name now but she used t' give me a bottle of buttermilk. One day I said that I didn't want it any more and she said, "That's good you must be fit now!" We used to smuggle in long loafs and we would sink them into our stomachs inside our belts. The guards would give you a quick search. You had your own guard, well he knew what game you were on because he was getting' stuff from y' as well so he never said anything to you. However, when you got to the guard camp, some of the guards would come out and run their hands over y' and I was caught one time with tomatoes and a loaf. Unfortunately, it was at the time when the camp Commandant was passin' which was only a 100 yards from the laundry where I had got it from. He asked me who had given it to me and I just shook my head. Then he told my guard, who was the double of my father and a fine man, to march me back to the laundry with the Commandant who then stopped all the women working. I had to point out which woman had given me the stuff but I said, "No, no, no I don't know." He then said, "If you don't tell us you will get one week in the bunker." The bunker was a four feet square tea box which was sunk into a wall with a metal door and a slide to look into. The women were all standin' there and I said, "No." So he said, "Two weeks in the bunker." I again said, "No." and shook my head again. He then said, "Three weeks in the bunker." I then

● A German platoon as guard of honour for the burial of a British prisoner. Courtesy Bill Reaper

said, "Three weeks, four weeks, five weeks, six weeks, no!" And d' y' know what he did David, he rubbed my head and told the guard to tack me back to the camp.

David Kilgour: He was testing your courage then?

Alex: Yes and there was another one who tested m' courage. A Corporal who was a beast of a bloke and he used t' go into the camp and inspect. Well, we were allowed a break from the laundry and we used to go in and have a bit to eat. We went into the camp and I went into the barracks which had all been cleaned and ready for inspection. The Corporal told me to get out and I said, "I should be here it's quite all right." But he said, "Get out of here, get out, raus, raus!" "I more or less said, "F off!" He said, "I know what that means." and he took my disc which was 16332. Weeks and weeks after that I had to get another one which was 26324 the only thing was these numbers were Australian numbers who had been captured in Greece and that places. So when the time came for some of us to be goin' home, myself and three others were put in charge of four mental cases. Real 'doolally tap' as we used t' call them. They were ex Indian soldiers, the sun must have got them, they shouldn't have been in the army. We used to look after them and when the time came for them t' go home the four nurses went home with them as well. However, we weren't the four nurses because they had taken us off to give us a breather. It sorted itself out though and I got home but they had been searchin' for me because the Aberdeen numbers were 163 something but mine was 26324. It resolved itself because the Germans then asked for those to put up their names who had not been called. So I got home and I was in Lockerbie before the second front had started on June the 6th.

David: So you were being exchanged then?

Alex: Yes, it was so many prisoners for so many prisoners. They put us in cattle trucks on Thorn station. I was a prisoner from June 1940 to September 1943, (when RAMC 'non-combatants' were exchanged with their German equivalent man for man).

● Christmas dinner at Fort 15, an underground camp. Alex Kilgour is shown at the top with Alex McLeod at his left. The Germans supplied them each with a bottle of beer for the occasion

● FLIGHT Seargent Morrison sits astride his Spitfire. One 'of the few' and a friend of Flight Sergeant James Murray, he was killed in the 'Battle of Britain'

" my mother got the impression that he was saddened by the absurdity of it all "

War in the Air

*T*HE ROYAL AIR FORCE, *although playing an undistinguished role during the fall of France, came into its own at the beginning of August, 1940. Until that time Hitler had enjoyed success after success but during the Battle of Britain he tasted his first defeat. Britain, moreover, began bombing mainland Germany as early as July, 1940, and after D-Day the allies assumed total air superiority over the axis despite the arrival of revolutionary technologies from the opposition.*

Bill Proven: Before D-Day our squadron along with another couple were then on a new roll. We weren't doing any fighting over London, our job was to fly at night to the German night fighter aerodromes from where they were attacking our bombers. If there was a bombing raid on over Dusseldorf or what have you they knew within the range of that bombing which of the German night fighters airfield they would operate from. So these British night intruder squadrons were sent on the basis of an hour and a half patrol it was just like a milk run. I went out at seven o'clock till half past eight and as I was coming away somebody else was commin' in t' take my place. So, in other words we covered that 'drome during the night and if any German night fighters took off or came back there was one of us waiting for them.

All the British aircraft carried what they called I.F.F (Identification Friend or Foe) but I don't know whether the German fighters and bombers had anything like that. Well, we could recognise one of our own because they had I.F.F 'cause they sent out that signal. We covered the Arnhem landings and there was two of us crossed for two nights and the second night the other one never came back. He was obviously shot down by either a night fighter or flak or something. To get through the war I put it down to one or two things, first of all if you're reasonably good at your job, obviously y' stood a better chance and secondly, if you didn't do anything stupid and thirdly y' had to listen to what other people told y'. What they used t' do at night - the Jerries used t' get a field miles from anywhere and they used t' put in all their trucks and lined them up t' look like a train and they got a boiler belting out steam and round this field they hung about eight balloons at 2000 feet and if you didn't know what they were up to you'd go belting straight into this train puffing out steam and of course if you hit one of these cables that was it, you'd had it. Another ruse was when the bombers were coming, they dropped this window stuff, foil, to confuse the radar then they did another trick over the channel. They used t' come over with a couple of

190's which were much faster than the Mosquito. They were about 10 miles apart and the first one would be picked up by our radar. We would put a night fighter, perhaps a Mosquito behind it to try and catch it so that when the Mosquito was chasing this 190 another one would come up behind and shot him down. We lost a wing commander that way.

William J McHardy: I was a child of five when my uncle, Alexander McHardy, an RAF gunner sent his sister Ruby the two letters (see p67). Shortly after she received the letters, he was killed on an operational flight on the 8/9th of April 1941. The letters only came to light in 1994 when Ruby died aged 92. They were still in their envelopes which were addressed to her at Candacraig House, Strathdon where she was working 'in service'. Coincidentally, shortly after Alick's death she joined the firm of Wilson Lightbody Ltd in Tullos which manufactured aircraft parts where she remained until the end of the war. The last letter is dated the 4th of April which was the day after they had to turn back from an operation to Brest where the targets were the German battle cruisers *Scharnhorst, Gneisenau,* and *Prinz Eugen.* At that time a lot of bomber command effort was directed towards the destruction of these ships with little effect however apart from the Air Ministries claim that the ships were

● Alick McHardy

prevented from putting to sea and therefore unable to participate in the Battle of the Atlantic. In the spring of 1941 the Battle of the Atlantic was going badly for Britain with thousands of tons of shipping being sunk by German U-boats. Thus the shipyards at Kiel, where the U-boats were assembled, were a constant objective for the bombers. On consecutive nights in April, 7/8th and 8/9th, forces of 288 and 159 aircraft were dispatched there on bombing raids. It was on the second of these raids that my uncle was lost.

Alick was 32 when he joined the RAF in 1939. He was almost too old as a newspaper cutting of a recruiting advert shows. The rest of the crew's ages were between 21 and 22. The subsequent six missives from the Royal Air Force records office not only interestingly demonstrate the procedure taken by the official body in these circumstances but also evince a seemingly personal and sympathetic attitude. Sergeant McHardy was an air-gunner in a Wellington bomber when it was probably hit by flak. Alick always declared that he would not bale out if they were shot down. However, the case was that he probably would not have had time to do so as all six crew members were killed indicating, perhaps, that the plane blew up or it crashed before they had time to bale out. They were buried in the Kiel War Cemetery in Germany where there are 1000 war graves of which 800 are British and Commonwealth aircrew. It was on his last leave that he told my mother how on returning from a mission where they had rained fire and destruction on some unfortunate German town they passed close by an English town which had suffered a similar fate from the Luftwaffe. My Mother got the impression that he was saddened by the absurdity of it all. She also said that he knew that he was unlikely to survive

> "Alick always declared that he would not bale out if they were shot down"

which is somewhat at odds with the upbeat tone of his letters. At the end of his last leave, his younger brother Charlie, also on leave at the time, walked with him to the bus. When the bus came Alick grabbed Charlie's hand and shook it, a gesture which took Charlie completely by surprise because "That was something that as a family we never did." As he walked home after seeing Alick off, Charlie, too, was convinced that he would never see his brother again. It was on that leave that I contracted chicken pox. Alick was disappointed that my spots didn't turn out to signify measles – defined as a communicable disease. The authorities wouldn't have wanted Alick back with the squadron until after the incubation period if he had been able to inform them that he had been in contact with measles. Who knows, if I'd had measles instead of chicken pox I could have perhaps saved his life, or at least prolonged it a bit.

The group photo below shows my uncle (extreme left, front row) and his colleagues taken, I assume, after training. There are 36 men in the photograph which is equivalent to six Wellington crews. Four members of my uncle's crew killed with him are in this group. They are Sgts. Rowland (Front row, 2nd from right) Hitchcock (2nd row, 4th from left) Cottell, a New Zealander (3rd row, extreme right) and Brown (back row, 4th from right)

● Alick McHardy.
Front row, far left.

Sergeants Mess
R.A.F. Station
Stradishall
Suffolk
8 March 1941

Dear Ruby

I've been a bit patchy in writing this time but you will see that I've been moving again, but I think this should be our last move for some time. I got five days leave when I got here and went home but had no time to let you know having only three clear days at home. I think this station is going to be OK, the grub is quite good and we have comfortable bunks of course like most aerodromes it is right out in the wilds the nearest town is Bury some 13 miles away, but being a country loon myself I don't mind this. Our Pilot is on sick leave so we have not done any flying yet, however he should be back soon then I expect we will get on the job. We did a "leaflet raid" on Northern France before we left Bassingbourn, this is by the way of breaking us in, it was quite an experience, the searchlights and gun fire was a bit troublesome in places, however we got through safely, the cold was the worst of it, but I've got one of these electrically heated suits now so should be warm enough on our next trips. I don't know what happens if you get a "short circuit" in these suits quite likely get roasted or fried. I found Mother quite well and cheerful but still as harassed with visitors. Aunt M came out on the Saturday and missed the last bus and had to wander away to Park she would not stay overnight in case her house got bombed. I did not see Bill or Charlie, Bill's crowd was moving into Aberdeen that weekend so he would have been pretty busy and Charlie was in Manchester spending his leave, young Bill has started school and seemed quite pleased with his first day but was doubtful if he would go another day. You will be a sort of clear of snow now you seemed to have had it pretty bad by the amount that was still lying about when I was home. Maybe you will be able to snatch a day at home or are they keeping you busy. I suppose you heard of the Durris bomb they are quite proud of it but are a bit doubtful if Kincluny's chickens will lay cracked eggs when they grow up, but seriously I don't like the way they have been snooping around Aberdeen lately I doubt they are in for a Blitz soon, they are always pretty active around here this being in East Anglia, however the nights are getting shorter so this should slow them down a bit, and now that the winter is over and better weather ahead helps you to face things with more confidence. Well I will close now, trusting you are well and hoping to hear from you soon.

All the best
Alick

Sergeants Mess
R.A.F. Station
Stradishall
Suffolk
4 April 1941

Dear Ruby

Thank you for the socks they were very welcome, you know what my feet are. I have to change my socks pretty frequently. I got your parcel when I came back off leave, you will be thinking I am aye at home but this was our official leave this time, the last few days were just on account of our Pilot being off duty. Was rather unlucky with weather and hardly got out of doors the whole time. I'm sure Mother was 'scunnered' with me mooching aboot in the hoose but still it was nice to be home. Mother was looking well and is very cheery. I saw both Bill and Charlie, they are not too well pleased in Aberdeen and their CO seems to be a nasty piece of work, we have some of his type here too but just manage to tolerate them. We had bad luck last night, set out for Brest but developed engine trouble on the way so had to turn back and just managed to reach home, I had visions of being dug out of a ploughed field, it was disappointing after being well on our way. Our new pilot is very cool and capable though he stands under five feet, the rest of the crew are all about my height so he looks a bit odd among us, but a very decent lad he is. We have got very little flying done lately the weather has been hopeless but now that it has cleared up a bit we will get on with it and I expect Jerry will resume his visits too. I knew a big difference in London this time the destruction is terrible and mostly living houses. The civilians are certainly getting the worst of this war so far. Well Ruby I will close now and hope to be able to see you next time I come home. I am due for leave about the 12th of May but might have to be content with a visit to Manchester the fare to Aberdeen is so big, however we get leave every six weeks so the next lot will soon come round. I don't know what Musso's sign means but a burst ballon would be more suitable.

All the best
Alick

William (Bill) Simpson: We needed silhouettes of all the different enemy bombers. We spotted them down at the coast. I was in the coast artillery down at Dover, a place called Hougham, halfway between Dover and Folkestone. We knew all about it there, Jerry used to shoot at us.

George Simpson: There is a photo of my plane there - a Shorts' Sunderland Flyin' boat. They say there's only one left in the world now. I ken where there's a few mair.

William Simpson: Aye, doon at the bottom o' the sea.

George: Aye we sunk them a', before we come hame. I'd just gotten four new wings, engines intil this plane. I knew this plane was OK, I could fly home in this plane but I was told to put a bullet through it. Sickening! Not only did they did they sink flyin' boats, but they threw tools intae the watter too, good tools like vernier gauges and micrometers. That was in West Africa. They just didnae want them.

Bill: Same as when I wound up wi' my unit in India. I was in the Special Investigation Branch of the Military Police, an' I wis the chief clerk. There was so many sent home that I got the unprivileged job o' windin' up the unit, which was quite a hazardous thing, cos no-one knew how tae dae it. We just had tae go bit by bit and it turned oot there was so many watches handed back intae ordnance that they would ruin the whole economy, so they put petrol o'er the top o' them.

That wis the pocket watches only, and they were first-class watches. We were a' issued wi' Omega watches. It wis the best o' stuff. Look, here's mine I bought in India afore I came hame. It cost me £40 recently tae get it repaired. The man that fixed it said that it was worth nearly £200, it cost me £7.

George: A' the crews had Omegas. They had the very best binoculars. They took them back aff ye, an' threw them in the sea.

Sinclair Slater: James Murray was my brother-in-law and he was killed in Aden in 1943 aged 27.

I don't know much about his war exploits but he was in the 74 Squadron, which were Spitfires and became one of the 'Few' by taking part in the Battle of Britain. He was stationed at Biggin Hill at that time. He was born in Portknockie, educated at Portknockie School and then he went to Buckie High School and later joined the RAF. He'd been about 18 a

that time. He was the first person at Portknockie to gain his wings and he was the only pilot in the Battle of Britain from Portknockie. So, he came through the Battle of Britain without a scratch. Then he got posted to Dalcross and from there he was posted to Aden. That is where he was killed. We didn't get much detail about his death. We don't know why but apparently, a volunteer was requested for a dangerous mission, he volunteered and he was killed on that mission in Aden. He flew there and was killed in a crash. We don't know if he couldn't get landed or what. Some one came from Aberdeen about it but maybe my Mother kept it from us. Then two men came from Inverness but they were wearing civilian clothes and I don't know what they said. It's a bit of a mystery.

Trevor: What aircraft was he flying?

Sinclair: It was an Anson, but for that mission I'm not quite sure.

Before the war he used t' come up in Tiger Moths, that was his first plane and he used to come so low and do all the loops and aerobatics over Portknockie. I always remember the old fishermen, he flew so low and he used to go round in circles round the town and he was comin' in from the sea one time and this old fisherman says, "Oh, he'll never make it, he's goin' t'

● Left Sgt Morrison,
Centre Sgt James Murray

crash!" Of course he didna crash and he came up two or three times in the Tiger Moth and then he came up in a Hurricane. There were two New Zealanders and himself ferrying these planes up to Wick. So when they got over Portknockie they gave a really good display! They did all the aerobatics that they could do at that time. It was really brilliant because no one had seen this sort of thing before in Portknockie, him being the only pilot. Even when they went to Dalcross he came down in an Anson. He was an instructor pilot and so he brought them down from Inverness to circle over the town!

Trevor: How did you know that he was goin' t' come down?

Sinclair: We didn't know, he just came and when the plane came down low we knew that this was James. I remember when he came in the Tiger Moth you could actually see his face a n d everything quite plainly.

Trevor: Did he land ever?

Sinclair: No, he used t' say to me when I was young, "I wish I could land somewhere and take you up for a wee flip." But that never materialised. During the war he took me down to Banff because there was a Messerschmitt there which had been shot down. There was this private soldier he was guarding the Messerschmitt and he says to the soldier, "Can the wee boy get aboard?" He said that he was sorry but the Officer would probably find himself on a charge if he allowed me on board. But he said that he could get in the cockpit. So he got in and tried the controls. It was a 109. My brother in law said that he could see that a Hurricane had shot down the plane. I asked him how did he know and he said that you could tell by the space of the bullets in the guns from the Spitfire to the Hurricane. He did get reported once for flying low over Portknockie but the local policeman just said, "Don't worry about that James

"no one had seen this sort of thing before in Portknockie"

C.O.'s View

Spitfire Pilot a Sinner

A PORTKNOCKIE fisherman told the North of Scotland Conscientious Objectors' Tribunal at Inverness yesterday that he would regard a Spitfire pilot who shot down a German bomber as a sinner because he had sent a brother into eternity.

The fisherman was Charles Wilson (40), deckhand on a steam drifter. He belonged, he said, to the religious body known as the Exclusive Brethren. He would not take up arms against his brethren, among whom he included the Germans. The skipper of his boat would not allow a gun on board. He would do any national work that did not conflict with his conscience. Wilson was registered as a conscientious objector on condition that he remained at his employment as a fisherman.

last Sunday it was doubtful which of them actually got the 600th victim, the honour and the station's prize were shared.

A group of sergeant-pilots (pictured below) are resting their feet on a stove while waiting for a call for action.

"Unknown To Any But God, They

it's just one o' these things." Portknockie got bombed durin' the war and James was at home on leave and he said, "I wonder, if I'd flown the Hurricane over Portknockie and shot the German down, if they'd have complained about me then!"

Most of the people from that time are gettin' old but lots o' people talk t' me about him.

What do you think about this?

Trevor: (reading the news cutting) Well, it seems churlish to say that of those chaps who were saving us from Fascism, but it is interesting to find evidence of conscientious objectors and they have their views.

Sinclair: So my sister sent that to him and wrote on the top of the cutting. 'So you're a sinner eh pet?'

I always felt that that there was something before he went away. I thought that he had a feelin' that he wouldn't come back. I don't know why but I think he sensed that there was something. Here is the letter that he sent from Aden to me. By the time I received it he had already been killed. I was a boy of about 14 at the time.

519400 J. Murray, 28 March 1943. RAF Aden.

Dear Sinclair,
Your letters to me arrive very regularly and I thank you for them. So you became a postman for two weeks! How did you enjoy the exercise? Perhaps now you have returned to sea - I'm sure you must enjoy that life a great deal. We shall continue our hunting at the first opportunity and I do hope you will learn to shoot straight in the mean time. Give your Ma and Dad my regards and I hope all the family are well. Douglas seems to be making great headway at school. Have you heard from George, and where is he stationed? You must write to him often. Are you helping Frances & Babs? They tell me that they keep you in pocket money but I doubt that very much. Do give Caroline my love, all the best.
James.

Trevor: Is that how the letters arrived?

Sinclair: Yes they were actually photographed and reduced in size.

It was a tragedy to go through the Battle of Britain where your chances weren't great and then get killed later on in Aden. One of his other chums was killed in action. That was SGT Morrison from Glasgow who was killed over the English Channel in February 1941.

● Above - Sgt. J. Murray
(and centre below)

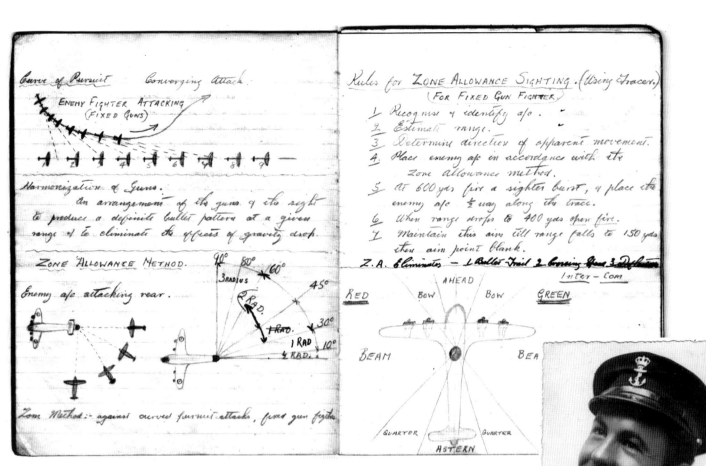

Top: pages from a training note book; courtesy B. Grassom. Right: Bert Procee in Scotland; note the Dutch Marine cap and the RAF blouson jacket

Bert Procee: I was born in the Netherlands, came to Aberdeen and married an Aberdonian lassie.

In the Netherlands everybody was called up for two years. I applied to go in the Navy voluntarily because the government promised to everybody who volunteered for the navy that when they came out after six years they would get a job. I wanted to be a sailor but I was 17 at the time so I was too old. 16 to 17 was the age range because they could get any amount at the time. But they told me if I gave my personal details, my height, weight and education and so on I might be considered as a marine if I so wished. So I agreed to go in as a marine. So from Amsterdam where I came from, I entered the marines in Rotterdam. I got my training there and also found a girlfriend but there came the time when I had to go abroad which would have been either the East Indies or the West Indies. So as soon as I had finished my training I had to go to one of the colonies to serve there and when I looked on the list my name was down for the East Indies. I didn't want to go to the East Indies because y' had to go there for three years whereas the West Indies was for two years.

I got my father to write a letter that my brother was going to work in the West Indies and if I could go there as well we could support one another and it worked! There were three islands there, Curacao, Aruba, Bonarie. Now, Curacao and Aruba are great big oil places, not that there is oil found there but the oil comes from Venezuela and is refined on the Islands. We were there as a force that could deal with any disturbances. *Mauritz Von Nassau* was the ship I was on. I got there in 1939 at sometime in April, I'm not quite sure but soon after war broke out. We didn't know much

'cause we heard very little in the West Indies then one morning at about two o'clock there was Reveille. "Everybody out of bed, everybody out right now! Full battle gear!" We were told that Holland had been attacked by Germany and had been overrun. What happened right away the same night the Corporal said, "You, you, you." and some of us were sent to the two cities, St. Nicholas and Oranjestad they kent all the people and they picked up all the Nazis.

David: Were you a part of those patrols?

Bert: No I was not. That was the blue eyed boys. They were always there and getting the best jobs. Well, they picked up the Nazis that they knew and they were interned in a camp. The Yanks had a quarter of the Island for refining the oil which came in from Venezuela and it was the Yank's intelligence which knew who the Nazis were. I was guardin' the turbines and every post had a soldier. Some civilians who worked there were also taken away. They were many different nationalities and we were in a 'home guard' situation.

I must have been there for about six or nine months. Then I was mobilised and as we were getting ready to leave other soldiers came in. They were the Scottish Highlanders and although we couldn't understand them very much we got on with them great. However, in each troop there was always the big boys with big mouths. We only had one canteen which was big enough for the marines but the Highlanders came in and they were a bit easier with their duties. They came into the canteen and overran the place and we couldn't get in any more. So some of the boys said, "Bugger them, let's get them bastards out of our canteen!" So there was a bit of bad blood between the two of them. The Scots were actually very, very good with respect to that sort of thing. They were visitors and they realised that. So instead of getting trouble they posted two Scots Guards with a rifle in front of the canteen but our boys weren't happy with that and they took their guns away from them! That was very dangerous thing to do because you never take guns off a sentry. Being the beginning of the war the Officers said that it had to be sorted out because it was a courts martial affair and eventually they did get it sorted.

We lived in a barracks which belonged to the oil company. You don't need too much in the tropical sun just a roof, a door and a couple of sides.

The Highlanders were next to us, in their own grounds and their own canteen so that eased things a bit. After that the Dutch and the Scots got on much better with each other.

We were then transported to Britain. There must have been 60 or 70 of us altogether including those from the other island as well. Some of the others who stayed behind set up a whole new corps because the marines that stayed behind went over to America and started a whole new marine school. We landed in Cardiff and when we sailed into the harbour we were standing on the deck and two Spitfires came over low and the noise of the engines was deafening. I'll never forget that. After that we went by train up to Holyhead. At Holyhead there was this Dutch merchant ship lying there which had been converted into a floating clearing camp. I had volunteered for air gunnery in the West Indies so I was sent from Holyhead to the airfield at Leuchars. I was an air-gunner but I had never been in an aeroplane! However, they gave you classes first then we fired guns on the range even though we could shoot already. I learned that the life expectancy of an air-gunner was four month!

● Two aeroplanes serviced by Bert; top the Consolidated PBY Catalina and bottom, a Handley Page Halifax GR mk. VI

David: What was funny?

Bert: We were sitting one day, ha ha, and as usual in the back, the only means of communication was an intercom. You weren't allowed to call the pilot he had t' call you. He'd call and say, "Are you still there?" and I'd say, "Fine". When you were two or three miles out you had to test the guns but you were nae allowed until the pilot tells y'. So he says, "Hello, hello, test your guns OK?" I sez, "OK". So I pulls the trigger, rrrrrrrrrrrrrrrrrrr. The pilot screams, "Hiiiiiya -you've shot the tail off! Stop, stop stop!" I scream back, "What the hell happened?" and he shouts, "You've shot through the bloody tail man!" Later on when we came back, we land and the pilot came round and looked at the damage and there was a neat line of bullets across the tail. I was told by this other chap that there is a device that stops you doing that but I didn't know that until then. So I said that the thing couldn't have been workin'. The plane was a Lockheed Hudson. Any way, the pilot asked if it was serious and I told him that it

> " I learned that the life expectancy of an air-gunner was four month! "

● Page from an instruction manual, circa 1939

wasn't and all I could see was these little holes. When we landed and the pilot went to look at the rear of the plane he went green, there were bits that size ha ha ha!

David: What was the main purpose of the flights that you were doing at that time?

Bert: The main flight at that time was to Norway which took two and a half hours there and two and a half hours back plus there was half an hour coasting. With coasting y' flew along the coastline and any shipping you saw you had to attack. We never actually attacked because any plane that had attacked previously had either been badly damaged or shot down. This was a the very beginning of the war and we did this to get into the war and another reason that we did this was that the Germans got a lot of iron ore from the top of Norway. On their way down they were attacked by the allies and you could see the smoke stacks sticking up out of the water where they had been sunk. Although we weren't attacked by enemy planes the ones that did get attacked were invariably shot down. Our plane was really only a pre war passenger plane.

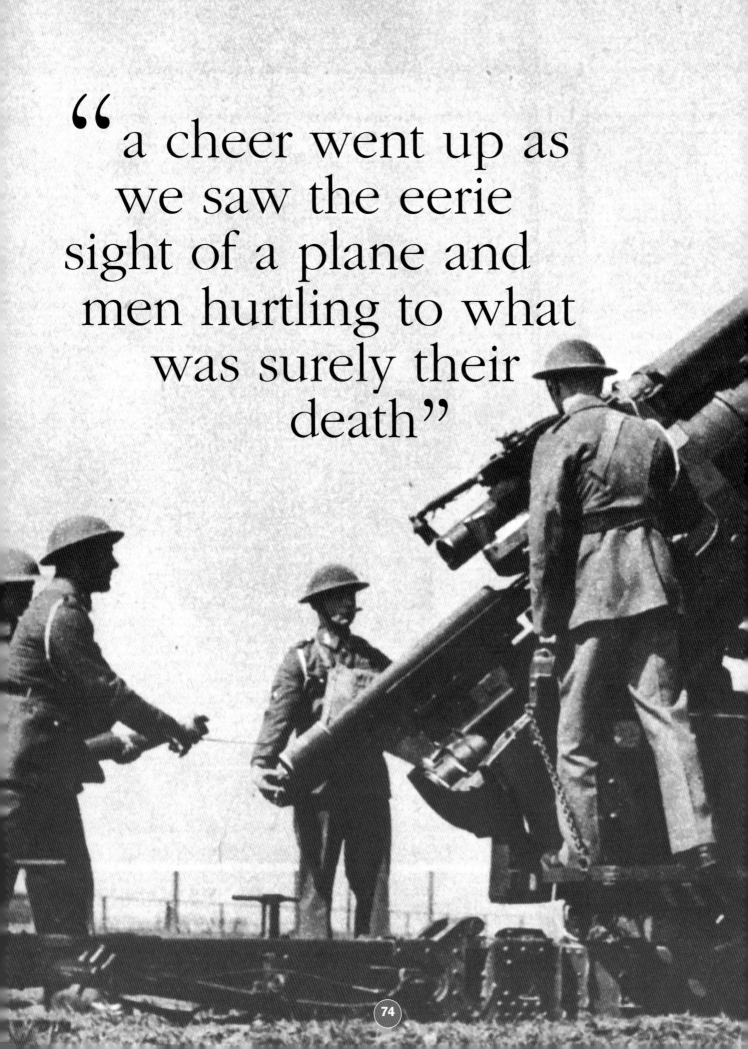

"a cheer went up as we saw the eerie sight of a plane and men hurtling to what was surely their death"

Anti-Aircraft Gunnery

WITH THE *GERMAN BOMBING CAMPAIGN ON BRITAIN* the demand for skilled anti-aircraft gunners was prodigious. Unwilling to redeploy their precious manpower from frontline regiments, the War Office ensured that these units often contained a large proportion of women.

Joyce Everill (Nee Mitchell): The 519 H.A.A. Mixed Battery was formed in Oswestry and it was divided into four sections: A, B, C and D. The Battery manned two sites, A and B one, and C and D the other. But before we were ready to man a site we had to have some real firing practice at a firing range, so off we went once more in Army trucks to entrain for Cornwall. There we were expected to put into practice all we had learnt at Oswestry, firing real guns at targets. We had trained on dummy guns at the training camp, but these were real shells we were dealing with now, or at least practice ones which didn't have the power of the kind we would be using for real. Nevertheless, they made enough noise to get us used to the real thing when the time came. The men actually loaded and fired them of course, we poor weak women could never lift those heavy shells. Mind you, the state of some of our Gunners made me wonder if they ever could either, for the male side of the Battery consisted of men who were unfit for really active service. In other words they were only a step away from their pensions or not long out of school. But I'm being unfair for they did an excellent job during the Blitz, and it wasn't such an easy job being under fire night after night, manning and firing guns that became red hot, while bombs rained down all around them. I'm being unfair too on the lads who made up our Battery, for they were a good bunch really despite their initial distrust of women doing what had been a mans job before the ATS were used on the instruments of a gun-site. They soon came round when they realised we were not shirking anything and were prepared to work as hard as them. We soon became friends and the older ones became like fathers to the girls, anxious about their welfare and giving us advice. Mind you they began to find it

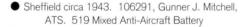

● Sheffield circa 1943. 106291, Gunner J. Mitchell, ATS. 519 Mixed Anti-Aircraft Battery

was an advantage having girls on site who were prepared to do a little sewing and darning for them. Oh aye, they were a crafty lot!

Firing practice meant firing at a long sleeve towed by an aircraft flying just off the coast. Now that was men who deserved a medal - the pilots of those planes - for how the majority of them didn't land up in the sea I'll never know, especially that first week! Mind you we did some pretty good shooting too, it's not everyone who can sever the towrope about 12 yards from the plane! Rumour had it the poor pilot had a nervous breakdown, and I wouldn't have been surprised, how they had the nerve to go up again I don't know, but with practice we improved as each day passed. Firing Practice over, we were finally given our first leave before we had to report to Huddersfield to take over our first gun-site. All too soon that oh so short leave was up and it was time to rejoin my unit in Huddersfield. Not quite so fearful of the unknown this time, but rather sorry to leave Mum's cooking behind.

I arrived at Huddersfield station to find the rest of the battery waiting at the station for the usual trucks to convey us to our new camp. After seeking out my friends we clambered aboard. I was getting to be quite a dab hand at climbing aboard these now without the help of some kind soldier who was always willing to give us girls a leg up. I soon caught on to their little game, we didn't wear our trousers out of camp you see, they were never so willing when we didn't have skirts on!

When we arrived at the site it was a relief to see how neat and tidy it was, and not too far from the town either. Nothing like the horror stories we had listened to from some of the old soldiers, away out in the wilds, no running water or toilets, etc. They did like to have us on, and a naïve gullible lot that we were, we

● Left: The crew of a British anti-aircraft gun, circa 1939

believed them. During my time with the Army I only stayed in one camp that came anywhere near their stories, but more about that later. The huts were quite comfortable, if you can call cement floors comfortable, but at least the paths were all laid out too. Oh aye, I later on had to dig and make the roads and paths of one of our camps, real old handy body was I during the war! Maybe that first site spoiled us for some of the others, but at least it broke us in gently for what was to be our life from now on.

We settled in quickly and accustomed ourselves with camp routine, drilling, marching, gun practice, P.T. And fatigues. Orderly duties and Guard Duty, and of course manning the guns when our section was on active duty. Our instruments had to be cleaned and lined up every day after we had attended site parade after breakfast. Then they were ready for any action that might come our way. Cookhouse fatigues were enough to put you off dish washing for the rest of your life, and as for spud pceling! There were mountains of them to feed all the Sections. Greasy floors had to be washed after every meal, and to think I used to try and dodge washing up the few dishes at home! At least cookhouse duty wasn't too bad in the winter, for at least you were in out of the cold, and there was always the chance of an extra cuppa depending which cook was on duty at the time. Some of them wouldn't have given you a kind look never mind a cup of tea or an extra bite to eat, but strange to say I don't remember ever seeing a thin cook all the time I was in the Army! We used to smuggle bits of bread back to the huts after supper, and toast them in front of the hut fire before bedtime, especially if we were hard up and couldn't afford the NAAFI. Grub. There were some peculiar shapes coming out of the cookhouse some nights I tell you, for it was forbidden to take food out of the dining hall. We would stick our loot inside our battledress blouses till we reached the safety of our hut, and my goodness those stolen pieces tasted better than anything else. They would have just been put into the swillbins for the pigs anyway, and my thought was, they were better inside us than any pig!

We never fired a gun whilst at Huddersfield, plenty of alarms and alerts, but no action, so most of our time was spent on the usual spit and polish and practice drills. The first time I was given a job in the plotting room was a real nightmare, for of all the jobs to give me, they chose the height board. Through my earphones I was given the height readings from the Ground Location team, G.L. for short then, but now known as Radar. It was in its infancy then, and was hailed as a wonderful thing,

> "I'm sure he went away thinking he had just seen a mathematical genius at work"

for before its invention the Ground Defences were helpless if the searchlights failed to pick up the aircraft. My job was to chalk the different heights given me on a blackboard until I had a certain number, eight I think it was, but after all this time I am not really sure. Anyway, once I had got the required number, they had to be added up then divided by the amount of heights I had written on the board. Now maths were never my strong point at school and why they chose to give me that job without finding out if I could count further than my 10 fingers I'll never know, but I was stuck with it. It's all very well doing sums like that if you have plenty time, but what you must remember is the fact that enemy planes would be approaching while you were busy trying to work out the mean height. They didn't travel at a snails pace just to let you get your sums right. I just about had kittens on the first run through, for try as I might I just couldn't get my brain to work fast enough. I could visualise the enemy planes being on their way back to Germany leaving a trail of devastation in their wake, while I was still desperately trying to work out my height chart! Then dear old Scottie came to my rescue. Lieut. Scott was our Section Officer, and he had been an Insurance man in civvy street so was well versed in figures. He could see I was having difficulty, so could the whole command post I expect by this time, and he took me aside and showed me a quick way to work out these figures with perfect results. Oh the relief! Anyway Gunner Mitchell became quite a dab hand at his system after a few more runs without anyone else knowing our secret, and was rewarded by being promoted to a Lance-Corporal. Oh the heady feeling of power! And all thanks to dear old Scottie and his insurance books. Bless him.

The camp became a real hive of activity when it became known that we were to have a visit from a Brigadier General who was coming to carry out an inspection. Talk about BULL——! If you stood still for two minutes you were liable to be either whitewashed, scrubbed or blancoed. We had to put on a dummy run for his Lordship of course to let him see how smart and proficient we were on the guns. Ha-Ha! It just had to be our sections turn for duty of course, so guess who landed up on the height board? Right wee duffer Joycie who was a dud at maths, and about to become the biggest con-merchant in the British Army. Luckily for me Scottie was the Plotting Officer that day, and he gave me an encouraging wink before we started which gave me all the nerve I needed to carry the excercise through. For once in my life I got things exactly right and was congratulated by the B.G. on my speed! It was only Scottie's twinkling eyes meeting mine across the plotting table that prevented me from bursting out laughing. I'm sure he went away thinking he had just seen a mathematical genius at work, if only he had known! But throughout my time in the Army that system never let me down, it worked perfectly every time.

We were never kept very long on one site. Just when you were getting settled in nicely, it was pack up camp and off to another site. We were a really fortunate Battery if that is the right word, for we usually went to relieve another battery that had really seen action, and by the time we took over Jerry had shifted his attacks somewhere else. The awful devastation of some of the towns we stationed at really shook me.

We manned two sites in Sheffield before moving again to Ecclesfield. Now there was a sight for you, not even finished when we took it over. Out came the spades and we were told to get cracking and dig! Thus your fragile Mother learnt the art of navvying! We dug out the roads and carted big stones in to make borders round the so-called gardens that were to be made around the huts. It was with some sense of relief when I was called to the Captain's office one day and told I was being sent on a course to Sheffield University. I came out of that office thinking it was a relief to get rid of that digging for a few weeks at least. Then it hit me - UNIVERSITY! What on earth was I going to do at a University? Heavens only knows why they picked me, for there were a lot of better educated girls on the site who would have been better qualified for the course. Maybe they just wanted rid of me for a while, well they could have sent me on leave couldn't they, I wouldn't have objected to that, but University, I ask you? It was termed as an 'educational course', so perhaps they had just decided I could do with a little more education up top. Some hope! I was supposed to take classes when I came back to the unit, but I never did. That was the Army all over for you, if they could find something useless for you to do, they would do it, and this was one fine instance. The camp was always too busy with other things to bother about education, and to be quite honest, this was one time I was relieved about it. It was a break away from camp at least, but it was with mixed feelings that I found myself standing in front of that awesome edifice the first day. What on earth was Joyce Mitchell frae Torry daen in a place like this? Oh Mither! It didn't help either to find out there were only two girls in the company, a Corporal from another battery and myself, all the others were men. Hooray! If the Army did nothing else for me, it at least broke open the shell I had been brought up in until I joined, and let me see a whole new world. The nearest I had ever been to a University in civvy street, was to sell newspapers in the hall of Aberdeen University at a conference once, when the shop had a kiosk there!

Back at camp again I discovered we were getting ready to move again to another firing camp, to be

● Joyce Everill (Mitchell), third from right, constructing roads to their barracks in Rotherham, 1943. Second from left is Corporal Newton, her best friend at the time

given the chance to knock another poor windsock towing pilot into the drink. This time it was to be Whitby, cheers from Joyce! Back to the sea once more. How I loved that wee place, I was amongst my ain folk again, and I haunted the quayside on my time off watching the boats coming in and going out, smelling the old familiar smells of fish and sea.

To get to the firing range, we had to cross the bridge that spanned the harbour, and climb the 199 steps that led up to the Abbey, then march another mile or so to reach the gun-site.

Once more we were to be subjected to an inspection by the Divisional Brigadier, another right carry on believe me. It was back to the whitewash brushes again with a vengeance. The Brigadier was an old soldier probably called out of retirement to do this job, and was a veteran of the First World War, so rats wouldn't have scared him off any, they were all too familiar with them in the trenches then. Section C was manning the guns this time, so Joyce wasn't called upon to do her height sums that day, thank goodness. We celebrated his visit afterwards with a camp concert, we had quite a lot of talent in our Battery, stage-wise as well as the usual kind! That was where Joyce wrote her first bit of verse. It was a parody on a well known song of the time and went something like this:-

> They've taken our old predictor,
> and even the guns as well.
> They've given us all a paintbrush,
> and told us to paint like H—-.
> We've whitewashed all the swill bins,
> and even the coke house walls.
> If it wasn't for the b——- old General,
> we wouldn't have to do it at all.

Ok, Ok, it maybe wasn't top of the pops material, but it went down a treat with the troops especially the other verses, which modesty and the censor forbids me to print here.

As I've said, it was a lovely place except for the rats. The grounds were beautiful with a big lake surrounded by trees, and the house itself was huge, with a window for every day of the year. In its heydey it must have been a really wonderful sight with the horses and carriages sweeping up the long curved drive. Now it was Army trucks churning up the grounds. I often imagined when I was on guard duty what it must have looked like long ago, with the gentry strolling in the grounds, the ladies with their parasols and long dresses. The carriages arriving with the guests for a ball. Oh I had a right good imagination when I let it run riot, but I bet I wasn't far out. I would have loved to have seen inside the house itself but of course that was taboo while the Intelligence Corp were stationed there. I believe it is a college or something like that now. It was some difference from the conditions we lived in though, I can assure you of that. Those blasted rats meant a lot more work for us in the cookhouse and dining room when we were on fatigues. Now there was a sight for you, us girls dressed up in our denims, ready for duty. These denims were never meant for anyone under six feet tall, and about the same wide. They didn't even fit where they touched, for they didn't touch any part of your anatomy unless you had on a belt. Guard duty now meant that you had to be dressed up to the nines, with buttons shining, and boots polished till you could see your face in them. Did I forget to tell you we wore boots? Oh aye, and gaiters as well, just like the men, and the boots had tackets in them as well!

We spent a short time at Corby, or Little Scotland as it was called, as there were so many Scots working there, but I never got a chance to see many of them, for we were on the move again very shortly, back up to Yorkshire, to make me homesick for the sea, all over again. However our next firing camp was at Weybourne, where once again I could continue my love affair with the ocean. It was a pretty dull camp after Whitby, no Canadians to lighten our lifes and no extra sweeties either. Now if you are thinking we must have been an awful lot of poor shots to need so much practice, you are wrong. It was just that if a battery was fortunate enough to see very little action as we were, they were sent to a firing camp to prevent them becoming rusty in their gun-drills, goodness knows we weren't rusty in all the other aspects of Army life, like cookhouse fatigues etc.

That summer of 1943 was a long hot one, so we took the chance in between firing off at another hapless pilot, to lie and sunbathe. We were all given leave before going to our next station, which was to be Hull, and I arrived home expecting another telling off for having a dirty

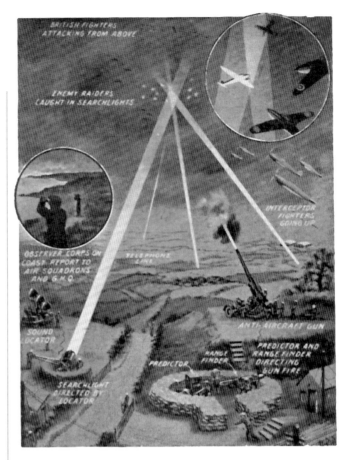

face. "No Ma, it's jist sunburn!" But poor Mum didn't have time or the inclination to look at my face, for when I arrived at the station I discovered that Aberdeen had once again been one of Jerry's targets. Luckily it hadn't been a bad one, but enough to upset everyone. Neither Mum nor Dad ever wrote very much about the raids in their letters, thinking I suppose that they were saving me the worry, but the fact was that in many raids we were called out to man the guns if there were enemy aircraft approaching the coast of Britain. We usually had some idea of the part of the country that had been bombed by the time we had stood down. It was always a relief to get a letter later and know they were alright.

For the first few weeks we were stationed in a camp, if I can call it that. On Spurn Point which is a long narrow piece of land jutting out into the sea from Hull. I have called it a camp with reservations, for that must have been the worst camp of all. Even Wentworth and its rats was heaven compared with this. Thank goodness it was summertime, I'd have hated to be there in the winter. It was the bare essentials, and barely that. Dry toilets which no amount of disinfectant ever sweetened. No sinks with running water, that had to be brought from the cookhouse and poured into little basins standing on a long plank. These basins doubled as baths as well when we took them into a corner behind some

> "The enemy plane appeared in the searchlights and suddenly smoke was pouring from it as it started diving earthwards"

blackout screens which we built up around us to hide our modesty, not that we had much left by now. One of the camp wags remarked that we washed up as far as possible and down as far as possible, then we went behind a screen and washed 'possible'! That just about sums it up. Hearing other stories of the dreadful conditions that some poor people had to live in during and after the war makes me feel a bit ashamed now of how we grumbled at the time, all with a lot of good humour mind you, but grumbling all the time. But at that time we didn't know any better. To make it worse, the guns and command post were away over rough fields which you had to plough through to get to your station. That was no fun in the pitch dark either, especially if it had been raining, it took nearly all next day to get your uniform fit for parade again. I do sound a right moan, don't I? From stories I heard after the war from ATS girls who followed the troops into Germany after D-Day, they had it much worse, and at least we were only there for a few weeks before moving in to our proper site.

We did see a bit of action though, for poor old Hull was still on the receiving end of the Luftwaffe's attentions. If I thought the towns I had been stationed at were bad with bomb damage, and my own town a mess, that was nothing to the sheer horror of Hull. Whole streets wiped out completely for as far as you could see.

One night on our new site we were called out, and soon the guns were all banging away with the other batteries round Hull. That was some noise I can tell for there were rocket batteries as well as our type of guns, and the awful scream they set up just about shattered ones eardrums. The enemy plane appeared in the searchlights and suddenly smoke was pouring from it as it started diving earthwards. We had been firing as well, and a cheer went up as we saw the eerie sight of a plane and men hurtling to what was surely their death. I guess the calculations on the height board were right that night. The full enormity of what I had done only hit me later. We were never fully accredited with the kill as there were so many other batteries firing at the same time, so I took some comfort from that, plus the thought that if it hadn't been brought down, it would have meant more devastation to the City we were defending. No more little houses smashed to smithereens with all the occupants, dreams of the future along with them. It was a strange feeling though and I'm glad to say the only time that I ever had to experience it, for though we fired off a few more rounds

before I left the Army, we could never claim a hit for sure.

Even though Aberdeen had the distinction, if you can call it that, of having the most Air Raid alarms in the country, it wasn't until I was posted to Sheffield and Hull during my service as an Ack Ack girl in the ATS that I realised how lucky my home town had been. We had bomb damage in many parts of the town and lives had been lost but nothing that could be compared with what I saw in these two cities. Whole streets had disappeared under the blast of many bombs. What had once been a row of happy homes was gone now, all that was left were row upon row of rubble, bricks, cement, torn pieces of curtains which had once been some housewive's pride and joy, the sooty mark of a chimney on a surviving wall, and most heart breaking of all, a child's toy now broken and dirty would catch my eye.

Did the bairn who had once cherished it survive? Did the housewife who had so lovingly polish that piece of furniture now fit for nothing but firewood live to shed tears over it?

I wondered too at the thoughts of a Hull fisherman returning home from a trip to sea to catch the fish so desperately needed to feed a country existing on rations, as he turned into what had once been the street where his home stood, only to be met by such a sight?

If I had any doubts or misgivings about giving the order to fire to the four Anti Aircraft guns on our site just out side these towns, they were quickly dispelled if I thought on what I had seen not only in these towns but my own as well.

I have never been back to Hull since the War but have no doubt it has been rebuilt and the scars of war eradicated.

But I did visit Sheffield recently and could not compare the town I saw then with the one I remembered from those far off days when I had had to choke back the tears at the scene of devastation I had seen then. Once VE Day and VJ Day were celebrated we drew a sigh of relief and thought - 'That's it, it's all over thank goodness, no more War!'

But I only have to watch the TV news nowadays and see the likes of Bosnia and other war torn countries and my mind goes back to the sights I saw back in the Forties, and it all becomes the more vivid to me. No, it's never all over for those of us who lived through it. You only have to watch the parade of disabled veterans marching past the Cenotaph on Armistice Day to realise that. Those of us who have gone through a war never forget. We remember!

● A British soldier guards the remains of a crashed axis plane. Courtesy R. Bauld

" Monty said –
All I have to tell you is
that it is going to be
easy. All my battles are!"

The Desert
The Middle East

*T*HE BRITISH AND COMMONWEALTH TROOPS *had fared extremely well against the Italian opposition in North Africa but had experienced serious reversals of fortune after the arrival of the Germans in February, 1941. By late summer, 1942, they were poised at the El Alamein position near the Egyptian frontier after a gruelling fighting withdrawal.*

Jack Kilgour: I was earmarked for what they called a Field Hygiene Section who tested the water and told them how many scoops of bleach'n powder to put into it to make it sterile. In the desert we also tested the wells to make sure that there wasn't any poison in them. We took a sample (of water) first, then we followed a process that was called the 'army way.' First of all you look for a 'box', then 'wooden', then 'water testing, sterilization'. So that if you're lookin' down the inventory, y' look for a box, then a wooden box, and so on.

There were 27 people in my unit. One Major, four Staff Sergeants, six Corporals acting Sergeant and the remainder were other ranks or privates. It was a fairly informal unit and a part of the Highland Division. We landed in Durban and we unloaded the ship because we were supposed t' be going to India, but unknown to us the South African division had surrendered at Tobruk. Smuts who was the South African Prime Minister, wanted to recruit a new division so he borrowed the pipes and drums of the 51st Division and beat the retreat in Johannesburg, Durban, Capetown and Port Elizabeth. At the same time, Churchill was over in America with Roosevelt. They decided to have a landing on the other end of North Africa and the idea was to squeeze between them. Roosevelt said that he would send some of his latest Sherman tanks if Britain would supply men for the Eighth Army side. Well, of course we were the nearest ones who could go there because we were already waiting on a slower convoy to take us to India sitting in Durban. So, we put everything back on board the *Stratheden* and went up the Red Sea and landed in Egypt. We were then taken under the wing of the New Zealanders who taught the Highland Division desert navigation. Then we went up in to what they call the 'boxes' which were the defences to stop Rommel coming through El Alamein.

David: Was there quite a panic on then about Rommel breaking through to Egypt?

Jack: No, but they thought he would. He'd come so far and then stopped and of course Auchinleck planned where to stop him because there was the Qattara Depression which was impassable to vehicles until Rommel came through and then the sea on the other side so you'd a 40 mile front. We usually operated from Divisional Headquarters except when we were sent out on detachment. I went through after Alamein and I went through a fair bit of desert up to Agheila with the 153 Brigade that one was the one that the Gordons were in.

Before Alamein, Montgomery was telling us what we were going to do. He stood up in his jeep and he said, "We're going to hit Rommel for six!" and when we were in Birkhamstead waiting to go over to France he said, "I said to you before Alamein we were going to hit Rommel for six and by God we hit 'em for six so now you're going to go over and do the same." He'd an extra bit for the Highland Division in the desert cause we'd to avenge St. Valery. It was a terrible thing that the Highland Division actually surrendered at St. Valery so it had to be blotted out of the records - it was never expected for the Highland Division to have surrendered.

T' get back to the desert, it was full o' flies; you'd travel maybe 600 miles West in a day then you'd stop and have tea and hard tack biscuits and a tin of bully between two and mid-day. Then when you stopped at night you had a proper meal. You'd stop and say, "This is great, not a fly in sight." But as soon as the tins were opened, zzzzzuph the flies were there. Some of them were travelling in the wagons with us. Through the day they were getting out of the heat of the sun and the canvas tops of the lorries - they would rest in there. If you had a mug of tea, the flies were very short of liquid the same as the troops and they'd be all round the rim of the mug and you'd knock them away. When we landed in Egypt first, there was a fertile bit where we were for a start. The women did all the work and the man rode out behind on his donkey, he would get underneath a tree and as the sun moved round he moved round the tree. We said, "Look at him, the flies are drinking the liquid out of his eyes and the corner of his mouth." But it wasn't more than a week before you saw your mate with flies around his eyes and he was fast asleep!

One time we were operating an Italian mobile bath at a well. A little way off there was an establishment of nomads, it was a great big tent and all the animals and everyone was in it. We had to go over to the cook house to get our evening meal, so we were driving back to this well where we had this big white canvas tent. A German plane came over, 'cause you would swear that he was firing at you but he was shooting at the wagons on the track miles away. So we jumped off the wagon and the driver he flapped down and it was a while later when we heard these bombs go off. Wumph, wumph WUMPH! and getting nearer. The driver looked out and said, "Jesus Christ I've left my lights on!" and they were blazing nicely on the side of this white tent but the bomb hit the nomads camp and what a carry on with all the animals, the bleating of sheep and goats and women crying. If there had been another one we would have got it but there was one, two and three. We heard them going over our dug out.

When I was up with the 153 Brigade, the one with the Highlanders in it, they got shelled occasionally and got bombed in El Agheila, and we went in to Mersa El Brega where they had all the Black Watch and Argylls hung up with piano wire. Every night there was a patrol going into Mersa El Brega trying to find out how heavily it was defended but the patrols, most of them, never came back. This went on for about a fortnight. When they finally took Mersa El Brega it was all booby-trapped and everything and not a German in sight, except for all these Highlanders hung up with piano wire.

David: Why?

● German Afrika Korps prisoners near Tobruk. circa 1942, courtesy R. Bauld

Jack: Well they went in with a patrol and were captured by the Germans and the Germans hung them up.

David: But why were they doing that, I thought that there was more chivalrous behavior?

Jack: There was, but occasionally you came across some of these SS units.

David: I didn't think there were any SS in the desert.

Jack: Well no, the 21st Light Division had some, not the kind that guarded camps. SS stands for Schutzstaffel y' see (Protection Squad). Anyway there were ones that were a bit - (sadistic?) There was a Swiss at our HQ at that time and he was investigating any cases like that. He got Montgomery to put a letter around all the divisions asking if anyone knew an SS, or a German Officer who had been bayoneted after his surrender. An Australian said that he had done it, him and his platoon had been winkling them out of a dugout and they came out with the Officer at the back. When they were being nicely disarmed, the Officer flung a grenade. However, it didn't go off and he said, "You think England is going to win the war, but you are wrong." This Aussie then says, "And you think you're going to be an effin' prisoner of war but you're not!" then he bayoneted him. So when he told the Swiss Officer, he said, "That's all right he asked for it." But he wasn't killed, that's why it came to light because the German Officer had reported that he had been bayoneted after he had surrendered.

> " When I threw the match at it my legs went on fire "

When we took Mersa Brega we had to ensure that it was free of disease, test the water, because amoebic dysentery was rife but there were no serious outbreaks. One thing that could be serious though was if you had a wound or a scratch, it then developed in to a desert sore and the flies used to live on the pus and it would be months before it would heal and sometimes it left a scar. There's people going about yet with scars from desert sores. They issued vitamin tablets and I used to collect them from mates and put them in my water bottle. I never got any desert sores but what I did have and was nearly charged with self-inflicted wounds was, once we started collecting Jerry cans (our petrol cans were made of tin and were square and inferior) we were operating this mobile bath and we'd a hydro burner. It was a boiler and by adjusting the flow of water you could make the water hotter or colder.

Anyway, I was to fill up this hydro burner and when I opened the Jerry can it had been filled right to the neck and sat out in the sun all day with the result that it spilled all over my legs. Well, I carried on and filled up the hydro burner and put on the top with the spanner and pumped it up. Then I let some water into the pan. When I threw the match at it my legs went on fire. A lad was going past with his wagon and he took the seat out of his wagon and wrapped it around my legs and put the fire out. However, we moved the next day and I had the hose tops on and when I came to take the hose tops off they were stuck and there was a great big scar. So I went to our own CO, "Well now," he says, "How did this happen because this looks like self-inflicted wounds, if you've burned that with petrol you ought to have known better than to have done that." Well, it looked dry and everything and with the heat of the sun I thought it would have evaporated. "Ha," he said, "I've got something new here, sulphanilamide powder all the way from America. Put it on, and those hose tops, don't put them on and don't touch it for about a week." Well, when I went back, the crust was ready to fall off but I still have the mark on the leg.

As to Jerry cans, they had them for water as well. These were marked with a 'W'. Some times the petrol was in the old fashioned two gallon petrol tin that you got in this country with a handle at an angle, you couldn't carry it for very long and it was only a little thing.

David: What other German or Italian equipment did you use regularly because they were much better than the allied stuff?

Jack: Well, when we went into Dabie (El Dab'a) airfield after Alamein we came across these big crates. Well, there was a lot of fake British money ready for going in to Cairo. But we also came across cartons of Italian Monopolo cigarettes. "Ah well," we said, "we can't smoke that shit." but we kept them and if we came across any native tribesmen we'd exchange them for eggs. They'd rather have tea than cigarettes and what we used to do was, we made the tea in a hanky so you could retrieve the leaves and put them out to dry then you put a sprinkling of good leaves on the top and flogged them!

When we got up to El Agheila we were miles ahead of our lines of communication and Montgomery said that only petrol, water, ammunition, and food, could come up. No luxuries, cigarettes no chocolate or anything like that so the Italian cigarettes became the finest cigarettes that were ever invented!

David: Talking about camaraderie then-

Jack: This well was about equal distance between the two lines and by gentleman's agreement from about 8am till midday the British drew water and were unmolested. From 12 till four was a kinda siesta because it was too hot to do anything and from four to eight the Italians and Germans drew water.

David: How long did that go on for?

Jack: Till our Officers heard about it!

When we came back to this country we were all taken down to the Army School of Hygiene. There was a Major there who was going to teach us how to test water for poisons because the testing should only have been made by an Officer but of course we'd been doing it in the desert for years. So there was a lad from the Guards Armoured Division and a lad from the 7th Armoured Division, a fella from the 50th Tyne Tees Division and me from the 51st. We all said, "What the hell does he think he's doing, we will have some fun with this bloke!" So, y' see the box mainly tested for arsenic and antimony and he's showin' us how to do this test and he says, "Common one for the Germans to poison all the wells." The Guards armoured boy sez, "Could y' tell us which well it was?" "Well, I don't quite have the map reference but I could get it." says the Major. "Was it arsenic or antimony?" "Oh it would be arsenic, the easiest one t' put in." the Major replied. So we had him right on toast and we said, "The four of us, have probably tested more wells than you've had hot breakfasts and we've never come across one that was poisoned. The only thing that we came across was in 1940 when Wavell's troops were retreating they put a 40 gallon drum o' diesel down a well. We were there two years later and we couldn't get rid of the damn diesel!

Frank Ledingham: From Port Taufiq we got ontil a train. What amused me most there was an Arab foreman with a whip and he'd about six Arabs who were unloadin' baggage and stuff and this foreman had this great long whip. Anyway, we got off the train and there was a big concentration camp full o' German prisoners.

● A Matilda Baron tank at work in the desert. This was one of the first operationally successful mine-clearing tanks.

Our trucks were stranded in Durban because the boat had broken down. We were taken out into the desert and they said, "You're a water truck, you're a five ton truck and you're a wireless truck-" and we had t' plod along in this soft sand till it almost killed us, it was like goin' through soft snow all the time. We were supposed t' be a truck not a soldier marchin' anyway it was just t' give us some drill before we got our trucks. That was in Ismailia and then we crossed the Nile into the western desert and went up into the blue. This was as near to the front line as you could get.

Trevor: Up near the boxes?

Frank: Yes, we were in the E box. A New Zealander was shot down into our box but he landed his aircraft in our box because he knew there were mines outside the box. It was an early Spitfire, this was 1942. Then came the battle of Alamein. At 9.20 at night, it was very dark, a lad came from the signal office and told me that the Staff Captain wanted a battery for his dug out. There was only one 12 volt battery so I took it. I was jist about 50 yards away from the truck when this barrage opened up and these shells were goin' over us like express trains, especially the older clapped out guns used by the New Zealanders and the shells went choo choo choo just like a train! We delivered the battery and

the Staff Captain says, "Well, are you scared?" and I sez, "Just a wee bitty." and he said, "Never mind boys, you're makin' history tonight!"

The main danger was mines. Y' couldn't go walkin', you had to keep t' tracks and there was no running around. Before the end o' Alamein there was the Stukas.

I drove from 12 midday t' 12 midnight if necessary and my pal he did the other 12. So I was waitin' t' get through the defences at Alamein and it was up a sandy slope and about 500 yards and the Redcaps controlled the traffic. It was only one truck at a time through the minefield. I remember sittin' and waiting for about an hour for my turn we had to leave a gap of about 100 yards between each truck because of the Stukas. I was just waitin' and the post Corporal come along and sez, "Ledingham?" and I said,"Aye." "Here's a postcard for you." Up in front of the mortars you could see the trail where they flew from the German lines. They were comin' across the top and dropping doon, you could see their vapour trails. Anyway, the postcard was from a Marian McDonald, a WAAF at Biggin Hill who came from Tullynessle which was close to Montgarrie where I came from. So I read it and I kept it for years and years because it couldn't have come at a better time. It gave me a boost before I went through a minefield.

> " if it hadna been for me hearing that Bofor guns I wouldna be here today "

I went up through the wire and the lad at the top said, "Left and park well away because you can't get over the top." So everything was becoming concentrated. We went along and we stopped at what had been a German trench and decided that would do us the night. When we got into it we thought that somebody had died in it so we gave it a good scrape out with a shovel and put on a sheet o' corrugated iron that we got off the railway station at Alamein!

Then the next mornin' I was sittin' connecting up m' batteries at the end o' the truck when I heard a Bofors gun goin' bump, bump, bump. I looked up and there were six Stukas. Two of them peeled off and were coming down and a big canister bomb left the aircraft. I'd only got 20 yards and I ran like a rabbit but my mate, he was about half that distance fae me but he'd a shovel in his hand because he'd been away t' the toilet. The shovel went up in the air, he dived - clunk on the top of his head and as soon as we got in, there was this almighty crash and then another big crash! The sun just faded out and there was complete darkness. We were choked with the cordite smoke, there was hardly any air so we sat an' pecked an' puffed. I popped my head out and I said, "Oh boy! You should see wer truck!" The bomb landed 10 feet from the axle and I would a been sittin' with my back til the wheel connectin' batteries. If it hadna been for me hearing that Bofor guns I wouldna be here today. There were six of them but the canister I had seen coming from the plane got the wireless wagon which was further down and it was the second one that was coming for me. The next one got a Bren gun carrier and the next Stuka got another. As to casualties; well the wireless truck, the bomb went right into a slit trench which fortunately he wasnae in but the truck was knocked out. He was a batman and he went off to the signal office to tell them he was fed-up up being a batman and he was wanting to get a job like what we had. We were digging out his trench to see if he was in it when he walked in aboot so he went right back and said, "Forget about me being a batman!" Ha ha ha! So we got a new truck in two days but that night we couldn't get over the hills because there was a tank battle going on, but the next day they got away. We had to wait for this replacement truck and then we loaded our stuff up. That was the last time we saw Alamein. It was a case of nose to tail all night and spread out 100 yards during the day all the way up to El Agheila. It was desperate bad for mines. As we were going up, we missed the Brigade road sign which was only six inches long by three and stuck in the road side. The Royal Engineers were sweeping the road but luckily we knew the Lieutenant, we got a good telling off for going too far, so he swept a bit so that we could get turned safely. When I was commin' up at the side of the road, I was shotguns, I wasna drivin, I was up in the hole in the cab and there's RE's diggin' out a mine. We were jist past him about 50 yards when the mine blew up. The poor man, he was about 30 feet up in the air. When I saw the puff o' smoke I ducked down oot o' the way and then the blast hit the truck and gid us a push forward. By the time we got turned back he was covered with a blanket.

A War Office lad came out and they'd invented a 'Bangalore torpedo' and they'd come oot t' let us see this thing. It was jist an ordinary down pipe from a house and it was packed with gun cotton and he then went up to the defences wire and he pushed it up intil it and lit the fuse an' run back, it jist blew the wire completely apart.

We were sittin' in wer truck again and here wis another bang! The Seaforths, they were back and they were going t' make a Bangalore torpedo but it had blown up on them. One of the men went up in the air and come down as though he was free fallin', it jist blew him sky-high! That was at El Agheila. We stayed there and we had Christmas there. We got a tot o' rum, aye the recht good stuff and wer tea. Then we had a wee concert. The next day we jist walked aboot where we knew where others had walked. This jeep came up the road wi four Officers and they jist went off the road to let something pass and there was this great bang. It was just like a 'Comic Cut' t' see them. The Jeep was up in the air about six feet! They were deep mines meant for blowing up tanks. They were down about three feet and the mine detectors couldna catch them. The mine detectors were Polish and made o' bamboo. It was basically a radio off tune with a coil in it and the valves whistled when it detected the mine. The Officers, they were off the seats an a', jist like a 'Comic Cut'.

Trevor: Did they survive?

Frank: Aye, they were taken away in an ambulance. They were alive then because they wouldna have taken them away, they would have just put a blanket on them. After that there was no more fightin' that affected us apart from a wee skirmish. We thought we wouldn't go into Misurata and the street fightin' to get the Germans outa there.

Then into Tripoli. Willie Sutherland got the MM at Mareth, his batteries were all shot up, they were two six volters and the only battery I had was the 12 volt that I had at Alamein so I offered it to him. However, the Germans drove them back and they

> "one of the men went up in the air and come down as though he was free fallin'"

had to retreat. Bill was a big bloke so he put his 19 set ontil his shoulder, that was complete with power pack and he picked up his battery and legged it right doon the trench and saved the set and kept the communications going.

The next een was Wadi Akarit. At five o'clock at night, teatime, Sergeant Clark told me that I had t' go with a Lieutenant of the Seaforths because there was an 18 set that had broken down. There was a platoon which was going to get into position for tomorrow mornin' for the battle to take Wadi Akarit was to take place. I took m' little bag o' tools, my meter and a set of valves. We went right up to the forward defence lines and he went forward and gave the password to get out into no man's land. He beckoned his escort and me t' go forward and told me that he wasn't going to give me the password because I'd have t' stay all night and in the morning, all being well, the brigade would move up and they contact me. So we went up and there was this group o' men. They were in the back of a bush lyin' in the sand there. I tested the wireless set but darkness was commin' down quick and the torch we had was next t' useless. Just then a German flare went up so I changed the valves by the light o' that! Later we heard these

engines runnin' and they were coming towards us and we thought tanks but it was four big twin engined bombers, they were Germans, and they were so low that it wasna a big drone and the engines were runnin' like sewing machines, so quiet. They came outa the hills at the back and along and over us and as soon as they reached our lines which was about half a mile, the Bofors guns and a' thing jist opened up and they couldna miss! One plane went up and come down on it's tail, another one cartwheeled and another een took a nose-dive and the forth went away t' the right and got away. The Seaforths then moved off and told me to stay till the next morning. There was a little shallow trench so I jist lay in one of them. After a while this little lad came along, a figure in the dark and he sez, "Hey Mac, which mob are you in?" I said, "I'm lying here till mornin'." He sez, "I'm lost can I stay wi you?" I says, "Oh aye plenty o' room here look!" In the morning we woke up and there was all this smoke. They were putting up a smoke screen because an attack must have been commin' in. We must have been hell of a near German lines because the Argyll and Sutherland Highlanders came trottin' past with bayonets fixed! Just then the barrage opened up to cover them. Wadi Akarit, that was a big battle for 152 Brigade, 51st Division.

Robbie Bremner: I was posted to a field regiment and eventually got a boat at Liverpool. It was one o' the *Strathaired* line that we gid on to. We landed in Freetown but we didna get off and then we went to Durban for about 10 days. Durban was a great city and at the time they really looked after the troops. Parties, street parties, it was a wonderful place. There was a great big open-air dance place an' we'd be there every night. Then we went up through the Red Sea to a place, I canna mind the name but there were salt lake and it was in the south of the Red Sea. By rail we travelled on further up to a place called Almarza (El Mansura). That was the RA depot there. I joined the 4th Field Regiment which was a regular unit. We went up the desert through 'Hellfire Pass' and that was the best push. We went up nearly as far as Tobruk which was the first time I saw action in the desert. Up until that time we were in 'boxes'. There was A box, B box, and C box etcetera and Churchill came out to see us at that particular time. The battle was at El Adem it was an aerodrome just outside Tobruk. The Panzers come on us there and we was duffed up. There were only 25 of us come back oota that and there was well over a thousand. They weren't all killed a lot of them were captured. Fortunately there was one battery that was left because they were late in commin'. Anyway, back from there, they joined us and everybody had come back to Alamein b'this time and there were very few regiments so we were right back up again and to the Qattara Depression.

This was the first time that I was a fightin' soldier. I was on a gun team there. Fen we were up at Alamein it was all go and at that time we hadna much equipment so that everything we had, like barrage balloons, they had tanks like 'at as well. They made things out of wood and sticks in the shape o' guns and tanks and things like that. Eventually the 51st Division came out an' jined us, then the Sussex and the West Kents. Then we'd Canadians, we had Poles all ready t' go. Before we went through Alamein, Monty came and gave us a big talk on how he wis goin' to do it. Then we went through the gaps in the minefields which took us about three days. We went on to take Mersa Matruh and then the next village and be that time the prisoners were commin' back in thousands. Then it was a great run through to Tobruk, through Benghazi. We then formed what they called 'flying columns'. I had to take turns with a Honey tank, a 25 pounder, a Bren gun carrier and maybe a platoon o' infantry. We went 50 miles into the desert right roond the back o' Jerry and shoot him up the backside and the jist piss off again. The Long Range Desert Group boys they were always up in front looking for positions for y'.

David: When you were in the flying columns what was your role?

Robbie: I was on the gun, the 25 pounder. We broke through Alamein 23rd of November 1942. We fired over five-hundred rounds that night and there was over a thousand guns. We had joined the 4th Indian Division then and we were attached to the 22nd Armoured Brigade. We felt important, keyed up and rarin' t' go. Although we were idle, we moved from sector to sector firing here and there night an D-Day. We called it 'kidology' because what we were doin' there is that we landed up in the Qattara Depression. We had a small front of about 21 miles and we were firing here in the mornin' and here at dinnertime and up here in the afternoon. All wer tanks were barrage balloons in the shape o' tanks. Later the made tanks outa sticks and covered them with sacking. So we were a decoy group. We weren't told that it was the big push, when we came up t' Alamein. It wasn't till Monty arrived that they said that this was it and we were goin' t' break through. That was when the big build up came and the 51st Division came out and joined us. We then had a running battle for the next three weeks with both the Germans and the Italians. We were goin' into the towns and capturing it. It was worse than comin' up Union Street wi the amount o' prisoners comin' back. There were thousands o' them. When we broke through there we then got into gun pits 'cause there was a bit o' resistance. The enemy knew exactly where we'd gone and they had our gun pits ranged and they were jist pumpin' at us and we got blown outa one gun pit. I was the only one that come outa that. I jist had my front teeth knocked out. It was very sad because there was two killed and one lost an eye and one an arm.

After goin' right up t' Tripoli we came right back down to Cairo.

I took jaundice up in Benghazi. That was a terrible thing, one o' my mates he wis a great character and he used t' go oot an' get eggs, grapes and fruit for me because I said, "I'm nae leavin' the regiment." Then after Derna we went to Benghazi, which was Mussolini's country, until we got to the Mareth line where we met the 1st Army. Our

> " The enemy knew exactly where we'd gone and they had our gun pits ranged and they were jist pumpin' at us' "

Colonel, he left and he said that if any out of our company wanted to go with him could go but there were very few went because we'd heard that we were goin' back to Blighty. Instead we come right back doon t' Cairo where we did more trainin'. At that time I was in the 4th Indian Division and I'd been sent on a gunnery course. I came back and got promotion. Then I went t' my Sergeant Major and said, "I've finished soldierin', you can shoot me, I'm finished." He said, "You are jokin'" I said, "No, I'm serious. What we've come through and you said this an' ar that. No, no, that's it." So he left me for three weeks and he came back and he sez, "We're goin' t' Baghdad. We're joinin' the 5th Indian Division. I've a job for y', you'll be in charge o' the cookhouses and the rations. I'll give y' a week t' make yer mind up." I sez, "Dina bother I'm takin' the job." I never looked back and I had more power than a Colonel. I was in charge o' the lot!

The next campaign for me was Burma.

Sandy McKenzie: After the long journey on the *Bergensfiord*, we landed and from the boat we took a train up to a place called Qassassin Camp. There we did more trainin', using a compass, map readin' and that sorta thing. The fly's werena good and the only time that y' got decent relief in the toilets was at dinnertime because the flies were all in the canteen! The flies they were horrible!

The first time we went into action was Aladdin. The vehicles were behind the lines a bit to create as much dust as possible to make Jerry think that there was a great load o' troops, material, etcetera, etcetera. At about 10, the barrage startit and they'd got some objectives by 2 am but we were in reserve but we were as close to the lines as you could get. It looked like a violent thunderstorm with all the gun flashes. We then moved from reserve to the second wave and I think that Wadi Akerit was the next objective. That was right up passed a lot of damaged and burned out vehicles through the Saloon Bends. I was driving and it was at night following the other vehicles.

David: How many men did you have on your lorry?

Sandy: Well I was carrying supplies such as ammunition, blankets and reserve water and maybe some reserve petrol. Daylight came and we carried on because we'd so long to use this track and they y' had t' get off on to the side and disperse and put a camouflage net ower the truck. The gun emplacements were the same, lower the barrel and put the net over. We supplied the troops with food rations after it was dark. Y' drove up as quiet as y' could. Sometimes we'd two companies to supply which took the whole of the night and into the mornin' maybe and of course we had no lights whatsoever they'd all been disconnected. They had a route marked oot wi old petrol tins and they had the number jist pierced oot and a candle inside which enabled y' t' see the way. We had numbers y' see, the Black Watch was HD 60, The 1st Battalion was HD 61 and our number wis 62 so all we had t' do was t' follow those signs.

● A hospital ship in the Mediterranean drawn by Jack Fleming. © G. Fleming

Something that comes to mind was when we were on boat duty in Tripoli when the harbour was cleared and new supplies were coming in. Petrol munitions food and boots. There was a time when the harbour was about filled with floating boots because the boys pit on new boots when they got in the consignment! Another time the crane took a container out of the hold which then burst and all the tins o' food come out and we'd as many tins o' food doon the back o' the seats! We were always on the scrounge!

Y' had what y' called a workbook for different tasks y' did on the vehicle. Some y' did every day and you ticked them off as you did them. The Transport Officer came round and would ask which task y' had t' do that day. I was drivin' a Bedford at the time and desert conditions seemed to be wearing the engines on them very quickly.

David: Did you ever lose a vehicle in the desert?

Sandy: No I didn't but two of my former mates did. They were blown up. They were reversing in, they tripped this mine and up they went. You werena safe goin' off the track. It was because they got killed that I was put on that same job. We tried not t' go off the track but y' had to at times. The Italians were great fellas for mines. They'd different kinds for example they'd square ones and they would detonate at any of the corners. They also had trip wires, something would pass and up they'd go. Some places which had been abandoned some of the boys would go round and see what was what. They'd pull a trip wire and off it would go.

Miss Allan: In June 1940, we set of from Aberdeen and went down to Liverpool from where we set sail on the *S.S. Aquitania*. The *Queen Mary* and the *Mauritania* sailed with us accompanied by an escort of warships. We stopped at Simonstown, Freetown, Bombay, and Colombo and eventually after 62 days sailing we reached Port Said. From there we went up to Cairo.

> " Some of them would come in without hands and others without legs "

● Miss Allan's section in Egypt on a trip to the pyramids. 1942

Now we were a base hospital and we were the 15th Scottish General Hospital and we were nearly all from Aberdeen. The doctors were doctors from Aberdeen Royal Infirmary and most of the sisters were from the Infirmary originally. The first day we arrived in Cairo we stayed on houseboats on the Nile, that was our digs and the hospital was directly across the street. There were hospitals scattered around Cairo and there were others in the desert. We'd have about the same number of beds as Foresterhill as it was then, before it was extended. Although the Hospital was new it wasna very clean so we cleaned up the place and then we got in convoys from the desert which brought the casualties in.

I was in a surgical ward and then later I was in an Officers ward. I used to say to Matron, "I'm not going back to that Officers ward, I just fight with them!" But she told me that I could deal with them so I was put back to the Officers ward, but on the whole we had a very happy unit. We started in the morning with breakfast until the convoys started to bring the casualties. Some of them would come in without hands and others without legs but they hardly complained they were very good. After we had operated on them an Officer would come round and decide who was going back to the lines and those who would go for convalescence. We gave the casualties jobs to do to make them feel needed and they did a good job. We had one, he was a deserter, he was a hard nut t' crack! We were detailing them all what they had t' do and he had to go into the kitchen. So he said that if he went into the kitchen there would be no one in there to upset him. I just told him that he'd t' go into the kitchen and do as he was told.

Trevor: Was he injured?

Miss Allan: No, he was down from the desert he was just malingering. Well, one day I was in the office and I could hear someone shouting, "Open that door Smith, open that door!" On board we had some of the Generals daughters or perhaps wives who would help with various things. Anyway, one of them, perhaps it was General

Wavel's daughter was trying to get into the kitchen. She was shouting, "Open the door Smith!" But he wouldn't open the door. I said to him, "Now just open that door." What a boy! Well he did eventually open it.

Trevor: But how did he get into hospital?

Miss Allan: Well, he'd have made some excuse like stress. Generally though, the lads were really good.

We had an inspection day, and they had to put all the boys blue suits and red ties, that's if they were going out, on top of the lockers in regimental order, what a lot o' rubbish!

Davey Adam: Eventually, after the training, I was on my way to Africa. Eight weeks, what a journey! The first five days, - see me, I rattle in the bath and I'm seasick! It was June the 22nd of June I think it was. There was a fog and the water was like a millpond and I was still sick. Anyway, we landed at a place called El Qassassin at the top o' the Red Sea. There was a great big camp up there and then on to the Alamein box. Then came the night. A few eventful things happened there, we lost quite a few.

There was the section commander, the boy Jamieson he was second in command, they went out on patrol, there were five of them. Ted G——, he got killed. He belonged t' the north o' England.

He went in to cut wire and it was booby-trapped and Jamieson was badly hurt and I never heard from him again. The first night I can remember the flippin' guns what a barrage. They were at the back of us and it was pitch black and y' hadna clue where y' were goin'. We walked over a minefield I'm sure we did. Suddenly, we were told t' dig in but this part they had picked for us was solid shale! All I had was a trenching tool and all I could manage was a very shallow scrape.

It was pitch black and shells were fallin' all round about us. I got a huge blister on my hand jist diggin'. Anyway, somebody runs in an' nearly falls over me. He was a company runner and he'd got lost and he said, "Can I get in your trench?" Well that was the two of us in this shallow thing. Eventually, we had t' use our blummin' picks to get in. We had t' lie there for about a fortnight. We got every bomb an' shell in the night and we'd really t' get right down in y' hole. We were in this holes long enough and eventually we had the word t' move up.

Right in front of us was this mine field and the Royal Engineers had made a path through for the tanks and we had t' go through in front o' the tanks t' guide 'em through. On the way we saw bodies lyin' a'way, that was the first horror things that I saw. This chum from Peterhead, Alexander was his last name, he used t' 'come wi me when we were goin' awar hame for a weekend. That's when we

● Valentine tanks, Courtesy the Tank Museum

were at Hayton camp - he got his head blown off, oh gee, I looked at him the next mornin' and I wis sick. We were both in B company; I was lucky that time. Anyway, we gets through this mine field and far we went I canna mind but we had t' get dug in and we stayed there for a few days getting' shelled all the time. We were advancin' bitty by bitty and then we were told that we were goin' to attack but there wouldna be any Jerries or nothin' there. Oh well, it was the efterneen and y' always had the sun in yer face. We found out jist efter, the tanks gave us a wrong reference point!

We were goin' well enough with our rifles over our shoulders. The ground was flat then you'd come to a bit wi sparse grass and then perhaps you'd come to shale. We were walkin' up in formation and all of a sudden there was a Brrrrup, brrrrup, brrrrrup. "In the name o-" It was a blumin' Spandau. There were two mounds and they'd made a fixed angle of fire. One of the Officers at the front cried, "Argh!" Well he got it in the chest and died a couple o' days efter. Then all hell broke loose when machine guns and this 75 pounder (sic) opened up. The tanks we had, we called 'em 'corned beef tins', they wis Valentines, they were useless. Well, it was mainly Italians that were there and a 75 pounder gun. The Jerries had gone and left them. They ay did 'at leavin' the Ities t' do all the work. They had a 75 pounder; well they started brewin' up. Fourteen o' these Valentines they brewed up. What a shame, boys burned t' death in these tanks.

Val: What did you do?

Davey: Well, we came to a bit that was sand dunes and down we went. Big Davey Gardine he was our company commander. A big sod he was t' me anyway. If you was up in front o' him, you were a criminal! He'd a castle doon in the borders, a real brought up soldier. Well, he comes up, his walkin' stick wis bigger than me, he musta been six feet four. Anyway, he shouts, "What's a doin' wi ye, what y doin' doon there?" We said, "It's that blummin' fixed Spandau firin' at us. We jist canna move." "Go a way wi yer. I'll go up and see." Ah, well big Davey, he goes up and the next thing we hears was this Brrrup! Brrrrrup! Well, he got a burst o' machine-gun fire and big Davey, he wis gone. We lost 75 per cent of our Battalion there. I buried 14 of our boys, they were on the back of the tanks y' see and when the tanks got hit they had t' get off and then they got hit by the Spandaus because they were left exposed. What a mess some o' them wi their heads blown off and I got the order to bury them.

> "we were in a wadi and these Mitchell bombers came over and flippin' well bombed us!"

Eventually night came. Night falls very quickly, the sun suddenly goes down an' it's black. The 4th Indian Division was ay wi us and I mind we heard a flippin' great bang and we got up on to the Alex. Road and lyin' jist waitin' to move. The next thing we knew was, we were being bombed by about 10 Stukas. We flew a' ways 'cause we werena dug in or anything'! There were a lot o' casualties there with the Stukas.

We were then told that we were goin' up to what we called 'Happy Valley' to lie for a fortnight. But to get there we had to walk 17 miles in the sand by the side of the Alex. Road. It was hell, the heat was terrible and it took us two days. Anyway, we were there for a few days and the next thing we were on lorries. Jerry had gone a long way retreatin' in a very short while. Then we went up this pass, 'Hellfire Pass' and up the top o' there we found a great big British cemetery.

We didna stop and we went up past Benghazi and across these salt flats what a terrible place. We were 22 mile in the desert near the Qattara Depression. Nothing could move in it because it was all soft sand. We were doon in there an' God I wis never in a place like 'at. We dug our trenches, we wis ae diggin' trenches, we were like moles! I've seen us in the same trench for a fortnight. When we wis there, from 12 o'clock till two, you couldna move y' just poured o' sweat. Well, they come one day till us and told that we were goin' awar to get a bath. Where did we get a bath? In the Med! It wis a laugh because commin' back there was a sand storm and the bloody stuff was stickin' to us and we were worse by the time we got back than if we'd never gone!

We were there with half a mug o' water t' wash, shave and mak tea. What we used t' dee was; there wis a heavy dew at night in fact it was kinda frosty at night there. Well, we used t' dig a hole, put wer gas capes in it, then in the mornin' y' collected the dew and there was enough water t' wash and shave. Tommy Morton was m' mate and we did a bit o' a recce around where Jerry had been. There were Jerry cans o' petrol lyin' all over the place but water? Oh no! Well Tommy and me comes upon this barrel so we tapped it open; pure, clear, cold water. The Jerries had brought it and then had t' leave it quick. You shoulda seen the scrabble for that water! After that we kept goin' because Jerry was retreatin' all the time and we weren't the troops at the front we were jist following up.

But eventually, we did stop at this place on the coast on the way to Tobruk, it had some Roman ruins there. Once we got to Tobruk we were informed that we might be here for a fortnight.

The Americans have landed! Great news. We were emptying lighters off the boats o' food and we had that much tins; tins o' bacon, tins o' fruit, tins o' God knows what! We were sleepin' in the open and the bivey was full o' this stuff! We couldn't let 'em see it y' see!

Well, we were telt that we were goin' t' move to the other side o' Tobruk but we never actually got intae Tobruk. All these guys that got inta Tobruk they never seen naethin o' the war, maist o' them. We had t' ging awar t' the other side. We were still telt we wis getting' a fortnight. So we dug a big hole an' put our bivey on the top o' it which gid y' mair room. The next thing we knew it bucketed doon wi rain. "Come on, get up, we've t' move, get y' bivey we're movin' in 20 minutes! 20 minutes God almighty! We never got wer claes off o' course an' it was bucketing doon wi rain. What had happened - the Yanks. Jerry had said, 'Get' and they pushed 'em right back up the Kasserine Pass. So we had t' ging up t' the line t' draw the Jerry awar and back. Y' never hear much about that, we wis forever pullin' 'em outa trouble. They couldna fight their way outa paper bags I'm tellin' ye!

So we went up there to pull the Jerries back so that the Yanks could get forward. We were there for about eight weeks and these planes used t' come, American Mitchell medium bombers and they used t' come roond maybe every half hour bombin' the Jerry who couldna ging nae where.

● Peter Evelyn's Company stranded in the desert near Palmyra, courtesy Lord Forbes

It's a wonder that they didna gie themselves up a long time before they did. Anyway, we were in what y' call a 'wadi' and these Mitchell bombers came over and flippin' well bombed us! The Germans had been in the same place for about six weeks, the Yanks shoulda known where they were. We lost a few men like that but I canna mind how many. Onywye, we gings fae this place to this place called Djidjelh in either Libya or Algeria. There were a lotta Yanks there. I got a hen there an' it wis layin' eggs for me but then it started cluckin' (Getting broody) and began to hide its eggs. I swapped it for a bag o' cigarettes with this Yank.

Lord Forbes: Our first taste of the Middle East, and desert conditions, was gained at Qassassin (in 1942). A number of the Battalion, including the Commanding Officer, went to hospital for brief periods suffering from jaundice or dysentery. I suppose that this was not surprising, considering the problems with flies and hygiene generally. At sundown there was a marked drop in temperature, and there was a Battalion order that sweaters should be worn from sundown. This was a wise precaution against tummy trouble.

From Qassassin the Battalion moved in its own transport through the Sinai Desert up through Palestine to join the 3rd Battalion Coldstream Guards and 2nd Battalion Scots Guards, who had recently been withdrawn from the Western Desert, and were now encamped near Qatana on the slopes of Mount Hermon. Said to have been the mountain of the Transfiguration, it appeared as an imposing mountain of 9000 feet high rising majestically between the Lebanon and anti-Lebanon ranges. It was whilst we were crossing the Sinai Desert that we encountered our first sandstorm, which was the worst one I can remember. When it hit one's face, the sand felt like a concentrated hailstorm. Each vehicle came to a halt while its occupants got underneath it so as to get some protection from the wheels, as well as having the benefit of having something over their heads. Having skin exposed to a bad sandstorm can be most painful.

The journey to Syria took us through all kinds of country; first the barren desert, then flat country and finally through mountainous scenery. Even the desert hills had their charms. At sunset and sunrise the colours were breathtaking. Each morning of this long drive we were up at 4.30, and our column was on the move by six o'clock. Except for a stop of an hour at midday, we drove on until about half past six. In reality it was a drive from dawn until dusk for three days.

On arrival at Qatana we found our camp in a bad state of repair, and even the doors and windows to the huts did not fit. However, the Battalion Pioneers soon got to work and dealt with the worst deficiencies. The location, amongst the bare lava covered hills 1000 feet above sea level on Mount Hermon, was a glorious spot, especially at sunset when the hills in the fading light looked as if they were covered in heather. It was moderately warm by day, but when the stoves went out at night the huts became freezing cold as we were almost on the snow line, and the huts had no insulation.

Because of the cold, during the night there was an almost constant stream of Officers and men heading for the latrines. As Adjutant, I was responsible for choosing a password each day, to be used when challenged by the camp sentries. Unfortunately, one night the Commanding Officer forgot the password. He was challenged and had to say he was the Commanding Officer, hoping the sentry would recognise him and not shoot him. Next morning Archer made it clear to me that I was not at all popular for choosing a password he could not remember.

In an effort to keep the frost out of the Officers' Mess hut, the Pioneers built a fireplace. This led to evening meals being bolted, as there was a stampede to get to the one and only fire. Those who were last to finish were literally left out in the cold beyond the human fire screen. During our time at Qatana, the Brigade was at 72 hours' notice to move to the Western Desert. Much time was spent in training at all levels. For us it was a question of gaining from the experience of the other two Battalions who had been operating in the Western Desert.

The three Guards Battalions were now the fighting units of 201 Guards Brigade, under the command of my old Platoon Commander at Sandhurst, Julian Gascoigne, who was now a Brigadier. At one period Peter Evelyn took his Company to train into the desert near Palmyra where, shortly after their arrival, the heavens opened with the result that not only did the dried up wadis suddenly become raging torrents, but also the whole area around the Company became a veritable lake, so that the Company was completely cut off. In no time at all some of the Company found themselves walking about in water up to their knees; the whole countryside round about appeared flooded, but luckily some of the men managed to wade to what had become a small island where they found a dry place to spend the night and wait for the floods to abate. Others less lucky found the water waist deep, so remained in their vehicles. Although everyone had plenty to eat, there was a shortage of drinking water, so that many were forced to drink the muddy floodwater,

happily with no ill effects. All vehicles had water up to their axles, and some had water over their bonnets. The Company simply could not move, and the only redeeming feature was the fact that they were still in radio communication with Battalion Headquarters, so they were able to ask for assistance.

On hearing of their plight, the Commanding Officer agreed I should request Brigade Headquarters to send the Light Aide Detachment, attached to the Battalion from the Royal Mechanical and Electrical Engineers, so as to help the Company out of its predicament. On arrival they laboriously and slowly winched most of the vehicles onto firm hard ground, so that the Company was able to rejoin the Battalion. It was five days before the last trucks were extricated and they had to be pulled out by a caterpillar tractor. Had the Battalion been given the word to move up to the Western Desert there would have been a lot of red faces, certainly in the Battalion and possibly also at Brigade Headquarters - altogether a narrow squeak.

In November the whole Brigade did a flag-showing exercise by touring Lebanon and the northern part of Syria. The object was not only to carry out desert training as a Brigade, but also to make a show of strength and Anglo-French unity to the Turks across the northern border, in case they were tempted to come into the war on the German side. We carried out an exercise devised by the Brigade Headquarters, known as 'Pretend to be an Army'. Each Battalion would be ordered to take up a certain position within sight of the frontier. Once established and seen by the Turks the Battalion, less one Company which would remain where it was, would move by night to another position and remain there till after dark the next evening, when the same procedure was adopted. This deception was repeated for three nights. As the whole Brigade was involved, the Turks must have imagined that the Allies had a large force to the south of them. Anyway, the ruse worked and the Turks kept out of the war. Eventually, on reaching Aleppo, a somewhat smelly town from which the French troops had recently pulled out, all three Battalions marched through the centre of the town.

It was whilst on this tour that I saw some of the really marvellous sights of the Middle East including places like Baalbek with its Roman temple of Jupiter built in AD 170 some 3000 feet above sea level and having 54 gigantic pillars of which only seven now remain. Also there was the wonderful 800 years old Krak des Chevaliers, a Crusader castle in a magnificent position standing north of the road between Tripoli and Homs, on a spur of the hills overlooking a marshy plain. T.E. Lawrence described it as - "perhaps the best preserved and wholly admirable castle in the world". Beneath the southwest tower there is a slanting wall of 80 feet thick. One marvels at its solidarity and the beauty of design. When fully garrisoned the castle held 2000 soldiers who

● "On the slopes of Mount Hermon we found woodcock and snipe to shoot", photo courtesy Lord Forbes

occupied it for 150 years. Kiak guards the approaches to the coast from the hinterland. Furthermore, in the Syrian desert we came across the spectacular ruins of the ancient commercial town of Palmyra, which was once the focus of the Syrian caravan trade. To have seen these three places really was a lifetime bonus. The tour was not only greatly enjoyed by everyone, but it also did much to cement together the three Battalions into what was to prove to be a formidable Brigade fighting unit in North Africa, and later in Italy.

Once back at Qatana the monotony continued, only to be relieved from time to time by visits to Damascus, with its famous 'Straight Street', the oldest street in the world. The street is extremely narrow and is lined with shops which nearly meet overhead. Many of the shops had lovely brocade and I bought some lengths to be sent home to Rosemary. It was quite difficult making ones way down the street which always seemed to be crowded with people, children, and donkeys. About the only alternative when off duty, was to go to Beirut where there were some excellent little restaurants.

The road to Beirut on the coast went through rocky gorges in the mountains renowned as places where robbers used to hide. We were advised to keep a look out when driving on this road, but did not have any trouble. All we saw from time to time during daylight were men in baggy trousers either tending their flocks of goats and kids, which had long ears hanging down like ribbons, while other men were just sitting on rocks smoking their hookahs'.

> " disaster nearly struck the Sergeants' Mess when the cooks used a tin of rifle oil in mistake for cooking oil "

Then, at various times, some of us managed to go off for a day's shooting. The guns usually came from the Commanding Officer, together with Bill Anson, Nick Villiers, Tom Butler, Geoffrey Gwyer, Malcolm Strang-Steel, Edmond Vaughan and myself, depending on who was off duty. Luckily I had managed to include a 16-bore gun and a thousand cartridges in the Battalion stores when we set sail from England. These items of undetected equipment came in most useful at times.

On the slopes of Mount Hermon we found woodcock and snipe to shoot, while the valleys held mainly chickaw and quail with duck in the marshy areas. Once we went into the desert to shoot sand grouse as they came in to drink at a tiny water hole. We also went to shoot duck on Lake Hula at the northern end of Lake Tiberias in Palestine. The best day was when three of us, Geoffrey Gwyer, Edmund Vaughan and I, shot 150 duck. My score between 11 in the morning and four in the afternoon was 61 duck. We had no dogs but all the duck were picked by Arabs who waded about in the water, which was not more than knee-deep.

Sometimes we took our small bivouacs with us so that we could spend the night near the lake after the evening flight, and then do the morning flight prior to returning to camp. On one occasion I remember spending the night in a grapefruit grove and the next morning plucking grapefruit off the trees and eating them for breakfast. Seldom have I had anything quite so delicious as a ripe grapefruit straight off the tree and eaten while the morning sun pours down from the clear blue skies above -

so much better and quite different from the grapefruit which has ripened in transit to a shop.

One task given to me was planning the Battalion's route through Palestine for our move to the Western Desert. Whilst doing this, I lunched at Government House in Jerusalem with the High Commissioner, Sir Harold MacMichael. I remember being very struck with Government House, and its fine garden and magnificent view over Jerusalem. Little did I realise, at the time, that I would be living there a few years later.

There was one unforeseen incident which occurred when the Battalion was told to practise making 'sangars' - these were rather like low stone grouse butts which troops used for protection on hard rocky ground, when it was impossible to dig trenches. Peter Evelyn wanted to try out a sangar made by his Company, so he got one of his subalterns, Johnnie Wiggin, to get into a sangar, while he, Peter, fired a shot at it with a rifle. The result was unexpected, to say the least, when Johnnie jumped up out of the sangar holding his bottom. Luckily the bullet had only just penetrated the sangar and it had only grazed poor Johnnie. Nevertheless he did have to spend one night in hospital, without being recorded as wounded in action. The majority of those from the Battalion admitted to hospital during the time we were in Syria, were suffering from malaria. Bill Anson had a particularly bad bout of it, and was in hospital for a number of weeks before being passed fit for duty.

Then just before Christmas, disaster nearly struck the Sergeants' Mess when the cooks used a tin of rifle oil in mistake for cooking oil. Luckily, only a few members of the Mess were cleaned out, and all were present and correct by Christmas. When Christmas Day came, we made a special effort to depart from the usual routine we had been following since arriving in Syria. In the morning we had a Drumhead Service for the whole Battalion followed by Christmas dinner when, as was the custom in the Regiment, the Officers served dinner to the men. This was followed by a hilarious afternoon of camel and donkey races organised

● A derelict Messerschmitt Bf 109F, possibly from Qasaba, circa 1942. Courtesy R. Bauld

● British troops inspecting a German 88mm. gun destroyed during the fighting. R.Bauld

● The remains of a British Crusader with Italian graffiti mimicking one of Churchill's sayings, "some chicken, some neck!" R.Bauld

● Inspection of the 6th Battalion Grenadier Guards by their Colonel-in-Chief, King George VI accompanied by Queen Elizabeth, Princess Elizabeth and Princess Margaret. Lord Forbes is front row far right

for us by the French forces. Company Commanders were mounted on camels, whilst junior Officers rode donkeys. The Commanding Officer umpired, perched high up on the largest camel, but his task proved impossible as the camels did not respond to any word of command. However, the main episode of the afternoon was a magnificent display of horsemanship by a detachment of the French Spahi Regiment stationed at Damascus. These colourful soldiers were wearing full-dress uniform with beautiful silver daggers hanging from their belts. They performed hair-raising and dramatic somersaults, balancing feats and, finally, a cavalry charge.

The pleasant autumn climate, though cold at night soon changed to wind and rain, to be followed by snow soon after Christmas, when we were warned that the only way to get supplies to the Battalion might be to drop them from the air, though luckily this was not necessary. Then, at the beginning of February 1943, we received the orders we had been waiting for, that the Brigade was to set off on 7th February to join General Montgomery who, after the 8th Army victory at Alamein, had now pushed the Germans westwards to near Tripoli in Libya. This meant we would have to move over 2,000 miles, much of it across desert country, which in itself would be no small feat.

It was at this time that I took on Guardsman Gray as my Soldier Servant. Throughout the time he was with me I could not have been better served, or had a more faithful companion. Albert Gray had wonderful foresight. I seldom had to ask him for anything; he nearly always anticipated my requirements, and everything I wanted was waiting for me.

On our way to the Western Desert we again spent 24 hours at Qassassin, drawing some essential stores. Also, whilst there, I paid a brief visit to the Royals who were encamped nearby. They had just been withdrawn to re-equip after fighting in the desert. I arranged to see briefly my two brothers-in-law, Jack and Desmond. Sadly, it was the last time that I saw them.

After leaving Qassassin, each day we covered about 150 miles when going through the Western Desert. Usually we would stop some time between 1600 and 1700 hours each evening, and then after a good meal we would bivouac for the night. The whole move proved to be most interesting, because we went either through or near so many places that became well known during the North African Campaign. We passed El Alamein where Monty had recently won his famous battle. Here we saw burnt out tanks, lorries and other vehicles, mainly German, which had become casualties during the battle. The sight of a substantial number of German tanks and guns put out of action gave us considerable cheer, especially as we had been told we must be ready for immediate action on reaching the 8th Army. After El Alamein we passed Mersa Matruh, Bug-Buq, Tobruk, Derna, Barce, Benghazi, Agedabia and Sirte. We went on past Tripoli, and it was to the considerable credit of the Battalion that we arrived at Medenine on 2nd March without having lost through any cause one vehicle during the marathon move from Syria.

The drive had taken us over 2,200 miles through vast desert country the whole way, except for the few inhabited areas where there were usually trees such as olives and date palms, and also near inhabited areas where one often found some cultivated ground. Somehow the desert was by no means monotonous, as it was full of interesting features. At times our route would take us near the coast and, on two occasions, we leaguered for the night near the sea, so that everyone was able to take a refreshing dip in the warm Mediterranean. Throughout the drive across the Western Desert we saw signs of the long ding-dong conflict that had already taken place. There was everything from burnt out vehicles, destroyed dumps, aircraft casualties, to crosses marking graves. Nights in the desert were often ice-cold in contrast to the scorching heat of the day which sometimes were made oppressive by the wind. One essential for everyone was water, to prevent dehydration. We had small canvas water sacks which we filled with water. The sack was then hung on the outside of one's vehicle, usually on the side mirror support. By this method, owing to evaporation through the canvas, the water kept cool.

On reaching Medenine, we were ordered to take up defensive positions at once as a German counter-attack was expected. The Coldstream and Scots Guards took up positions to the west on hills overlooking flat ground, whilst we were to be in reserve, in an area like a large basin to the rear of them.

Sure enough, on the morning of 5th March the Germans launched their counter-attack with three of Rommel's Panzer Divisions, across open country towards the Coldstream and Scots Guards who excelled themselves by destroying enemy tanks as they trundled towards where the two Battalions were dug in. Meanwhile we were having a tantalising time, as from our area in the basin behind the hills, we could not see what was going on. We could hear gunfire, and from time to time we could see clouds of smoke going up into the air as German tanks were hit, and we could also hear reports of success on the radio. At one moment I managed to walk up to some higher ground from where I could get a glimpse of part of the battle. Later that afternoon the Germans withdrew leaving 52 tanks knocked out by the Coldstream and Scots Guards - a truly magnificent result.

After the battle of Medenine, the Battalion sent out a patrol to ascertain just how far the Germans had withdrawn. Also at this time the Commander in Chief, General Montgomery, visited the Brigade to say how pleased he was that the Germans had been so successfully repulsed at Medenine. He said that now the plan was for the Eighth Army to break through the Mareth Line, a defensive position constructed by the French to guard the approaches to southern Tunisia.

Prior to reaching the Mareth Line the plan was to dislodge the Germans from their outpost positions on the hills of Sidi El Guelaa, about three miles to the south, and this operation was to be undertaken by 201 Guards Brigade. Monty, as he often did before a battle, visited the Battalion. He stood on the bonnet of his jeep and told us he never launched an attack until he had the necessary

troops and equipment to bring about success. He ended by saying - 'Now this is your first major battle in the 8th Army. All I have to tell you is that it is going to be easy. All my battles are!' The plan was for the 8th Army to break through the Mareth Line, and then join up with the 1st Army in Tunisia. The Mareth Line consisted of a series of fortifications extending from the coast to the Matmata Hills, about 22 miles inland to the south. I have never seen soldiers leave an address by a Commander with such high morale as all ranks did that day. The thoughts and dread of battle had been put aside by Monty's confidence. It was all very moving.

Later, I found that many who had not served directly under Monty, criticised him for being a showman. What they did not appreciate was that this showmanship was all part of Monty's technique that produced his great leadership. He would at once get everyone's attention, and then explain how victory was to be achieved. Nobody was left in any doubt that they were part of a victorious army and, furthermore, everyone knew the outline plan of battle. He was greatly respected by Officers who served under him and was revered by his troops; he was both boastful and abrasive at times. Monty made it clear that now he had got both the troops and equipment and it was Just a question of going on and on till the Axis troops were forced out of North Africa.

Julian Gascoigne, the Brigade Commander, decided that he would make a night assault on the German positions when there would be a full moon on the 16th of March. His plan was that the 6th Battalion would lead the assault, and from intelligence reports available it was not anticipated that the Brigade would have a very formidable task. How wrong this turned out to be!

Patrolling was carried out during the night of 14/15th March and it was during that night a Gunner Officer of the 51st Highland Division was captured whilst doing a reconnaissance to locate a suitable observation post, from where artillery fire could be controlled during the assault. However, what was not known at the time was that the captured Officer had marked maps on him, so that the Germans knew just where and when the artillery barrage would come down. This gave away the whole battle plan, and there is no doubt that during the 15th and 16th March the Germans greatly strengthened their defensive positions. Little did we know that the surprise of a night attack had been lost, before the attack began.

The area occupied by the Germans' crack 90 Light Division, was where the desert gave way to more broken ground. In between the Battalion start line and the high ground of Sidi El Guelaa, held by the Germans, was the now dry Wadi Zess. The Wadi had a steep bank on our side, and consequently it could only be crossed in a few places, unless prior excavation was carried out.

During the somewhat tense afternoon of 16th March our Padre, Reggie Leadbeater, a heroic little man, went round the Battalion holding short services wherever a number of Officers and men were gathered together, preparing for the night assault.

At 1930 that evening the Battalion moved silently by moonlight up to the start line, previously marked by Douglas Phillips the Battalion Intelligence Officer, and Edmund Vaughan. The air was still, with a freshness from the smell of the wild flowers, especially the rosemary. It was just as the various units got to their markers at the start line that a German aircraft came over and dropped a flare, which lit up the whole Battalion area. This episode again confirmed the fact that the Germans knew about our plan - which was that it would be a two Battalion attack with us on the right and the Coldstreamers on the left. The Scots Guards were in reserve.

Battalion Headquarters was located near the start line. My task was one of communication both forward and backward. For this I had in the command vehicle, which looked like a rectangular box on wheels, two radios, each on a different frequency. With one I could communicate with ~ Brigade Headquarters, and the other was on the Battalion frequency. With the latter, I could hear the talk going on between the Commanding Officer and the Companies, and I could also contact the Commanding Officer with any orders which I received from Brigade Headquarters.

The leading Companies of the Battalion then proceeded to cross the Wadi, which they did with very little opposition. Indeed they were able to reform on the far side of the Wadi for the final assault as had been planned, but then soon ran into trouble as the Germans' 90th Light Division reinforced by a Battalion of Panzer Grenadiers, had laid minefields in thick belts. Mines were exploding all around the leading troops. In spite of the very heavy casualties sustained in crossing the minefields, the Battalion objectives were reached, but pockets of Germans had been passed in the advance. These Germans had either been stunned by the barrage, or had decided to lie low. During the assault, the supporting artillery fired barrage after barrage - in all some 24,000 shells were fired. At Battalion Headquarters we were on a piece of featureless ground, overlooking the Wadis, with the artillery right behind us. Later in life, it was not surprising that my hearing became impaired and I have little doubt that this was due largely to the Mareth artillery barrage.

Unfortunately the assault had passed by some German positions, and these now began to counter-attack our assault Companies from the rear. The Companies were very depleted, having already suffered heavy casualties. To add to their difficulties, many of their radios had become defective during the fighting, making any form of communication extremely difficult. This resulted in the Companies being unable to ask for further artillery support. At Battalion Headquarters we did not dare request Brigade Headquarters for more artillery support, as we had been receiving insufficient information from the assault Companies, that we did not know the exact position of all our troops. We might have brought the barrage down on some of them - such was the fog of war.

At this stage the few remaining Officers and men of the three leading Companies were virtually surrounded, and to make matters worse our Bren gun carriers, as well as our anti-tank guns, were being shot to pieces as they attempted to cross the Wadi Zess, in order to reach the forward Companies through the minefields. Mines had proved an obstacle to the infantry, but they spelt disaster to the vehicles. The banks of the Wadi were anything from five to 30 feet high. Vehicles which were set on fire by enemy action, lit up the whole area, with the result that our Bren gun carriers and anti-tank guns became easy targets for the Germans.

At about 0300 Battalion Headquarters began to come under mortar and rifle fire and, to guard against a German counter attack, Billy Kingsmill the Battalion second in command told Bill Anson and I to organise a defensive flank around the Headquarters. The battle continued. The forward positions were becoming untenable so the Commanding Officer asked Brigade Headquarters for two Companies of the Scots Guards to help hold onto our Battalion objectives, but probably wisely this was refused as they might be needed to cover a withdrawal. For this their support could be vital.

All this time at the Regimental Aide Post the Medical Officer, Captain Anthony Winder, and the Padre, worked ceaselessly tending the wounded, and at times were under heavy mortar fire. Later on in the campaign in North Africa the Padre, with some Guardsmen in his vehicle, was trying to rejoin the Battalion, and lost the way. The next thing they saw was a German armoured vehicle. On seeing the German vehicle the Padre turned to the driver and said- 'I think we need a little help from above'. They got it! And managed to extricate themselves and reach the Battalion.

Peter Evelyn, who was a master of foxhounds,

> "to have taken part in such a battle and to have survived was indeed an experience, and one that will not be forgotten"

rallied his Company by blowing his hunting horn; alas Peter, my best man at our wedding, and a very gallant Officer, did not survive the battle. Communication was becoming more and more difficult, and in the final stages of the battle the aerial of my control radio was shot away. This severed the link with the Commanding Officer and the Companies. Luckily, this happened just after I had radioed the Commanding Officer to say I had received orders from Julian Gascoigne at 0525 for the Battalion to withdraw. Once the aerial had gone, all I could do was to communicate with Brigade Headquarters by means of the rear link radio.

The battle weary remnants of the Battalion, on orders from the Commanding Office, withdrew under cover of a smoke screen put down by the artillery to a point near our original start line. During the course of the battle the Commanding Officer had been wounded; in addition 24 Officers and 255 men were battle casualties. Of the Officer casualties, no fewer than 14 had been killed on the battlefield. To have taken part in such a battle and to have survived was indeed an experience, and one that will not be forgotten. The leadership shown by the Commanding Officer, Archer Clive, was superb. Throughout the battle he had been up with the leading troops. He was awarded the DSO.

For the remainder of the North African Campaign the Battalion was little more than a skeleton fighting unit, as there were not enough reinforcements readily available to bring it up to the strength of a fighting Battalion. Owing to the shape of the terrain held by the Germans, the battle became known at the time as the Horseshoe Battle. There is little doubt that, had the Germans not been forewarned of the attack, the outcome could have been very different. Even so, Monty praised 201 Guards Brigade for drawing so many German crack troops to the Horseshoe area and thus enabling him to out flank the Germans holding the Mareth Line with the New Zealand Division. Once outflanked von Arnim, who had taken over from Rommel, was forced to continue to withdraw his troops westwards.

On 1st April, Rosemary's birthday, the Battalion, having followed the withdrawing Germans, took up a defensive position along the Wadi Akarit in Southern Tunisia, in case the Germans put in a counter-attack on the 8th Army. We spent the day digging slit trenches and that night we remained all night in our trenches until after stand-to at dawn, when we could see that the Germans were not going to launch an immediate attack.

It was after stand-to was over that I walked back to have a news with our Reserve Company, who were behind Battalion Headquarters. I was just walking back to Battalion Headquarters along the desert road when a German Messerschmitt fighter aircraft suddenly appeared from nowhere, flying straight down the road. It came from behind me and was flying at not more than 100ft. I just had time to throw myself flat on the ground before the pilot pressed the trigger, and a hail of bullets sprayed right down the middle of the road. Luckily I went down across the road, as the next moment one bullet hit the ground less than a yard on one side of me, and another hit the ground on the other side of me, again less than a yard away. By pure luck I had gone down across the road and not along the road; it really was luck as I did not have time to think. If I had gone down along the road it was almost certain I would have been hit. It was all over in a flash and I certainly had had a very lucky escape. Oddly enough almost exactly the same thing happened in the desert to Roddy Heathcote-Amory in the Royals. He also escaped untouched by bullets which hit the road on either side of him though, unlike me, he fell face down along the road. He also had luck on his side.

From the Wadi Akarit, the Brigade formed part of a force whose task was to do a left hook south westwards into the desert. It would then join up with the 1st Army, which had landed in Algeria and advanced into Tunisia. While this operation was in progress, the remainder of the 8th Army were to remain in position near Enfidaville, to prevent the Germans escaping back into Libya. It was here that Desmond, Rosemary's youngest brother, was killed whilst serving with The Royals. An outflanking movement across the desert, such as this left hook, was a role ideally suited to a Motor Battalion. I shall always remember this size of the desert, the light nights when the moon was full, the multitude of stars and the great depth of the sky at night. Often the nights were cold, the sand was hard to sleep on and there were endless dawns as well as false dawns yet, when I wanted to sleep, I slept.

It was whilst doing this lightening outflanking movement under cover of darkness, which took us by Kairouan and Le Kef, that the Brigade outran Army Supplies. However, we came on an abandoned Italian dump, containing hundreds and hundreds of large tins of gherkins. The Battalion stocked up with gherkins, and was able to continue the advance for three days until army supplies caught up with us again. Ever since then I have never wanted to touch a gherkin again!

"they had a
gentlemen's agreement
to stop firin' until they
buried the dead"

The Desert

North Africa

*A*NGLO-AMERICAN ARMIES LANDED ON THE NORTH COAST OF AFRICA *between Casablanca and Algiers, on 8th November, 1942. It was an operational feat of the first magnitude in its planning and execution and trapped the German Afrika Korps between its 117,000 troops and the advancing British/Commonwealth Eighth Army.*

Major William MacHardy: After training, I was at the Gordon Barracks for just two months then I was sent out to Algiers. One thing I was looking forward to, was seeing my brother who was serving in the 51st Highland Division and I was hoping that we would meet. I was posted to a training school just outside Beirut as an instructor. I was six months there at that school. I was teaching the type of things we were going to be involved in North Africa.

The main thing that I learned from desert warfare was, if only we had good maps and aerial photography because the maps were very very poor. If you had good maps taken from aerial photography, then you were able to see all the little bits where you could creep along and not be seen. Reconnaissance was something you had to do a lot of, putting out patrols, putting them out at night and lying up and trying to find out what the ground looked like then come back again and report what they'd seen. There were clashes at night sometimes because the Germans were doing the same thing and their patrolling was also very good. I enjoyed patrolling, creeping about and that it must have come from my stalking days in Scotland. Before we went out on a patrol we had to be sure that our kit was in good order because you were always involved with sand. Making quite clear that the patrol knew exactly what they were going to do. Sound carries over a long distance in the desert, I don't know why it is but the least little noise, a clink up against a stone, a rifle or something you could hear it but it was sometimes difficult to know exactly where it had come from. Hissing was the usual means of communication between us. If there was a long hiss for example then there was something bothering us, there was something in front of us or we were coming up against a patrol or we were coming up against something that

would eventually give us trouble. I found that if you were doing that for a couple of hours at night it was a great strain, you came back very tired.

The patrol I always remember was that one night we went out and we knew Jerry was pretty close but we weren't quite sure were he was. We got so far, probably as five or six hundred yards moving very slowly and suddenly we heard a noise so we signalled to stop. This German patrol came up and past us just within yards and they never spotted us. The funny thing that came out of this was this; I could smell Germans and I believe that what I was smelling was what they had eaten, sausages etc. And they had their own peculiar smell and I suppose that we did as well. I always tried to move with the wind so that I could get their wind and therefore their scent so that we could get warning of them in good time. The job of reconnaissance was to find out as much as we could, here was a German patrol on the move, we kept quiet and then we started to move back keeping close to them all the time to see how far they would go. But that night, they didn't go very far and down they went and we lay with them quite close. Then they got up and went back. There was a chance, that if they'd have seen us, there might have been an armed confrontation. We didn't want that because I felt that the more they felt that we were not putting out patrols the better. If they think that, then they are likely to get a bit careless if they think there is no one going about and run in to them. However, there were times when there was a firefight. In fact there was one time that we had caught a few casualties because what happened was, the Germans had come over the top and it was an English regiment that was there at the time and they were thrown off. With the poor communications we had we didn't know that they had been thrown off so instead of meeting the English regiment we landed

● Left: British troops landing in North Africa. Courtesy J. Pelella

with the Germans. They were waiting for us so we had to make a quick move. That happened often and of course there were times when we got the better of them. The Germans were very good at that sort of thing, they were very quick.

David: What was your first experience of the desert?

Billy Henderson: The first experiences I had in the desert was diggin' holes for toilets! We were based at Alexandria after El Alamein and we were following the 51st Highland Division. We were the Royal Corps of Signals attached to this 65th Medium Artillery from the Newcastle area. We stayed in tents and what we did was, we dug a trench in the tent and we slept in that just in case we got fired on. There was always the flies o' course and y' jist had t' put up wi them but our tents had mosquito nets so we were all right at night an' that.

The first battle we had was the Mareth Line. That was bad for us. I used t' look after the switchboard. I was once called in to do a repair then suddenly barrage went up and we all jumped into the hole. You ae dug a hole wherever you went and after that the artillery barrage went on all night long and yet y' slept through it!

David: Where were you mortared then?

Billy: Oh, that was up at the top, Enfidaville just before they capitulated. During the day there was not much to do if you were in the Signals. Perhaps you'd have to charge a battery with a battery charger. At that time I was looking after the batteries. A funny incident that I remember was that I was drivin' a truck along a road when a lot of German planes started comin' over. There were a lot of Americans at that time and they were all jumping out of their trucks and divin' into the ditches. They werna firin' on us though so I just took no notice and drove on. The only good things the Americans were good for was the food they had. Our Sergeants always had a ration o' whiskey and they used t' trade it in for sugar for wer tea. We didn't see the Americans in the desert it was mostly in Italy that we saw them.

We were under shellfire once and our Colonel was runnin' helter skelter. I was following him and I jumped into the same trench. You were always diggin' trenches. The army was a good life I enjoyed it.

I remember, in Chorley Wood, we were in a barracks there an one mornin' I was in m' bed and the Sergeant comes along, "Come on wakey wakey, rise and shine!" and I said, "Oh, fiddlesticks!" so he put me on a charge for that. Y' couldna disobey y' see. I think I got seven days pay stop for that. I never did it again. You had t' watch when you were comin' in anar. I've seen me creepin' in because you only got a pass till 11.59 y' had t' be in before 12 o' clock. The guards would charge y' efter 'at. Durin the time I was doon in Shepton Mallet we used t' do a lota guard duty. We did other things as well but you always did a guard anar. Funnily enough if you had money y' could pay for someone t' do guard duty fa ye. But I never had nae money so I used t' do guard for some o' the boys. I never had any money cause I used t' send ma mother. Before y' went away, y' signed a form saying what you would leave at home. So, I left half of my pay at home. Some fellas didna dee that so they had an extra bit o' cash. So I wis aye short o' cash.

David: Did you ever buy presents for people?

Billy: Well there was that girlie I used t' knock aboot with, that was in Blandford. I went abroad and I sent hame jewellery t' her. I bought it in Alexandria but that wis the finish o' the romance, I never seen her efter 'at. It wis the same in Aberdeen an' a, I had a girlie in Aberdeen before I left and I used t' write til her but when I came home I couldna settle doon so I lost her an' a.

David: Have you been strafed?

● Ernie Mundy

Ernie Mundie: Yes in North Africa and it wasn't very comfortable but there were no casualties. We also got bombed by American Mitchell bombers in North Africa and we had casualties then. We didn't have a very good opinion of the Americans after that and when we went into action they were in a place called the Kasserine Pass and they had Stuart tanks which was a light tank ('Honey' in British parlance; ed.), before the Shermans came out. Anyway, they were confronted by Tiger tanks and they stood no chance and the Americans took to their heels and ran. I don't blame them but the discipline was so lax that the American General was sacked and Patton was put in his place. Patton pulled them up and they never ran again.

David: It was British artillery that stopped them at Kasserine I believe.

Ernie: Aye, with six pounders firing over open sights. What I was always at a loss to understand, the Germans had an 88mm gun which was an anti-aircraft gun originally but they changed it's purpose to a field gun. The British never thought o' transferin' a 3.7 into an artillery gun. If they fired an 88 at you, you had very little warnin' that it was commin'.

My worst experience in North Africa was what they called Longstop and it was well fortified by the Germans and they slaughtered hundreds o' British troops at Longstop and when we started advancin' we finished up at the bottom of Longstop for a day and a half and you could hardly breath for the stench o' dead bodies. None of them had been buried but we had pioneers to do that job. There were Coldsteam Guards, Scots and Irish. There was a scheme later on whereby if there was heavy fightin' and heavy casualties they had a gentlemen's agreement to stop firin' until they buried the dead. That was the first place that I knew of Germans firin' on stretcher-bearers.

David: How did you get from being an infantryman to becoming a driver?

Ernie: 'Cause I fiddled the books! Well you see when we were Special Service it was all under control of the War Office and because we didn't sign on at the end of the six months I was sent back to the depot but your records didn't follow you. So after six weeks at the depot I was transferred to the 6th Battalion and the records still did not follow me. I asked for an interview with the company commander and told them I'd been doing a transport-driving course in the Special Service so I was transferred to transport. That's how I became a driver in the 6th Battalion.

I drove the cook's truck which towed a two-pounder gun. We carried rations, utensils, stores, tinned food and stuff like that. Each time y' stopped the cooks would prepare the meal and the drivers also helped them. When we left Pantelleria and came back to Soussese in North Africa. We went from there to Misurata and from there we went on

> "the civilians were starvin' because the Germans took everything with them"

● British Troops landing in North Africa

an American Liberty ship to Naples. Naples was terrible, what actually happened was, we sailed from Misurata up through the Straits of Messina out into the bay of Naples and they couldna get landed for three days the Germans had sabotaged all the ships which were in port and sunk them against the quays so we couldn't get alongside the quays to unload. The engineers had to build wooden quays above the superstructure of the boats.

David: It only took three days to construct all that.

Ernie: Yes, but you see it was the Americans, the CB's which was a different thing. They had got all the equipment, mechanical saws they had everything from British engineers. I'm not decryin' them it was a different role of life. We got the freedom to go into Naples and the civilians were starvin' because the Germans took everything with them. We could however, get in touch with an Italian civilian who would ask us if we wanted anything to eat, steak, eggs and chips. They could take you into any of their houses and get you steak eggs and chips whilst the ordinary civilians were starvin'. Do you know why that was? Because they took a man from the Mafia in America who was deported into Italy and he was put in charge of the distribution of rations for civilians. His name was Lucky Luciano and he

was goin' about in a big powerful car that the Americans gave him. They sold everything that the civilians were supposed to get. They sold it to anyone who could afford to buy it. The troops didn't really need it because we had adequate rations. Eventually we went from Naples to a place called Spinazzola which was just south of Foggia on the east coast of Italy. We spent Christmas and Hogmanay night in Spinazzola. We set off on the 1st of January 1944 to go up into the Eighth Army front but they changed that on route and we finished up just outside Salerno. I was taken off the cook's truck and I was given a Jeep and a trailer. There was myself, the Quartermaster's Captain, the second in command and Captain Donald. There were three Officers and myself. I asked the Quartermaster where we were goin' and he told me that we were goin' to Army Headquarters at Caserta. They were readin' the map and tellin' me how to get there. We eventually got to Caserta Palace and that was the plannin' for Anzio. We got to Anzio on the 21st of January.

We boarded the *'Duchess of York'* in Liverpool in March 1943. We went out into the bay and there were 10 troop ships all the same size and there were submarines, destroyers and cruisers in the escort. Each of these ships held about 3000 - 4000 troops. They sailed right out into the Atlantic and sailed south then in through the Straits of Gibraltar. We landed in Algiers in the late evening and we marched 20 miles to an Arab village called Mason Blodge (sic) It was the first time that anyone had seen an Arab. It was an eye opener these Arabs in their djellabas' and that. They didna look very clean but I think they were.

The name of the ship which our supplies were on was called the *'Battle River'* and some of the sailors were not keen to sail in her because they had filled the bottom up with ammunition and they filled up the next section with fuel and transport above that. My truck, which was a Bedford, was on the top deck. They were brand new vehicles and had only done 20 or 30 miles. They were good transport vehicles although they were only two-wheel drive. They loaded them up with stores and there were guns on the back of them and we drove in convoy from there to where the action was in Tunis. We went up in two or three days. There were people

● Supplies coming ashore for the British Army, North Africa

● Stuart 'Honey' on the move in the desert; note the unusual 'sun-shade' hatch cover

coming back who had been wounded going back from the front. Some of them were shouting, "You'll find out all about it, you'll find out!" and that let us think what we were going to find. What we didn't know was that the two-pounder gun we were given was absolutely hopeless against the German tanks because the ammunition just bounced off. What we actually did was drive across a part of the Atlas Mountains towing the two-pounder gun which wasn't a big problem driving up hill and down dale. As I say my vehicle had only done 20 or 30 miles and at 5000 miles the whole set of the ends went, absolutely ruined because they had not been run in. They were speeding and pulling heavy loads up the mountains without any consideration for the new engines. They took three days instead of five but we ended up in North Africa with four big ends broken out of the six. They were taken to a workshop and had their big ends replaced. Oh goodness me it was a disaster! Then we were expected to go to Pantelleria with these vehicles when the fighting had stopped. You were expected to receive 95% casualties if you went to Pantelleria. We only had one casualty. He was wounded by trying to grab an Italian Officers revolver, the safety catch happened to be off and he shot himself in the foot!

> " So here was us stuck in this tank landin' craft with dive-bombers and Messerschmitts' coming across and strafing us' "

What we did in Pantelleria when we landed was we went on in landing craft. It was only the drivers of the vehicles who went out on landing craft and we were told it was going to be sticky and an hour before we landed they came across with a 150 Flying Fortresses and bombed it. They had cruisers there as well and they also started firing. You couldn't see anything but what we had in the front of the landing craft was a big bulldozer powered by a diesel engine which in turn was started by a petrol engine. Well, they couldn't get the petrol engine started with the result that we couldn't get the diesel engine started. So here was us stuck in this tank landin' craft with dive-bombers and Messerschmitts' coming across and strafing us. The door of the craft was doon on the quay and eventually they got it off and we disappeared along the quay and into the village. I saw everybody disappearing behind buildin's and I said, "What's goin' on here?" I soon discovered it was Messerschmitts commin' across strafin'. I stopped the lorry, put on the hand brake and dived round the back of the gable end of this buildin'. I sensed there was somebody at the back o' me and I looked over m' shoulder and there was a British soldier and I said to him, "This is a bit of a B... this isn't it?" He said, "Yes it is rather." I then saw it was a Divisional Commander!

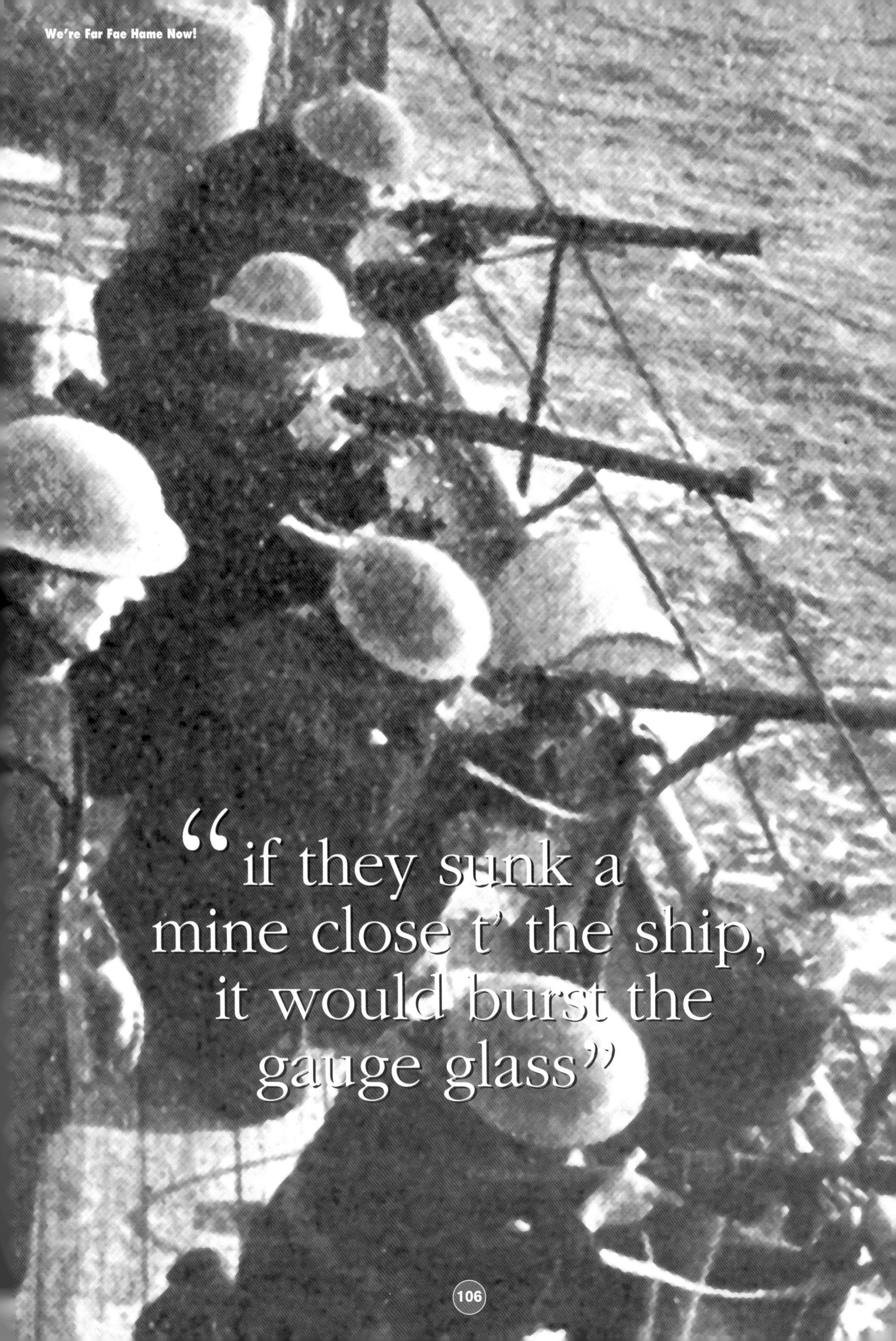

"if they sunk a mine close t' the ship, it would burst the gauge glass"

Mine Sweeping

AN IMPORTANT COMPONENT OF THE SEA WAR was the use of mines by all belligerents. The process of sweeping for mines – of trailing cables and paravanes to cut and lift the devices that they could be fired at and sunk or destroyed – was the role of specially kitted-out boats. However, such was the similarity of minesweeping to trawling that many Aberdonians and North East fishermen became involved.

Ted Munro: From Port Said we had t' sweep Suez Canal which took us two days. Although there was naebody puttin' mines in the canal, there was always the suspicion that Hitler would drop mines in the canal because it would have made an awfa difference because the ships would have to go all round the Cape and that wis dangerous. First of all you'd go out mine spottin'; y' went outside the harbour and y' lay out all night keepin' a watch. Then you'd start at about three or four o'clock in the mornin', y'd put out y' sweeps and sweep recht through Port Said doon the first half of the canal t' Ismailia and by that time we stopped. Then, you'd do the other half and the same commin' back which took you about four days.

They tried t' break the monotony by putting us to a holiday camp for a fortnight, but I'd rather a bin aboard ship because everything that flew, walked, an' crawled wis in this holid'y camps! The only thing that bothert me wis roon ma ankles wi bites. Even though y' had a mosquito net they used t' fly right through without closin' their wings! That carried on for two or three month and then they

discovered that the flotilla had a new job and they attached us to the American Navy.

They were sweepin' - openin' the gates o' the minefields - t' the Med. and the south o' France an' we were markin' off where they had swept t' broaden the gate in the minefield and it took six ships. We had a marvellous time. Y' had a day off in every six. You'd be on one o' the American minesweepers, y' got a' yer food aboard 'ere. They did everything there, our cooks had a day off. We swept first of all up at Elba. Of the six ships one would lay markers as they were clearin' a part o' the gate in the minefield. They dropped Dan buoys. There was another one behind that, he had t' do the same thing then be that time the sweepers had started another sweep on the next lane linkin' up with the first. The third boat lifted the mines from the first clearance.

David: What's happening to all the mines at this time?

Ted: They're jist commin' t' the top. This third

● A trawler equipped for minesweeping

● Left: Sailors shooting at 'trawled' mines in an effort to sink or explode them

boat was supplied with a rifle to shoot at the mines t' blow them up. The fleet sweepers cleared oot and this whalers were left t' sink the mines. They also had this (permission granted) that they could stay within the clearance because a whaler wasn't the same value as a fleet sweeper. So, we were left t' clear all this stuff that they were sweepin' up in our whaler.

With whalers, you'd a good height t' the top o' the casing. The stokers - there wis two stokers and I was one o' them, we jist put on a burner t' keep it alight. Then we went on deck because it was no use bein' doon there. So they used t' tell y' to check the gauge glass which told y' how much water wis in the boiler 'cause y' can't let the water doon too far. They used t' tell us t' shut aff the gauge glass. If y' didna and they sunk a mine close t' the ship, it

> ## "the third boat was supplied with a rifle to shoot at the mines t' blow them up'"

would burst the gauge glass and you had an awfa job t' get the gear t' shut off the cocks and replace the glass.

David: Did you lose many boats in your American flotilla?

Ted: I only saw one being lost. The ships practically had all the same name, the *Satsa*, *Sarra*, and the *Santa* and there was one of them lost out of that flotilla but we weren't there when it sank. It was an Aiberdeen skipper that I knew on the lines, (Long-line fishing), who was on that boat, William Wood. The other whaler in our flotilla (was skippered by) John Mair, he was an Aberdeen fella too. Anyway, the boat hit a mine and that was the end o' it, it didn't get a ghost o' a chance. It was a common thing to steam up atween the mines and a lot of 'em said that they started joining mines agether and they were dropped in a 'cradle'. When the cradle hit the bottom the distance that the mine rises is set before the mine is put owra the side. The mine would come up to a certain height. Now, they started to tie two of them together and if you sailed up between them you were bound to get it because they would come together.

After we went to Elba we took the Yanks into the south of France and after that was finished, the Americans got all cleared like, they advanced at an affa rate in the south of France because I dina think the opposition was there. They brought us back to the Eighth Army and the east coast of Italy at Anzio, going up that way. We went open as far as Leghorn then they changed their minds so we went through the Messina Straits.

David: Did you see any Italian boats?

Ted: We were in Taranto which was a naval base in the heel of Italy, at the instep and we saw a lot of the Italian Navy in this one man subs. There was a lot of them there. Then we moved, we did nae work as we went up past Brindisi and up the east coast of Italy as far as Ancona. We swept round Ancona because the Eighth Army was just up that distance; we were sweeping ahead of them to get a base without too much of a distance for them to travel for the supplies. Then we went across to Split in Yugoslavia.

Before we went with the Yanks, we went to Beirut, Haifa, Famagusta, Alexandria then Turkey and the place I remember best was Port Said because I was there longest

● Ted Munro

● Mine priming and launching.

and I was ay lookin' out for somethin' t' send hame to the wife and family. But I very very seldom went ashore. Haifa - I went ashore twice in Haifa - maybe three times in Beirut, which I thought was the most immoral city I'd ever seen.

David: In what way?

Ted: Maybe it was the company I kept. As always there were the boozers and you couldn't go to the boozer without seeing a brothel that sorta thing an' it never interested me. We didn't get at ashore in Alexandra and Turkey and from there we went across to Famagusta and Cyprus. There was a party at one time which left Haifa to go to Jerusalem on a three-day break. But I was not lucky enough to be picked as there was ay a standby crew needed there on the boat.

David: How did you and the crew greet the end of the war in Europe?

Ted: We were at home before VE day because things got so quiet in the Mediterranean that they didna need mine sweepers s' much. When we were in Split we hit a submerged blockship and we'd t' limp back to Malta. When we got back to Malta, the ship went into the dry dock to get an extensive repair so they said, "Right, you, Alexandria." so I was put aboard one of those little troop carriers and finished up in Port Said. Then we steamed from Port Said to Alex. and put intil a camp there at a place called Siddibish.

Frank Ledingham poses with a set of bagpipes at the brickworks, Barcelona, Sicily, Oct 1943.

"I found a German helmet and I thought, "A souvenir!" but the man's head was still in it"

Sicily

THE CONQUEST OF SICILY, OPERATION HUSKY, was to be the jumping off point for an allied assault on mainland Europe. It was carried out as a logical development of the victory in North Africa and in response to Stalin's request for a Second Front to take some of the pressure off his forces in the East. 160,000 men of the British Eighth and U.S. Seventh armies were pitted against some 300,000 German and Italians in an action that lasted from 9th July until 17th August, 1943 and precipitated the resignation of Mussolini, the Italian Fascist dictator.

Frank Ledingham: After Wadi Akerit we went t' Sicily. Enfidaville, we were mortared a few times at Enfidaville. That was a place similar to Edinburgh castle, up a sandy cliff. The batteries had t' be pulled up the cliff every night but Sergeant Clark from Anstruther, he did the donkeywork there and he got the MM for that. I was up in Enfidaville twice because an engine wouldn't start and we were greeted with mortars both times. After that we went t' Philipville. We were supposed t' do mountain training but the brigadier said, "The only thing that you lads are going t' do is to learn to swim 'cause we're going to Sicily." So every day we were lyin' on the beach in the sun learning to swim. We then went down to Sfax from there and I went onto a naval landing craft. It was a ship actually, quite a big thing. I put on all the wireless sets and every day I checked them to make sure they were working.

For three weeks we sailed up and down the Mediterranean and every afternoon they opened the front doors of the landin' ship and we went doon the ramp and had a swim with wer life jackets on. It was jist like a holiday! Then we came back into Sousse and picked up all the drivers, operators and Brigade infantry and then went to Sicily. There were no problems except it was very rough goin' over. I was goin' to pinch a box of compo rations which included about 12 tins of steak and kidney puddin's, aye American style, we'd never had it before. But when I went down into the hold it was awash with water and there was a big bulldozer on the loose and the blade had gone into the ballast tank. However, it didna make any difference to our landing 'cause we went up these flat slopin' rocks and we got off completely dry and we went up intil this big field of tomatoes. We were told not to eat the tomatoes by the field padre because we would get upset stomachs but we all said we'll chance that!

The next mornin' there was a bad smell hanging around so I went away and I found a German helmet and I thought, "A souvenir!" but the man's head was still in it. I looked round and his body was lying elsewhere. Whatever had hit him must have hit right on the side of the head. The padre from the 2nd Seaforths came with a burial party and buried him. We then moved off only to have the Herman Goering dropped on us - the paratroopers. The drill was that there was one man that slept whilst the other lay under the truck with the gun. We had a Bren gun at that time but there was no room to operate a Bren under a truck. Anyway we didn't have to use it 'cause the paratroopers were further off but the lad, he slept while I kept watch wi the gun.

The Intelligence Officer, the next day, went into this farmhouse over the road fae us. We were in a beech wood, and he went in there and he came out with his jeep, his driver and his escort lad and they'd got this fair headed lad dressed like one of the Mafia, white shirt and all the rest o' it. Apparently he was a paratrooper and he'd changed into these clothes. He must have been promptly shot at the side of the road because when we moved that day his body was lying in the ditch shot through the forehead. So, he'd been shot as a spy. As we went on we came across quite a few civilian unburied dead. We lost a few of our reconnaissance lads when we bombed this town and the coffins were lying open at the side o' the road with the blasted bodies an' that. After that everything was goin' fine.

Sicily was nae problem except Catania Plain of course, where we took four Italian paratroopers prisoner. They were easily taken, they wanted t' give themselves up! We'd jist newly got Sten guns and we'd never used 'em. We were standin' practicin' shootin' at empty beef tins and this lad came to us and told us that there were

> **"we lost a few of our reconnaissance lads when we bombed this town"**

paratroopers in the dung midden of this croft up the hill. So we said we'll jist leave them there then! Ha ha! Well, he went awar and told the only Officer available who was an RASC Officer, Captain Archer. Of course somebody would have t' go and get them. So he came along and said, "You've got the Bren gun," but I told him that my Bren only shot three shots before it jammed. He says, "Oh well, but it will scare 'em." So off we go up the hill, the three behind us had Sten guns and the Captain was in front. His legs were a bit shaky with his shorts on. We got up to the top but we were still a field across. We knew exactly where they were and the Captain told me to run to the back of a big stone and fire a burst. I said, "Oh no, no way I'm going to run across there, they would jist mow me down before I got anywhere near that stone." So he says "OK" and he got some o' the others to cover the house so they couldn't escape and then told the batman t' go to the 5th Seaforths, they were restin' at B echelon. Well they had an anti tank gun and they

● As the war progressed the soldiers were given more and more information concerning the countries in which they were to be engaged

FOREWORD

We are about to engage in the second phase of the operations which began with the invasion of North Africa.

We have defeated the enemies' forces on the South shore of the Mediterranean and captured his army intact.

The French in North Africa, for whom the yoke of Axis domination has been lifted, are now our loyal allies.

However, this is NOT enough. Our untiring pressure on the enemy must be maintained, and as this book falls into your hands we are about to pursue the invasion and occupation of enemy territory.

The successful conclusion of these operations will NOT only strike closer to the heart of the Axis, but also will remove the last threat to the free sea lanes of the Mediterranean.

Remember that this time it is indeed enemy territory which we are attacking, and as such we must expect extremely difficult fighting.

But we have learned to work smoothly alongside one another as a team, and many of you who will be in the first ranks of this force know full well the power of our Allied air and naval forces and the real meaning of air and naval superiority.

The task is difficult but your skill, courage and devotion to duty will be successful in driving our enemies closer to disaster and leading us towards victory and the liberation of Europe and Asia.

Dwight D. Eisenhower,

General, U.S. Army, C.-in-C.

SOLDIER'S GUIDE TO SICILY

SICILY is the largest island in the MEDITERRANEAN—roughly the size of WALES. Its importance, however, lies not in its size, but in its position. Situated at the narrowest point of the MEDITERRANEAN, where only 90 miles of sea separate it from TUNIS, it has permitted the Axis to attack East-bound convoys. Thus it has forced us to send the greater part of our shipping 12,000 miles round the CAPE.

With its dozen odd aerodromes, SICILY gave Axis forces air support in NORTH AFRICA, and until recently permitted a stiff blockade of MALTA and the "narrows." CATANIA and GERBINI in particular have long been strongholds of the Luftwaffe in the MEDITERRANEAN. Indeed, in SICILY is Air Marshal KESSELRING's H.Q. (KESSELRING who invented the word "Coventrize" after his too successful raid on that place).

On the other side SICILY is separated from ITALY itself by only two miles of water. In our hands, therefore, SICILY would be a vital threat to the Italian mainland, and of course to SARDINIA and CORSICA. It would offer our fleet SYRACUSE, AUGUSTA, CATANIA, PALERMO, TRAPANI and MARSALA as bases. And it would bring our bombers within 2 hours range of ROME, 3½ hours of GENOA, and 4 hours of MILAN and TURIN, the nearest we have ever been.

The Story of the Island

The Island has a long and unhappy history that has left it primitive and undeveloped, with many relics and ruins of a highly civilized past.

1

fired it over the top of this dung press. There were about 50 men coming up either side in a pincer movement! I said, "Here, you've got all these men to take four paratroopers and I was t' be doing it by myself!" The RASC Officer got mentioned in despatches for this and went about with his oak leaves!

Trevor: When you should have got them. There's always somebody ready to take the credit for others actions!

Davey Adam: The next move after North Africa was, we gid onto these Landing Craft Infantry vessels. We were goin' round the coast and assaulting the beachheads and things like 'at. Then we went t' Malta for a couple o' days then the big one came – Sicily. The boats were flat bottomed, y ken, and the sea was murder. Seasick? Torpedo us or something! Onywye, we jist walked on to the beach, nae bother. Three or four miles frae us, the Yanks were getting' battered t' death. The fightin' that was goin' on there, gee whizz and we jist walks on! On the sands were rows and rows o' figs and grapes so we had a good feed there.

We had t' move before night because Jerry woulda bombed us on the beaches and when we wis movin' we came upon two or three bodies o' Canadians. The Canadian Paratroopers gid in first and they had been caught as they come doon in all this trees and were shot there. Further on we came to these low trees and we went in and they were absolutely full of peaches. I was sick eatin' 'em, ha ha ha! In Sicily the roads were lined wi almond trees. Y' jist shak the tree an' doon they come, it wis great. Then started the real fun.

We went along es road and we'd t' cross a bridge. Now, Jerry had an OP. up on Etna. When you were up there you could see all around the Island and if you'd got yer glesses on y' could see onything. So they knew where we were. If a truck tried t' get over the bridge Jerry fired three shells and they were that accurate that the first shell landed in the front, one in the middle and one the other side and they hit the truck every time. There was nothing moved through the day hardly. That was up into Sferro, well I'm tellin' you, we got shelled three solid days and nights every second of the day and night. It was the marshalling yards for Catania which was about 20 miles on the coast. Fit wis in these marshalling yards wis these railway tankers full wi either petrol or oil. Ha well, Jerry was brewin' them up be the minute and there wis dozens o' them and he wis haein a hay day shellin' them. Ah me, we lost a lota men there, that was one o' the worst

> **"we got shelled three solid days and nights every second of the day and night"**

places I was ever in. God, y' didna ken far the shells were commin' from.

Trevor: Were you takin' cover all the time or were you able to fire back?

Davey: What? We couldna do nothing it wis the big guns that wis firin' at us. SP guns - self-propelled guns - they were the 88's, they were some gun. They pit 'em on their Tiger Tanks.

I think it was at this time Patton and Montgomery were at loggerheeds aboot who would mak fer where up at the top o' Sicily. Anyway, we ended up in this marshy kinda place which wis riddled wi malaria. There was an awfa lot o' oor boys got malaria there so I was glad t' get awar frae there. There was nothing there y' ken, then we went from there to Catania and eventually got onto boats and taken back to England to a place called Chalfont St. Giles.

● Syracuse, a drawing by Jack Fleming. © G. Fleming

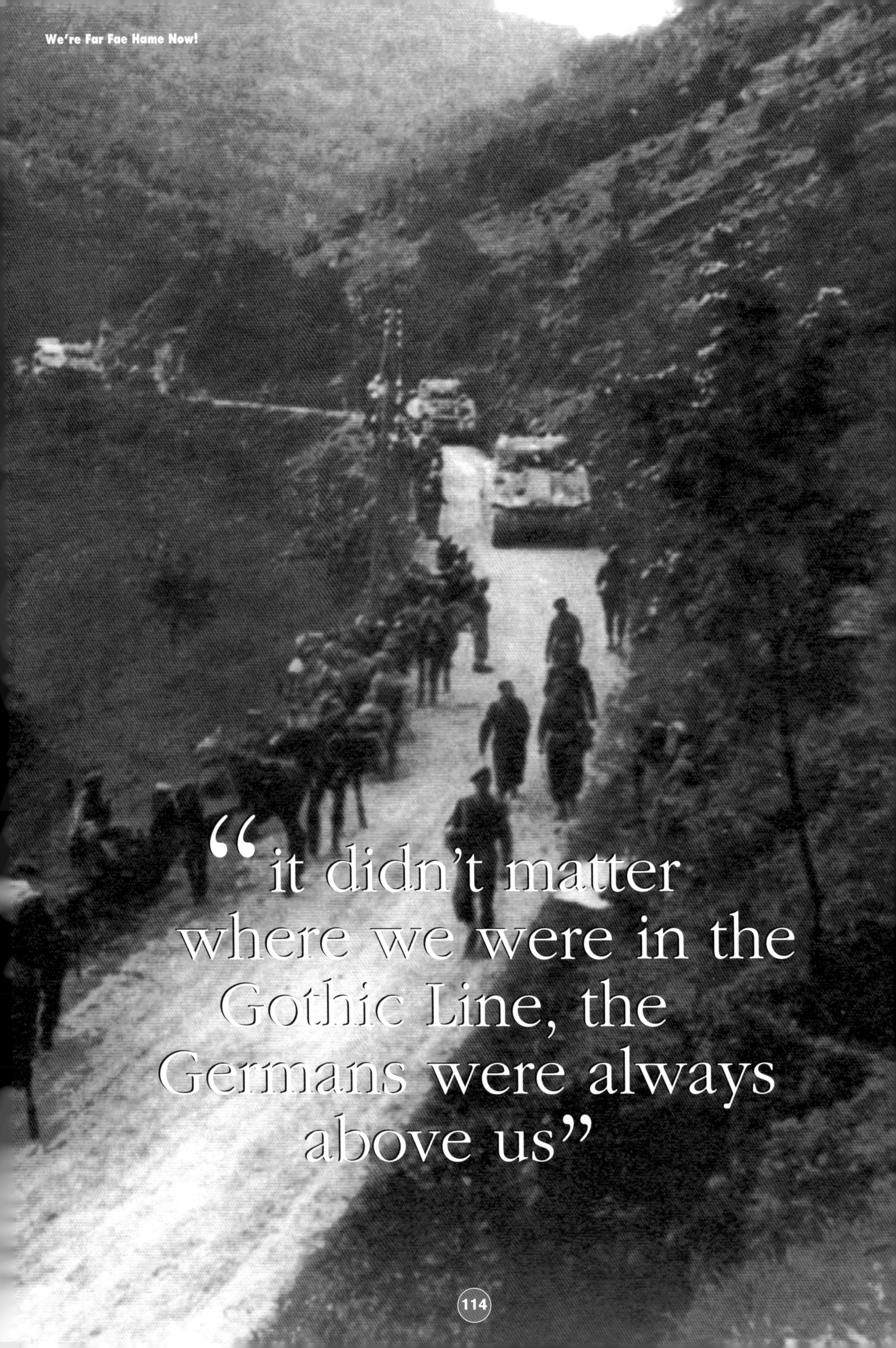

"*it didn't matter where we were in the Gothic Line, the Germans were always above us*"

The Italian Campaign

ITALY CAPITULATED TO THE ALLIES ON 8TH SEPTEMBER 1943. To the surprise of the Badoglio government, (Mussolini's replacement leader), the American Fifth Army landed in force at Salerno Bay whilst the British Eighth Army sailed across the Messina Straits and took Taranto – the Italians had expected, and indeed hoped for, a landing nearer Rome. With their customary efficiency the Germans in Italy quickly disarmed their erstwhile co-belligerents, commandeered all their best equipment and fought a protracted battle against the allies until the final surrender of Germany.

Mr. Fowler: My father, John Dunbar Fowler, who was from Aberdeen, was in the artillery durin' the War and he was part of the 6 AGRA army group. This book follows the Italian campaign conducted by that Artillery group. The written part of the book is very small but the rest of the book is full of these drawings. My father told me that this is a drawing of his gun crew. My father ended the war as a Sergeant in the Royal Artillery. These were the guys that went up through Italy, Casino and all that. My Father said that the artist (F. Ward) was going round all the units and doing these drawings. He was also in the North Africa campaign and at the start of the war he went across to France with the BEF. After Dunkirk he came back through the Gordon Highlander's lines at St. Valery and he met a chap out of the Gordons that he knew who told him that they had got orders to wait there and surrender. My father said that he didn't have any orders to do

that and he said, "We're outa here". and out they went; they got away. I can't remember which port it was but they destroyed their guns, got on board a ship which took them out into the channel but then got dropped back off in Cherbourg! They were issued with a rifle and five rounds of ammunition. After six days, Winston Churchill was on the radio announcing that the BEF had been evacuated from France, they were still digging slit trenches between Cherbourg and Paris! They got away after the seventh day after the BEF had gotten out of France.

● Above, Mr. Fowler and below, far left, standing.

Left, cover of the publication mentioned

● Left: Infantry and tanks advancing up 'Arrow' route in N.Italy. Infantry being held up by enemy fire from a tunnel so tanks going up to engage. Gordon Highlanders Commanders with leading tanks

This contribution is taken from George Lieper's unpublished book called, 'Soggiorno Italiano. An Uphill Struggle.' This excellent personal account which is taken from his diaries made during his time in Italy is viewed from the infantryman's point of view. As a contemporary document written by an ordinary soldier it is unique in that it was considered illegal for the ranks to keep diaries.

To
The Poor Bloody Infantryman

Here's tae us wha's like us
Damn the few an' they're a' deid

George Leiper: The six-barrelled mortars are the worst - more like a game of deadly Russian Roulette. If the first bomb to land is a near miss the other five will almost certainly miss as well but if the first one falls some way off then all we do is to crouch even lower and pray, because we know the rest will fall slap bang amongst us. Then the inevitable shout of 'stretcher-bearer' foretells another bloody casualty to be manhandled back down the hill to the RAP*.

It's bad enough being mortared by the enemy but when you are shelled by your own people it is even worse especially when they are bang on target. This happened to us the other day and it took us about half an hour to convince higher authority that it was true. We could hear the damned things coming from behind us in shoals and tempers were really frayed when we started taking casualties. Talk about doing the enemy's job for him and very little apology for doing so.

*Regimental aid post.

The second incident which still sends shivers up and down my spine every time I think of it concerns a German hand grenade. That I am still in one piece is because the German grenade works in a different way from our Mills type. With our grenade it is live from the moment it leaves your hand and the spring lever flies off; the length of time before it explodes depends on the fuse time delay - five or seven seconds depending on what you are using it for. With the German stick grenade, however, the whole operation is controlled by a weighted tape wound round the top of the handle. As the grenade flies through the air the tape unwinds to its full length and then pulls out the release mechanism ready to make it explode on impact.

What happened was that we were out in a ration party job and due to the heavy shelling we struck off the main path up the mountain to try and find a safer way up. Needless to say we got somewhat lost and ended up nearer the enemy lines than we should. As we edged our way round a rocky outcrop to have a better look at where we were, a German popped up from some rocks in front of us and a stick grenade came sailing through the air and landed in front of me before I could get flat on my face on the ground. It didn't go off and I suddenly realised that the tape was still not completely unwound so without thinking I picked the damned thing up and tossed it right back where it came from. It exploded with a satisfying bang but we were not interested in finding out what damage it had done - we were on our way back down as fast as our legs could carry us. I found that even as I was sliding and slipping about on the way down I was shaking like a leaf at the thought of my audacity or stupidity. On 99 cases out of a 100 we should have all been killed or wounded but in this case our names couldn't have been on it. I have promised myself that I will not stray off the beaten track in future if I can help it.

Our nightly perambulations consist of water carrying, ration parties, occupying defensive positions in and around the town and of course patrols.

> ❝a stick grenade came sailing through the air and landed in front of me❞

The water point for our platoon is a well in the side of a house which is covered by enemy Spandaus apparently firing on fixed lines. Great care is needed in lowering the jerricans down the well; if one lowers away too fast the can clangs against the sides and creates the most horrible racket This is a signal to Jerry to open up and arcs of tracer criss-cross the square. He seems to be firing too high but we take no chances; we are flat on our faces hugging the wall of the house cursing the unfortunate who caused the trouble in the first place. However we discovered a ploy to make the enemy waste ammunition and leave us alone to fill our water cans in peace. There are a lot of stray dogs in the town hunting ravenously for food and we tryst them into our house in the evening and feed and amuse them until it is dark, then shoo them out to run barking through the square. Old Jerry reacts instantly and presses the trigger hosing his tracer harmlessly through the dark. After two or three such excursions, it seems he realises he has been conned and thereafter is not so ready to react to any noises.

We had a big flap the other night in one of our outlying positions when Jerry decided to test our defences with an attack. Fortunately for us they got their initial directions wrong and went across our front instead of at us. We let them have everything we had - rifles, Brens, Tommy guns, grenades - and stopped them cold forcing them to retreat. However, they came back at us for another go and the fun started again. Bullets buzzed about

us like bees some thudding into the beams and sandbags which protected us and their 'Tattiemashers'* exploded with a sharp crack. Once more we stopped them and this time they had had enough and pulled right back to the sound of a whistle blown by what appeared to be an Officer who was leading from the back. When we went out to look for dead and wounded we found that they were not Germans but Poles and Russians who had either been impressed or volunteered to join their conquerors - perhaps that was the reason for their Officer leading from the back. We had suffered one or two casualties and the strange sense of exhilaration and blood lust which keyed us up during the attack very quickly subsided and we all felt totally limp and drained and the nagging sense of fear returned to the pits of our stomachs. We were all quite glad when the time came to return to the relative security of our house in the town.

*'Tattie-mashers' - Scots troops name for a German hand grenade which looked for all the world like an old-fashioned potato-masher.

Following our successful repulse of the enemy's attack on our outlying position we have had one or two deserters coming over to us and last night I was involved in helping one on his way. It was my turn of duty as lookout beside our Bren gun position and not long after I had taken over I heard someone moving about in front of our positions. I alerted everyone and waited tensely for any further moves. Suddenly a voice called out from the darkness in front of us "Nicht schiessen" followed by a string of further unidentifiable words. I remembered enough German from my school-days to know that the first two words meant "do not fire" so without relaxing my grip on the Bren I shouted back "Hande hoch! Kommen Zie hier". Suddenly a flare went up and the source of the voice was revealed, a woebegone looking specimen waving a piece of paper in his right hand about 20 yards in front of us. He staggered up to our position and practically fell into the trench yabbering in some totally strange language to me. I took the paper from him, and pushing him in front of me made my way to our main position where by the light of a torch we discovered that the piece of paper he was waving was a Safe Conduct pass. (We continually fire special shells containing these passes into the enemy's lines in the hope of inducing desertion). He grabbed the paper and turning it over pointed to the translation

in Polish - not much wonder I couldn't understand him. Having handed him over I purloined the pass and returned to do my duty stint - no one was getting that pass from me. It will be kept as a souvenir.

After we had been allocated our quarters and had a good shower the two other lads from the Company and myself decided we should go out on the town to sample the local delights. After sampling these delights in a goodly number of the local vino establishments we decided that the pleasure of a woman's company would help our morale no end. However, Bari seemed to be devoid of any fair sex desirous of our company so after some 'judicious' enquiries we decided to take ourselves off to Barletta just outside the main town. Needless to say it was out of bounds to British troops because of its 'evil' reputation but nothing daunted and following the devious instructions some kind soul gave us we set out on our merry way.

No sooner had we got there than we were approached by a rather ragged urchin who knowing the ropes, conspiratorially whispered "Ya wanna a woman, Joe?". On receiving an affirmative he immediately demanded "Cigarette for papa" and then led us to a house nearby. The occupant of the house was a good-looking woman in her late 20s and was perfectly willing to accommodate us, so after agreeing terms we decided to toss a coin for the order of batting. I wasn't even in the hunt coming a poor third.

Imagine my horror when in due course I entered the boudoir to find her lying on the bed waiting for me busily munching a large apple of all things. I am totally allergic to apples and even the smell coming from a half-eaten one can make me feel queasy in the extreme. Having drunk a considerable amount of vino only made matters worse. I hastily demanded

> " we had suffered one or two casualties and the strange sense of exhilaration and blood lust "

"Dove Ia cucina" and once there deposited the contents of my stomach down the kitchen. Feeling somewhat better I returned to the bedroom and as best as I could, explained to her that it wasn't her fault, it simply was that I was 'un po malato' having just come from the front line. I gave her a couple of notes and told her to get something for the bambino and went outside to meet my friends, trying as hard as I could to look like a satisfied customer. Their enthusiasm as we wended our way back to Bari only made matters worse alas!

Our Company sniper is really enjoying himself here in Arielli and is doing great execution amongst the enemy opposite us. He is much older than the rest of us and in civilian life he is a ghillie and a deerstalker for a highland estate, and is a fantastic shot. He treats his sniper's rifle and all its telescopic paraphernalia like a newborn babe, lavishing the utmost care and attention on it every spare moment he has. His judgement of distance is unerring and he can pinpoint the range to any target within sight to the nth degree and is reputed never to miss when he gets anything in his sights. Whether this is actually true or not I cannot say but if what happened when I was with him this afternoon is anything to go by then I can very well believe all that is said of him.

He had already found himself a nice roof space in a substantial house facing towards the enemy when I went up to join him. A mortar bomb had hit the roof at some time and the explosion had left a convenient but not too large a hole to give us both good cover and yet ideal observation of the whole of the Jerry lines to our front. He was already scanning the whole area with his binoculars when I settled down beside him. I hadn't been there for more than a few minutes when he suddenly stopped and a look of eager anticipation came across his face and he grinned quietly to himself. I asked him to share the joke and he handed me the binoculars, gave me instructions where to look, and started to adjust the sights on his rifle.

With some difficulty I eventually managed to pinpoint the location he had indicated and lo and behold there in the lea of a house I saw some tiny figures moving about. After I got them into proper focus I saw that they were busily engaged in filling a large bath with water. I felt like a Peeping Tom as I watched them, utterly fascinated as they went about their business blissfully unaware that they were under scrutiny. I heard a grunt of satisfaction at my side and there was my colleague in the prone position, rifle cuddled to his cheek, gazing intently through his telescopic sight. I asked him what he was going to do and he quietly said "We'll just wait for the Officer."

I managed to find the house again and watched the last of the water being tipped into the bath by a Jerry in his shirtsleeves. He then went into the house and almost immediately after, a rather corpulent individual emerged from the house naked except for a large towel round his waist. I

● 'Road under shellfire'. Drawn by F. Ward

watched him test the water in the bath and as he straightened up I was startled out of my wits by a shattering explosion beside me and I dropped the binoculars. I immediately realised that our sniper had fired and I hastily picked them up and re-focused on the house. The corpulent figure was lying sprawled on the ground beside the bath and through the glasses I could detect no movement in the body. In the meantime my colleague had reloaded his rifle and was still lying there, eyes glued on the target. We seemed to wait ages before anything stirred round the house. Eventually a Red Cross flag was waved from the back of the house and two figures appeared carrying a stretcher. They ran to the body and lifted it on to the stretcher and then doubled back behind the building, leaving the bath alone in its lonely splendour.

When I asked my colleague how far away the target was he merely grunted "Och it wisna very far" - he wasn't giving any of his secrets away.

We eventually reached the slopes of a low ridge and lay down to await further orders glad of the breather after our exertions. We still had no idea of where our objective was or what it would entail but we suspected it would be the usual chaos before it was all over. Still we were content for the moment to lie where we were and enjoy the sun.

However Nemesis was fast catching up with us once more thanks to the eagle-eyed enemy who must have spotted some movement from our forward platoon. Down came the mortars once more and this time we had no protection.

I was already face down on the grass and I turned my head to where the bombs were landing and I was petrified to see one land at my feet and knock a twig up in the air without exploding. I turned my head away in utter disbelief and through gritted teeth wheezed, "Thank Christ its a dud" when another one landed in the same place. There was an almighty crack and I found myself flying high in the air with searing pains shooting through my back, my hips and my legs. The next second I thumped back on the ground amidst the smoke gasping like a stranded fish to get some air into my lungs flattened by the blast. The pain returned and I put my hand round my side and felt a bulky object sticking out of my back. I quickly withdrew my hand and saw it covered in blood and shouted "Stretcher Bearer!"

The two lads on either side of me were quite untouched and were absolutely flabbergasted when I shouted for help. They were quite convinced I had been killed when they saw me flying through the air. I half turned on my other side and looked down at my legs. My trousers had been shredded

"they were quite convinced I had been killed when they saw me flying through the air"

by the blast and blood was seeping through from my hips to my ankles. One of the Company stretcher-bearers arrived at the double and started dusting me with antiseptic powder and bandaging the worst affected parts as best he could. He told me he could really do nothing with my side as the object sticking out was a piece of the tail fin of the mortar bomb and he didn't know how far in it had penetrated. The blood appeared to be already coagulating round about and to try to pull it out could be disastrous. The force of the explosion had caused it to burst my webbing belt but the broad German leather belt (purloined from a prisoner and how I blessed him) I wore underneath had withstood most of the force and only a long sliver of steel attached to the fin had gone through and into me. He did, however, bind a large bandage round and round me to prevent the fin from moving about too much. Two of the other lads some distance behind me had also been wounded; one had a large chunk of shrapnel in his thigh and the other a badly sliced hand and fingers. No stretcher-bearers were available to take us back as they were all needed for the attack still to come so the other two wounded were instructed to help me back to the RAP.

The stretcher-bearer climbed a small knoll behind us out in the open for all to see and bravely waved his red cross flag while we three crawled past his feet and thus proceeded on down the hill still on all fours. At the foot of the hill the other two helped me to my feet and we struggled on for a while but the pain was too much for me and I told them to carry on and send somebody back for me. After they had gone I rested for a while and then started to crawl again; I felt that as long as I kept moving I would be all right. I lost all count of time and, in my confused state, direction as well because sometime after mid-day I ended up at an Indian machine-gun position. There they gave me the most wonderful cup of tea - you could almost stand a spoon in it there was so much condensed milk - and then helped me back to their aid post.

The aid post was in a farmhouse and the room I was helped into was rather dim and dingy and full of wounded and moaning Indians. The harassed MO had a quick look at me, decided he could do nothing for me there and directed that I be taken by the next ambulance back to the hospital at Vasto. He then shot a massive dose of anti-tetanus into me. The atmosphere in that room was so depressing that I crawled outside once more into the warm sun and climbed onto a stretcher attached to a jeep and sat there propping myself up on my left elbow and my legs dangling over the side.

A Padre appeared and started fussing over me trying to get me to lie down but I refused most vehemently because I was already convinced in my somewhat delirious state that if I lay down I would die. He then contented himself with re-powdering me with anti-septic powder from a large tin with a massive powder puff. While I was sitting there in a dream-like state an Indian orderly appeared with a crate of beer and asked me if I wanted a bottle. I helped myself and asked him if anybody else wanted any and when he said no I ordered him to leave the crate on the end of the stretcher and he did so meekly.

The ambulance duly arrived and after another five Indian casualties were carried in I was helped in to the bottom stretcher complete with crate of beer. The ride back was a nightmare over rough shell catered roads to the accompaniment of much moaning from two of my Indian companions. When we arrived at the hospital I was carried into a corridor and laid down at the end of a queue of stretcher casualties all awaiting attention. I hadn't been there long when a pompous orderly attempted to remove my precious beer and I kicked up such a racket that a passing MO came to see what all the fuss was about. My pleas were listened to and the orderly was duly sent packing- that crate of beer, along with my refusal to lie down had become a symbol of my will to live and I like to think that the MO recognised the fact.

I must have passed out shortly after because I was suddenly aware of being carried into a brightly-lit room and being placed on a lead table and my trousers being cut off me and a masked figure bending over me. I remember asking him if my beer was OK and telling him that I did not like ether. He assured me that my beer was under the table and that they were now giving casualties a new anaesthetic called Pentothol and it was so good that I would be back for more. He then started cutting off my battle-dress jacket carefully avoiding moving the protruding tail fin. The anaesthetist then placed a board under my left arm tied a cuff bandage round my muscle and started to pump until the vein above my elbow began to swell like a balloon. He then produced the biggest hypodermic syringe I had ever seen in my life and asked me to start counting. I watched him place the needle against the vein and can remember no more. When I came round I found myself lying in a bed completely surrounded by a mosquito net. The room was in semi-darkness and I panicked for a moment in the strange surroundings thinking that I had been captured when the sound of an English voice in the next bed re-assured me. The owner of the voice was shouting loudly for some food so I joined in. A nurse bustled in and demanded to know what all the noise was about and to be quiet forthwith and not disturb the other patients.

I dragged myself up into a sitting position in bed and recognised the other patient as the Sergeant of one of the other platoons. He had been hit quite a time after me but he had been brought via our own Battalion RAP back to hospital to arrive at about the same time as I had. He told me that there had been more casualties after I had gone and the whole affair looked as though it would be pretty dicey and despite the fact that we had both copped a packet we were better off out of it. He was sure a lot of the lads would be killed by the time it was all over. Our conversation was interrupted by the return of the nurse carrying a couple of trays with plates of chicken and potatoes, custard and prunes and a bowl of tea. I suddenly realised how ravenous I was and scoffed the lot in double quick time. Thus satisfied I put my head down and was out like a light until I was shaken by an orderly, told it was morning and was handed a bowl of tea.

The euphoria of the Pentothol had worn off and I was aching all over and felt as if I had been run over by a steamroller. I explored the various parts of my anatomy and was amazed at the amounts of sticking plaster and padding adhering to me- however I seemed still to be in one piece which was all that mattered. What was even more comforting was the fact that my precious beer had been put under the bed.

After breakfast the MO who had operated on me came to see me on his rounds and told me that although he had taken out the largest pieces of shrapnel there were still many very small bits left in the fleshy parts of my hips. These were not dangerous, he said, and would eventually work their way to the surface in the years to come. He pointed to a small cloth bag hanging at the head of my bed and said that everything he had managed to get out was in the bag for me to keep as a rather grizzly souvenir of the event. He said he was sorry that he had to cut up my German belt in order to get at the bit in my side but he was sure that I could get another one to replace it in due course.

"the euphoria of the Pentothol had worn off and I was aching all over"

I thanked him for looking after the beer and said that there was a bottle for him and that the rest would be shared out in the ward. He said that he had been quite amused at the sight of a rather dirty tattered and bloody figure vehemently protecting a prized possession and he asked me how I had come by such a treasure. I told him and he shook his head, helped himself to a bottle and continued on his rounds. After he had gone I grabbed the bag and opened it and was rather staggered at the amount of metal he had extracted from me. I must have copped most of the bomb and miraculously none of it appeared to have hit any of my most vital parts.

June

The Company has got the dirty job as usual - we have to take Pescara and we have been given to understand the whole place is lousy with mines of all descriptions and the buildings are booby-trapped into the bargain. The old tummy is knotted once more and you can feel the tension in the air despite the somewhat forced good-humour and banter. After all it's been a piece of cake so far, but the thought of mines - especially these blasted wooden "schu" ones with their hundreds of pellets - is not very comforting.

A novelty has been introduced into the plans for the attack. We are to do a sea-borne right hook with God knows what kind of crazy results. The powers-that-be have obtained a DUKW from somewhere and one platoon is to embark, sail up the coast, land behind the enemy lines and close off Pescara from the north while the other two platoons come up from the south by land. Thank God the sea job has been given to one of the other platoons - what good one platoon will do if the place is anything like strongly defended I just don't know.

The luck has held out; the event was a complete anti-climax. Jerry had pulled out after demolishing the bridge across the river that runs through the town. The place was filthy with booby-traps and while a crossing of the river was reconnoitred the platoon had a rest in a large building housing a bank. The floor was paved with large marble slabs and showed no signs of being tampered with so we parked ourselves down on it with reasonable confidence and had a brew up. No exploring was allowed so souvenirs were out much to the annoyance of one member of the platoon, the greatest looter I know. His specialty is churches and large houses, which are usually sure to contain the objects he wants especially if they are made of gold or silver. According to some of the lads he already has a fortune in loot and I know he is carrying a gold candlestick and a chalice in his rucksack. I wonder who will inherit his spoil if he cops a packet -the nearest one to him I suppose if they are that way inclined. Still he is confident that he will survive! However its a good job we stayed put as I understand that a couple of lads from another platoon were badly wounded by a booby-trap whilst nosing around another part of the town looking for loot. They opened a drawer or something and bang!!

Crossing the river was a real hairy business and we were grateful that the enemy had pulled out. The 2 I/c of the Company had seemingly explored all up and down the river bank and could find no other way over except across the partially demolished bridge. There was still one girder intact and the CO insisted that we use it despite the fact that the blasted thing was less than a foot wide. God knows what would have happened if Jerry had decided to shell us in the middle of the crossing. Still, somehow or other, we all got across without anybody falling off. Some bright boy got

hold of a rowing skiff and the 2 I/c and a couple of other lads rowed backwards, and forwards just downstream from the bridge to pick up anyone who fell off. How they expected to pull anyone out of the water into a skiff without tipping themselves up I do not know. I don't suppose anyone thought of getting a hold of the DUKW from the other platoon and ferrying us across

The other day I got advanced warning of our withdrawal from the line in a most horrific yet amusing way. I was sent from Company HQ back to Battalion with a message and was strolling merrily down the road when Jerry started a most awful 'stonk'. There I was, absolutely petrified on my own, lying in the ditch at the side of the road as the shells shrieked and exploded all round me. The noise was absolutely deafening and the blast was whipping branches and bark from the trees at the side of the road just above me and sending stones and dust showering on me. In a lull in the bombardment I got to my knees to look around me and saw to my amazement about 50 yards or so further down the road a couple of men in army uniform and black berets working on a telegraph pole on top of the bank at the side of the road, quite unconcerned and apparently quite oblivious to the shelling. I shouted to them not to be bloody fools and get down as there was sure to be more to come but they paid no attention to me whatsoever.

Luckily no more shells arrived, so I got to my feet and angrily strode down the road to give them a piece of my mind at this stupidity. When I reached them, the reason for their apparent indifference became clear; they were a couple of signallers from the Polish Corps pushing their telephone link forward and hadn't understood a word I said. They seemed quite amused at a British squaddy getting a pasting all on his own. However I managed to extract from them in a mixture of German and English the information that the whole Polish Corps had arrived on the Adriatic front and it was obvious that they were taking over the sector. This was better than any Padres Prop, I had seen them with my own eyes and gleefully reported the fact when I got back to the Company. Elation had replaced the terror I had experienced not long before but for how long? Where are we bound for now; some other dirty job I suppose.

There is a rule that at dawn in the line everybody stands to for an hour as it seems to be the most favourable time for an attack especially after a long and weary night with everyone dying for some rest. After stand-to we normally wash and shave and make preparations for breakfast but our Company Commander has decided that things have been too cushy lately and we are in need of some physical exercise before we start on our daily routine. This wouldn't be too bad in the conventional sense but unfortunately he is a Scottish Country Dance fanatic and has decided to substitute PT with Scottish Reels. We are detailed off as opposite sexes and off we go to the sound of bagpipes from our Company piper. The Englishmen amongst our recent reinforcements think it is absolutely crazy and outlandish - what trouble they have with their "paddie-bas" and "birls". Personally, I like to keep as near cover as possible in case Jerry attracted by the skirl of the pipes in the still of the morning decides to liven things up with a few shells. Word of what we are doing has leaked out to other troops in the area and we are now known as "Ma C's Dancing Girls". What a sobriquet for an Infantry Company; it will take a lot of living down.

The different attitudes to discipline in and out of the line is really quite amazing. In the line the good NCO or Officer leads by example and exercises an almost paternal influence over his men despite the fact that he may be only a youngster himself. He must be an ever-ready prop and a friend to everyone. Out of the line NCO's and Officers all seem to feel their rank more and must always be seen to be exerting or exercising discipline to justify their position in the eyes of their superiors. The British Army's obsession seems to be that regimentation and skill in ceremonial breeds courage and discipline in action; if you are good at one you are good at the other.

What this tenet fails to take account of is the fact that we are all different in our make up. The breaking point under strain in all of us is different and no matter how brave we are there comes a time - and it can be totally unexpected - when we can no longer contain our suppressed fear and then discipline becomes a thing of the past.

The ordinary British private has a great reputation for being able to stick it out under the most terrible conditions but I often wonder whether it is discipline or fear that inspires him to do so. I often suspect it is the latter. Not so much fear of the enemy - although that can be just as unpleasant - but the fear of the consequences of doing anything other than stick it out. In this kind of situation there are two alternatives, surrender to the enemy or retreat. The former can be an attractive proposition to end the misery but there is always the nagging thought that if there has been desperate fighting the enemy may not be disposed to respect the Geneva Convention. Indeed, no prisoners may be the order of the day as far as he is concerned.

The other alternative is to get the hell out of it, but if the order has been to stay put then to do so lays the soldier wide open to a charge of cowardice and desertion in the face of the enemy with all its attendant unpleasantness and possible death. The poor private is thus on the horns of a terrible dilemma and I think that what sustains him in such a position is hope and good comradeship and above all superb leadership rather than discipline.

" in this kind of situation there are two alternatives, surrender to the enemy or retreat "

July/August

It is now high summer and the Battalion is once more back in the Line in Central Tuscany, just north of Arezzo with the Company HQ operating from a little town called Puglia. At one point we took over positions from the Gurkhas but rapidly moved out when we discovered that the remains of their handiwork with their kukris were still in evidence and the place stank to high heaven. Quite a number of stomachs turned over I can tell you.

Patrols are the order of the day and since they are, in the main, fighting patrols, we have already started taking casualties again. In fact, a couple of nights ago I had a repeat performance of the patrol I experienced at Arielli. We stumbled on a German forward position and they opened up with a Spandau and immediately we had a Platoon Commander with both legs smashed and another member of the patrol also hit. This time, however, we did not quietly steal away, but charged straight in and killed all the occupants of the post bar one whom we took prisoner. The return to our own Lines was a totally exhausting business, because we had to carry our wounded all the way back, and the Platoon Commander was no light weight I can assure you, - in fact he was built like a bull and seemed to weigh as much. However, we had achieved our aim according to the Powers-that-Be and congratulations were the order of the day.

It is amazing how amidst all this mayhem and slaughter, the Italian farmers try to carry on in the countryside cultivating their vines, fruit and vegetables and producing their innumerable offspring. We had a good example of this a couple of days ago when the platoon was in positions round a fairly substantial Tuscan farmhouse. Despite the sporadic shelling, the farmer was out in his fields trying to salvage what crops he could in order to keep his family going, whilst inside the house his spouse was in the process of giving birth to her sixth child. Two of us were trying to act as midwifes - producing hot water and clean linen - but truth to tell we were far more nervous than the mother herself, she seemed to accept the strange circumstances with complete resignation and wanted the whole affair over as soon as possible so that she could get back to her everyday chores. Whether our presence was more of a help or a hindrance I do not know, but the outcome was a bawling healthy boy. Needless to say, some of our rations were left behind to help them in their struggle to survive. The proud papa in return produced a nice Chianti type wine to celebrate the happy event; he must have had it well hidden from old Jerry.

The Division was visited by a VIP yesterday - no less a person than His Majesty himself - and this meant that some of the lads were withdrawn from the line and had to get all 'bulled' up for this so-called auspicious occasion. All their webbing equipment had to be made spotlessly clean, battledress to be properly tidy and pressed just for his inspection. What a waste of time during a war! Not that the Brass think so; - "Awfully good for morale, what"! Is it heck! As far as I am concerned I am glad that I was not among the chosen few. In all honesty I must confess that some of the lads used it as an excuse to get out of the Line for a few hours, - nothing more.

● George Leiper, centre back

We go around saying "poor old so-and-so Company isn't half catching it" but secretly we are very glad indeed it is them and not us. Again I noticed how during the heat of the attack the sense of fear quickly recedes into the background and everybody is caught up in the bloodlust of killing and the strange exhilaration it brings. However, once it is all over back comes the feeling of depression and the old nagging returns to the pit of the stomach.

Darkness eventually arrived and as zero hour approached we started to move up to our start line with the usual exhortations to keep the noise to a minimum. As we passed a house on the way up the occupants wished us the best of luck and we knew that we would need it. On reaching the start line we got down and waited until the barrage started, fervently hoping that the deception would work and we would be in amongst them before they realised they had been fooled.

As soon as the barrage started the two forward platoons melted into the darkness and almost immediately heavy firing broke out in front of us and our right hand platoon was soon calling for assistance as they were heavily outnumbered. The CO decided to commit our platoon and so we duly dashed up the hill to render support. Alas just short of the ridge we ourselves ran into so much heavy fire from well dug in positions that it became obvious to all of us that we had come a real cropper and were on a hiding to nothing. Still we got down and began to swop (sic) fire with them at the same time trying to edge our way forward and blasting away at anything that moved on the skyline. Indeed, it took the combined fire of two of us to stop a huge Jerry who kept on coming in spite of the bullets that were obviously hitting him. He was either a very brave man or it may be that he simply went berserk and lost all reason.

As we were making little or no progress and taking unnecessary casualties, the Company Commander decided to pull back and ordered me to instruct the other two platoons by radio to do the same. (I had picked up the platoon radio from one of the lads who had been hit.) I did as I was told but got no reply and he told me to keep on trying. By this time we were suffering heavy mortaring which was becoming more accurate all the time and I can assure you that we were really glad to be on our way back down the hill. We retired in good order until we reached the area of the house from which we had received the good wishes on our way up, when suddenly we were greeted with a hail of bullets. Not waiting to find out whether the occupants were now enemy or merely jittery friends we belted round the house at speed and were eventually halted by the CO in a small hollow behind a comforting and substantial dyke. There were only about 20 of us in that hollow and we were instructed to take up defensive positions to fight off any German attempt to rush us or try to outflank us.

From my position near the Company Commander I could hear the Colonel loudly demanding to know what had happened over the Company radio and being rather plaintively told that half our Company was missing and we were hanging on in the hope of recovering stragglers or any survivors from the two forward platoons. The Company Commander kept asking me if I could raise the other two platoons on my radio, but all I was getting was the crackle of static. I knew it was pretty hopeless as I only had one small section of the aerial attached, the other sections still lying on the ground where they had fallen when the original wireless operator had been hit. I didn't have the heart to tell the poor man in his distraught state and kept on with my impossible task. (We found out later that it would have been impossible anyhow because both the leading platoons' radios were out of action - in one case the radio was u/s and in the other the radio operator had been killed.) Whilst all this was going on Jerry was actively mortaring the whole area. Some of the bombs were dropping ominously close to our position causing quite a few remarks among the lads as to the wisdom or the strategic necessity of our prolonged stay in the area, as the chances of picking up any of the missing in the dark were pretty remote.

Eventually I heard the Colonel give our CO a direct order "to get the hell out of it" and only then did we retire back to Bibbiano. When we got there we found that the survivors of the other two platoons had already made their own way back and they in turn had been wondering what had happened to us. However, we were very glad to see them and to learn that our casualties were not as heavy as we had feared in view of the opposition we had met. Although there was no real comfort in this in view of the fact that we were very much below strength before the attack had begun and dreading the thought of what would happen if we were committed again.

Yesterday, the 9th of August saw the last fateful act of the drama played out by the Company in the battle for Monte Grillo. The day after our unsuccessful attack the whole Brigade was committed and it took about four days of very heavy fighting before Jerry was shoved off the ridge. In the meantime we were still stuck in Bibbiano being pounded at regular intervals by very heavy guns - someone said that they were 210's - but the houses we were in were well built and stood up remarkably well to the bombardment. This is more than I can say for our nerves and I feel that if we had been subjected to too much more some of us would surely have been candidates for the trick cyclists*.

A sustained 100-plus stonk is very frightening indeed and with each succeeding scream of the shell followed by its shattering explosion you find yourself drawing in your neck more and more and cowering lower and lower against whatever protection you can find. You find yourself wanting to scream out loud to relieve the tension but some inner reserve restrains you from letting your emotions run riot; the thought of letting the rest of the lads down usually looms large in everybody's mind. The explosions from these large shells were

tremendous and especially close ones caused everything in the houses to crash and rattle and dance about and of course anything in the way of the blast was simply ripped apart. Outside the street was a mass of rubble and the usual litter of war, shattered glass, broken tiles and chimney pots, smashed wood and other domestic flotsam.

*Troops slang for psychiatrists.

Wednesday, 13th September - what a strange day for coincidences. Whether good or bad I still have to decide. Thirteen is my lucky number; I was born on the 13th and today I received some belated birthday wishes and presents - a month late but better late than never. We have also been told that we are being put under temporary command of 46th Division to help them out in the attack on Gemmano, definitely a bad coincidence. Even worse, I understand that 12 attacks on the mountain have already been made by both 56th and 46th Divisions and all have failed. The Battalion has been given the honour - unwanted as far as I am concerned - of attacking it for the 13th time and taking it they hope. The attack is to take place tomorrow night.

The Company Officers have come back from a recce full of forebodings (sic). The Gemmano feature is a ridge some 2-4 miles long and we are to attack the highest part, a steep knoll over 1400 feet high with a large wooden cross planted right on top. Before we get there however we have to take a small village called Zollora on the left of Gemmano. It seems that almost all the artillery of the Eighth Army will be lending us a hand, over 250 guns in all. Bofors guns firing tracer will be used to help us keep direction in the dark. We will attack behind a creeping barrage at 3 o'clock in the morning. The powers that be are confident that after that lot has fallen on the enemy there will be very few of them left to bother us. If this is the case we wonder why all the previous attacks have failed.

For once the big brass were right, - it was a complete walk over and it was nice to be complemented all round for a very competent piece of work by the Battalion. What bothered me more than the enemy was the absolute inferno of noise caused by so many guns - it was absolutely ear shattering, so loud at times that even shouted orders were difficult to hear. Just over an hour before we left our start-line every gun for miles around opened up on Zollora and simply blasted it out of existence. The tracer from the Bofors guns arched lazily towards the enemy positions and it appeared that it would be easy to dodge the shells as they seemed to be travelling so slowly. They were however a great help in keeping the right direction in the dark. The creeping barrage behind which we advanced from the crest of the spur to the south of Zollora was spot-on as far as we were concerned because there were no shorts.

As we followed the leading Company up the hill we were astonished at the lack of real opposition

● 'Getting into action' Drawing by F. Ward

and within an hour what was left of Zollora was in the Battalion hands. We passed several very bedraggled and dazed prisoners being escorted back down the hill. Beyond the village we re-organised and stayed there until some tanks arrived. The tanks were then deployed amongst the leading companies and we began the stiff climb to the summit. Opposition was negligible and by mid-morning we were dug in along the whole length of the ridge.

The devastation on the ridge was unbelievable. The ground was pitted with shell craters of all sizes and both the enemy and our own dead lay around in dozens. It reminded me of some of the pictures I had seen of the First World War. Shortly after daybreak we came across two British soldiers crouched behind a low wall with their weapons still trained on the enemy. I clapped one on the back and told him everything was OK now that we were here. You can imagine my horror when he slumped forward and tumbled over - he was stone dead, as was the other. It looked as though they had been killed by blast and somehow or other had remained in an upright position. When we mentioned it later in the day someone said that in the early attacks naval units in the Adriatic had also fired their big guns in support and the blast from these guns had done a great deal of damage to troops on both sides. I don't know how the infantrymen of the First War could have faced this sort of thing day in day out for as long as they did.

October - It is over a month since I put pen to paper, because I have been lying incapacitated in a hospital bed. However I am putting down in chronological order the happenings of my last three days in action while they are still fresh and clear in my mind.

The attack went in at one o'clock in the morning in buckets of rain driven by a full gale into our faces. The slope was extremely greasy and slippery from the rain and the noise of the guns was ear shattering. Enemy small arms fire was pretty accurate and we were forced to dash from one bit of shelter to the next until we got into a position to charge the house itself. The darkness, the rain and the noise of the guns hindered the enemy as much as it did ourselves and we were able to get right up to the house before they realised we had got so far.

Showers of grenades sailed through the ground-floor windows and we burst through the main door with all guns blazing to find the enemy diving out through the back door and bolting for the rear. We did fearful execution as we got rid of our pent-up fear and emotion. We methodically cleared the positions round the house and pushed on for another couple of 100 yards where we consolidated and waited for further orders. The whole affair took about two and a half hours but the action had been so intense and concentrated that it had seemed so much shorter than it really was.

As I sat alone soaked and miserably cold in a slit trench waiting for the dawn to come up, I let myself go in a wave of self-pity and suddenly found myself shaking like a leaf and very close to tears. I had come through another attack unscathed, had been at very close quarters with the enemy and had killed those who had got in my way, but I was now certain that I couldn't go on much longer. Most of my old friends had been killed and I wondered when it would be my turn. If I was to be killed then I hoped it would be nice and quick or alternatively let me get a nice arm or leg wound and get a month in hospital by which time things might be a lot different. A voice shouting "tea up" aroused me from my misery and never was a cup of char more appreciated - all the more so because of a large spoonful of rum decanted into it. The effects of the rum being circulated by the hot tea created a tingling sense of warmth which lasted until first light.

Shortly after dawn the tanks came up and started firing from amongst our positions and Jerry immediately replied with his 88's. When things got too unhealthy for them the tank crews battened down the hatches and disappeared whence they came. They always seem to bring us bad luck because we had one or two lads wounded by the retaliatory fire.

Later on during the morning we were ordered to move forward to take over Borghi so that the Sikhs could continue the advance. We reached the village after some desultory shelling on the way up. The Platoon took over the left flank of the Company and installed itself in a nice strong two-storey house with a flat roof and a nice deep cellar. Much to the Platoon's disgust the cellar was immediately commandeered by the Platoon Commander who had only recently taken over.

During the night the Sikhs captured the village on the hill away to our left flank, but during the morning after they were heavily counter attacked and driven back. Borghi was very heavily shelled but luckily our house was not hit although we had quite a few near misses and the shutters and doors were banged about. By this time we had acquired a large number of Sikhs from their reserve Companies who didn't know what was going on and the place began to feel unhealthily overcrowded in the event of a further counter-attack.

Just before mid-day we received a message from Company HQ which filled most of us with evil foreboding. The platoon was to supply cover party for the Indian Sappers while they attempted to clear the road of mines so that tanks could go forward in support of the leading Sikh Companies on the hill to our left in front of San Martino.

We went out on the flat roof to have a look at the situation and were appalled at the sight which greeted us. From the crest of the hill down to Borghi itself the road was a mass of erupting stones and dust from the curtain of shells being laid down by Jerry. It was obvious that he intended that no relief of the Sikhs forward companies would come via the road. You literally couldn't see the road for the explosions and the dust. We went down to the cellar and suggested that the Platoon Commander come and have a look for himself but he declined and said the operation would have to go ahead. In the event of insufficient volunteers section commanders were to detail sufficient men to make up the numbers. Needless to say most of us volunteered but I heard mutterings that the Platoon Commander was not to lead us - he couldn't leave Platoon HQ!

In the event the order was cancelled and we were ordered to put out a strong piquet to cover the extreme western edge of the village to give warning in case of any enemy encroachment on Borghi itself. Whilst making our way there we were heavily stonked and we threw ourselves to the ground. The last thing I heard was the scream of a shell and knew no more. When I came to I was lying on a bed with heavy bandages round my eyes and the mother and father of all headaches.

For the moment my war is over.

Dougal Milne: We left from Liverpool and sailed out into the Atlantic and came up towards Gibraltar and we still hadn't a clue where we were goin' and then we were goin' through the Straits of Gibraltar which was a fascinating sight. The lights shinning across the water from Morocco. Gibraltar was all blacked out and you were cuttin' through the rays of the lights. Light, darkness, light, darkness, it was the most fantastic eerie feeling. Something is going

> " we were all in tents with rush mats and mud up to our ankles and dysentery and diarrhoea was common "

to happen, we thought, and in fact once we got through we did get attacked. Bein' the curious devil that I am I poked up the thing to have a look but somebody yelled, "Get yer bloody head down below!"

We landed at Oran and the first thing I saw, it was a beautiful place but all along the one side the British had sunk all the French ships. Anyway, we were in a base camp before we joined the Lancers. Out of the 120 of us in the camp, at least 40 every day were up for sick parade! We were all in tents with rush mats and mud up to our ankles and dysentery and diarrhoea was common. We eventually moved to another camp.

David: You said you had an interesting story about Pantelleria

Dougal: Pantelleria, well, you know where it is, it's between North Africa and Malta. The Gordon Highlanders were there and the Allies took the island without a shot being fired until the surrender was signed and because someone let off one of those little Berrettas and then pandemonium broke loose! There is a pistol in the Highlanders Museum to this day, could it be <u>the</u> pistol?

Well, we left Algiers and we thought we were coming home but as the ship veered left, then, I think, right about, we knew we weren't. We went all the way along the coast between and then Sicily and Italy and up to Naples. After landing there we went on to a little place called Afragola.

David: Can you remember any of the actions in Italy?

● Allied troops and tanks landing in Salerno
Drawing by J. Fleming
© G. Fleming

Dougal: Five Troop had been hit near Perugia. The first armoured car was burnt out. The tyres on my vehicle were all shattered but there was a hard core of rubber inside the tyres which meant that you could run for 100 miles. The steering was very difficult but you could manage. In fact I drove through a river on the way back with a patrol of Argylls who climbed on to keep dry; it was on the 19th we were hit. A few days later my pal was killed. I was up havin' breakfast with him on the 23rd; we only had the one armoured car, his Sergeant volunteered t' go down again. You should never volunteer. Anyway he'd t' stop his breakfast and his last words to me were, "It's not our turn t' go first." Well they didn't get a quarter of a mile down the country road and the Jerries came back waitin' for them and hit them with a bazooka which killed Alec Bain outright. Alec Taylor - he tried t' get out of the little wee side door and as soon as he got out they jist machine-gunned him. So that was the two of them Alec Taylor and Alec Bain.

Between the winter of 44/45 the line was static for about six months and on most occasions in Italy there were rivers between you and canals but on this occasion just north of Forli at a place called Mezzano we were on open ground. On New Years morning '45 we crossed over onto a bridgehead and we were standing there; it was very early in the morning - 6.45am. - and we were chatting with the Canadians. This was the place that the last Canadians fought in Italy before they came out t' prepare for France. We were doin' flank for them. They were there with their tanks and we were with our armoured cars. We looked up and saw this Yankee plane come over. "Good God they are up early!" Then I said, "Christ, they're commin' down!" We dived for cover as it strafed us! Fortunately it missed us but it hit the first aid post, there were some casualties, I don't know how many.

I think it was the next day we heard this Panzer tank coming and oh my God we were messing ourselves! What he didn't realise was his engineers had blown the bridge further inland and had left him stranded. There it was the next mornin' the crew had gone of course and that was the first time that I had a close look at a Panzer. The only other time we bumped intil a German tank. It was pourin' wi rain but we had t' keep goin 'cause these cavalry Officers were always after medals. The Germans had cut a trench right across the airfield so that the aeroplanes couldn't land so we couldn't cross and fortunately neither could the Panzer facing us, so I said, "Let's get the blazes

● German Panzer III Ausf H, in Afrika Korps livery

outa here!" Our 6 Troop did run into a self-propelled gun once. It was a 105 or a 150. With this gun you could elevate it but you had to move the whole thing when you wanted t' swivel it. Actually, they were in a farmyard and the Sergeant and his driver left the operator with his earphones on listenin' for instructions but then of course he didn't hear this self propelled gun coming round the end of this buildin'. This vehicle had a bunch of Jerries on it, about eight or nine. Well, the wireless operator (suddenly realised that there was a German A.F.V.) and fired the two pounder and how he could have missed a vehicle that size I don't know. However, he hit the aerial and the Germans all ran. The Sergeant ran out of the house and here was the thing there for the takin'. So he drove it back. That wireless operator got an immediate mention in dispatches ie. The old Oak Leaf. What they did that for I don't know; he fired the gun and missed! The same as that 'do' when my mate was killed. The lad fired the Bren from the rear scout car didn't hit anybody, didn't capture any Germans and didn't kill anybody. He got the MM! I fired a Bren gun for five hours at the battle of Casa–di–Mezzo and got nothing; not even a mention! We were firing on SS troops and there were two Battalions of them and there were only nine in our position. There were no vehicles, we were just infantry and there was nothing between us and the Jerry.

In my diary it says, '3rd Jan. Weather, cold but fine, move on, hurried meal. Off in (armoured) cars and *Dingo's* so far, then on foot with all gear, self with Bren, one of two in troop. Took over position in C.di M. from friends, (the Kings Royal Rifle Corps), who were overjoyed to get away having been heavily counter attacked in the morning. Dark – very dark – by the time we take over. Took up position in the upstairs room; two windows, both Brens there. Standing-to from 6pm. Frozen stiff through night. Heard explosions; learned that 'gaffer' Lt. David Middleditch had stood on a mine while looking for a break in the tel. lines just outside; down to nine men!' On the 4th it says, 'Heard Jerry, held fire.' Y' heard them hammerin' all night they were building bridges t' get across the canals. It has never been explained to me why they were never shelled or mortared. 'Early morning (4th Jan.), still very dark. Suddenly a flare went off, (to me a Jerry had stood on one)' - I recollect that moment vividly; in the flat white glare I saw three Jerries pulling a small gun and many, many more crouching around them becoming larger as they approached us. To our surprise –

they must have passed one of our platoons in the adjacent house – they were only yards away! I wonder what the gun was?

David: Probably 37mm or *panzerbuchse 41.*

Dougal: Yeah, 'Heard Jerry, held fire, opened up 5am' is how I noted it. It really was Bedlam: We just fired at everythin'; bullets were flyin' all around me and the wall behind me was disintegrating. After the flare extinguished we continued to fire at their gun flashes – it was pitch black – presumably they were firing at ours. At one point my Bren jammed – Lt. Taberer came up, (Middleditch's replacement), and seriously shouting, poised above me to fire his Tommy gun; it did not go off, he said something, dashed off, we never saw him again in that 'do' but he still got the M.C. for it! I got firing again and just as things got really hairy three tanks came up to assist us. The first, placin' itself below my window, was knocked out straight away and the crew killed. I can still remember the moaning coming from that disabled machine. One of the tankies survived for some time after he had been lifted out, but how he did with half his face blown away I will never know. The Sergeant was dead outright but only had a small hole in his stomach – you remember these strange things. In my diary I wrote: 'Tanks and artillery to the rescue. Plenty of prisoners; chaps killed. 10.30am. finished. Relieved at night.' And that was us. Later we went back (5th March) and the German bodies were still there but the reason why they weren't buried was that they had been booby-trapped. I've met and kept in touch with one of the tankies from the 4th Hussars since then; the officer used his radio to direct the artillery fire which, with the tanks, saved us. If it wasn't for their help and the Honey (light tank) that brought us up ammunition supplies when we were dangerously low, I'm sure we'd have been overrun and wiped out. Our only casualties were later in the day – in fact just after the battle finished at 10.30 - when two Sergeants and the Lance-corporal from our other position in the steadin' and farmhouse opposite were 'searching' and gathering prisoners; the Jerries mortared them and killed everyone including their own troops.

David: Was that the end?

Dougal: Yea; after 10.30am. grub and relief came up but we weren't relieved until night. I wrote 'Very tired; walked back to vehicles, loaded up and I started to drive only to complain to the relief Sergeant that I couldn't see. He groaned and walked out in front with a torch until we had cleared the vines and fields. Still on bridgehead. Billeted in loft – Knackered! Two visitors before kipping; first the padre trying to console us whilst ducking every time a shell came over, then S.S.M. to say that 'gongs' (medals) were going. Freddie (Bohler) first, then the rest of us, said "Stuff them!"

Billy Henderson: We used t' listen into the Germans - that was when we were in Rome. I was a part of a clandestine organisation putting microphones into prisons. We were recording the prisoner's conversations on big records.

There was a black market for radio parts such as valves and the Italians were clammerin' for parts. We had an Officers radio - I don't know where it came from - and I was asked if I could get rid of it. Well, I took it to see what I could get for it so I took it to a shop and asked, in broken Italian, how much it would be. I canna remember how much it was but let's say it was 20 pounds. Well, I went back to the Officer and told him 10 pounds; that way we made a bittie of money! That was only one occasion but sometimes we did get hold of some valves to sell. They were all at it. It was the same if you got a hold of some sugar or chocolate. They were desperate to buy stuff including our ration of 50 cigarettes which, we also sold. I did smoke at that time but I saw the other fellas sellin' their cigarettes to the Italians and sendin' the money home so I stopped smokin' and did the same as them. See, what happened was that I'd said that half my wages could be stoppit' to give to ma parents; other lads had plenty of money to buy stuff and I had little; this was a way to make ma life slightly better.

William MacHardy: They told us we were going there (Pantelleria) as soon as we left the shore. There were briefings then, the maps came out and we saw what we were going to do but I never expected for one minute that we would land practically unopposed. We knew that there was an airstrip on the island - that's why we wanted to get there, to stop the Germans using it. I thought, if there is an air lane there then it is bound to be very well protected. But fortunately it wasn't because the Italians had taken it. As soon as we landed the Italians just put up their hands. There was some fighting but very little to that which we expected. I wasn't involved in the fighting there, that was on the right of us and we had to move to the left. We never came up against the forces that started the fighting. However, it didn't last long and we only stayed for a few days then we were back to Tunis. What happened after that was that we were organised and made ready for another move, which was by shipping to Taranto. We then became part of the Eighth Army. First we went to Salerno, then when we came out of there we were told that we would be involved in an assault somewhere. After that there was a couple of weeks practising getting into and out of landing craft so we knew something was going to happen but we didn't know where until the night we moved out. That was on the 21st of January and that was to Anzio. Anzio is just south Rome and I felt at the time that we were going to have a real problem but it didn't work out like that at all. The 6th Gordons and the 2nd North Staffs, we were together and we were the first to land on the actual shore. We were unopposed there. The first prisoners we took were in their pyjamas! Yes, the first two German officers were both in their pyjamas. It was a complete surprise.

David: Which Battalion were you with then?

William: From Tunis I went to Taranto trying to catch up with the Sixth Battalion. I caught up with the Battalion after Anzio, which was on the 22nd of January 1944. After joining the Battalion I did a lot of reconnaissance work. When I went out on patrol I took very little equipment with me. We would black up, put on the woollen cap, plimsolls, long trousers, commando knife and pistol. I always carried my pistol but I carried the rifle as well and ammunition in my belt. We sometimes carried grenades in the belt pouch. We had to investigate the land very carefully before going and coming back - that was always a problem - you had to be very careful especially where you went out. Then if it was not through your own lines - maybe you had to patrol somewhere else - there were great difficulties coming back. You had to be very careful. There was no noise whatsoever; no speaking and we didn't carry anything that made a

> ## " the first prisoners we took were in their pyjamas! "

noise. Going through minefields was difficult because lots of the minefields were not registered and sometimes accidents happened but there were a lot of risks taken. There were quite a few accidents particularly when mines (that) had been laid indiscriminately. Florence was a particularly bad example of that. On the outskirts of the City, Germans not staying to fight, (they) would mine the outskirts. They played a dirty game with the mines they were bad for that.

David: When was it that you had your first taste of action?

William: The first time was when we were moving out of Anzio, after the 3rd and 4th of February and we had lost a lot of men. March, April we were moving out from Campoleone into the hills. The beginning of April roughly, the Germans were beginning to pull out. It made things easier but they still left a tremendous amount of minefields. The Germans were experts in booby-traps and minefields. For example, I lost my best pioneer Sergeant with a mine. There was an olive grove and he was bending down to defuse this mine and a civilian had gone over a trip wire - which was leading to another one - and he was killed instantly.

● Allied troops and tanks landing in Salerno

David: What do you remember about Anzio?

William: There were a large number of German tanks and the positions that we were in - we were supporting the Scots Guards on the right - and the tanks came in between us and they got in behind B company. B Company could not get out which put C Company out of action and practically the whole of C Company was lost. They were cut off, every one of them. That was about 150 men. Fortunately, I wasn't in C Company, I was in A Company and we managed to get back.

The fighting was really severe. It just made us a half battalion because we lost all these men and we re-formed. We had to disband C Company altogether and make just three little companies A, B and D then we got reinforcements from various regiments. The thing that saved the day to a good extent was the London Scottish; (they) had disembarked and were thrown in and they helped to stop the gap. It was a disaster. In the confusion of the battle when the Germans were taking away the British (they'd captured), some of the British were lying low and coming back and getting caught by some other German unit. This went on quite a few times and some did manage to escape and they were able to tell us what really had happened on that night. The official report was that we had 319 people missing. Over and above that we had casualties - the wounded and the dead - so we were down to three small companies after that. After re-forming we pushed towards Rome and then towards the Gothic line. We crossed the Tiber into Florence and out to the Gothic Line where the real fighting happened.

My sniping skills were used to good advantage here and I trained (many of) my chaps to be snipers, although unfortunately in a battalion you were only allowed eight sniper rifles and to me, that was stupid. I thought we should have eight rifles in each company because in that type of warfare sniping was something that was needed. You can pick people off.

Germans were sniping at us from the tops of houses and all sorts of places and we retaliated with that. It certainly worked because when our chaps started sniping, the Germans beat it pretty quick. You could never quite tell whether you had hit him or the splinters had or that he had had enough and backed off. That was always a pleasure when that happened.

Unfortunately, it is not often realised by historians that it didn't matter where we were in the Gothic Line, the Germans were always above us and they could always see you and your fighting was uphill - uphill to the next ridge. You'd think that was the last ridge but then when you reached that there would be another one so you were at a disadvantage all the time.

We cleared quite a number of places just north of Florence; we cleared the Germans out of quite a few places. Sniping became quite a thing then. I remember one incident when we were fired on by a section of Germans from a railway tunnel - it

● Maj W. MacHardy, centre, with Mingham on his right and Corporal Smith on his left. "Smith was one of the finest Corporals that I ever had; a few days after the photograph was taken he stood on a mine while we were out on patrol. The explosion blew his foot off, knocked me over and destroyed the radio being carried by another soldier. A local woman, although very upset, motioned me to use her wheelbarrow to get Smith away. This we did and he was uplifted by an American ambulance after withdrawing about 500yds".

happened all of a sudden. The tanks that were with us daren't close in on it because of the fear of *Panzerfaust* so my patrol was sent in. It was a strange thing; you had to get forward, listen, get forward again; it was pitch dark. They were firing at us and tossing their 'Tattiemashers'; we were doing the same. There are lots of niches in these tunnels and it was a difficult job, my, it was good to see the light at the other end! Street fighting was really a dirty game. You would move up the streets in the open and you know that probably on both sides of the street there would be snipers trying to pick you off. You are watching, and the least movement, you would fire. When you got out of the end of the street and had cleared the area you would always have suffered casualties because there were so many windows and doors. We also used grenades – thrown or rifle launched - in street fighting and we also used the Piat if you felt there was more than one in a building. A Piat round through the window soon settled things.

We had to use the Piat quite often in Italy against tanks because the Germans had a great preponderance of tanks in Italy at that time. The first time I saw a Tiger, oh my goodness! When I think of the Sherman and the others we had. When it came round the corner it was a fearsome sight and we just had to get out of the way. We had a Piat at the time and we fired at the Tiger, it hit it but it did very little damage but at least it made them think and turn back.

David: What were your other experiences with tanks?

William: We did exactly the same as the Germans did. We followed as close behind them as we could. You can just imagine a section - seven to 10 men - keeping as close to the tank as they could and just following it up. It was dangerous when following a tank, or riding on one for that matter, because bullets would ricochet off the tank and hit the men. We had lots of casualties that way. Also, riding on a tank, there was always the possibility that you would be thrown off when the tank went over a bump.

An experience we had with a tank, well I think the first was when we were pulling out from Anzio on the road to Rome and Florence and we came across German tanks who were withdrawing. We had a lot of fighting there between our own tanks and German tanks. We had nothing to compete with their 88mm gun, if we'd had that we'd have been all set because that was all we needed. What was the worst thing though was the weather, which started in August and got so bad in September and October that the tanks were bogged down and they couldn't move.

As to sniping, the Germans went in a lot for sniping maybe not quite so much in Italy, the real sniping was in France after D-Day. The casualties were savage from sniping after D-Day.

A typical day in the Italian lowlands would usually start very early in the morning and there had to be a pretty close liaison with the tank commanders and the infantry. We would need to know exactly what they were going to do, at what speed they would be doing it and what their objectives would be. The whole thing went round the advancement of the tanks; how far the tanks had gone forward and how far we the infantry had gone forward. Sometimes maybe, we would be left behind a little bit where the tanks might have sped across flatter ground and then we would catch up with them again. Then if you went in to higher ground you would be able to keep up with them much easier. We would never get divorced from them completely

● Above - A ruined hilltop known as Calderare which was the first position taken over by the Gordons from the Americans. The church in the picture was obliterated later in the week.

Left - the Gordons awaiting further orders at the top of hill 1197. The 6th Gordons CO. (Lt-Col. JB. Clapham) is shown pacing up and down.

because the tanks machine guns could deploy fire on the Germans and also, on the top of the tank, you had a better view compared to what we had dealt on the ground itself. The battle might go on for two or three hours and it depended entirely how well the tanks got forward and how poor the German defensive positions were. If the 88s were there, which was their main weapon, there was little hope of the tanks getting through. We could speak to the tank commander through our net but that was the only means of communicating with them. In the better weather it was quite enjoyable moving through the foothills in the Gothic Line and clearing villages and so forth, but when we moved later on to go into the mountains the rain then started it was dreadful. From the weather reports at that time, that kind of weather was unknown in Italy before. It had started early that year - July, August, September; it was far too early. The higher up we went, the more the rain and sleet changed to snow and of course the conditions became appalling for the simple reason that no-one could keep dry and as the weather deteriorated the mules couldn't come up the mule tracks so everything had to be man handled. The only good thing to come out of that was that the commanders decided that the tanks and the artillery be taken out because they couldn't function, and the crews were then made into stretcher bearer parties and ration parties to serve us chappies on the higher ground.

I remember once it was a very bad time in Italy at Il Casoni (West of Monte Romano). We had taken the feature and I was sent round the other side of it to find out what had happened to the Royal Scots. It was a dry day and getting towards dusk, we came to this lonely farmhouse and not knowing whether they were Germans or who in it, we crept up to it carefully. I had a patrol with me of about eight men. Nobody had appeared at the windows but there was smoke coming out of the chimney and I thought that I would take a chance so I told the chaps to spread out. We got forward to the farmhouse and got into the door. In the kitchen there was a fire going and in front of the fire were three Royal Scots. One was seriously wounded and was lying in agony in front of the fire. He'd been machine gunned in the stomach. The two others were not hurt but had volunteered to look after their Corporal. I asked what had happened and they said that they had been caught unawares and the Germans had fixed them up. I said, "Let's have a look to see how he is." I looked and I could see that there

was no hope. I, as an Officer, carried ampoules of painkillers so I said, "I'll give you this and it will help you." He wanted to drink but I said "no just keep his lips moist". I bandaged him up and I gave him a dose of the ampoule. Well on the way back next day on the track back out of that area we came on this grave on the side of the track which was the Corporal who I had attended to. The other two had tried to take him back but he had died on the way. This sort of thing happened time and time again.

> " it was always enjoyable to me to get a target and to see the Germans scatter all over the place "

David: What accommodation was there?

William: There was no accommodation, we just dug a slit trench and got in there. You were never dry in a slit trench, as soon as you made a slit it filled up with rain. We tried to make channels to run off the water but the rain was coming down so fast (that) it was filling up as fast as we could dig and that's what we had to live in. It was a question of trying to get shelter to keep warm; that was the main thing. You were sodden and you were soaked and then of course when night came you became very uncomfortable because of the cold. However, at night you could move about and try to keep warm. During the day you couldn't, you had to keep down because there was always someone above you watching so you had to lie doggo during the day. If you moved during the day you got fired on. Any movement at all and you could bet your boots that shells would come over and the bombs would come just to let you know that you were seen. Conversely, if a target presented itself - which at times it did - it was always enjoyable to me to get a target and to see the Germans scatter all over the place.

The main targets I saw myself were patrols approaching farmhouses or some other place and then we'd stonk down on them and see them scatter left right and centre and see a few left lying on the ground; that was good. It let them see that even though they held all these positions, they were still vulnerable. My last days up there by the Gothic Line were in October of 1944 when we took the main features there overlooking Bologna. Then we moved from there to Monte Grande on the American side and took that over. After that we got our Christmas dinner on the 4th or 5th January 1945 at San Lorenzo at the bottom of the Gothic Line. Then we moved from there to the (Garibaldi) Barracks at Perugia and then by cattle trucks from Perugia, (which took about three days) to Taranto and then from Taranto to Haifa in Palestine.

Dougal Milne:

Before the last attack in Italy, my pal came to see me - he was the orderly Corporal at the time – while I was workin' on my vehicle. He says, "Dougal, job for ye, you've t' pick an armoured car, get ready you are goin' on special duty." I said, " I'll take my own." "Y' canna do that Dougal look at all this (mess)!" (Being a painter I'd adorned my Daimler with drawings that were rather frowned upon by the officers; I was known as 'Little Haggis', so I'd drawn one on my car; I'd drawn a wee haggis and other things too. We'd condensation tanks as well - little two gallon tanks for getting' condensation water and they were also painted). "You'll have to get all that off Doug." I still said, "I'm takin' my own armoured car", so I cleaned it up as well as I could and went off to represent 'A' squadron. A,B,C,D, - four armoured cars inspected by all the ranks until it came to the Colonel and 'C' squadron's vehicle was bulled up to ninety nine even down to the inside of the two pounder! Mine was rather sad in comparison. Anyway, when we came to drive off, 'C' squadron armoured cars' engine wouldn't start and had to be left behind! Where we went to was the 8th Army TAC Headquarters at Cesena north of Rimini. The rumour was going round that the King was coming to inspect the troops before the last push in Italy. So all the big shots were there of course. Anyway, we had special zip suits at the time that you could make into a sleepin' bag. Well, we are standing there and this Minister came over to us - it was the Archbishop of York, Doctor Garbett - who had come out to bless the troops. He told us that it was so miserable when he left England, cold and that, but out here everything was so beautiful and everything else. He asked the Corporal what denomination he was and was told that he belonged to the Church of Scotland. My wireless operator at the time was a Welshman. I can't remember his denomination but it was something Welsh and although I was brought up as an Episcopalian, when he came to me I said, "And I'm a Scotsman too Sir!" He said, "How strange in an English regiment, not one of you an Englishman." That was the first time we saw Alexander. They were all there, the Kiwi commander (Freyburg), the Polish commander, Anders and 13 Corps Commander, Sir John Harding.

After the battle we were in Trieste and we moved out of the centre of the square; it was a three sided square because the sea was on the other side and we moved up because of the political situation. The Yugoslavs couldn't take Trieste but they by passed it and we met them at a place called Monfalcone. They were all marchin', no vehicles.

● 02/05/45; the main square in Trieste. Vehicles of the 12th Lancers are lined up in front of the town hall. "We billeted on the right hand side whilst the Communist Slavs were on the left, across the piazza. We had our guns trained on each other for three days before we pulled out to safer surroundings" (Dougal Milne)

There were women as well with bandoleers. I'd no idea who they were but they weren't shooting at us but they were salutin' us with their fists so we did the same back! The political situation became so bad that that they moved us out of the square. (Photo here) We were in this building here (indicating) and the Yugoslavs were in there and we were pointing .5 Brownings at one another.

The very first night that we were in the line (we were in the badly ruined village of Capracotta) they asked for volunteers to do a listening post about 500 yards in front of our positions and of course three Scotsmen volunteered! Well actually, the Germans come through that night, passed us, cut the telephone wires and we never knew a thing. That was our first experience of action.

Dougal reading from his diary: 'The 18th was a Sunday, moving 5am. Had powdered eggs and bacon. Windy and sunny at times. On job in afternoon.' That means that we were in action. 'S all night.' That means a mortar stonk. 'Still out, pouring rain, bedding wet, Nabbed.' That means that we were hit. There are two armoured cars in a Troop and the other armoured car had two direct hits. How he got out I don't know. He actually got out from behind the steering wheel and up past the two lads in the turret before they could move!

The position that we passed through was held by the Argyll and Sutherland Highlanders and they were damned annoyed at us for coming in about 'cause the dust was knockin' up, a sign for Jerry saying, "Look we're here!" The Troop Leader went in to get the information from the commander and he said, "Come on we are going out." Well in the early days he didn't discuss things with us. He just got in, started up and down the road and BANG ! BANG! BANG!

David: Tell me about the story of Mirano.

Dougal: We had a Kiwi commander, Freyberg, with whom we'd t' crack on to Venice with. As we went we were to secure the bridges and make sure they weren't booby-trapped. The partisans were appearing all over by this time in northern Italy and we'd put them in charge of the bridges and crack on. We were about eight or 10 miles from Venice. It was a Sunday; a bad bleak day but the civilians were walking along the side of the road to church all dressed in black. There was a slight bend in the road and we were bummin' on, we were so confident and at this slight bend in the road it happened. As I say, that business runnin' into a German column happened so quick. We went round the corner and there was the Germans. We fired the two pounder – the gunner didn't even wait for me to close my hatch - and it's not a very nice experience being fired on that close. I sez, "T' hell wi this, let's get the blazes out o' this!" There was only one road and the poor civilians were jumping into the ditches at the side of the road. The Germans were walking with horse-drawn vehicles pulling eight field guns. So we went back the way and then met the partisans who asked to go in with us. So, the Sergeant 'volunteered' us to go in my armoured car and I went in over this bridge as I say, with these partisans climbing all over the vehicle. (It's still there to this day) We came round and as soon as I looked up the straight bit to the square there were (all) the Germans.

My mate Freddie Bohler he sez, "Dougal, we'll keep on goin' because we'll never reverse back over that bridge, keep on goin." It was about 150 yards and I kept goin' up and it was a funny, funny feelin' that they might open up on ye. I was very fortunate that my wireless operator Pete Day, this is him here, (referring to a photo) - him and his brother had been entertainers and they did a bit o' song and dance and they'd travelled through Europe before the war and Pete spoke quite good German. He was wearing my duffle coat which I had acquired from my old Officer. He spoke to the Germans and they took him for the Officer. They thought we were leading a whole squadron of armoured cars and we didn't realise that we'd killed their column commander when we fired on them on the way up. They all came up to hand over their weapons and Freddie in his Aberdonian sez, "Oot ye ging an' tak up their weapons!" Then

> " when they saw a little wee divil like me wearin' a Scots tammy coming out I don't know what they thought "

when they saw a little wee divil like me wearin' a Scots tammy coming out I don't know what they thought, they were smart the German Officers, salutin', surrendering their weapons and laying them in front of the armoured car.

There were rows and rows of weapons and the Germans were laying them down and Freddie wirelessed to the Sergeant who was outside the village. He sent in a scout car whilst he still sat outside the village. So by this time the Germans were getting a bit suspicious. They were all lined up be then and it was very fortunate for us that three Spitties came over. Before we'd left we had this thing like a blind to swing over the armoured car because we were out in front more than 15 miles, these blinds had air identification markings on them so that, in theory, our own planes wouldn't attack us. In fact we were about 30 miles in front. We weren't supposed t' use these blinds unless we had orders from TAC headquarters. Anyway, I took the thing and slung it over the back of the armoured car. The Spitties immediately recognised it. The Germans were flappin' by this time and the civies were running in all directions! Up they came and they come doon jist rooftop height, wagged their wings, went round, waved, around again and gave us a salute and that was it. By this time an infantry troop came in aboot (Photo here) there woulda been seven o' them and that was our support so that now, there was the three of us, two in a scout car and seven o' them. That was 12 of us opposed to 600 Germans with eight field guns! How we got away with it I don't know!

That's the reason that I was taken back here as Guest of Honour with expenses paid and everything done for me and I'm invited back again in the year 2000.

● Left - Germans, British and partisans; line of German weapons on the flagstones. To the right, obscured by telegraph wires, is a White Scout Car, a favourite general purpose vehicle used by the British and here debusing infantry of 7 troop, Dougal's support group, to guard prisoners.
Right - part of the same sequence; note that the German transport is horse-drawn.

● An extraordinary sequence of photographs taken by Italian, Leo Pavan, of Dougal Milne's AC taking the surrender of an entire German artillery column in Mirano. Below - Dougal, the driver, is to the right with his hand in the air. To his right and going off the picture is Cpl. Freddie Bohler, the AC Commander. Pete Day, the wireless operator, is walking back towards the 'car.

Inset - Proud Italian partisans and behind them members of the Lancers infantry support group; note the Scot in the beret is Jock Irvine from Glasgow. Left - Dougal feted by the villagers in 1996; to his left is Franco Marchiori, the mayor, behind him in the glasses is the British consul from Venice, to his right, with glasses and umbrella, is Francesco de Gaspari, former district head of the partisans.

Above - Mirano square today, little changed.

"It wis getting' dark and the sea wis bubblin' with the spent shrapnel falling down"

D-Day
and the Battle for France and North Western Europe

***T**O ACCOMPLISH THE FINAL DEFEAT OF **G**ERMANY an invasion of France had to be orchestrated. Commitments in the Mediterranean and further East delayed this, even though Stalin was constantly clamouring for a 'Second Front' and the British had created a plan on paper before the end of 1941. It was 1944 before millions of men and women based in Britain moved into action. On 5/6 th June three airborne divisions, five infantry divisions and their supporting armour moved across the Channel to land in Normandy under the protection of largest naval/air umbrella ever assembled.*

George Johnston Duguid: Landing in Normandy, we lay off shore for about 12 hours. We saw shells comin' over. There was a railway gun further up the coast. When we did land, the ship landed at the same time as us and a shell came over and hit a wagon. It was a direct hit.

Dod Martin: Y' see the OP landed with the commando boys there – I was an OP driver. They were directin' the naval gunfire before our ain guns came ower. There wis a church tower an' we went up on top o' there and a course there was a sniper up there, a commando boy an' he wis sick when he seen us commin' up an' wis off sayin' it wis too dangerous.

As an OP most o' the time y' wis in a vehicle but y' couldna sit in a vehicle the wireless operator sat there but what y' mostly did was t' dig a slit

trench an' get intilt. The Officer in charge, he always picked the spot an' we had t' dig the slitters an' get in there.

Johnston Duguid: I think I showed y' a photograph o' my gun at Colleville-sur-Orne that was the village that we went through and we were bein' sniped at from the church tower and we were held up for a wee while. Before 'at we were on the beaches an' we went into a corn park as a rendezvous. We followed the tracks round so that we wouldn't hit a landmine. So we waited in this field and we were bein' bombed so we dug slit trenches to be under cover. One o' the lads said, "Sarge, there's a hole under the muzzle of our gun." Well, we knew before that we had been bombed durin' the night and an unexploded bomb had gone off somewhere else. So I

● Courtesy J. Pelella

● Left: Allied troops, with Bren gun carrier, preparing for a landing. Courtesy J. Pelella

sez, "There must be an unexploded bomb doon there under the muzzle of our gun." I didn't like t' show that I was scared or onything like that I jist said, "OK boys outa the trenches it's time t' go!" The D.R (Dispatch Rider) came back, "Start up!" Whooosh! We couldn't get outa there quick enough. At the end o' the field goin' through the gate the bomb exploded! Then we were fired at from the church spire at Corgill. The next troop along unlimbered their gun an' shot the bloody spire doon. Then we went up to wer gun positions an' we were seven weeks in that position. We were the first guns ashore and we were right at the front near where the Pegasus Bridge was. We followed the cart tracks up into a tattie field. Where my gun position was to be, someone had stuck in a stick. I looks at it an' sez, something's bloody funny here. There were two sticks stickin' up where my gun position was meant t' be. So I sez, "Jesus Christ, there's a bloody mine there!" So I crawled on ma tummy owra across to it -it was a mole trap! Ha, ha, ha!

We dug in our gun position behind the boundary of two fields where there were little trees and bushes. However, we were quite happy with it but there was a hell o' a lota diggin'. Anyway, next day Captain Dickie cam up t' me and said, "Sergeant, you're in the wrong position. You should be in the hedge, you'll be in the hedge tomorrow." That was the last I saw of him. We were supportin' the Highland Division and they parked a Bren carrier against a wall then a mortar cam over an' killed this two. The Lance Bombardier Angus and Captain Dickie were killed outright. In fact fen we went back for the fiftieth anniversary we went to see the graves and took photographs. They got buried with the paratroopers they were killed wi the Gordon Highlanders. Dickie, he definitely wanted medals. I'll gie y' an' example, I wis in the OP. At the time, this Gordons Captain come doon an' he sez, "I've got a right spot at the top of the Seine where the Jerries is crossin', if we get an OP. up 'ere we'll mek a killin' 'ere."

David: Dod, you were a driver; what did you drive?

Dod: The vehicle we used for OP was a Bren carrier, with an ordinary wireless set. I drove it, I was the cook I hid t' dee arthing. Wilson Spence, who was a barber, was with me he wis from Montrose. He was the OP ack , the Observation Officer y' see an' I was the driver come - I did arthing. The other guy did the ranging an a' the rest o' it.

David: How close would you have to be to the enemy?

Dod: Sometimes in front of the infantry. Only once did we get caught in an ambush. After D-Day all the Officers wanted a medal, they all wanted a Distinguished Cross or something like 'at with the result that - there were four OP's, one to each battery. So, onyway they chased us up to get across the Seine - the Germans were firin' across the Seine - so this Gordons Officer he wis in a Bren carrier (at the front of the patrol), there wis a Bren carrier, a jeep, an' then me and a 15 hundredwecht behind me. So this Officer sez, "I've got a recht place for an OP." Wilson sez, "Right, we're on!" There wis jist a long road and there was hedges either side. All of a sudden I sees the first motor blew up and then the second one.

It was jist two shells y' see. I whirled the Bren carrier roond, I didn't ask him, I whirled it roond aboot and as I whirled I hit a telegraph pole, broke et an' it broke ma track. The boy behind us he managed t' get turned but he was shot up in the tail. I never seen these guys again, they were Gordons. They were shot up wi rifles. We baled oota the motor because we could hear 'em firin' they were hittin the apron o' the motor. Sammy English went into the ditch at es side an' me an' es boy fae Norwich – Mike Jarrett - we went itae the other side an' the Officer – Captain Spencer - he cam inta the same side as us but when I looked he

● Transporting sections of the Mulberry harbour across the channel. Drawing by J. Fleming. © G. Fleming

wis gone, couldn't see him. Mike an' me we were lyin' in this ditch an' I sez til him, "Dinna let us bide here 'cause I can nearly see this guy." He wis firin' over oor heeds. So we were crawlin' along this ditch; we crawled along the road a bitty an' we come til an entrance intil a field. So it meant we had t' go over the top. I don't care what anybody sez that guy coulda shot us. We crawled aboot a mile, when we got out we got a lift back wi a motor t' the regiment. Our Major said t' me "Where's y' steel helmet?" An' I sez, "On the motor." "Where's y' gun?" "In the motor." I sez, "Wait a minty now, I'm a driver d' y' expect me t' hod a Bren carrier on the road an' carry a gun at the same time?" He put us on a charge for leavin' ma weapons. I said, "By the way there's a lad left up there I don't know if he's wounded or not. I'd like t' go up wi two or three lads wi rifles an' hae a look." "No, no leave him we'll go up in the mornin'." When darkness cam, Sammy cam back hi'sel; he wasna touched but oor Officer he'd ran awar. Eventually we met him, I sez "You're a fine een y' didna even see if we were a'right!" We phoned back next mornin' aboot the motor, the mechanic was t' come an repair the track. An anti-tank shell had gone through the front o' the motor and had sprayed the seats with shrapnel. If we'd stayed in the motor like the Major had wanted us t' dee we'da all been killed. What annoyed me was they had stole all ma chocolates an' ma fags! I've nae idea what happened to the other lads but their motors were aff the road. They were deen awar be the time we got up. They were infantry; Gordons they were. We found, with another OP,

another old boy Ernie Angus frae Aberdeen (who wis later killed) that every time we went with the Highland Division we lost men, why I don't know. There wis mony a time we had t' go forward in front o' the infantry t' find a place. But this place had been reconnoitred an' swept clean, it was safe enough, there were nae mines or onything like 'at. Fen they telt us t' ging up 'ere we understood that they would be in front o' us but they (must have) retreated back. There'd been a patrol oot y' see an' we had t' ging up by oor selves and once y' got nearer the Germans you'd t' be very, very careful but sometimes if y' med a bitta stew an' if Jerry seen this he fired on y'. We were very lucky, as I said, efter we left that action an' we went up wi the Gordons that's when we started losin' men. We never lost men wi the Airborne. We went ashore wi the 42nd Marine Commandos and everyone o' them come outa Barlinnie!

What hit us was an anti-tank gun - a PIAT gun or something like 'at - they had laid a trap for us.

Dod Martin: I slept in a garage to the right of the cafe' (hotel) on the corner (see below) and although we were only there for three days, the French remembered us very well. It was in the winter (1939-40) and we were sleeping on straw which was warm and cosy. In those days I liked a drink and we were in the bar as much as possible. At the time I had false teeth and one morning I couldn't find them. I got our friends from the cafe' and my fellow gunners to search - which meant moving half a ton of straw bedding! We found nothing. Some

5632. BEAUMONT-sur-SARTHE (Sarthe) – Place d'Arme et Route d'Alençon

● The village remembered by Dod Martin

BELL'S "Afore ye go"

Evening Express

LATE FINAL

Still the Best! BIRD'S CUSTARD

No. 20,643 (Estab. 1879).   ABERDEEN, TUESDAY, JUNE 6, 1944.   Three Halfpence.

ALLIES ESTABLISH BEACHHEADS

Now Slashing Their Way Inland

Soldiers Sang "Road To Isles"

There was no tension about the troops as D Day approached, wires a B.U.P. war correspondent who is with them.

On the last night before embarkation a number of the troops in my area attended a camp film show, "Holy Matrimony," and before the start of the show had a sing-song.

There was scarcely a military tune to be heard. Instead, there was "I Don't want to be a Soldier," "The Road to the Isles," "Annie Laurie," and when they ran short of a tune they sang the song their fathers sang when they went out on the same brave journey nearly thirty years ago, "Tipperary."

ALLIED TROOPS HAVE LANDED IN FRANCE, FORMED BRIDGEHEADS, AND ARE SLASHING INLAND.

The location of these bridgeheads has not yet been revealed by the Allied C.-in-C., but the Germans assert that they lie between Cherbourg and Le Havre.

"The greatest concentrations of invasion forces detected so far are at Cherbourg and Havre," said the German News Agency.

"Obviously both these towns are wanted by the enemy as his principal disembarkation ports."

The following details of the invasion were given by Mr Churchill to the House of Commons to-day:—

An immense armada of upwards of 4000 ships with several thousand smaller craft has crossed the Channel.

Massed airborne landings have been successfully effected behind enemy's lines.

Landings on the beaches are proceeding at various points at the present time.

The fire of the shore batteries has been largely quelled.

NOT SO DIFFICULT

The obstacles which were constructed in the sea have not proved as difficult as was apprehended.

The Anglo-American Allies are sustained by about 11,000 first-line aircraft which can be drawn upon as may be needed for the purposes of the battle.

There are already hopes that actual tactical surprise has been attained, and we hope to furnish the enemy with a succession of surprises during the course of the fighting.

The landings, it is understood in London, were made in Normandy between 6 a.m. and 8.15 a.m., minesweepers clearing a way. Naval bombardments, in which U.S ships took part, were carried out, and airborne landings made, first reports being described as "good."

General Montgomery is in charge of the army group carrying out the assault, with British, Canadian and U.S forces under his command.

The Allies have established beachheads in Northern France and are slashing inland, according to photo reconnaissance pilots back from the landings.

Since the invasion began Allied fighter-bombers have been dive-bombing, glide-bombing and strafing German defences and communications.

They are hitting any target that has a bearing on the strength of the German armies at the front

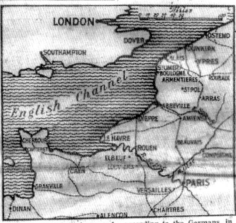
Allied landings have been made, according to the Germans, in the Cherbourg Peninsula and at various points between the peninsula and Le Havre.

HARD FIGHTING AT CAEN

But Allies Are On The Advance

"THE Germans are putting up very stiff resistance in the Caen area," said Paris Radio this afternoon. "The town area itself has been sorely tried. The enemy appears to be penetrating deeper inland."

The Germans say that landing operations are at present from Cherbourg to Le Havre, with bombing attacks on Calais and Dunkirk. Among places mentioned by name are Arromanches (midway between Cherbourg and Le Havre) and Marcouf.

Scaling Cliffs

"More than 200 craft approached Arromanches nine hours after the first landings," said the German News Agency. "The enemy are trying to scale the steep coast with the aid of special ladders."

Black-out: Light-up Time

	p.m.		a.m.
Begin	11.56.	End ...	4.17

		a.m.		p.m.
Sun —Rises,		5.18	Sets,	10.56
Moon—Rises,		10.23	Sets.	5.37

To-morrow's Tides

Aberdeen 3.19   3.41

Hard fighting is going on everywhere.

"Landing barges penetrated into the estuaries of the Orne and the Vire.

"British 1st, 2nd and 6th Airborne Divisions took part in attacks in the Seine estuary area."

The Overseas German News Agency this afternoon reported Allied landings on Guernsey and Jersey in the Channel Islands.

Nazis Expect

The Berlin military spokesman said:—"It is quite possible that within the next hours or days the focal point of the battle will shift to another sector of the French Atlantic coast.

"Further sea transports of the Anglo-Americans are at present en route, partly in the Channel and partly north of Cherbourg. One cannot say at this hour where they are going to land.

"The invasion army stationed in England is strong enough to undertake landings on a large scale at other points."

Pitiful Plea By Petain

Marshal Petain, in a broadcast on Paris radio, said: "Frenchmen, obey the orders of your Government. Everyone must stay in his place.

"Frenchmen, do not pile up misfortune by act which will bring about terrible reprisals.

"France can save herself only by observing the most rigorous discipline."

Beachhead Quickly Secured

The umbrella bombardment from Allied warships began to-day as soon as dawn broke, reports a military observer who landed with the first assault forces.

It seemed that hell itself had been let loose, he said. From left, right and centre our guns opened up, and from our vantage point at sea we could see that targets ashore were being pounded out of existence as the assaulting infantry sailed slowly and surely ahead to let bayonets do whatever work remained.

Magnificent

From sea and sky the bombardment continued, until our infantry went ashore. It was a magnificent sight.

Wave upon wave of khaki-clad figures surged up the beaches overcoming any opposition in their way and surging on.

Within a very short space of time the immediate bridgehead was ours, and shortly afterwards beach parties and the like were ashore and putting their organisations into effect.

Organisation

When I went ashore, the organisation was complete, and as vehicles, guns, infantry and equipment of all sorts quickly landed with the sea, it was obvious that well-timed plans had been put into effect.

On both sides of us divisions stormed ashore, or rushed in their reinforcements to coincide with ours.

After months of waiting and wondering—on both sides of the Channel—our plans have been put into effect.

HITLER IN CHARGE

Hitler is taking personal command of all anti-invasion operations. He is surrounded by a staff, including four marshals, and is believed to have moved his H.Q. to a place somewhere in Northern France.

The news reached London from underground sources.

Hitler's marshals are Rundstedt, air forces, and Blaskowitz, Acting Deputy to Rommel.

Gen. de Gaulle Here

General de Gaulle is in this country. He has been here some days. He is accompanied by Mr Duff Cooper, M. Massigli, M. Le Trocquer, M d'Astier, Gen. Bethourd, M Palewski and M. France.

King Holds D Day Investiture

To-day, D Day while his troops were fighting again on the beachheads in France the King held an investiture at Buckingham Palace.

In the uniform of Admiral of the Fleet he gave medals to nearly 300 soldiers, sailors, airmen, men of the Merchant Navy and civilians who had won their decorations during the long uphill struggle before the invasion could begin.

His Majesty To Broadcast

The B.B.C. announces that the King will broadcast at 9 o'clock to-night

2 Killed In Bed: Plane Fell On House

An elderly woman and young girl were killed in bed at Gillingham Kent early to-day when an American plane crashed on a row of houses following a mid-air collision with another plane.

The second plane fell in an orchard.

The bodies of five airmen have so far been recovered.

Highlanders In Grand Trim

MEN of famous Highland units who are taking part in the early assault operations are in splendid trim, wires a B.U.P. correspondent at one of the marshalling areas. They joked and laughed although knowing that their formation was to be first on he beachhead with no light task.

One Highland officer told me—"My men are disappointed about one thing. They are not going to see enough Germans.

In the last few days before the invasion the pipers of this unit could be heard nearly all

hills of Scotland whence the pipes came.

Sealed Off

The troops were completely sealed from the outer world while they waited for reembarkation. The bar to all communications with the outside world was so complete that you could see troops playing cards within a hundred yards of main roads with only a few strands of wire between them and the outer world.

The success of the security measures was tremendous, helped by the inhabitants of the coastal areas.

the time practising for the final piping of the troops into battle.

More than once the sound of pipes sounded strangely from the midst of a great concentration of armoured equipment—strange contrast to the

time later we moved on and I found the missing dentures in the pocket of my greatcoat much to the annoyance of my fellow gunners! After D-Day I returned to the village, much knocked about by now after days of shelling and of bombing - as a driver of an OP in an unattached regiment I had some freedom movement. The owners remembered me well, firstly because I was accompanied by a lad who'd played the piano and secondly because I was the soldier who'd lost his teeth!

Johnston Duguid: I was on a Bren gun carrier once an' this was up about Kleve in Germany and we werna doin' nothing. I forget the name of the river but anyway we were harein' around t' see what was in the area 'cause we were jist restin' for a couple o' days. Well there was a chap wi a Bren gun, the driver o' the carrier an' meself and we come back wi 41 prisoners! We come up t' the river bank and there was a farm there and there was a little boy there and he came up to us and said, "Deutschen, Deutschen other side o' the river." So I crept up the bank o' the river an' had a look and saw them all millin, around on the other side o' the bank. They were tryin' t' give themselves up anyway. So, I gets the Bren gun carrier right up and still they couldn't see where we were. Him with the Bren gun tells 'em t' get on the bank then I stood up in the front wi my Sten gun rrrrrrt across the lot o' them. All, the lot o' them, up wi their hands! There was a little boat which woulda held about five so the young lad he rowed the boat across. There was a Sergeant and Officers in charge of the platoon, or whatever it was, and eventually (they) rowed themselves across. As they

came across, they were disarmed. They were armed but they dropped their guns and rifles. We were restin' in a school at the time and the next mornin' we decided what we were going t' do with the Germans. We were supposed t' send them to H.Q but I said, "That's a bloody long way a way. T' hell, they are quite willin' t' walk themselves so let 'em walk!" I told the Officer in charge to walk to H.Q., which they did, and surrendered there. We went t' bed in this school, the next mornin' I woke up an' I thought it was a guard outside - it was another bloody Jerry sittin' on the doorstep!

David: Do you remember the Battle of the Bulge?

Johnston Duguid: The Germans had broken through the Ardennes and there was a fresh American Division come over from the States and they couldna hold the Germans. The Jerries just came right through them. They switched the Highland Division over and they stopped it. We were used as infantry then, getting them outa the houses.

Back as Artillery we were selected to go and advance one night to harass the Germans. So, we set off this night, it was dark and we travelled on for miles and miles and miles. We had two escorts on motorbikes, but seven miles on they went very quiet; "This is bloody funny this." I thought, so we stops and find that we are lost. Lt. Sacco was in charge so he came back down the line an' sez, "We are lost and there's no one here t' tell us what to do." I said, "Where's the escort?" He said, "They were here a minute ago but they are not here how." They'd just buggered off! They'd left, took the bikes the whole lot. So there were four guns deserted *miles* behind enemy lines. So he sez, "We've been deployed t' get t' within shootin' distance." So we got down so far as Udenbosch and there's a railway crossin' there. There were covered wagons there. So we went into a field beside a stream and I remember that in front of my gun was a great big wall like a garden wall. Well, we were there an' we knew that we were in German territory. Some o' the lads were afa nervous an' there was this one boy from Newcastle, he said, "Hey Sarge, let's get the hell outa here!" but a 'cause we had a job to do so we stayed. Anyway - so we could hear the Germans shoutin' an' all this sorta business. So they were getting ready t' move but the bloody English were there and the Highlanders were here. So we started firin' every few minutes from 10 o'clock until about 1. Someone said that someone was firin' from below. I looks down and so they were. I said, "Alright, we'll fire back from where it's comin' from." They were four Tiger tanks! We didn't know that at that time and they were only about 400 yards away. So we took the bull by the horns and eventually we stopped at daybreak. Then all the locals came outa their houses and invited us in, gave us beer an' drink an' food t' help us. We were left there for about two days before the rest of the troops came up. Then the Americans gave up and dug in behind us.

David: How do you think Montgomery changed the conditions between Dunkirk and Normandy?

Alex Ross: The thinking from 1939 was from 1914. The generals were right behind in Paris or whatever and let the troops get on with it. There was jist nothing for the lads. Once we got back from Dunkirk to be de-loused. It was scabies we had. Anyway it's an indication of how Montgomery thought of his troops (he ensured that they were kept healthy) but one thing he wouldn't have was this: it was so warm in Normandy the boys were apt to strip off at the guns and he didn't like that. It was shirts on, sleeves rolled up an' no beer wasted or onything like that.

● A gun of the Fish Troop somewhere in Belgium

The only time I saw Montgomery was, we were on the road and he was commin' through. It was a great thrill t' see him. He'd got his black beret on with his badges and he'd on a jersey - a commando jersey - just a fightin' man. Before Normandy he cleared out the unfit people, Officers especially. Officers who were over age or were a wee bit unfit.

(?): Our regiment - I'm not tryin' t' blaw or onything - but they musta thought a lot o' the 65th because there was two regiments before the war started but the other, 56th regiment, was disbanded after Dunkirk. We were kept goin' and we were the only North East regiment that landed on D-Day but I didna realise that our guns were the first guns there.

Charlie Low: Well, on D-Day I was drivin' a rations truck wi Johnny Taylor an' some o' the lads. We travelled and got this position and we were told t' stay there. We were being shelled but we didna have many casualties in fact I thought that we had it pretty easy gettin' ashore to be quite honest. It was just a case of gettin' organised and getting everything oot for the lads on the guns. We were lucky in a way 'cause we were gettin' shelled but I didn't think we were in dire danger.

David: Alex, how did you end up in the Fish troop in France?

Alexander Ross: I enlisted in 1938 in the Territorial Army. We knew there was going to be a war (the way young men thought at that time) and wanted t' do something about it. In 1939 I thought I was a member of the 56th medium regiment but it didn't happen that way. There

were too many of us and they formed a sister regiment the 65th Medium and I was delighted to go all through the war with my comrades of that regiment. We come off at Dunkirk - that was a nasty business - that was a defeat for the British army, no question. From there we defended the Northumbrian coast and kept training. From there we invaded the French coast at Normandy and that was quite a remarkable experience and I'm sure all my comrades would bear me out on that. We went all the way through, at each river crossing, the Seine, the Maas and the Rhine. I met my brother three times, he was a member of the 51st Highland Division. On two occasions we couldn't talk we just waved to each other. Things were moving fast. On the third occasion, before we crossed the Rhine, we managed an hour of a chat which was excellent. But t' be with the comrades here, we had comradeship and it's never been lost since then all the way through it all.

> **" I stood up in the front wi my Sten gun right across the lot o' them. "**

David: Johnston, what do you remember?

Johnston Duguid: We were the first artillery regiment to be in action after D-Day. Once we opened up with our guns the Jerries got the shock o' their blinkin' lives, they never expected for guns t' be firin' on them. We were firin' three shells to the minute when we got goin'. They weren't long finding out that we were the only regiment employed in counter battery fire and so they started poundin' us. They tried t' knock us out an' we tried t' knock them out, but we won most times. We got the works the second day we were there. A shell landed just outside the gun pit and broke the site gear at the side. So we phoned ordnance at the beach, or wherever it was, and they said that we were in luck; the small

A photograph showing a battery of S S' Gun Howitzer Carriages in an assembly bay at King's Works

In war or peace HENDERSONS productions for all-round efficiency

JOHN M. HENDERSON & Co Ltd
King's Works Aberdeen

Hendersons have been responsible for the production of many weapons. They have made ammunition hoists for destroyers, lifting jacks for bombers, anti-submarine devices, special cranes for mine-sweepers, boat traversing gears for aircraft-carriers and warships, parts of Bailey bridges, turret rings and bogie frames for Churchill tanks, 'plane propeller shafts, etc

Peacetime productions
Aerial Cableways, Cableway Dragline Excavators, Cable Drag Scrapers, Cranes of every description.
Write for new literature.

Page Thirty-six

Polsten guns had not come ashore yet (which were in demand for air defence) but they'd got a new gun for us. (Amazingly) it was a McKinnon's gun, (from Aberdeen), number 500; it was a brand new gun. Next day I went down t' the beach (and) left the old one where it was. They didn't want it, they jist left it. So that's the one that's <u>still</u> on Pegasus Bridge. Anyway, we picked up the new one from the beach and we fired about 10,500 shells before we'd finished.

There's one episode that I will always remember an' that was; we were in BHQ so I had t' take all these stores up to the gun positions. I was drivin', like, an' Bill Fraser he wis in the back. It was a 30 hundredwecht van - Bedford I think it was. There was a Bren gun mounted in the back o' the truck so I was drivin an' he was in the back wi the Bren gun. So, we got along es road then all o' a sudden a' these shells started fleein' aboot so I stopped an' I was in a ditch. Then, as the shells landed there was smoke commin' up. God, I thought it was gas so I shouted, "Gas! Gas!" But

● Above, Sergeant Johnston Duguid in 1939.
Below, Johnston (left) in 1994 beside his gun left at Pegasus Bridge

it wasna gas it was jist the smoke commin' off the shells but I thought we were fair away wi it that time. Anyway, I gets up an' there was Bill in the back with the Bren gun, he hadn't even moved! I've seen it bloody well snowin', freezin, an' a that, he'd <u>still</u> be there wi his Bren gun it probably werena even loaded!

David: You were involved in quite a lot of the major actions around the British sector then?

Johnston Duguid: We were just outside Caen at Colombelles and we shelled it over open sights. There were 13 chimneys which the Jerries used for observation posts so we had t' knock 'em down. We put shells through, unfused to explode on impact, but they just passed right through. We tried t' blow them up - we never did. We struck 'em and struck 'em and struck 'em but we never destroyed them.

We were in a cornfield facin' the enemy. They could see us an' we got bombed t' hell at that place. We were dug in and things like that. Anyway, at the corner o' this field was a little orchard an' a cottage and a barn. Well that was our HQ in there but we were never in this bloody barn except Dougie Davidson and somebody else. Well they came back. I said, "Where the hell y' been?" They mumbled some reply and just fell asleep they couldna do nothing. Anyway, there was this barrel and it was full of wine. The Officers there wouldna touch it in case the Germans had poisoned it but *they* had drunk it. But we had bottle fulls after 'at, aye

Dod: Were you there when the Fortresses came over an' bombed the factory?

Johnston Duguid: We were actually about a quarter of a mile from the factory in a straight line from it.

Aye, there was two 1000 bomber raids on et. That was the day we left when they were bombed out.

The Canadians were in the area as well so they took over Colombelles an' used it for a dump for all their equipment - trucks an' guns were stuck in there - the Yankees came over and bombed the bloody place again an' blew the hale lot up!

(?): A Spitfire shot doon a Fortress, that's the way they stopped the bombing. It cam owra an' shot doon the first Fortress doon.

David: Why?

(?): Because they were bombing our troops. Oh there was lotsa that!

Johnston Duguid: There was a sayin' 'We shell the Germans, the Germans run. The Germans shell us, and we run but when the Americans shelled, everybody runs!'. The Americans bombed the 51st when we were advancing into Caen. The Americans came over and bombed the Gordon Highlanders when they were walking in, there was a lot of Gordons killed there.

David: What was the relationship between the British and the Americans in your experience?

Johnston Duguid: Well, I'd say that it wasna very good. Y' couldna believe what y' heard from the Americans and y' couldn't believe what they did. They used t' boast what they did and what they didn't do. We were talkin' about that awful business with the American planes bombin' the Black Watch which was supportin' that area there then all of a sudden the infantry came along. I said, "What's the matter boys?" They said, "The bastards are bombin' us." All this in spite o' the fact that they had their markers out. An' that was typical o' the Yanks.

Dod: Y' see this here, (referring to a newspaper cutting of 4th August 1944) it sez 'American aircraft bomb Colombelles factory area.' That's efter we captured it! We aine troops were in it an' arthing! That's why the Spitfire shot at it! It wis Flyin' Fortresses.

Johnston Duguid: There were 13 chimneys at the factory and I fired at some o' them but the shells went right through. The day the Germans went every chimney went down. They did it themselves.

We didn't use fuses it was direct fire (shells exploding on impact) so the shells went right through. After the Germans had gone the Canadians came and occupied it. Then the Americans came over thinkin' the Germans were still there and the Canadians were bombed.

Dod: Here's another example; we were supportin' the 104th American Airborne Division. There was a big attack on Le Havre. The Americans were advancin' from Antwerp in Holland. They were walkin' and we were wis in an OP an' we watched these guys walkin'. We'd bin shellin' before these guys come along. There was also the West Riddin' Division - the 49th - an' the 4th Canadians. Now the Americans come along an' they said, "We're up t' help you lot out" - that wis usually their patter – an' we watched em an' Spencey sez, "Look at 'at idiots they're all gonna get killed." Sure enough, in no time there were heaps o' them gettin' shot doon. They were walkin' along as though they were on a picnic.

> "there was a sayin' 'We shell the Germans, the Germans run, the Germans shell us, and we run but when the Americans shelled, everybody runs!'"

● Drawing by J. Fleming of the Mulberry harbour, Arromanches. © G. Fleming

● The Fish Troop, 'somewhere in Holland'. Dod Martin holding a copy of Bon Accord. Clockwise from top left: Bob Jeffries, W.G. Fraser, D.M., Bill Prestcott, Bill Card, Unknown, Sgt. Bill Gunn, 'Butch' McLennan, Dod Pirie

David: You were put in charge of a concentration camp at Kleve ?

Dod: It had Red and White Russians in it. Because they were invadin' Kleve, they were comin' out an' cuttin' holes in the wire robbin' the shops an' shootin' the Germans. We were sent - about 30 of us – with an Officer that came from Malta.

Alex: Sacco.

Dod: Yes that was his name, Sacco. He was put in charge and we were there for about a week and we sorted 'em all out. Wis you there the day that the Russians attacked the woman with the pitchfork? Killed her. You wis ere 'at day?

(?): Aye, Aye

Dod: I wis ere anar. We catched the guys. We catched the guys in the efterneen. Y' see these Germans were in the fields cuttin' hay. There wis nae machinery, they wis usin' scythes. The Russians cam inaboot t' them afore we got there, robbed 'em then stabbed this man and killed the old lady with the pitchforks. We went doon wi four 'White' half tracks and we did what we could for them. But she was a gonner - well er bubbles o' blood was commin' outa her mouth - I've got photygraphs o' some o' the internees.

Johnston Duguid: The Red Russians were OK. I met a Russian in the toilet one day, he was full o' drink - they made their own drink - anyway, he started o' me so I give him one or two bumps on the chin an' that wis that!

Dod: That's when y' were fit! Ha, ha, ha!

Johnston: Anyway, we were there another week an' Sacco; we sorted 'em all oot. Dougie Davidson from Blacks buildin's he was a little bugger. He got orders from me that if onyone went near the wire he was t' put a bullet up through the vents to let them know what was right. We filled all the holes in the wire nettin' and they were all content. There were about 5000 of them. We organised dances and things like that. We had wer own dance band which came from Montrose anyway we organised things t' keep 'em quiet. Sacco had t' go away this particular day t' see somebody and all the bigshots cam up, a big General cam up an' a big car cam inaboot. I was just a Sergeant and I was in charge! Well, all the guards turned out an' everything went great. We shook hands and I got three days devotion t'duty for that!

Dod: Big deal 'at. Ha, ha! - The nearest I got t' bein in that situation was when the war was finished. At Delmenhorst there was a Spandau barracks there. There was a Sergeant, me drivin, and four men in the back an' we'd take residence in a German farm. Our job was to protect the Germans from the roving bands of escaped POW's. We'd go in the evening and stay the night and all the farmers had hooters because the 'displaced persons' were raiding the German Farms. They were roaming wild and raiding the farms for food. A siren would go then some of us would go out. But sometimes we wouldna. We felt that these people (the prisoners) had such a bad deal. They were starvin' maist o' the time an' they were tryin' t' get some food - an' good luck t' them! So sometimes we'd go out and sometimes we'd let them get on with it. We were quite sympathetic to them but they thought it was their right to kill the Germans which is wrong.

Alex: There was a farm at Kleve which was burnt out and we'd done all the firin' we had t' do an' we were more or less standin' idle and all of a sudden - there were corn stacks in them days - two Gordon Highlanders appeared! Where the hell had they come from? The truth was they had a shelter underneath where a corn stack was. From the regiment they had disappeared an' they had stopped there overnight and got lost. So, they came out an' they didn't know we were there an' they got the shock o' their lives!

Dod: Deserters!

Alex: Yes, and they had two guns. They *said* they'd got lost and just wanted t' return to their unit.

Dod: Mind you, I couldna blame nae guy fer desertin' some o' the actions they were in. The Gordons lost a lotta men in the rear guard actions. That young boys went through a lot.

Johnston Duguid: There was a regiment of German infantry seen goin' into a wood - our aircraft spotter had seen them, an unarmed light plane - and he phoned down that this regiment had gone into this wood. Well, I was the only gun in action, the rest were out of action; some were disabled, others were doin' maintenance an' things like that. We fired about 30 rounds into that wood. About two or three days after (that) we moved out, we went through that wood, there were dead lying all over the place. They were airburst shells. It was quite disturbing that.

Dod: When we wis movin' up t' the Siegfreid Line d' y' remember the amount o' Germans that wis lyin' at the sid o' the road deed?

Johnston: Aye an' as y' went through, the bodies were hangin' from the trees.

Dod: They were lyin' a' ower the place. The Commandos had been there an' strung (some of) them up in the tree after they had been killed. (They put up) a big notice up an' it said, 'This is the Siegfried Line'!

● British LCI's lining up for a landing. Courtesy J. Pelella

Frank Ledingham: We finished up in Messina and I was reserved for the Italian campaign. Then Montgomery told us that we were goin' home so we came back for the Second Front. We were back in Britain for Christmas 1943. We were in Harpenden to get presented with our African Star Ribbons only to start another battle with the Yanks over the ATS, WAAFS and Land Girls that were in abundance! We were then preparing for June 1944 and the D-Day landings. I was in the south of England then, doing trainin' and waterproofing trucks and that sorta thing. What is now the M11 was all lined up for Tilbury Docks and we went onto a 'liberty ship' and went doon through the Channel on the 4th o' June.

We were fired on and we got a shell from the Calais guns, which fell 100 yards astern but his distance was bang on. I had a wireless truck t' drive ashore, the one that I'd waterproofed and ready t' go but it was late, late, on before we could get stevedores to come on board to take them out o' the holds and on to the lighters. There were four of us on this LCT, an assault landin' craft (Landing Craft, Tank). We were jist commin' in when there was an aircraft raid. It was butterfly bombs they were using. The anti aircraft fire was colossal. It wis getting' dark and the sea wis bubblin' with the spent shrapnel falling down. The skipper of the landin' craft was an American, he stopped and told us that it was no use us goin' in there, so we eventually went in with only a wee bit o' water to go through.

So we got on to Sword Beach; there was nobody there! They had all drifted away down towards where they got off the beach. There wis nobody to take us off. Once we'd got the waterproof kit off ready for goin', Lieutenant Buchanan, he said he'd go down to see where we'd get off but when he went down the beach master told us that we couldn't get off tonight and that we'd have t' stay there all night and come off the next morning! This was D-plus-two!

Trevor: So it was two days later than planned?

Frank: Aye. The instructions were to follow Buchanan's map and go to this location and stop for nobody. If anybody tried to stop us we just had to carry on regardless. So we went out and we got up on to the road and there was a house and they were trying to get a little six pound anti-tank gun manoeuvred in the road t' blast this house. There'd been a sniper in it. Anyhow, I'd got to get past this without stoppin' so I went on and it was a good job we didna stop 'cause there were Germans everywhere. I then got to TAC Headquarters and got into a trench jist the other

side o' Pegasus Bridge in a defensive position. We were mortared there and a dispatch rider took me back to collect a wireless set complete wi power pack and take it out to this location at the 5th Seaforth's TAC HQ. I had t' go through a hedge with the wireless on ma shoulder and there was absolutely no one to be seen. I stood and looked and eventually I saw a wee curve in the ground and I thought there must be a signal office under here somewhere.

So I walked up and Sergeant Farr was standin' white as a sheet and I said, "This is the wireless for the armoured truck." He said, "It's over there in the hedge." Sure enough it wis in the hedge camouflaged up wi a net. So I went over to it and saw two operators in a slit trench and I said, "What's wrong wi ye wireless?" and he said, "Nothin', we're nae operatin' a wireless up there, you shoulda been here this mornin'". I said, "At five o'clock, was that you?" It was a terrific concentration of mortars that time. In fact I was scared in my slit trench, I didn't know it was them. Anyway, I said, "I'll see if I can put it underground." So I walked back over t' the signal office and out came a Lieutenant in his kilt not battle dress. He'd his tin hat on though and I asked him if he wanted the wireless underground. He said, "Well, we are under observation here and we might have t' move from here so I'll ask the CO." Just wi that there was a flash and a bang and I was on my back with the wireless and I'd landed right in the tracks where the armoured car had been. So I went like a snake along there and went right up and underneath the

> **"just wi that there was a flash and a bang and I was on my back with the wireless"**

armoured car. The driver Patsy Gallacher, he was under it as well and he said, "We had a fair do this mornin' and this is goin' t' be the same." He sez, "I'm countin', that's 36 mortars." That was very concentrated considering the little wee orchard we were in and they were still commin' in. Well, there were 42 mortars in all. I think there musta been two boxes of 25 or something like that

Trevor: Were there any casualties?

Frank: The mortar landed at the Lieutenant Hector's back so his kidneys and back we opened up, - there was six dead altogether. I says, "Well, I'm off." When I looked, the wireless set had got five holes in it and I got away without injury apart from a singing ear! So I went out through the hedge and there was the Jeep sittin' by it's self, no driver. There was a tree the other side of the road and there was a hole where the roots had grown up where you could get underneath and here's this face lookin' oot. I said, "Come on let's get outa here!" and he said, "Oh you drive." So I drove all the way back down to Pegasus Bridge and over a Bailey bridge.

The Paratrooper Padre was in front o' me on a little Corgi motor bike, well I sent him down the bank! A Redcap stopped me the other side o' the bridge and he said, "Did y' see what y' did?" I said,"Aye" then I started t' shake and the driver said that he would drive from then on. The driver told the Redcap what we'd come through but suggested that we go back and apologise to the Padre but the Redcap said, "No, it's OK I don't think he's awfa good at the motor bike ony way!"

That was the last really bad time but later we got shelled by those really big railway guns. What a noise! And what big holes they were takin' out. Luckily they were missin' by several 100 yards. Then we went right up and crossed the Rhine at Rees. Crossing the Wilhelmina Canal I had t' go out there into no man's land again with a speaker in m' bag which I connected ontil a pylon. Then I took a wire from it and led it down to an amplifier into a forward position dug-out and the Lieutenant - aye the intelligence lad who could speak Polish - he was tryin' t' get the Polish lads t' give up. (It would appear that in a number of campaigns the Germans employed Polish troops – see our section on Italy). That was at the Battle of Best.

At the end we liberated a concentration camp and the folk were jist like skeletons.

Trevor: Where about was that then?

Frank: That was at Bremervorde that was just at the end of the war. We passed Belsen but we didna stop there. We were to the left o' them and we went back up into Holland makin' for Bremerhaven and we finished outside Cuxhaven in Bremervorde. A day before the war finished I had to escort a woman and her daughter who (like all the other civilians) had been conscripted to dig graves to bury the dead of the concentration camp. She was a young lookin' dame but her husband, he wis about 55 and stout kind and she says, "Oh no y' can't take him he's got a bad heart." I said, "Oh, yes we can, he can dig like the rest of them". So they all went away in a truck to dig this mass grave.

At night the Sergeant came and said, "Here's a fine job for y' tak this dame and her mother hame." Because the Russians, when they got out of the concentration camp, they were jist mad and would have perhaps killed any Germans they could find. So, I took 'em right home and told them to bolt all the windows and doors and he said "I'll see you in the mornin'".

> ## "they had been conscripted to dig graves to bury the dead of the concentration camp"

Trevor: Was he inviting you to stay the night then?

Frank: Aye, then I said, "No way, with the war only one day finished and bidin' in the house o' a German. No way!"

The Russians who we had let out were like skeletons. They'd got sores on their hands and they came round and we were givin' them biscuits. A lad came up in a Jeep, some Intelligence Officer and shouting, "Don't feed the prisoners." It was killin' them because it was too much, they hadn't had food for so long.

On the 1st of September 1946, exactly seven years after I was called up from Hendersons, I returned to finish my apprenticeship there. All told it took me 14 years to serve my time as an engineer!

Miss Allan: I thought I was going to be posted to the desert but I was going to be a bridesmaid to one of my friends. She was a great pal of the matron so she wouldn't let me go to the desert she wanted me to be there for the wedding, so I never went to the desert. There was great friendliness amongst us, we worked together and it was a good unit. We were shifted out to a place called Helmich which was a few miles north of Cairo. Although we were posted there we weren't working there, we were just sort of gatherin' together on our way home where we were supposed to go to the Second Front. I came home in November or December and I decided to ask for a home posting. So I asked for a home posting, so where did I get sent to? Aldershot! I hated it, it was so regimented and when you went into Aldershot you were supposed to salute all that troops and it didn't go down well with me, so I requested to go away again and I landed up in a hospital ship.

We started off and it was D-Day plus 1. We were supposed to start off on D-Day but it was such terrible weather, the boats were getting loose from their anchors. We set sail for Caen just off the beaches but all of a sudden what a blooming bang! This was us landing in a mine field (sic)! It was our intention to get to Caen (via the) Arromanches beaches but now we were unable to take on casualties because we were out of action because of the mine damage. But the boys - if anybody deserved medals - their boats were sunk and they were on platforms for the troops to get across and get into the landing craft and they'd come across to our boat and ask where they were. They'd no idea where they were and yet they were going away to fight and they were soaking, I used t' feel sorry for the loons.

Although we couldn't take injured, there were other ships that could and they were taken back to somewhere like Southampton, or somewhere that there were beds. However, we were lucky and before you could cough one of the smaller boats came along side and took us on, then took us to the beaches. Unfortunately through the night they started to shell Caen.

Our matron wasn't a regular matron and she said that we could go upstairs (on the ship). The Officers were very good, they gave us their cabins and we lay on the floor and all the rest of it. So the others went away up the stair whilst the shelling was going on in Caen. We didn't go up because our matron said that if we were going to be sunk we would be nearer the water! Anyway, we eventually went from Cherbourg, on to a landing craft and back to near Portsmouth. So, we got our boat sorted and off we started again and blow me if we didn't hit something else! So back we went. However, we eventually plied between Southampton, Cherbourg, Dieppe and Mulberry Harbour (Arromanches). The work was similar to that which we did in Cairo but we had to try and get dressings done before we set sail from the pick up point because the Channel could be very rough.

Later I was posted to Norway and spent six months there. We were right up in the north at the top and one day we were taken on a trip to see the German pocked battle ship the *Tirpitz*, which had been sunk near Murmansk. And who took us to see the *Tirpitz*, two Germans! We got absolutely soaked!

Trevor: How could there have been two Germans?

Miss Allan: Well, by this time the war was over and we'd had VJ and VE day. Although we had little to do with the Germans they were always respectful and gave us our place.

Trevor: Which was the nicest place you visited when you got away on leave?

Miss Allan: Well, y' see we'd no money and if we went away we would come back broke. But we would go up to Alexandria or up to Palestine and Syria. Apart from not having any money we had good times.

I was a patient for a while, I had jaundice which was very prevalent. That and dysentery. One of the Colonels used t' say to the boys, "Do you know why you've got dysentery?" "No sir." So he said, "Well, the flies don't wipe their feet before they go onto your food!" Oh, it was true. So, some of them were quite ill. It was quite sad.

● The hospital ship 'St. Julian', on which Miss Allan served, berthed at the Mulberry Harbour

The lads had very little comfort, - that was another thing; hand towels and bath towels, the troops went away with the towels, I'm sure they did. But what did it matter, it was for a good cause. We'd inventories and the lad that did it would say, "It's your ward again." We had the bulk of them, I can't remember the numbers but there was a back stair and when we knew there was an inventory we used t' set out all our stuff. We knew fine we were short but we went upstairs and got more from there by sneaking up this back stair!

Davey Adam: From Sicily we got on to an American boat. What a rare boat, it was a cruiser and we went back to Britain to a camp called Chalfont St. Giles near Slough. We were thrown into this camp, the Yanks wouldna bide intil it. It was built o' stone and it was cold. Oh no, they had t' get better billets. What a bunch they were! They got awar wi murder ower here. I did some more trainin' for a couple o' weeks then back t' the vash camp.

Val Plante: How long had you been away altogether?

Davey: Aboot two years but I got a pass for about a fortnight in between t' get hame.

The next thing was D-Day. Then from Chalfont St. Giles we went down t' Tilbury Docks. The 6th Airborne and the Americans were in fields. They musta been in bivies but I canna mind. The next thing we were on the boats and goin' over for D-Day which was actually put back a day because the

weather wis that bad. So, it started on the 6th rather than the 5th o' June. When we went over it wis the efterneen and we missed the worst but let me tell ye. I'm standin' on the LCI an' I'm lookin' at the boys aboot a 100 yards away. All ye could see wis their heeds an' their bonnets. I sez, "I'm nae goin' aff on 'at, there's no way I'm goin' aff on that because I'll get drowned, I canna swim." The Officer sez, "Come on Adams!" and I said, "No way, you can go away." So, he went away. So I'm standin' on the side o' the boat holdin' the wire that's meant to keep y' steady. The next thing I kens is, Ping! Es bullet gis right atween my legs and hut the back o' the boat! So, I wis down the stairs and I sez, "Well they can tek me back and get me Courts Marshalled I'm still nae goin off on that!" Y' see you had t' go off doon a ladder on the front o' the LCI intae the water. Somebody shouted if there wis anybody wanting off and I sez, "Yes but not intae the water." "Come on we'll take you off." The Mulberry Harbour - maybe you've heard o' that - well there was a bit o' that and he sez, "Come awar." An' I steps on t' this thing, got onto the beach and I was bone dry.

I walked along the beach and there were two rows, as far as the eye could see o' dead bodies wi ground sheets on them. So I gid up past that hoose which is on a' the photographs showin' the British goin' up and caught up wi the boys. What we then had t' dee was, the Canadians had gone that far up that they had run outa petrol for their tanks. So we had t' ging in front o' them wi a petrol tanker which was no good to anybody. It wis like sittin' on a bomb!

That was some time D-Day and efter 'at. I canna mind much aboot it but gee - anyway, we went up to this box place. The 6th Airborne was lyin' doon the river and we had t' ging up an' consolidate them. They'd deen their job and they were on their way back.

Trevor: Was this near Pegasus Bridge?

Davey: Coulda been aye but I'm nae jokin' y', y' didna ken far the shell wis comin' fae. The Jerries were on a' sides on yer, all roond about ye. Then, as far as I can mind, we went doon into es village we crossed the road and I canna mind the name, but we were stickin' oot like a sair thumb an' Jerry didna like es, us bein' oot frae the line. We wis there for aboot a couple o' days then all of a sudden there was - "Come on, get movin' get outa this!" and we had t' run back t' wer line. Jerry wis attackin' us in force but we jist made it back. The next thing I ken was that we moved and we were over lookin' this great big shoe factory in Caen. Y' could see the Jerries goin' along this road, nae bother. It wis aboot two mile awar. Anyway I wis nearly killed there again, stupid me.

There was the Seaforths and the Camerons and they made an attack. They hanna got dykes along their fields they'd got trees and silly me I decided t' hae a look. I was company runner and stood

● Davey Adam

next t' the company commander so I picked up his glesses. He wis awar t' see some body an' the next thing I ken a bullet lands at m' blummin' feet! Pissshoo! I thought, "Get back in the hole. I didna think there wis any Jerries left!" It had bin a sniper. There'd been a few times I'd been lucky like 'at.   Next was the Falaise gap and that's where I got wounded. On the 12th o' August we were swathin' a path to meet Patton who was circlin' roond so we could capture a' this Jerries. The Yanks got the credit fer that but we wis dein a bitty anar. There wis ae things like 'at, the Yanks wis ae forgettin' that we did our part. They were the ones that won the war. But we ae had t' gie 'em a hand. Anyway, I got wounded. The bit's still in ma back. Fit happened was, we gings doon and we were all in es village called St. Sylvia (St. Sylvain). We had t' ging up es hill and up on the top was a great big forest o' trees. Jerry was in there. We had about five or six tanks on baeth sides o' the fields and when we got up the top there was a Tiger tank. We managed t' knock out one o' his tracks so he couldna move but other than that a Tiger against a Sherman was like a flippin' fly against a spider. Anyway, we get up there and oh, what a time, I'm nae jokin' ye! They had a bit swathed through the trees about 30 feet wide. Then they were in trenches and they wouldna come oot. Well, I was company runner and there wis two Jerries and they come over and

my Company commander sez to tek them back. I gets em in this clearin' and the Sergeant Major shouts, "Adams! Stop these two!" 'cause they wanted t' search them. I said, "I'm nae stoppin' here, no way." 'cause they were firin' rifle grenades. Well this een landed. The two Jerries were here and the Sergeant was there. This is nae a word o' a lie, I don't know how I got awar wi it but I did. It landed there just t' the left o' ma and I jist saw one o' the Jerries drappin' like a log. I looks roond and all I sees was the Sergeant Major with his heed split wide open. I felt the blast in m' leg which wis a bitty numb so I ran over to where the Company commander was, "You'd better awar and see t' y' Sergeant Major he's been badly hurt over there." but he asked me what was up wi me. I'd felt es bit, it wis right where y' jacket meets yer troosers there's a couple o' buttons t' fit on y' troosers for y' battle dress. It was jist aboot there. So I sez "I dina ken fits a do wi me but ma back's awfa numb." He sez,"Oh, you've bin hit, where's y' field dressin'?" "It's in ma pocket. Will I have t' go back Sir?" "Oh no, I'm afraid you're oot o' this!" was his reply. So I gets doon and there's a jeep and I gets on es jeep. We were on the main road and suddenly this 75 pounder (sic) starts firin' at us. If he'd hit us weeda bin splattered all over France. So he drove like hell t' get oot o' it. Anyway, that day the Yanks had bombed the Canadians silly wi B17s.

● Pegasus Bridge

● The 'Bocage' country in Normandy. Courtesy the Tank Museum

They'd got pom-pom guns shootin' at the Yanks and the Typhoons were goin' in amongst 'em and tellin' them if they didna stop they'd shoot them doon. We were across the road and there were huge bomb craters in the road an' I was as sick as a dog. Well we gets doon t' the advanced position and inta the tent an' I wis sick so I went out side and a nurse followed me oot and said, "What's a do wi you?" "I've got a bit o' shrapnel in m' back." "What! Walkin' wounded! You shoulda been on a stretcher." I sez, "Well – er - I wis only…" "I don't want no excuses." She said, "You should have been on a stretcher." Well, that was alright and then I got x-rayed, bathed and put t' bed, that wis fine.

Val: Did y' get your leg done as well?

Davey: No, that was jist the blast fae the grenade. Well I lay there, how lang I canna mind but the next thing was, "You're goin' awar back t' Blighty." "Oh", I sez, "That's great. May be I'll finish up so that I won't have t' come back." They were feart that the shrapnel wis touchin' ma kidney. It wis only the size o' a sixpence and it's still in my back noo. So I wis took doon t' this tank landin' craft. There was a lot o' wounded on it. I eventually landed up in Cherry Knowles (sic) in Sunderland and fae there to another hospital in the Borders then I got back to Aberdeen 'cause my sister died.

Efter about two or three weeks I got word t' go back to the barracks in Edinburgh. The next thing was I was shipped over t' France. Do you remember the film 'The Longest Day'? Well, the 6th Airborne got slattered there. Well, we were in Eindhoven and we had to go up and try to give the 6th Airborne a hand but it wis too late. We went

up to Nijmegen Bridge and then up in to Belgium. It's winter now and at the time o' Battle o' the Bulge. The Yanks say they won that, dinna believe 'em. We had t' come doon a' the way fae Belgium right doon. I've got a photey of Esnoo and Ardennes. The next thing we were on 'em, we went that fast that the Yanks had a place they caed the killin' ground. The Jerries were runnin' and the Yanks had their guns trained on this place and they had 'em trained on us! We'd gone that fast that they didna ken we were in there! Oh gee, what a bunch they were.

Val: Did you get shelled though?

Davey: No, we didna get shelled but they only jist stopped in time. They would have if we hadna stopped. We gave them a good hand then t' get rid o' the Jerries. Fae there we went back up t' Belgium again and up into Goch. Now this village Goch, that was on the border o' Germany and the Allied forces had bombed it flat and y' couldna get moved with all the rubble. Jerry had got these SP guns in an' they were nae mair than half a mile awar and by the time the shell was outa the gun it was on ye. It was a disaster 'at.

Jist t' let y' know, these SP guns were 88's mounted on tracks and oh boy they were mean. We got into the square at Goch and we were sneakin' by and there were snipers and the boy that had the Bren gun wis jist in front o' me. Ping! Next thing I knew he wis down, he wis killed. Eventually we got through Goch and up to Delmenhorst. That was declared an open city by the Germans because they'd got that much wounded in it. I got bleezin' drunk in there. We went intil es distillery and there wis vats, great big vat barrels and we were takin' a suppy o' this. But we couldna cery onything because we were on the move all the time. I did take some little dagger swastikas an' they were jewelled and I had a chenille cover. It was a beautiful thing. There were one or two other things I canna mind now. After Delmenhorst we went t' this place and we were lyin' in the street. It was a bonny place and all of a sudden it came through, "The war is finished!" Well, we were goin' to attack Bremenhaven the next day but the war had finished. We thought some body wis kiddin' us but somebody else shouted again, "Oh yes, the war's finished, it's been finished for two hours!"

When the war was finished and I wis commin' hame and we went intil Belgium and intil a barracks 'ere for the night and we were goin' home on the ferry the next day. Es fella he sez t' me, "Commin' oot t' night?" but I sez, "Na, I dinna fancy it." He sez, "Come awar, come on." "Ha well, ok." I wished I'd never gone now. I had a big clip thing that y' fitted a lock on til. But that didna stop 'em. A knife ripped open the top o' ma kit bag. Stole everything oot o' it, even my great coat.

Trevor: Who would that have been?

Davey: Oh, the Belgians, they jist come in an' nicket a' they could. I had 't pay for a flippin' great coat fen I got hame!

The 51st Highlanders were on the go all the time and I woulda been at it continuously (apart from a 52 hour pass in Brussels) and the fact that I was wounded.

Sandy McKenzie: After the Italian campaign we were sent from Taranto back to Blighty to train and re-equip for D-Day. We went to Chalfont St.Giles in Buckinghamshire for trainin' for D-Day and we were issued with new vehicles. They were British Ford V8's and wer job at that time was waterproofing the engines. That meant the distributor and the leads had to be sealed with waterproof tape and the plug holes had t' be filled with some putty like stuff. Then that had t' be taped up. The carburettor had t' be tapped right round and see that the accelerator parts were not jammed. The air cleaner had to come off and a piece of corrugated piping added on. The brake drums had t' be sealed up. Then we had t' tested in about three feet o' water. All this was jist in case we were dumped on the beach in the water but lucky enough we didna need that and as I say, we went right off and up the beach.

David: When and where did you land?

Sandy: D-Day plus 1 at Arromanches. There was a lot of shellin' and boats bein' hit and down they went. There were lots of smoke and the support ships, probably the *Rodney* and the *Nelson* they were firing back. Oh, it was horrible! Bein' away from active service then back again, you'd had enough be this time.

The counter attack woulda started at about five o'clock in the mornin' I think. It wis the multiple mortars - 'Moanin' Minnies' we called them - and they fired right down into the ditch to where we were with their Spandau's. Some of the boys got shot and wounded. Two stretcher-bearers went out to get them - Red Cross - and I think they shot his flag. They then opened up with the machinegun and jist split him right down with gun fire. At night we had to go back a bit across Pegasus Bridge again.

David: Tell me which was the worst one you can remember? Was it the occasion when you got the MM.

Sandy: Well, there were short and sharp skirmishes - over night affairs - with maybe five of six casualties. There was mortar fire and we were in a jeep at that time. It was a Company commander's personal vehicle. It had a couple of irons front and back which you could hang a couple o' stretchers on. The drivers eardrums had burst or some such like and I had t' take over.

The Company was up in front and it was Canadian Company commander at this time. You couldna get across the canals because the bridge was blown. However the Company got across with two or three rubber dinghies. There must have been some information passed back. The Germans knew the range that these Royal Engineers were workin' at. It wisna jist pitch dark and they had search lights that they beamed right up and it was like the moon comin' through a cloud so it was nae jist absolutely dark. The Germans peppered the place wi shells. There was an old buildin' in which I was takin' refuge and this Officer named Orton came up and asked me to take this injured fella back to our own regimental post. So I took him back then drove back to the bridge and there were another two waitin' to be taken back. I bandaged them up as best as I could then I took him back to the regimental first aid post where the Doctor gave them morphine.

David: You are being very calm about it but apparently you were being heavily shelled and mortared.

> " it wis the multiple mortars - 'Moanin' Minnies' we called them "

● British crewed Sherman tanks approaching the Rhine. Courtesy the Tank Museum

Sandy: Well y' jist did it; 'grin and bear it' as they used t' say. The engineers put a couple o' dinghies in this stream and a couple o' planks, jist like scaffolding planks they were, and you had t' straddle y' vehicle on this. I thought I was goin' to go doon in the water but no, no they held y' up. So that's they way we took the casualties back. But this fella he wis badly hurt and I had t' strap him onto the stretcher, he wis in agony. Then I went back for the other two. That was in October so we went on up towards the Ardennes.

David: When did you get injured yourself then?

Sandy: That was after the Ardennes in March. With the Ardennes we had t' wait for hours and hours at the roadside. It was cold miserable and wet and the Christmas dinner had t' be cancelled. Then when we got up it was near the Herz mountains and we were in this village, there was snow and what a frost! We were there a few days policin' the area. On patrol, we went doon this street and we come on this half track and in it were eight bodies. They musta got a direct hit. There were four on each side sittin' on the benches and they were frozen stiff. That was the time of the flyin' bombs and we saw them going across they woulda been launchin' them further up I suppose. They were the ones with a flame at it's tail. V1's, that's what they were called. Anyway, when I got injured at the time we were takin' prisoners. There were stretcher-bearers - oh they were guy lads - they were on the jeep with their arms up and they were handin' them over to the Military Police. That was commin' back from the cross roads, we were goin' up when this jist German shell hit it, burst the petrol tank. I got a wound in here and in the groin. I drove on until the petrol in the tank came

all oot and I had t' run and hop like a shot rabbit efter 'at. Some o' them were wimmin' in the hoose they were Jerries. I was nae afa keen on them puttin' on bandage and stuff. However the ambulance came and I was taken right doon to the casualty clearance station. Then I got my first operation. That was on the Friday and the next one was on the Sunday. That was down around Bruges. I don't remember that much about it 'cause I was awfa doped up and dazed. The shrapnel musta hit the jeep on the panel about here. The petrol tank was here and y' sat on the top o' het. There was a bitty folded up like 'at. It must have come through the panel, we were lucky it didna go on fire. The passenger was uninjured and the jeep jist went a few yards and there musta been a big hole, I don't know. Anyway, when I pressed down the accelerator there was no response 'cause the petrol tank had burst.

Lord Forbes: During the winter of 1944, I suffered a bad attack of bronchitis resulting in the Battalion Medical Officer saying I must go to the Field Hospital near Amiens. After being in the tented Field Hospital for three days, the Medical Officer in charge said that I was fit to be discharged but that I should not rejoin the Battalion for 48 hours, and during that period I could do anything I liked. It so happened that the hospital was very close to the supply airfield. Having walked over to the airfield where I soon met up with a Canadian pilot who said he was about to fly to Northolt and asked if I would like a lift. This suited me admirably as I knew Rosemary was living and working in London. I jumped into the Dakota and sat amongst mail bags for the flight. On landing at Northolt I said good-bye to the Canadian pilot, who assured me I should have no difficulty in hitching a lift back to Amiens. I then telephoned Rosemary, who was working at the Red Cross Headquarters in Belgrave Square and luckily found she was in, so we met and were able to spend the night together. Next morning she accompanied me to the gates of Northolt airfield where she had to leave me, as civilians were not permitted to enter without a pass.

Once in the airfield I went to the Officers' Mess to enquire about a lift back, and was told that this would be no problem. However, I was horrified to hear that the Army Supply Base had been moved from Amiens, but the congenial RAF Station Commander reassured me that he would soon find something flying to Amiens or nearby. This proved to be somewhat optimistic. I waited all morning without any news, then the Station Commander invited me to have lunch in the Officers' Mess where he introduced me to a young Spitfire pilot, who had been shot down when operating from France and was about to ferry an Auster plane back to France. The pilot said he could easily go via Amiens. This seemed almost too good to be true, and after lunch both of us climbed into the little one-engined aircraft, the smallest plane in use by the services. It was used by the Army for spotting.

The Auster could hold a pilot and a spotter, who sat immediately behind him. As we were strapping ourselves in, my pilot friend announced that never before had he flown an Auster, however he thought it would be quite simple as it would be much the same as driving a baby Austin car; both the car and the aircraft were absolutely basic!

Having found out how the controls worked, the pilot started the engine by swinging the propeller blade and off we set without any trouble. Almost at once he announced we would land at Lydd as Austers could only carry a very limited amount of fuel, so he would re-fuel there. Having landed at Lydd and refuelled the pilot asked control for permission to take off. It was then that he was told orders had been received that no Auster was to cross the Channel unescorted, as recently some had been lost, either through enemy aircraft action, or through running out of fuel if there was a head wind. We were told we would have to wait till a number of light aircraft had assembled and then an RAF escort would be provided; this might be in two or three days' time. My heart sank. However, without a word more, my splendid pilot pretended he was taking the plane to a parking bay but instead suddenly headed for the runway, and in a minute we were speeding for our take off.

We crossed the Channel without any difficulty and saw France beneath us. It was then that the

pilot pulled out a map and said he would head for the nearest airfield, which we did, only to find that it had been well cratered by bombs. Out came the map again, and we headed for another airfield, only to find that it too was cratered. It was then that the pilot announced we were about to run out of fuel so we simply must land. Almost at once he looked over the side of the plane and asked me whether I thought the field below us looked reasonably flat. I replied that I had not got a clue, as I had no experience of looking at fields from the air. The next thing was the flaps went down and we were heading for a landing in the field.

We touched down without incident, but in running along the field we did have one big bump which made me wonder whether we would nose-dive into the field or take off again. However, we did neither and soon the undamaged plane came to a halt. Then, to our horror, out of the blue a French farmer appeared wielding a hay fork in a hostile manner, thinking we were Germans, so quickly we made it abundantly clear we were not German. We then found we had come down in a field which was quite close to a road carrying a lot of army transport, so we went over and stopped the first army lorry we saw. Luckily it had a spare Jerry can of petrol which the driver agreed to put into the aircraft tank. Again it was fortunate that the aircraft would run on any petrol, so the Jerry can was perfectly adequate to enable the pilot to complete his journey.

I was now back with the 1st Battalion for the great advance through Belgium, leading to the liberation of Brussels by the Guards Armoured Division. For those of us who had marched through Brussels in 1940 on the way back to Dunkirk there was a certain nostalgia. There was a race for Brussels between the Grenadiers and the Welsh Guards Units, which was just won by the latter. On entering Brussels at daybreak, there was a considerable amount of sniping from Germans, with the result that we were ordered to consolidate an area of the city before moving on. The area allotted to the Battalion contained a vast German store having, amongst other things, cases and cases of champagne. The result of this was that not only did everyone, including all the Guardsmen, have champagne for breakfast, but later we filled up any half empty Battalion lorries with crates of champagne for future use. I think that Peter Carrington, a Squadron Commander in our 2nd Battalion, showed the greatest initiative. He left Brussels with 21 cases strapped to the back of his tank. He later said 'It gave me quite a taste for warm champagne.'

In Brussels we had a great reception from the

> "it was cold miserable and wet and the Christmas dinner had t' be cancelled"

● A German Panzer IV photographed by Sgt. J. Duguid in Arnhem

population, who had last seen the British Army retreating westwards towards Dunkirk. From Brussels we continued to spearhead the advance through the lovely area of hardwoods to the east of the city, and then on through Louvain into Holland, where we met stiff opposition at Nijmegen. Here we captured intact the last vital bridge before Arnhem, where the Germans had decided to make a stand. The leading troops to take the bridge were Peter Carrington's Squadron of tanks from the 2nd Battalion supported by my Motor Company from the 1st Battalion.

Montgomery's plan was to take the town and bridge at Arnhem with an airborne landing, with the idea that once the paratroops were established the Guards Armoured Division should advance and link up with them. However, the Germans were holding Arnhem in such strength that the airborne plan failed. It was at Arnhem that my Sandhurst room neighbour, Digby Tatham-Water, led his men on to the bridge wearing a bowler hat and carrying an umbrella. After the war I was not altogether surprised to find Digby in Kenya, as I do not think a conventional life in the United Kingdom would have suited him.

Jack Kilgour: Because I had completed a M.T. course (Motor Transport), I was instructed to accompany Idle - a lad from Leeds - on his motorcycle. This 'bike had developed an engine problem which oiled up the spark plug regularly every 25 or so miles at which point the machine had to be stopped, cooled and the plug cleaned. We were thus well behind the rest of the unit who were making their way to Brest in Holland.

As we were travelling through Son (Zon) we made one of our scheduled stops for a smoke and a bit of cleaning up. We noticed, however, a profusion of HD signs (Highland Division) and one indicated that our unit had been held up and

were billeted nearby. Sadly, by the time we arrived all the accommodation had been taken but we were given orders that since we had a 'bike we could find our own. I suggested to Idle that we go back a little way to the turning we had passed where we had seen no army vehicles, there had been a shop there that I felt might be able to help us. At the corner of the Njimagen road was the shop - a butcher's, I decided to ask if they knew of somewhere we could stay. The owners - a family called Schutjes - invited us to stay with them and whilst they lived in the cellar we were given the master bedroom upstairs. Eindhoven power station at that time was working at quarter capacity, having been blown up by the retreating Germans. As a result the Dutch were only allowed limited consumption. For our family this meant burning one 100-Watt bulb or four 25-Watt bulbs in the evening. Obviously they had the light in the living room and for that reason Idle and I began to spend considerable time downstairs with them. Now it had been our intention to spend three days in these digs but as it happened we spent three weeks with them! I found that with my Buchan accent I could understand them and they me; furthermore, Karol, one of the three sons, could speak French, which I also had a good knowledge of. At the end of the stay Frau Schutjes gave me a note to pass on to her fourth daughter living in an adjacent village - that of Schijndel - and through which we were to pass during the next few days. They then bid us a fond farewell.

The army vehicles at that time travelled slowly; we would do 10 miles then halt, another two then halt again. At one of these halts we found ourselves in the village of Schijndel wherein the woman had said that her daughter, Cato, lived. I decided to try to find out whether I could find her in this bombed and shell-blasted ruin and spying a man with an orange armband (signifying Dutch Resistance) I called him over to get assistance. In my finest Dutch (?!) I asked him about the daughter to which he replied "yes, I know her and she is here!". "Where is she?" I asked; "Here" he said pointing to the house we were parked next to, "Here in this cellar!".

The Dutchman called out for Cato and I gave the letter - it was all very emotional -s he scribbled something on the back of it and implored me to take it to her family even though this was obviously impossible for me to do. The unit moved on and after another few miles encamped beside a seminary in a wood. I gave the note some thought and decided to ask permission from my commanding Officer to deliver it to the family. His reply was, not unnaturally, a point blank refusal but he added "We leave at 10 tomorrow morning, if you can get out and back by then, I don't know anything

about it; if you get caught I don't know anything about it!". The encampment was well cordoned with a guard piquet all around it, however I managed to push the 'bike through the wood undetected and set off. On the way the battery became disconnected from the 'bike and I had to rev the machine to get any beam at all from the headlights - this had implications later since it meant that I decided to stay the night with the family rather than get shot at by our guards when travelling towards them on an unlit vehicle. In no time I was back in Son with the Schutjes and they were ecstatic with relief; I was feted and was told in no uncertain terms by the mother that I was now part of the family - I was even offered a job in the family meat business for after the war, a job which although I declared I knew nothing about was told that I could be the book-keeper!

After the war I made a point of returning to my family in Holland and although the old lady died a few months before the visit, I was met at the station by one of the daughters. I arrived just at the time the district was preparing for a local festival - with banners and flowers and various other regalia - and was pleased to be part of such a happy event after all the horror. What I didn't realise was that the festival was all for me! All for the first allied soldier to return to Eindhoven after the cessation of hostilities, Jack Kilgour!"

● 'My billet in Emmerich', painting by I. Fleming. © C. Fleming

● British Victory parade in Berlin, 1945
  Courtesy J. Palella

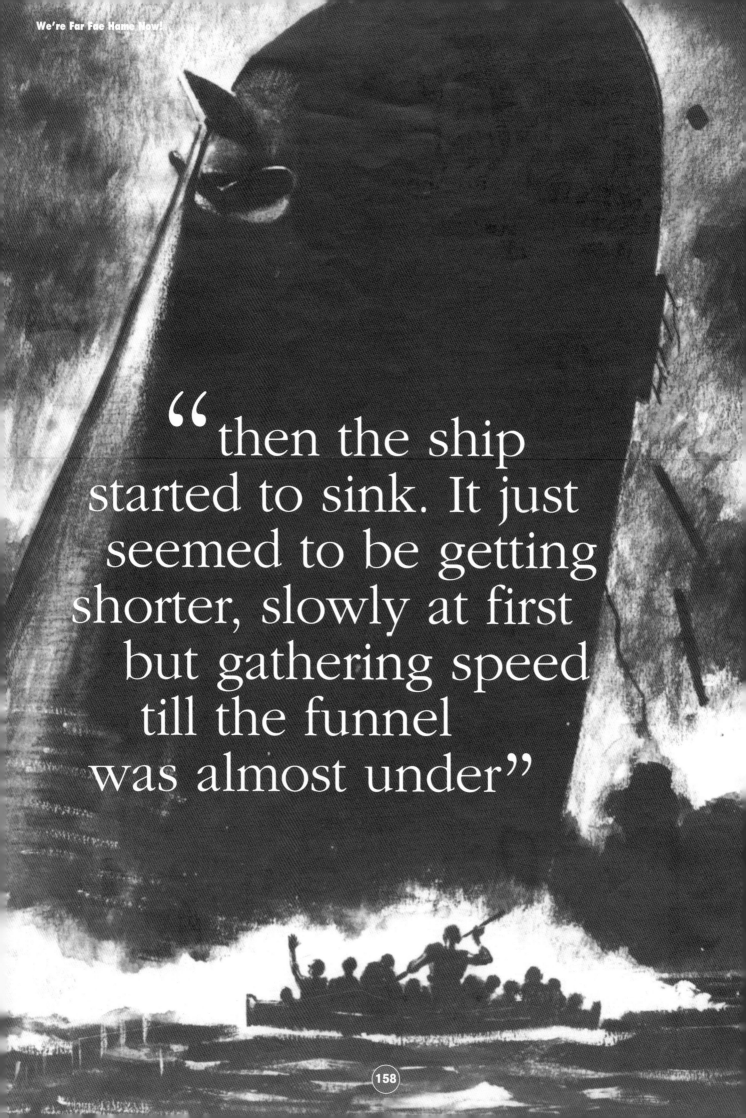

"then the ship started to sink. It just seemed to be getting shorter, slowly at first but gathering speed till the funnel was almost under"

At Sea

AT SEA THE WAR CONTINUED WITH UNABATED FEROCITY. *This letter was contributed by Miss Mackie whose brother was torpedoed in 1941 in the Atlantic off the coast of Africa.*

573696 Cpl. Mackie,
RAF GHQ,
SIERRA LEONE
WEST AFRICA.

Saturday 19th JULY 1941.

Dear Mam,

Here I am still to the fore. At present we are right in the middle of Sierra Leone at a town called Bo, (It was called BO before the Lifebuoy soap company started their latest advertisements) However this may be a fairly long story so I'll start at the beginning. Once upon a time, well, you see, it's like this (No, it's not the heat that's supposed to be funny (ha ha) not funny (peculiar). Anyway, we went to Wilmslow to be equipped with our tropical gear and spent a week in the tents there. After that we went by train to ZXXXXXXX from where we were introduced to our boat, stuck on board and told to stay there or get shot. We sailed to Glasgow and sailed with four corvettes to look after us. The Irish Sea was as calm as - well it looked as if somebody had ironed it. However, the Atlantic was a bit different, but it wasn't bad at all. After a few days it got a bit rough, and a lot of the blokes were pretty seasick. I avoided that by eating as much as possible. The old boat, a converted merchantman wallowed on at a steady speed and we were just beginning to get fed up when the escort started depth-charging a Sub. We never saw it, though it was confirmed as sunk. That, however was very tame compared with the next morning when a sub. Thought we would be a fine target for a couple of torpedoes. That was at half-past five and we were all sound asleep in the hammocks we had just learned to be comfortable in, when they hit us. I fell out of mine on to the floor and woke up as it is about six feet off the

deck. The lights went out and blokes were yelling, screaming, and shouting, and the water was roaring as it rushed in. I looked round, got my lifebelt and climbed up the hatch, as the explosion had blown the cover off. Then Curly Baker (my new "oppo") and myself doubled smartly for our Boat stations. Our position was up on the boat deck. The screaming and shouting had died down and from the boat deck we could see all that went on. We then found that were stationed on the top deck to lower all the boats. Nobody had thought of telling us before, and we certainly didn't know how. The first boat was so heavy (about 70 blokes in it) that the rope on one end slipped and it went into the water end first, turned over spilling all the blokes into the Atlantic. One of the crew came to the rescue and showed us all the art of lowering a boat and we lowered the next one quite successfully. The ship had had a decided list and we thought it

● Above, explosion of a depth charge.
Below, German submarine surrendering to
British naval vessel.

● Left: Drawing by J. Fleming. © G. Fleming

● J. Fleming. © G. Fleming

might get worse and turn over. However it straightened up and started to sink by the nose. The stern coming up further and further up out of the water. By the time a corvette had come up with her nose to our stern and a lot of blokes jumped the gap. It soon had to withdraw as the stern rose too high, and they were scared that our ship might do something funny. We had lowered five or six boats, including two overturned when it gave a lurch and the forecastle slipped under as a wave came rushing up the deck and broke against the upperworks. The chief steward came around and told us we hadn't time to lower any more boats and to abandon ship if we valued our skins. Well, we did value them so I took a look at the water and it seemed a terrific distance down. However, the ropes that had lowered a boat were hanging down from the davits and I did the Tarzan act. I took a run and jumped out over the side and caught them. I slid down quicker than I ever went down a rope before, and caught hold of the pulley block. The ship was about twice as far out of the water as normally where I was (in the centre). The front part was all under and the stern was sticking up in the air. I dropped into the good old Atlantic and swam for the nearest boat. I wished it was nearer, but when I got on it I wished it was farther away, as we were almost under the stern and smoke floats started to fall off round us. They are

> ❝ by this time the ship was standing vertical on its nose, sticking three quarters out of the water ❞

in an iron casing and must weigh some 3 or 4 hundredweight each. If one had hit our little boat it would have knocked at least half a dozen blokes through the bottom and the rest would have gone swimming again. By this time the ship was standing vertical on its nose, sticking three quarters out of the water like the tower at the Exhibition, and we were far close to it to feel comfortable. Rowing a heavy boat with four oars and about 40 or more blokes is a very slow business so we hardly seemed to move away at all. Then the ship started to sink. It just seemed to be getting shorter, slowly at first but gathering speed till the funnel was almost under. The water reached the furnace and there was a hissing boom and grey steam and smoke poured out of the funnel, but only for a second or so as the Atlantic claimed the rest. Looking up we could see the rudder lying on one side and the propeller getting bigger as it came down from where it had no right to be. We expected to be sucked down with it but there was a bit of an anti climax. The stern made a little ripple which nearly swamped us and disappeared. We could hardly believe that a ship had been there as it didn't even leave a hole. The rest is pretty tame I'm afraid but we didn't think it funny. The corvette normally took about a hundred men now it had over XXXXXXX extra, all shivering and running round in their birthday suits, waiting for their clothes to dry.

The sailors were very kind and supplied us with bully beef and bread. Next morning we were woken up at five o'clock - well we hadn't been to sleep actually - to change on to an armed xxxxxxxxxxxxxxxxxxxxxx which had come up in an answer to an S.O.S. It was very big compared with our first ship, the late lamented, and terrific compared with the corvette we were on. We got on board and had a good time as we had plenty of room. There was even a picture house on board and the food was good. We saw flying fish by the 100, porpoises by the score, and sharks occasionally. We arrived in Freetown on Wednesday morning and got on the train that afternoon. If you look at a map of Sierra etc. You will find two railway lines connecting dozens of towns making it look quite developed. Well the railway is the same type as the one in the sawmill, about three feet gauge. The carriages have a long bench down each side for seats. We started off in high spirits with niggers running alongside as we puffed along past shops and through streets into the jungle. Fifteen hours later we arrived here after a night of trying to find the most comfortable of a few very uncomfortable positions, and picking imaginary mosquitoes off our necks, arms and legs, seeing imaginary scorpions and snakes in the dark. Twice we came to hills in the railway that the old engine couldn't tackle even by putting sand under the slipping wheels which are about one foot diam. We got up both by taking the brakes, off and freewheeling down to the bottom to get up steam and taking another run at it. We are 160 miles, from Freetown here so the train is even slower than the Wick to Inverness expresses. I'm afraid I'll have to shorten, the rest as I don't want to have to send it in two instalments and I'm feeling sorry for the Censor. The camp here is not an aerodrome and there are no planes so we won't be here long. It is right in the middle of marshes where mosquitos breed villages where they get malaria from the natives and here we are to get it. We eat two quinine pills daily, wear mosquito boots (like leather Wellington) in the evening, and sleep under 'squito nets at night. Other nice inhabitants are, snakes with a guaranteed single ticket to wherever you're going given with each bite. Tarantula spiders ditto and scorpions which make you quite ill for a day or two and umpteen insects, lizards and centipedes which are poisonous.

The millipedes which are quite harmless are about six inches long round and fat about the diameter of a thumb. When you stand on them you balance for a minute and they suddenly give way with a loud squelch. What a thrill! The scorpions are just like lobsters with a long armour plated tail and sting curling over the top. Grasshoppers are about two or three inches long and at night they, with the aid of millions of crickets, frogs and other insects make a row like Henry Hall's Band only louder and continuous. The spiders are very small (compared with elephants.) both being about half an inch across and legs two or three inches long and hairier than a Black Watch Drum Major. Apart from these few insignificant things this place is fine. This is the cold rainy season It comes down like a shower bath about once a day. Last time the weight of water brought a tree down across the road just in front us and it is as hot as _____. Still, it gets warm in summer -Sept till June. Everything is twice as dear as in England except Bananas, four for ld, Pineapple 1 1/2d each and mangoes about the same. The huts are mud walls with a leaf thatch in which the lizards, spiders and etc. Stay. Sorry finished paper. Writing paper pads 1/3 Envelopes 8d for 20 all stuck with heat and damp. To get back to normal subjects, I hope you are all well and getting on O.K. How is Allie liking the RAF? Please send his address and tell him I've been torpedoed as I don't want to write all that again. The heat doesn't help in letter writing. Can you find out if I can claim any insurance for stuff lost by enemy action, as the RAF don't replace personal items and I got away with trousers shirt and socks? Personal stuff, £16 in notes. Bank book (post office registered at Cranwell, number lost). Fountain pen, 7/6. Toothbrush, tooth paste etc. Approx 7/6d. Total lost £17. Can you find out if I can get a new bank book, and please find out how? It had £13 in it. Well I'm afraid I'll have to stop now so ta-ta.
Love from James.

P.S. Tell Mrs. Webster that I could do with somebody here to hold my hand I see spiders etc. But I don't know when the boat sails. Still she can find out herself. It's worth coming to as you don't have to pay to go to the Zoo it's on your doorstep - inside the house as well.

Adios.

Censor.
W.G.Horton.

● Mr J. Mackie

"it was the wet heat
in the jungle, durin' the
monsoon period that
beat us more than
anything"

Burma

ITH MASSIVE ENERGY AND RESOURCES BEING EXPENDED BY THE ALLIES on the war against Germany, Burma might have been regarded as a neglected area. However, as supplies and equipment gradually began to arrive in that theatre and the Japanese became vulnerable to the increasing allied air and sea power, the tide began to turn.

As a part of the British Empire, Burma was considered as an adjunct to India. Burmese culture had been seriously subsumed by the British, which caused the disintegration of the indigenous civilization. A serious revolt (1930-32) by the Saya San, an anti modern movement, was put down despite being well supported by the populace. Separately, a nationalist movement under the guise of such bodies as the Young Men's Buddhist Association incited student strikes and agitated for political representation, the separation from India and later, for independence. Thakin,(meaning Master) a name only used for the British was then re-applied to these emerging political movements. One of these, the Thakin movement, formed a Burmese Independent Army who gave support to the Japanese during the invasion of 1942. Towards the end of the war, curiously, the BIA began to resist the Japanese and became known as the Anti Fascist Peoples Freedom League (AFPFL). These movements virtually dominated political power and with the return of the British, Aung San, former student leader and BIA head under the auspices of the AFPFL, negotiated independence for Burma by 1948.

Albert MacIntosh: At that time in the police y' had t' be taught how to drive all the vehicles that you might come across. When you got on to the road in Burma it was like round a huge hill and the road started at the bottom and it went round and round and round until it was thousands of feet up. Now you could only keep the traffic goin' one way and you had to let so much traffic up one way and then you had to let the ones coming down have their turn. It was all in a big circle. Now we had TCPs (traffic control points) on the roads (to Kohima and Imphal) and we knew what we were doin' but you'd get - it's a shame to say it - mostly Officers tryin' to come down in a jeep when you had 10 ton trucks goin' up the way. There was nae room for two lots because the kerbs wouldn't allow it and on one side there was a drop of perhaps two or three roads down thousands of feet. We had to keep control of that but being police we had the authority; I mean, we could arrest the Officers and actually I did one or two myself and they were taken in front of General Stockford. The Officers knew that they shouldn't do it but they just did.

David: You said that you'd learnt to drive every thing available; like what?

Albert: We learned to drive all kinds of trucks and tanks including jeeps and motorcycles. These motorcycles were BSAs and they did give you one; they were horrible. BSAs were too low in the sump for that sort of work. The Nortons were better because they had a high sump. When we were at this training - I forgot to tell you - we were put into the Great North Road to watch for any speeding army trucks and things like that and we were there and we had 'Indian' motorcycles. They were American motorcycles and they could do a 100 miles an hour even in those days. We were the only ones that had bikes like that, mind you they used to catch fire and all kinds of things like that!

I remember pushing one, I must have pushed it a couple of miles after it had caught fire and I was absolutely knackered. I had tried to start it up again, I had got the fire out and I remember taking it in into the garage. The mechanic in there he just sat on the bike, kicked it and away it went; it started fine! We did a lot of training after that. We did rough riding, through water and stuff like that and if your bike stalled you just had to strip it down, clean it out and put it back together again. Then I drove jeeps, 15 hundred-weight vehicles, 30 hundredweights then 10 tonners. I think they were Bedfords. I also

● Left: Fitter squad, 9th Gordons, 116 RAC, India 1943.
  Courtesy the Highlanders Museum

learned to drive a tank. It was a medium tank - probably a Grant - but I also had a shot at a Sherman tank. We had to be able to drive those things because if anything got stuck on the road, we had to be able to move it.

On the way to Burma the train was held up for about a week. The train was shunted down into a siding. Rations were what you could steal out of the stations or off the top of the native food-bearers baskets as they went past. You were lucky to get dinner which was probably a can full of dehydrated mince. You went up to the engine with this and put it under the steam thing and got the driver to put on the steam and that heated the mince.

David: What food did you get each day?

Albert: Y' didna get food. We just had t' steal off the natives as they went by. Y' see we were in the police but we were put into the 5th Indian Division. I was four months eating raw 'pyahs' - wild dogs. We couldna cook anything y' see because y' couldn't light a fire or light a match in the jungle. Everything was eaten raw. We used t' get a little box everyday which were called 'K rations' which consisted of concentrated prunes, two salt tablets, four little hard tack biscuits and one cigarette. That was your ration everyday plus what you found or caught all was eaten raw.

David: How could you tolerate that?

Albert: Y' just had to. Y' see, when we went into the Indian Army the British rations didna come through to us at all. The regiments got their rations and cooks but if they were in the jungle fightin' they werena allowed t' have fires and things like that.

Peter Rennie: the 'K rations' we had had quite a good selection of items even though the cigarettes were either Camels or Marlbourgh. They contained chocolate, glucose tablets, *bouillon* powder – for making soup – and were in waxed paper containers to keep them dry. But then being in the 10th, (Gordon Highlanders), Anti-tank Regiment R.A. we were entitled to British Army supplies. (Being with the 5th Indian Division. Albert wasn't).

Albert: We were in Dimapur and there were only a few of us (Police) there and I was with the 33 corps, 14th Army in Burma. It was about 120 in the shade but it was the wet heat in the jungle, durin' the monsoon period that beat us more than

anything. There must have been a period of between six and eight weeks that we didn't see daylight because the forest was so thick. Our job was to keep the road open in the jungle, which was just a single track. You had to keep your eyes open just in case there were any Jap snipers around - and there were quite a few.

We had two Gurkhas and they were (attached to the) TCP's so that if there were any snipers about the Gurkhas went out after them. When they came back they always came back with a couple of heads to you and that was your snipers. They did this to prove that they had caught them. One of the Gurkhas that was with me took me through a ceremony in which we became blood brothers. He cut his thumb with his Kukri and then cut mine. We put both our thumbs together and that's what he decided was a blood brother. I would say that those two Gurkhas kept us safe whilst we were there.

One time we were out in a jeep and there was this telephone operator who was laying telephone lines and we came upon them when they'd just been hit by a small Jap patrol. They'd been knocked out but he was still livin' and I got him into the back of my jeep and took him back to his unit. About 10 years ago, we were down at the Park Hotel and we were havin' a meal with two friends who were up from Peebles. We were sittin' at this table having a meal and I saw this fella and he's lookin' at me and I'm lookin' at him eventually he says, "God almighty Mac, it's nae you is it? De y' mind pickin' me up on the road in Burma?" I says, "Oh no Jock It canna be you?" And he sez, "Aye, So you're still on the go then." That was the first time I'd seen him since I was oot there.

David: But you must have seen some dreadful things during the war in Burma?

Albert: Aye, we did: I remember one time we'd gone out to find some missing soldiers. We discovered that the Japs had captured them. We found one of them tied to a tree and the barbed wire was all round about right through his skin right round and it was tightened at the back. Now, when we found him - and they found another one in the TCP towards Tammu - we got him inside and we were lucky that we werna blown up wersels because it might have been booby trapped. He was dead. We had big machetes and I did things with my machete ; there was one point that no troops were supposed t' go past because apparently the Japs had taken in tanks somewhere above us. They had taken the tanks in parts on the back of elephants and put them together in the jungle! We come across a place there where there was a pipe stickin' out which was outa place in the

"I was four months eating raw 'pyahs' - wild dogs."

● Albert MacIntosh: before Burma, after Burma and 1998; note he still has the same bush hat

jungle altogether and we were sittin' on our motor bikes and we were at the end of our particular patrol. I was saying, "What's that up there?" He – my pal -had a look and I had a look although we didn't go nae where near it and then the blasted thing started t' move! This was one of their tanks! There were a lot o' incidents like that.

On one occasion we were last to get billeted and we went down into this field - well it was *like* a field - and we put up our little bivey. I had two metal boards which we slept on and in the mornin' they had opened the sluices and the water was right up underneath! We'd gone into a paddy field! These things jist happened. Those metal boards I just mentioned were (road) signs that we had and there was one particular sign that I never forgot and it was, 'No troops past this point.' We made two holes through the metal and we put a little light in so that it would shine on it. Then they took a pole and stuck it in the back and put the Jap head on the top, a gas mask and a helmet. They took off the Japs head jist like that, nae bother! They never give it a second thought.

David: If the Gurkhas thought nothing of bringing back two Japanese heads then surely the Japanese weren't going to worry about choppin' off your heads.

Albert: Oh, they didn't worry about that, nae body worried aboot that. I've got this (showing a photograph of a dead body) and I shot him stone dead. That was in his pocket. (indicating a thing

which looked like a medal or an ear-ring) I thought that I had shot a member of the Kepiti Police who were the terror of the Japanese army.

David: You seem to suggest that the conventional part of the war, like Italy, was a completely different world from the jungle both physically and mentally. When you were talking about fighting in the jungle there seems to be a change of attitude where you seem to move into a more dream like state.

Albert: That's exactly right. Survival takes over.

David: Can you remember the point at which you saw the change in attitude?

Albert: Well I think that it was when we were on the road to relieve Kohima and we were patrollin' the road and we were takin' rations, shells and all kinds o' things

> " we used our machetes on them just in case they were playing possum "

up to Kohima. At the same time as we were lettin' those lorries up the road we had t' close the road t' let the ambulances down with the wounded. When they came down from Kohima you could hear the screamin' and yellin' (of the injured troops) which was horrible to hear but the Sikh drivers just put their foot down, the pain that those men must have gone through was really terrible. After we captured Kohima things died down a bit because that's when we met Vera Lynn.

We left Kohima and carried on towards Imphal and the same thing with the ambulances was happening. You were getting lorries goin' up loaded with stuff and ambulances commin' back, it was a horrible thing. There was quite a bit of Jap infiltration. You would never come across more than about half a dozen Japs at a time. I've Jap snipers wi half their backs out and still snipin'. If I came across a patrol like that I just shot them and that was it. It was nothing to do with regiments and soldiers and things like that. It was things we came across and had to deal with to survive. They were shot and then we used our machetes on them just in case they were playing possum. Y' jist did away with them and that was that. It's awful when I think of it. Here's me at my age now and I've got through all this stuff. We did take prisoners on the odd occasion though and we once brought in these two Jap prisoners and it must have been near to Imphal because these prisoners were taken across to the special investigation branch and we left them with them. Truthfully, they spoke about the 'forgotten army' and they never spoke a truer word and they still dinna ken a thing about it.

Robbie Bremner: After Iraq we sailed from Basra to Bombay then we were transferred to Calcutta. We were an experimental unit at es time and they put us out to some camp. We threw away the pith helmets and later on we got bush hats. We had shirtless days and they were testing us out. They found that we could stand the heat better than the natives, so we were guinea pigs testing us out for heat endurance. Here's a story; we got so many leaves and I was out one night in this hotel havin' a quiet dram and who should come in was this chap Ferguson from Banff and y' jist couldna believe it. Well, we were jist chattin away and who comes in but anither o' our pals frae Banff! Leslie Gibson, well I can tell you, what a night we had! We pinched a horse and cart an' we were in es an' roond the toon, cerryin' on an' the Redcaps chased us. Then we met a Canadian or American and he took us into this hotel (to hide) then I went back to Gibson's unit. He said that their Padre had come from Foggie and his name was Buchan. I said that I would like t' see him but I didna manage to. I then went back to my ain unit because m' leave was up. Another time I was out wi m' mate Jack an' I dinna ken fit wye we got picked up but they picked us up for bein' pimps! We wis pit inta jail and all our claes wis teen awar fae us. We was marched up in front o' this guy and I sez, "I want t' talk to my Commandin' Officer." "Oh, y' can't do that." However, I did eventually get Captain Garret to come along and certify who I was so eventually we got oot. It wis quite an experience in the jail.

> " we were all goin' til a film show. We were watchin' one side o' the screen and the Japs musta been lookin' at the other side! "

They were feedin' us through the door on the fleer an' I wis doon on ma knees barkin' like a dog! After a few weeks we sailed from Calcutta to Chittagong and that was us into the jungle. The battle at the time was Arakan and the first job we had when we got there was on the Naf river. It wis a bit tidal there and we used t' go out wi the guns when the tide wis oot, we'd fire away then wait till the tide come back oot before you could do it again. The Japs were having it all their own way, it was completely different warfare being enclosed in by the jungle. The mosquitoes were bad and although we had nets we couldna use the 'cause the Japs jist looked for the nets and put the bayonet in.

Then we went for the battle in Maungdo and we managed to capture it - which was aboot the first time that the Japs had been stopped - and there was a chap there from Banff and he wis on a barge and they were the OP which was directin' oor guns where t' fire. The Royal West Kents, they were there, and with them we had the job of keepin' the Naf river and the peninsula clear o' Japs. In the jungle, y' didna ken where y' were. There were fortress's and they built them of bamboo and there were trenches around so they were very well protected. There was a battle for the tunnels. There was a range of mountains and the tunnels were through them. That was the famous Nockydoc (Nyakydauk) Pass. We stopped the Japs there but I mind the time before that when we were all goin' til a film show. We were watchin' one side o' the screen and the Japs musta been lookin' at the other side! Once the film wis finished there wis hell let loose but the most of us were all back to our units but that was some battle. That wis a terrible night that! I got back nearly t' my position and I was separated anyway but I had my ain Tommy gun. I jist got my head down because if you were standin' up you were going to get caught in the crossfire. The fight was goin' on all night and I was blastin' away which was a dangerous thing t' do 'cause you could hit your own boys. There was quite a lot of heavy fighting but for the first time we had stopped the Japs. We flew into Imphal - I can always remember that night - they were shoutin' "Bremner! Bremner! Get into the plane". I wasna goin' t' flee in that Dakotas was I? Well, I thought I'll have t' go so I went intil the plane and I wrapped a blanket round me. There wis no winders in these things, they wis freezin'! I had 12 tins o' bacon in this pack and I thought that the Dakota wouldna take off ! I wished that I'd never taken this bacon! There were three

CAMPAIGNING IN BURMA: A "HOME-MADE PUB,"

Drawn by Captain Hugh Ecob, of the R.A.C., whose Unit was attached to the Fourteenth Army during the Great Push thr

THE "GORDON ARMS," A "PUB" BUILT ENTIRELY BY OFFICERS OF THE 116TH R.A.C. REGT. (THE GORDON HIGHLANDERS) FOR THEIR HO
IT NOW STANDS EMPTY IN THE BURMESE JUNGLE AS A MEMORIAL TO THE DETERMINED CLINGING OF EXILED SCOTSMEN TO THEIR N

● Courtesy the Highlanders Museum

landin' strips but the first two we got to were occupied wi Japs. The third one we managed to land then we'd landed in Imphal. We occupied the places that the Chindits had been in and we were like reinforcements for the Chindits. They went away out to get ready to fly in with an aeroplane with a glider towed behind. We were in 'boxes' at Imphal for about six weeks then the 2nd Div. Came up and that's when the battle of Kohima went on. When we broke outa those 'boxes' I started wheeling and dealing with the Nagas - the head hunters. I was buying potatoes, cabbages and ducks or hens t' feed the troops and I was tradin' back with tinned fish, sardines and herrin'. The time came when things became more mechanised and they were doin' away with a lot of the mules. So we used to cook the mules. The

" I started wheeling and dealing with the Nagas - the head hunters "

meat was very dark but it was good food. I have eaten dog and the way the Nagas did it was they had big pups and they fed them up and then they starved them for about a week. Then they put down a big bowl o' rice, the dog then ate all this and then it was stuffed. Then, they killed it and cooked it and it was beautiful.

David: What about fruit?

Robbie: Mango's were the most frequent fruit that we had. We also had bananas but not on regular supply. So, I did all that wheeling and dealing after we came outa the box then after the battle we went back and that's when I went away. There wis a chap from our village and he was a Silchar which is the name of a district and it's up beside Shillong where the people there are a different tribe again.

Their skins are nearly white - similar to a Pattan. When I come outa the box I had forty Pattans attached to me. They were great lads and very loyal. When Kohima was finished and all that side o' the battle before we started t' go down the Irrawaddy. I said to the Major at that time that I'd an uncle who was living in Silchar and could I get leave to visit him. That wis the best six weeks o' my life in the army. So I travelled about 1500 miles on this old train. There was a buffet on it, it was rice and something cooked and I landed up at this tea garden. I phoned up from this gate on one of those old wind up phones saying I was at this gate and someone came out t' meet me. This chap who was called Cookie McKay ran three tea gardens and he had his own mill there for grinding the tea. It was all made out of wood and he used t' turn all these things and he said that he would teach me all about tea making if I wanted to come out. He also kept large fruit and vegetable gardens. This chap came from Foggie and his family and mine were very close. That was a great experience in my life.

> " I could have settled down in this place but it wis time t' go again "

After about six weeks I went back to my regiment and we wis on the move south to Tilin which was the last stronghold that the Japs had before we crossed the Irrawaddy in home made rafts. Then we were on the road to Mandalay. There were some raidin' parties which were mainly at night but durin' the day the Japs were very quiet. They were depleted at this time and the big battles were mostly over. Then we went to Rangoon, which we took, then we came back to what we called the Shand States(Shwenyaing?) It was a hill station where I set up a permanent camp. I had an old Indian guy and a few coolies and we built tables, seats and a cookhouse out of bamboo.

David: You must have been quite a character up there and the Infantry must have said something like, "Let's go to Bremner's hotel for the night."

Robbie: Ha, ha! Yes, that's right. At this place - it was a beautiful place - there was an Indian village, there was a Karen village they were all different

● Courtesy the Highlanders Museum

ANOTHER ASPECT OF THE BURMESE CAMPAIGN: A SCENE TYPICAL OF THE MONSOON, WHEN TARPAULINS BECOME ONE OF THE MOST IMPORTANT ITEMS OF ARMY EQUIPME IT IS IMPOSSIBLE TO KEEP ANYTHING DRY, BUT TARPAULINS AT LEAST MAKE POSSIBLE SOME SORT OF BIVOUAC SHELTERS FOR MEN AND MATERIALS.

peoples and there were others who were more educated. One time I was out shooting water buffalo for the boys so we ate well. I bought rations, veg, and firewood every day and sent the food up to the forward brigade that was on duty. I used to have perhaps forty women comin' up wi sticks, vegetables and all this. They are all dressed in their saris all in different colours.

The climate was wonderful and similar to Scotland with pine and fir trees; and flowers grew everywhere. I met the 6/9th Gordons there and played football wi them and met a few boys that I knew from Turriff, Keith and Huntly. I could have settled down in this place but it wis time t' go again. We then went down to Rangoon where the British were getting' everything goin' again. When we landed in Rangoon there was what we called 'Kasber'(sic) which was a special part o' the army. They were all Colonels and Lieutenant Colonels and they came and took over the workings of Burma, the railways, everything. I set up canteens for these Kasber people. I was put second in command of stores and rations and I was responsible for three thousand men t' feed. Can you imagine I'd a breakfast dinner and tea to find. I had to improvise and make our own ovens and fires. There was worse t' come because we were landed with the allied prisoners comin' back from the far east. God, there were in a terrible state. They were the ones who were caught in Singapore, we were feedin' 'em and getting' them

> ## "they were an awful sight and I thanked God for not being in enemy hands "

away. I was lost for about six month oot there. Worse t' come still was (when) we were landed with the prisoners of war from Thailand and Burma road. They were an awful sight and I thanked God for not being in enemy hands. We were promised a ship to take us home 'cause we were overdue but then the prisoners got priority and rightly so. It was another six months before the 'forgotten army' landed in Glasgow. I looked at the import of bikes and sewing machines because they were the prize possessions at that time and we settled down quite well in Rangoon. I landed in hospital (at one point) that was the best time I had since leaving home. I got to be 'ward boy', it was a great job. The nightcap was Horlicks, Cocoa, or a dram. I can tell you I used to advertise the Horlicks and Cocoa so we could build up the booze! Eventually we did get a boat and landed in Glasgow. We jumped ship, we cleared oot and I said that I was goin' t' my uncles and I phoned Banff to speak to my wife for I had been missing for about a year! With all the hullabaloo the 14th Army had indeed been forgotten. We went to the Plaza dance hall in Glasgow. We had oor bush hats on and they thought we were Australians and they gave us a wonderful time. We went back to the ship in the morning and was put on a charge! Then we went by rail to Aldershot to get our passes and then home to Foggie after being away for five years!

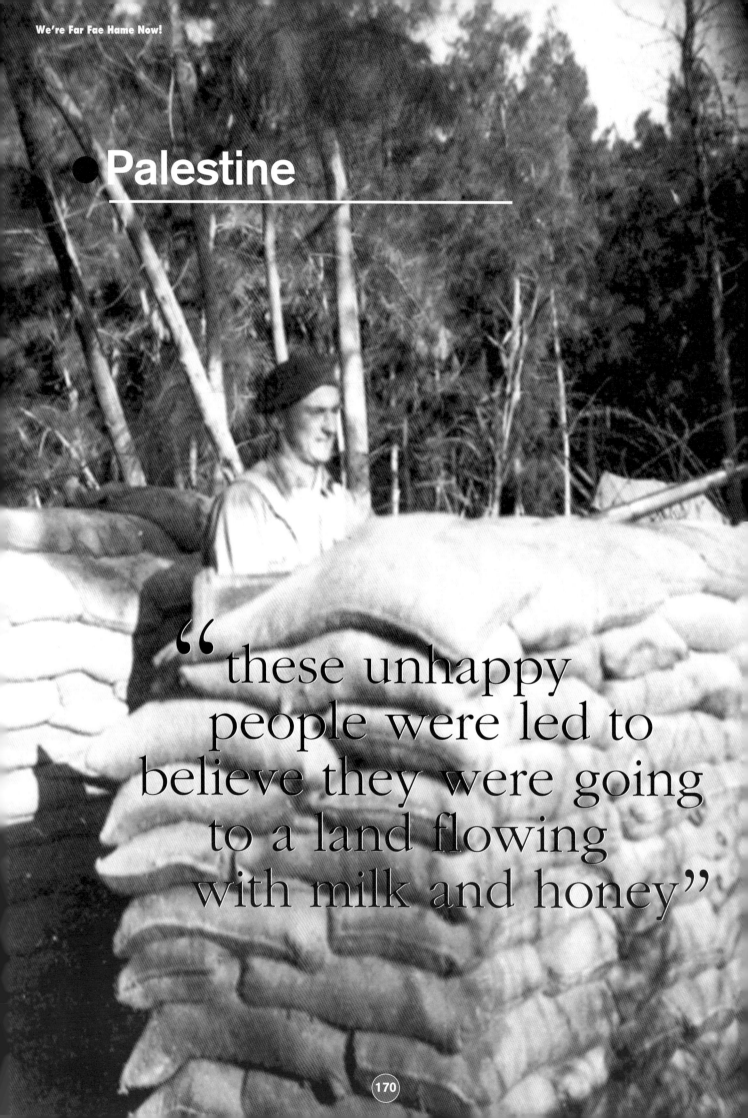

●Palestine

"these unhappy
people were led to
believe they were going
to a land flowing
with milk and honey"

Palestine
1948

WITH THE FALL OF THE OTTOMAN EMPIRE *during the First World War, Palestine came under the jurisdiction of the British in 1917. November of that year saw, through the Balfour Declaration, Britain giving support to the notion that the Jewish people might achieve a national home in Palestine. In this declaration, Britain made promises not only to the Jews but also to the Arabs and the overlapping of some of these promises sowed the seeds of the discontent that followed. The inter-war period saw the first outbreak of violence with both Jew and Arab suffering casualties. With the advent of immigration, the Jewish nation (which numbered 83,000 in 1921) doubled in five years.*

The anti-Semitism, which had grown with intensity throughout the Second World War, had caused the Jews to become preoccupied with their nation's settlement in the Holy Land.

The conclusion of the War - in which both Arab and Jewish Palestinians served with the Allied forces - saw the question of Jewish resettlement reappear; it was pursued by the Zionists with considerable vigour.

Following Jewish guerrilla activities during 1947, Britain put the Jewish question to the United Nations who voted for partition. 1948 saw the proclamation of the Jewish State of Israel. Since then, a series of Arab/Israeli wars has seen the total loss of the Arab State and the emergence of the Palestine Liberation Organisation, which fronted guerrilla warfare against the Israel. The problems have yet to be resolved.

Walter Watt: In 1945 I finished my apprenticeship as a plater in the shipyards. M' dad wisna very pleased about it 'cause money wis short but I just wanted t' go into the services cause I hadna travelled very far except t' Dundee on a bike. So, I got it inta m' head that I wanted t' jine so I went up and joined the RAF at Woolmanhill. I got called up in January in 1946. So I had t' report t' Padgate near Warrington so I did m' square bashin' there. I didn't mind it too much but some o' the lads, oh me, broken hearted what with blood an' thunder an' bullshit. They cam t' me one day and said, "You've passed the physical test, y' mental test an' yer grade one, how would y' like t' be a gunner?" An' I sez "Ya", and I said, "An airgunner" but he never said that, he jist said, "- a gunner." So I said, "Aye OK."

Some way or other I found m'sel in Grantham in Number One depot, RAF Regiment. We got a rude awakenin', they took away our nice RAF bloose an' gave us kaki, big boots an' a rifle and we had t' go through the assault course jist t' let us know what we were in for. Well, I finished ma trainin' there - an' it was rough - but I did a whole battle course and quite honestly I enjoyed it 'cause bein' in a shipyard climbin' ropes an' a' that, I thought it was great.

Eventually, we were posted and we had t' make our way t' London then we got posted t' Dover. They took away our rifles and gave us Burma hats an' mosquito nets. We didn't know where we were goin' we really didn't know. Then they took our Burma hats back an' left us with the mosquito net. Well they took us across t' Calais by ferry we got bunged on a train at Calais and then down through the whole length o' France to Toulon.

● Left: photo Walter Watt

Well, we went to the troop ship, it was one of them Liberty ships an' bein an ex-professional shipbuilder, I'm afraid I was very wary of it. It was very calm, it was quite nice. All the glamour boys were lyin' about the decks gettin' sunburnt but not the RAF Regiment, no, we got the job o' cleanin' shit houses an' all that stuff. We got a ticket t' go t' the cinema on the ship. They'd only got one film, 'Show Business' with Eddie Cantor. Where my bunk was, I looked right into the screen an' I knew every bit o' the bloody script be the end o' the trip. We landed in Port Said and then we went t' Cairo and still we didna know where we were goin'. They then put us on a train. We'd no guns an' they did warn us between Cairo and Haifa there were terrorists and stuff like that. The Sergeant said, "If there's any shootin' jist get your head doon." There was two Arab Egyptian soldiers one at each end o' each carriage. Poor buggers, they'd only .22 rifles. Well, we got t' Haifa and we suddenly realised we were in Palestine. We went to the airport which was very active with Lancasters and Spitfires and their job was t' guard the pipeline. Also, the planes were used t' spot illegal immigrants along the coast. We didn't have to deal with that because we were inland. I think it would have been a terrible job t' deal with these people 'cause some of them had come outa concentration camps, they were kissin' the ground an' that and they had t' be sent back t' Cyprus t' concentration camps there.

We realised that we were in a situation far there were terrorists and Palestinians, they didna want y' there and we were often on red alert but sometimes we were alright. There was these Jewish gangs operatin' - there was the Stern gang, The Irgun Zvei Leumi and the Hagganah who were underground military Jews. Not a week after we left Haifa somebody rolled a 40 gallon drum inta Haifa railway station an' blew it up. It was Hagganah that did 'at but they did phone in like the IRA do but the Stern Gang they woulda jist killed y'. They had no morals about killin' y', they hated us. The Palestinian police they had a very difficult job because they were neutral, they were in between us and them people.

Trevor: What nationality were they; were they Arabs?

Walter: Some o' them were but some o' them were British. I tried t' join 'em one time but somebody intercepted ma papers so I didn't get.

There wis times that it wis quiet but you were armed at all times. They say in the army, "Y' rifles y' best friend." Well you sleep wi the bloody thing with a lanyard round yer wrist, (but) it's not y' best friend! And there's always one up the spout, even when y' went for a shower y' tek yer rifle wi yer. Arabs wanted weapons but they didna have weapons. The Israelis had because the Jews were sponsored by the Americans. They used t' go about in big cars and they had better weapons than we had. We still had the old Enfield .303. A lota lads got wounded through having a loaded rifle, they weren't accustomed til 'em. I remember one day I was sittin' in the billet cleanin' the rifle and the lad next t' me never thought, (he) pushed the bolt down, BANG! there's a hole in the roof. Oh God! I was on wi a charge. One night there was a bit of a dance on, it was in Jerusalem as far as I can remember. These two army lads got into a bit of an argument with drinkin'. They went oot

> **"you've always got a silly bugger who'd come along an' pull the trigger when it wis in the holster!"**

the back and had a duel with Sten guns and they killed one another. There was a few things like 'at. We were given pistols, they were Smith an' Wesson and Webley's. We knew about guns because that wer our job. The RAF didna know much about guns, and I didna like t' go by an RAF gunpost. There was no love lost between us, d' y' understand. They hated us, we were bullshit regimental and they didn't like bullshit. Even on Christmas Day I was on guard duty and they were out enjoyin' themselves. One day they cam doon an' started teasin' me so I gid 'em a burst on a Bren gun and wi a bloody pistol. Anyway we got this pistols y' see an' we knew the pistols. An' we knew that Smith an' Wesson or Webley, I'm not sure which now, but the barrel giz clockwise and the other one anticlockwise. So we always kept an empty chamber 'cause you've always got a silly bugger who'd come along an' pull the trigger when it wis in the holster!

I was in this German hospital in Jerusalem and two RAF lads - military policemen - they'd jist got made up with their stripes, they got pistols. Well they got the story about clockwise and that but they didn't know which was which amazingly enough we were lookin' at them and they were on about John Wayne the cowboy and this lad pointed his pistol at his friend. He pulled the trigger and it went bang! The look on his face he'd shot his friend in the guts, just the one bullet and he sez, "It's not supposed t' do that." Y' know the famous song "I didn't know the gun was loaded!" I sez, "Laddie, y' don't go round pointing pistols at anybody." Well, the lad kept shoutin' that he wis dyin'. I said, "Yer nae dyin'." He wis pretty ill for a while but he did recover. Another incident I remember, there was a very quiet day in a street in Jerusalem, there was an RAF headquarters there. I'll always remember the name, it was Ben Yehudie Street! A real Jewish name, as I say we were just stan'in, the sun beatin' doon watchin the talent. I must say the Jewish girls were very beautiful, very beautiful, the most beautiful women in the world - till they get married! We were jist standin' at the gun post an' this Lance Corporal, he wis nae long oota Blighty. He was standin' aboot wi a Sten gun and he was pullin' back the cockin' handle and off it went in a burst and instead o' tiltin' it up the way, he tilted it down the way and one o' ma friends was standin' havin' a fag. He got five Sten gun bullets right from his shoulder right down through him. We didn't think he would survive, and his Mom was sent for, it was pretty dodgy. Then there wis a Courts Martial for it.

So, in Jerusalem there wis a big private school with Jewish and Christian Arab girls, an' they were quite nice and they used to show their passes an' some o' them would mumble t' ye, "English pigs." I sez, "No darlin' I'm a Scottish pig!" Everthin' was fine until y' put on Marshall Law and once you'd put that on there'd be barbed wire on the streets and everything. The Jewish couldn't do business nor the Arabs for that matter and then they got angry and then you would expect trouble and then the bombs cam over. One night, we wis in the camp and they'd made this home-made bomb - they were made outa old fire extinguishers - luckily none of them went off and one landed in front o' the armoury. We had t' go an' look for 'em and we found an old RAF van made up as a milk van but we never found the bloody terrorists. You were always a little bit on guard and y' were never sure. I used t' sit in that gun post on my own early in the mornin', I was more worried aboot somebody throwing a knife or a hand grenade y' don't hear the bloody thing. T' say y' werna windy I'd be tellin' a lie.

This is strange, I was sittin' there at Ramat David - this was a valley where a thousand Arabs died of malaria one time and the Arabs called it the Valley of Death. I was sittin' there and I saw this light commin' up over this hill. It was very bright like a big star and it actually looked like a big cross. Everything was silent and I could a see it movin'. I was listenin' t' see if it was one of the bombers coming over. I couldna hear nae engine. I was a bit dubious as to what it was so I got on the old field telephone to the next post. I sez, "What the Hell's that thing commin' over!" He sez, "Walter, you'll never see that in your life again, that is the Bethlehem Star I've heard about it but I've never seen it. It's a very rare sight". It's true, it did look like a shiny silver cross an' you could actually see it move. I sat there, y' think a lot when you're on your own at a gun post an' I said t' mesel, "I wonder whether it means anything, is there somebody up there watchin' me? I hope they are good t' me." That was a very unusual thing.

Then there wis these green eyes glarin' at me. I didna ken fit they were so I got on the field telephone an' I sez, "Fits es buggers oot ere?" He said, "Piads; they're wild dogs. They run about the desert." I sez, "Will they touch ma?" He said, "No, but if there's a Hyena he might egg 'em on a bit." Oh Christ! I was shitin' mesel! They said, "Dinna open fire fer Gods sake, if y' open fire the whole camp will turn oot. Jist throw some steens at 'em." When y' pit on at night it was creepy. There wis snakes, scorpions and there was this flyin' beetle about two or three inches an' it used t' come doon the beam o' yer Aldis lamp hut yer glass, like a steen!

Trevor: Did you have terrorism in equal amounts from Palestinians and Jews or what?

● photo Walter Watt

Walter: Well, at that time I would say it was pretty equal. There was a lota villages and in one of them there was a swimming pool there an' we used t' go to it but y' had t' take your weapons wi yer. So, somebody had t' stay and watch the weapons. There was Arabs and Jews and they were all livin' side by side. Jews had their own bus routes and the Arabs had theirs. Anyway, we met Jewish people, American Jews and British Jews and they were quite nice and I got t' know a few o' the kids. I had sweeties an' that 'cause I hadna become a smoker by that time and one day the kiddies come up t' me an' said, "Hello Jock." I said, "Hello boys and girls, how y' doin'?" Their mother came over t' me and apologised and said, "I'm very sorry but I prefer it if you didna speak t' the kids." I sez, "What for?" She sez, "The Gang says that we are too far in with you people. I'd like to invite you in for a cup of coffee but we could be punished." As I was sayin' earlier there were Christian Arabs and one o' them was friendly with one of ours. We didn't see her for a while but she was burned by acid. Then there was a Jewish girl who became very friendly with one o' my Corporals and when we saw her again she had a big scar on her upper lip. This was a warnin' t' say, "Not t' be." When y' went t' the beach off Haifa, the beaches were segregated. There were Christian Arabs and Jews then there was us, the services. Y' were scared, y' got t' a gun post and your imagination runs wild.

I remember one day, I was sittin' in a gun post an' I was half a mile from the tent. I'm sittin' there and I decided that I wanted t' go to the toilet. Well tension was high, 200 Jews had broken outa prison, we didn't know where they were but we knew they were needin' arms and they did threaten t' blow up all the brass and blow up our planes. Anyway, I decided t' go t' the toilet but there was a fair bit o' walkin' in the dark and there was no lights in the toilets just big holes in the ground with concrete. Well I was convinced that somebody was followin' me, I thought I heard footsteps at m' back. I stopped, I went on a bit, then I stopped and I was gettin' windy and my hair wis standin'

● Life in Palestine. Courtesy Walter Watt.

up! I went into the toilet wi ma shorts half doon an' ma pistol sittin' in ma hand. Y thought y' saw shadows and I was gettin really windy an' I was shoutin': "Piss off I don't know who you— piss off or I'll blow your bloody head off!" I didn't enjoy that shit, I can tell you that much!

We had t' guard the aircraft, Spitfires, Lancasters, Stirlings and everything else. It was a big air park. This night we were wonderin' around the airplanes, we were supposed t' board the aircraft to make sure there were no bombs. How did we know what a bomb would look like? It coulda been a corned beef tin - in fact we knew that they made bombs with corned beef tins! All that equipment in a plane, I used t' sit up in the cockpit of a Stirling bomber, hae a smoke an' hide outa the road. I used t' sit in a Spitfire as well, it's a good job I didn't touch the gun button 'cause they were loaded up wi ammunition! I used t' sit there kiddin' mesel, Battle o' Britain, Douglas Bader an' a' that. Aeeeerrr! Imagination gone mad! Anyway this night, it was quiet, there was no flyin' and this other chap who was wi me said, " Hey Jock, steady, there's somebody lyin' under a Spitfire." I sez, "What yer on aboot?" " There's a bloke lyin' face doon under the wheels o' that Spitfire over there. Go over an' see …" I sez, "I'm nae goin' awar." "Well, I'm nae goin', you go, you Scotsmen are supposed t' be mad." I sez, "Well I'm nae bloody mad!" I sez, "I'll tell y' what I'll dee, he's nae a mechanic 'cause he's got nae lights on, he might be a terrorist. I'll tell y' what I'll dee, I've got a revolver and you've got a Sten gun, I'll get as near as I can and you cover me, but for Christ sake dinna shoot me." So, I got t' within' aboot 20 feet from him and shouted the usual challenge, "Halt who goes there!" He didna move. "Halt who goes there!" Be this time ma hand wis waverin' aboot. "Halt who goes there!" Whoever he was he got up an' he made a break and dived over the barbed wire. Well I opened up and so did the lad wi the sten. We don't know if we hut him or no but we did find bits o' cloth an' that. We got on the blower t' see what he'd been up to. There was three

Spitfires with bombs strapped t' the wheels. So they got in the bomb disposal boys an' they said that if that lot had gone up the whole airfield woulda went up. It was 100 octane petrol and what with the ammunition it woulda been some bloody explosion! Very brave lads, an' I sez "Do I get a medal?" And I laugh when the boys say that us Scots men are mad! Well that was one nasty one.

Well y' speak about bein' brave, I hadna long been there and they had these big bowsers for fuel, well this bowser come along an' they put the hose intae the tanks o' the Lancaster which had just landed. Unfortunately, the hose touched the hot exhaust pipes the flames went right doon and right into the bowser. The flight Sergeant jumped right into the cab and drove it away from the airfield. One o' the lads had pulled him outa the cab, he was on fire be this time and he died. It seems that this was the second time he had done it but he didna get awar wi it this time. We read in the 'Palestine Post' that he'd got a George Medal. It wis a great thing t' dee but y' dinna play aboot wi that stuff.

There was this airstrip where the VIPs came in for their conferences. Count Bernadotte - he was the founder of the World Peace Organisation and I think he was Swedish - an' they used t' come in on their planes. When they shouted, "VIP!" oor job was t' go oot inta the hills an' protect 'em. It wis only a little airstrip an' Arabs come in in Mufti, civilian and it wis oor job t' guard 'em. Bloody laugh this airstrip; the ambulance and fire brigade had t' go up and doon every mornin' back an' forth in case any mines were laid. D' y' know what they paid fer that? Four pence a day extra for danger money! The Airborne - they had a truck wi train wheels on it an' they used t' do the Haifa - Cairo run in case o' land mines - they got four pence a day extra money. Oh! Well paid for the danger! Anyway, when Bernadotte got off that plane and being a peace commission, the laugh of it was there were jeeps, (with) 'point-five' guns an arthin! That was one o' the posts and we were under canvas all the

time an' it was a bitty rough. We had t' go out t' get water in a bowser so we sent some of oor boys t' get water. Well, they had t' go up t' the Jewish settlement t' get it unfortunately some of the Jews shot 'em. It was three days before we could get t' them t' get them oot. We didna ken far did it, it was nowhere near a Jewish settlement. When anything like 'at happened the Airborne came in very quick, they'd the newest repeater rifles wi the short bayonets instead o' the old equipment that we had. That was the agreement and when that Jews escaped from Agra prison. There wis a dozen o' us one night and we had t' go up an' doon an orange grove at one o'clock in the morning an' I was last in line wi a Bren gun. It was terrible 'cause ony o' this buggers could pop up an' knock y' on the heed! The Officer was a National Service Officer (and) he wis a bloody idiot, I'd not much faith in him but the old Sergeant there, he'd a few ribbons on his chest, an' I sez, "I'm bidin' wi you! You've bin through the war an' I'm bidin' wi you!" You wis windy but y' had a job t' do so that wis that. We went up an' doon

> ❝the Officer was so nervous when he pulled that trigger o' the Very pistol he fell in the bloody ditch! ❞

● A dead terrorist in Palestine

this orange grove and the agreement was once we got through and everything was alright the Officer would fire a Very pistol - a green flare - t' let 'em ken. If y' got intae trouble y' fired a red one then the Airborne woulda bin there in nae time. So we were goin up an' doon es orange grove and this friend o' mine, a Cockney lad, a barra boy an' in typical Cockney humour he said, "Can't you smell the orange blossoms?" I said, "Bugger the orange blossoms!" But that wis good, it broke the tension. Well we got through the orange grove an' luckily nothin' happened and the Officer was so nervous when he pulled that trigger o' the Very pistol he fell in the bloody ditch!

The Palestinian Arab is a nice Arab; we were twice invited t' a Palestinian home and the first thing we had t' do was t' apologise that you'd got weapons. This Arab lad who dealt wi the water, he spoke very good English an' he invited us to his home. Now one o' oor lads, he was a miner from

Newcastle some way, he made a great study o' the Arabs and he learned the language. He told us how t' behave ourselves when y' go to an Arab home. "Now, y' can speak aboot his horses, his situation and things like that but don't mention the women. You'll hear them gigglin', they'll be there in the background but they won't come out. Now, you'll get offered three little cups of coffee or tea, there's nae sugar and milk but there's lemon in it. Now when he offers y' third one it's time t' go. Y' take y' shoes aff before y' go in an' when y' leave don't look back 'cause it shows y' don't trust 'em." O, fair enough, but I can bet we had half a dozen cups o' coffee before we went! One time a little Arab boy came over, he kneeled doon an' he took one o' ma friends hands and kissed the back of his hands. Ma pal felt a bit daft about it and then the boy said something in Arabic. I asked the man what he was sayin' and he said that he wis blessin' us all, hoping that we get home safe. That was very nice, but o' course when we went we forgot and turned around and shouted "Cheerio". Typical service men at their best!

When I was in Egypt I nearly got mesel jailed. I swam across the Suez Canal from Smyrna to the other side. I didna know I'd left the country illegally an' gid into another country. Mind you I wasna such a good swimmer, it's about a 100 yards an' when I got t' the other side I had a breather. I swam back an' there wis two military policemen waiting' f' ma. One of 'em said, "Do you know what you've done?" I said, "I swam across the Suez Canal." "Y' know y' left Egypt illegally and you went inta Saudi Arabia?" I sez, "I didn't realise that." They said, "We could put you in trouble y' know, fit woulda happened if y' couldn't get back?" I said, "I'm sure I woulda found a bridge somewhere." An' he sez, "Yes, about 90 miles up the Suez Canal!"

● Government House Jerusalem. Courtesy Lord Forbes

Lord Forbes: Being Military Assistant was not only an extremely interesting appointment, but it was the nicest possible job. I was serving an utterly charming master (General Sir Alan Cunningham). How lucky I had held out about being posted to the Far East only a year ago. As Military Assistant I was responsible for the High Commissioner's personal safety, and also for advising him on security arrangements being made by the army and police, so that the civil administration in Palestine could function properly. The High Commissioner was not only responsible to the United Kingdom Government for the administration of the mandate of Palestine, but he was also Commander-in-Chief of the Forces in Palestine. This title was rather confusing, for while Palestine functioned under civil and not martial law, Alan had the Armed Forces under his control, but not command. It was he who had to sanction their use if hostilities broke out, but it was the General Officer Commanding who took command of them.

Alan and I were very close to one another. Each morning I would accompany him to the King David Hotel where he would talk to the head of the civil administration, Sir Henry Gurney, the Chief Secretary, a first rate man who was one of the best civil servants. The High Commissioner headed the Government of Palestine and under him there was an Executive Council, like the Cabinet in Whitehall, over which the High Commissioner presided. Its members consisted of the Chief Secretary, the Attorney General, and the Financial Secretary plus a few nominated members. Then there was an Advisory Council, consisting of the District Commissioners and Heads of Departments, to advise the Chief Secretary. The departments in the administration really mirrored, on a smaller scale, departments in the United Kingdom administration.

Each morning, while Alan was having his discussion with the Chief Secretary, invariably my first meeting would be at the Intelligence Unit located in the King David, the only entry being through a locked iron door, rather like doors in a prison. Here my contact was Colonel Bill Megan, a really talented Irishman. Having got the latest news from Bill, my next visit was usually to see the head of police, styled the Inspector General, Colonel Nicol Gray, who had previously been a Royal Marine. Nicol had a great reputation for training, both in the army and the police; however Alan Cunningham felt on occasions that he was not getting enough information about Jewish terrorist activities so from time to time we would both have discussions with Richard Catling of the CID - the man most feared amongst the terrorists.

On our return to Government House from Jerusalem, quite often Alan would have a meeting with someone whom he had summoned to see him. On these occasions I would meet the person at the front door before escorting them to Alan's study, where I would sit in and take notes on the talks. This task was not only extremely interesting, but also very necessary.

The person most frequently summoned to an audience with the High Commissioner was Golda Meyerson, head of the Political Department of the Jewish Agency, as it was she who had to try to justify any Jewish acts of terrorism. These meetings with Golda were predictable. She would offer her apologies on behalf of the Jewish Agency to His Excellency and then say the Agency had no control over these terrorists. Then, with tears in her eyes, she would say that the Agency would do all in its power to see that such a thing did not happen again. Then the end of the meeting the time would come for me to escort her from Alan's study. On reaching the front door her tears would have vanished, and on driving off she was all smiles. She was a marvellously plausible actress.

On days when there were no official engagements in the afternoon I often went riding, which was an easy and very pleasant form of exercise. Then in the evening it would be a case of office work till dinner time and, after dinner, if there were no guests, invariably the Private Secretary, ADC, and myself would play snooker with Alan. He loved his game of snooker and had a pretty good eye for it.

The food at Government House was excellent - really far too good especially so soon after the war. The contrast between wartime meals and Government House meals was immense. Alan, a bachelor at the time, was himself a proficient cook and always maintained that a good cook should never have to use a tasty sauce as a strong sauce merely was a cover up for something not good enough under the sauce.

The person who did much for the comfort of us all at Government House, including visitors irrespective of their rank was Mardell, the English butler, who was always dressed in a black suit or wore tails if there were guests. He was both charming and efficient, and had served two previous High Commissioners, Sir Harold MacMichael and Lord Gort. On one occasion Mardell came to me to say that the chef was chasing one of the kitchen boys with a carving knife. Luckily my

responsibility was for the safety of the High Commissioner and not the kitchen staff so the ADC had to sort out that little problem!

Sundays were different. I would accompany Alan to St. Andrew's Presbyterian Church in Jerusalem, except about once a year or on special occasions when he would announce that he must support the Bishop and we would go to the Cathedral. Then on Sunday afternoons, Alan and I would sometimes do some improvement to the garden, but more often we would thin and brash a young Corsican pine plantation in the grounds. Alan was not only a knowledgeable gardener but also was very keen about trees. I often wonder what that Corsican pine plantation, which we put so much effort into, looks like today. Anyway, we had some excellent Sunday afternoon exercise, and the satisfaction of a job well done. It really was well done, for the plantation was greatly improved.

Since the 1939/45 war, Jewish immigration had been sanctioned at 1,500 a month and the Zionists now did all they could to increase the number through illegal shipments of Jews. This illegal immigration was organised by Zionists in Europe, who made use of their experience in underground movements during the war. To enable the would-be immigrants to get across Europe, these Zionists acted as guides as well as seeing to their documentation necessary for them to proceed to various Mediterranean ports to await shipment to 'God's chosen land' - Israel. The ships used were anything that the Zionists could lay their hands on. It really was a case of- 'any old tub will do!'

On two occasions, accompanied by the Naval Liaison Officer from Army Headquarters, I went down to the coast to see the Royal Navy dealing with an illegal immigration ship. On both occasions I looked through my binoculars. What I saw of the conditions on the ships was appalling - really beyond belief. With 'Standing Room Only'

● A blockade-runner with Jewish immigrants.
Courtesy G. McRae

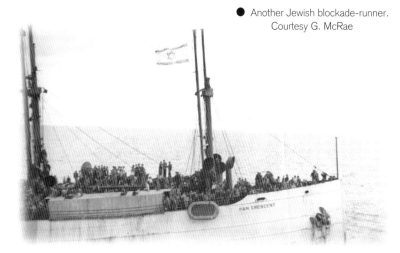

● Another Jewish blockade-runner.
Courtesy G. McRae

there was no home awaiting them. Our Navy had orders to stop but not to fire on ships with illegal immigrants. This they did to good measure, and it was only a few small boats that escaped detection by the Navy. Any ship with illegal immigrants stopped by the Navy was escorted to Haifa, where the immigrants were transhipped over to Cyprus to be put into camps.

The Colonial Office wanted to find out more about the conditions of the Cyprus camps for the Jewish illegal immigrants, so they sent out a senior civil servant, Trafford-Smith, to Palestine. On arrival, he came to Government House to be briefed by Alan on the Palestinian situation. After the briefing, Alan asked me to take Trafford-Smith to Cyprus, where we would spend the night. The Colonial Office had been in touch with the Head of the Administration in Cyprus regarding Trafford Smith's visit so, as everything seemed to have been arranged. He and I flew to Cyprus where we expected to find the red carpet down for his arrival, and the Head of the Administration waiting to greet him. Far from it!

the ships were loaded to their gunwales and were desperately low in the water. I was told that drinking water invariably ran out halfway through the voyage and that the lavatory facilities were totally inadequate for the numbers aboard.

The squalor that these Jews endured was unbelievable. These unhappy people were led to believe they were going to a land flowing with milk and honey. Those few who did get through the British net and stepped onto Palestinian soil, were quickly disillusioned. There was nobody to welcome them with open arms and

> " in Jerusalem buildings were dynamited; bombs exploded; bullets flew and people were killed or maimed "

There was nobody waiting to greet us. Trafford-Smith was livid and at once got on the telephone

● Damage to the King David Hotel, Jerusalem.
Courtesy Lord Forbes

to the Cyprus headquarters to ask why we had not been met at the airport, and got the reply that nobody was available to speak to him. Then, just as he was about to ask the RAF pilot to fly us back to Palestine, a Cyprus District Commissioner happened to turn up. This young man had been a civil servant in Whitehall and Trafford-Smith knew him slightly. As a result of this meeting, we spent the night in his house

As was to be expected with the vehement rejection of the United Nations plan by the Arabs, the Jews and Arabs once more began to fight each other. In Jerusalem buildings were dynamited; bombs exploded; bullets flew and people were killed or maimed.

The end of the mandate was now in sight as was my retirement from the army, but there was, however one more special occasion in which I played a part. This was the visit of King Abdullah to Jerusalem, and to the High Commissioner. The army provided a Guard of Honour at Government House, where I met the King and accompanied him during its inspection. After this I took the King into Government House to meet Alan. After the two heads of state had exchanged greetings we walked around the immaculately kept and beautifully designed garden with its really splendid panorama of Jerusalem and the Judaean hills, while the King and Alan chatted through Alec Kirkbride, who acted at interpreter. As so often in Palestine, it was a day of brilliant sunshine, with not a cloud in the sky, yet it was a sad day. Here were two great statesmen meeting together for the last time. One was about to relinquish the appointment of High Commissioner for Palestine and not be replaced. The other, during his next visit to Jerusalem soon after the termination of the mandate, was to be so cruelly and sadly assassinated, not by a Jew but by a disgruntled Arab. It was a plot by West Bank Arabs who blamed King Abdullah for trying to reach a peaceful settlement with Israel. Both the King and Alan had done their utmost to further a peaceful solution to the Palestine problem, but to no avail. The King was a delightful little man with a great twinkle in his eye who, although he was not supposed to speak or understand English, I have a suspicion he understood quite a lot as whenever a joke was made a smile would come over his face.

Inevitably, with all the uncertainty, our movements became more and more restricted. The British were now not only the enemies of the Jews, because of the restrictions on Jewish immigration, but also of the Arabs because of the United Nations plan. In spite of this, on Christmas Eve Alan and I went to the carol service at the Church of Nativity in Bethlehem which, owing to the large numbers attending and to the fact that the church had a tiny door- made so small in former days to keep out a mounted assassin wishing to murder worshippers - was held outside. It was a poignant moment when we sang about 'Peace on Earth'. One just wondered when that peace would come to this historic country steeped in Christian history. That Christmas Eve was a beautiful starlit night without a cloud in the sky. The air was warm and an overcoat was not necessary. There was a smell of rosemary and other herbs in the air. The lights of Jerusalem were twinkling in the distance, and the city was in silence, for once; not a shot rang out. Finally, the great bell above our heads struck midnight, after which this peaceful gathering of worshippers dispersed, and we returned to Government House.

Early in 1948, at a time when a few flakes of snow lay for about three hours on the high ground around Government House, John Pawle, a civil servant, took over from James Blewitt as Private Secretary. When the weather was cold, Government House could be quite chilly. The only fireplace to be found was in the main reception room. Alan's study only had a miserable one-bar electric heater. Obviously the Colonial Office architect who designed the building was unaware that there could be quite a drop in temperature in the winter.

At Government House there were two big functions each year. There was the presentation of honours and awards to those in Palestine who had been mentioned in the Sovereign's New Year's Honours List, by His Excellency, acting on behalf of the Sovereign. It was a big occasion as relatives of the recipients also attended the ceremony. Then, during the summer, there would be a garden party. With its fine rooms and lovely grounds, Government House was ideal for this colourful function, which was modelled on similar ones held at Buckingham Palace. There was even a military band playing on the terrace.

About this time I was informed that my release from the army had been approved. Alas, it was to be before the date of the mandate ending. As there were only a few more weeks to go before the mandate was terminated and Alan would be on his way home, I pleaded with the Military Secretary at Army Headquarters to get permission to remain on with Alan till the very end, and come home with him. However, my release was gazetted, and I was told it could not be altered. I was thus forced with great sadness to comply, as I desperately wanted to continue to serve Alan till he was safely back in England.

David: Tell me about leaving Taranto for Palestine.

Major William MacHardy: I never felt so good as when I landed in Haifa in the sunshine. We were completely exhausted and we were all terribly thin. With the sunshine in Palestine and the climate, we were soon bucked up. It was quiet when we landed and we got time to do sports, athletics and so forth. We got good food to build us up but then when V E day came and V J day came in August, terrorism started. There were three main terrorist organisations, The Stern Gang, Irgun Zvei Leumi and Hagganah. The Arabs were all right to us, they were no problem, it was only Jews we had problems with. There were a lot of skirmishes and quite a number of casualties. British soldiers being hanged - they found three British chaps hanged in an orange grove. Then they came and shot up the Airborne Division boys in Tel Aviv. They were sitting in a tent playing cards and they shot the lot. It was a bad time that. This day was a Sunday and the alarm went off and I was at the crossroads in Tulkarm. My job was to stop all traffic and in conjunction with the Palestinian police, search all the vehicles. We raced down to these cross roads, stopped all the traffic and then the police went down the line with all the trucks and cars. I was going down the line with the chief of police and we had looked at some cars, there were lorries filled with oranges and things like that and then I came on this chap sitting on a motorcycle. He never moved and he kept his goggles on. Immediately - it was probably intuition - I said, "Take off your goggles." He took off his goggles and his helmet. I didn't like his face and I said to the police, "I think you should take that lad in." He wasn't armed and we didn't find anything on him at the time. They took away the motorcycle and took him to police headquarters and it turned out that he was one of the big boys in the Irgun Zvei Leumi! It was the way he looked at me, it was pure intuition. That was successful that day but that's the kind of things we got. It was very frustrating and it took hours to go through all the traffic and go all through the papers etc. Mostly, it was about arms been moved from place to place. They were hiding arms in schools, in classrooms, in wells and anywhere they could hide them. Unfortunately, I seemed to fall in to a lot of these sorta things.

There was one day in particular just outside Tel Aviv where there was a village, it was a bad village and was full of these characters. This alarm went and I was sent out, with my platoon. There were

> " they were hiding arms in schools, in classrooms, in wells and anywhere they could hide them "

● Major William MacHardy, Sarona, Palestine, 1946

armed people floating about so we went out and we came on this bunch of characters and we called them to halt but they paid no attention and they started firing. I then gave the order to fire but I had a policeman with me. You had to be careful, you had to make sure if you gave an order it was understood. So I gave the order to fire and through that we inflicted nine casualties and of course there was a hue and cry about that. So when we went back to camp that night, the CO sent for me and he said to me, "We are in a spot of trouble here, they were all gangsters but a couple have died and the rest were wounded. The unfortunate thing that has happened is that your name has been put (out) over the Jewish radio (and) when that happens you have got to go." "Well," I said, "I'm not going I'm staying here with my men." Before this situation was resolved there was another that I got involved in. My CO had to go home and report to the War Office on the situation. He came back and he said to me, "This still obliges you to get out of the country for fear of being killed." I said, "No, I am not leaving my men but if my platoon commanders wish to go they can." One of my platoon commanders was a Jewish boy and the other one was an Italian. So I explained that they could go home but they wanted to stay with me. But I said, "No, better you go home and then you're out of this conflict altogether." Anyway, I managed to get through it and they didn't get me in the end.

There was one case where we were landed with an insurrection. There were two or three hundred Jews in this sports stadium. All we had was this coil of barbed wire to keep them in. Then of course they started to get violent. It wasn't the ones at the front it was the ringleaders at the back. So I gave the order to fix bayonets. That caused a commotion because some of them complained that they had been pricked with the bayonets. I said, "Certainly they were, they wouldn't stay within the wire and if they were going to come out over the top of the wire they would get pricked alright." So of course that sort of thing got out and caused problems.

● 17 Platoon, 'D' Company, 6th Gordons. Palestine 1946. (MacHardy is in the centre of the group)

You had to carry on and abide by the law at that time - which we did - but when you are confronted by people who are determined to escape you had to do something. An Argyll patrol was shot up just outside Jerusalem and if I remember rightly there were a couple killed and two or three wounded. The CO was so angry at this happening that he called a press conference. In the course of giving details of what had happened, he had used strong language which was recorded and passed on to the Jewish radio and of course it all came out loud and clear. There was such a hoo-har got up that he was called to apologise but he wouldn't do that so he was sent home. I was in Palestine from January '45 till December '46. It fell upon me to disband the 6th Battalion in November 1946 and that was the end of us. It was a sad day for me.

I came back in 1947 and unfortunately I had suffered rather badly with dysentery and was hospitalised for three months in Aberdeen. I had decided to give up army life because I had been told that I wouldn't be accepted for an overseas posting after having amoebic dysentery. So I applied for work with Scottish Agricultural Industries in Aberdeen. They were a big agricultural firm at that time. I was taken on as a trainee manager and I was with them for two years becoming a manager of one of the departments. I enjoyed it but I still had a longing for the army and the pay was not good. It was a time consuming job and in 1952 I decided to go back to the army. At this time the Malayan emergency was on and I thought whether I could get passed to get abroad. I went to see the medical Officer at the Gordon barracks. I explained to him, I didn't try to conceal anything and he told me that I stood every chance of getting better since a couple of years had passed.

● 'My Brigade winning sniper team; Camp 524, Gaza, June 1945' MacHardy in Glen Garry in centre of picture

● The pyramids, Cairo, 1945. L to R – Curran-Douglas, M.O. Edwin Hall, Donald and MacHardy

●Malaya

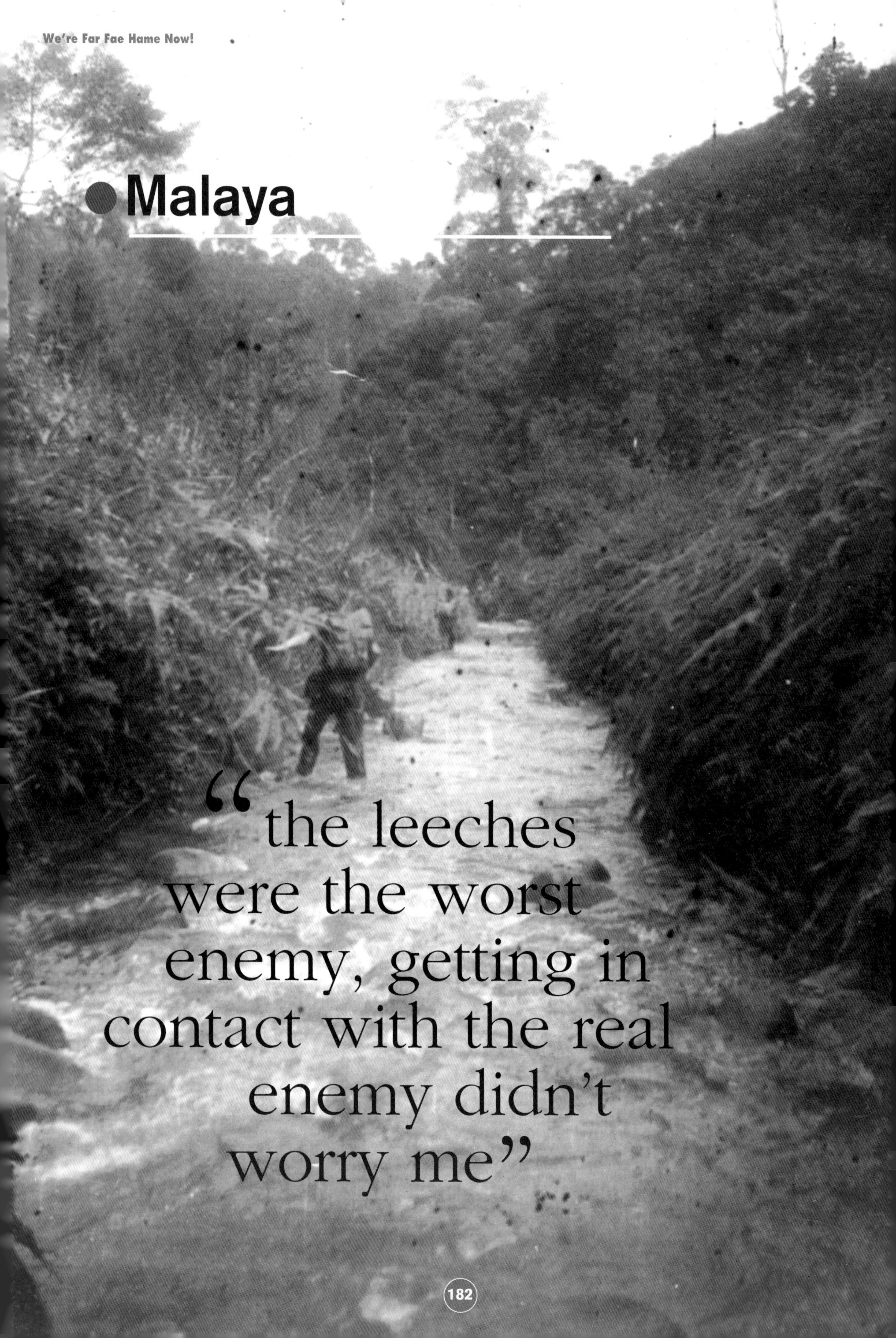

" the leeches
were the worst
enemy, getting in
contact with the real
enemy didn't
worry me "

Malaya
1948-60

*T*HE COMMUNIST INFILTRATION OF MALAYA BEGAN IN THE EARLY *1920s and in 1929 the Malayan Communist party planned to overthrow the administration and establish their own republic. Despite being declared illegal and without any enthusiasm from the people, the party was strong enough by 1937 to instigate a series of strikes with the intention of crippling the economy.*

As the Second World War loomed the MCP (Malayan Communist Party) effected an increase in its numbers by forming anti-Japanese groups which gave numerical strength to the anti-British strikes which had ensued by 1940. With the Japanese invasion of the Malayan peninsula late in 1941 the British saw it expeditious to enlist indigenous agents to perform a subversive role for the Allies. It was found that only the MCP could supply the personnel for this campaign and 200 men under British instructors became the motivating force for the resistance to the Japanese after the fall of Singapore. This became the Malayan Peoples' Anti Japanese Army (MPAJA). In 1943 the MPAJA still provided the only effective resistance to the Japanese and by the time of the Japanese capitulation the MPAJA had become a highly organised and equipped force of 4000 men with 6000 ancillary personnel. The Allies disbanded the force in 1945, however this merely meant that the MCP now reverted to it's original aim, that being, to install a communist state in Malaya. Whilst most MPAJA had forfeited their arms, several hundred guerrillas remained in the jungle to become the nucleus of an insurrection. By 1948 the MCP had begun a vigorous campaign of labour unrest, however, this campaign proving less than effective the MCP instigated a regime of murder and sabotage. These actions were opposed by the emergency powers invoked by the Federal Government of the British colony on 16th June 1948.

The Malayan emergency lasted for 12 years and occupied over 250, 000 men.

Major William MacHardy: I was only a month in Gordon barracks before I was posted out to Malaya as a Captain to the 1st Battalion. I joined them at Tampin I had to come down a rank because I was going back. I was in the Battalion for only two months and at this time I was commanding D Company of the Gordons because the company commander was ill on leave. Brigadier Henecker of the 63rd Gurkha Infantry Brigade came along one day and said, "How are you getting on, you have just arrived but how would you like to become my Intelligence Officer?" I was completely stunned. "I will be passing here

● Left: Bill Bain's platoon following a stream, one of the few recognised tracks in the jungle in two days time and I will expect your answer." Well, he came back and I spent two years with Brigadier Henecker. So I became his Intelligence Officer and it proved to be a most illuminating job that I thoroughly enjoyed. At that time things were bad. '52 and '53 were the two years where there were tremendous casualties. The High Commissioner, Gurney had been ambushed and assassinated. Lots of people had been killed and quite a lot of Gordons had been killed and it seemed to go on and on. So, I felt that I could do something here and I stayed with the Brigadier and the work was thoroughly enjoyable because you were on the hop all the time and we were also responsible for a lot of units.

The emergency started in 1948 and at that time there were thousands of communists in the jungle. There were tremendous casualties and uproar everywhere. The great thing that changed the whole proceedings was when General Templar became our GOC. He was a very hard man and if he said that something had to be done it had t' be done. I believe that a lot of the good work that was done in Malaya which dispensed with a lot of the terrorism, was due to Templar's ideas and methods. One of the first things that he introduced was (the building of) new villages, which caused a lot of hoo-har amongst the civilian population. He said that all these villages on the edge of the jungle were to be dispensed with because there would always be a food supply for the terrorists in the jungle. So he brought the people out of these places and put them into new villages surrounded by wire and with a home guard put on to patrol and keep the commies out. That was the first stage that the Communists were really getting hard hit. As you can well imagine, when you're looking down it's just a vast area of 100s and 100s of miles of jungle. Once you were in the jungle you could get lost and

> ## "the first night I was out, I had 30 leeches on my back"

once the Communists got the food taken away by destroying those villages it became very difficult for them. This made them come out into the open more where we could ambush them and kill them. This method got stronger and stronger and people started to see that Templar was right because the killing of the civilian population went down and down. At the same time we kept a very close liaison with the aircraft so they flew over the jungle continuously and when they saw a clearing and a garden patch it was reported to us and we then put out patrols to sort it out. We burned the gardens and dwellings.

David: Where were the Communists coming from?

William: From the North. They were training up there and coming down which was proven by photo reconnaissance. The Americans introduced photographic material, which would show what was happening under the foliage, and aircraft were put out the whole time, on the borders photographing. We could see the camps, huge camps where these characters were being trained. Over a period of time we bombed the lot. The main bombing that I took part in was when Brigadier Henecker went home, I still stayed on as Intelligence Officer to Brigadier Vickers. He was quite a character and was known as the Fuhrer but I got on well with him. He had just come from being commandant of Air Infantry School in England. His main thing was aircraft so when he came out, his first thing he said was, "We've got to bomb these beggars out of this!" I pointed out to him that pin-point bombing was not very easy in the jungle and there was always the chance that there could be casualties among our own troops. He managed to convince GHQ in Singapore that bombing was a good thing.

When I went on my first patrol, I'd never done

● Indigenous Malays, courtesy B. Bain

● A British serviceman - probably Malayan Police - instructing local people in the mechanics of ordnance. Courtesy B. Bain

● Erskine Camp at Kuala Kabbu Bharu in about 1950. This was their first permanent camp after living under canvas for the soldiers. Note the white building in the background, which was Bill's accomodation.

anything in jungles before, it was quite interesting going into that vast area of trees and darkness, covered in sweat. There were also great swamp areas, which were full of malarial mosquitoes, and the worst thing was the leeches. The first night I was out, I had 30 leeches on my back. Each evening you took your shirt off and the chaps would go round and put a cigarette on the leech and that was him finished. The worst thing you could do was to pull them out because if you left the head it immediately erupted and you got the poison. They seemed t' clamp on to you if you hadn't been in the jungle before, or you had white skin. There was no way of keeping them out, the water was alive with them. The leeches were the worst enemy, getting in contact with the real enemy didn't worry me, I enjoyed the creeping and not making any noise and get as close as y' could to them.

We didn't meet a thing on that first patrol but the one thing I discovered was trying to cut the undergrowth to get through. This area that we first went through on our first patrol, you couldn't move through it and you had to hack which made an infernal noise. People within a considerable radius could hear us hacking but you still had to cut a way through. That was very tiring. On our next patrol we were luckier and we made contact and killed a couple. It was a small area with about half a dozen of them there but the good thing was that we got right up t' them and caught them unawares allowing us to get their packs which was personally important to me. When we got back and the documents produced from the packs with the help of the Chinese translators we could find out who it was, which unit it was and where they were likely to go. We had to do that sort of thing all the time. In the OPs. room we had this wonderful map on one side there was all the known Communists and as they were killed we put a red line through them and the date when and where they were killed. One thing that always fascinated me was that we lost a lot of weapons when troops were ambushed. However, when we killed the Communists, the rifles came back, the Tommy guns came back, the

binoculars and the compasses. We could then trace where they had been lost on the map and where they had been found when the Communists had been shot. It was an interesting puzzle putting it all together.

Something happened which frightened Kathleen my wife. She came out to Malaya y' see, six months after I had arrived. The first day I went to meet her at Singapore where we stayed in the transit camp. We moved up on the train the next day. Well the train was ambushed! A few shots were fired and my youngest son Roderick was with us, he was only about three or four. So when the shots rang out I told then to get into the bottom bunk. There were a number of soldiers who went round the train to see and combat anyone who came near the train and to check the lines for booby traps. Then we set off again so that was the first scare she got. The next scare she got was, she came down to me at Police Headquarters. That day one of the patrols had shot three Communists and the procedure was that when anyone was shot they were immediately brought to the police station and deposited on the pavement so that they could be identified. People would come and identify them and that was one way to discover who they were. That frightened her when she saw that!

David: Can you tell me about the weapons you used?

William: Well yes, some units used the Sten but I didn't like it - especially in Malaya where there was dampness and everything was wet and it could jam. The Tommy gun was good it suited Malaya well and I still carried my .303 rifle, I still believed in that. I also carried the revolver on the back just in case. One thing about the Chinese, even though they were wounded they could run and get away very quick. If you didn't get onto them quickly you lost them. You'd get a trail of blood and you could follow that for a while and then it would disappear. They would commandeer vehicles on the rubber estates. That was one of our jobs to go round the estates, see the managers and consult

An officers club in Malaya, courtesy Major William MacHardy

Bedford 3-ton trucks ('Frankenstein' and 'Dracula') armoured for counter-insurgency work. - Cap Reid, one of the drivers, survived several ambushes in Frankenstein before being killed by a hit-and-run driver on his way to the pub in rural Aberdeenshire.

with them as to their own protection. They were responsible for their own protection but we liked them to feel that we were close at hand to come quickly if something went wrong. That was quite interesting because many of the managers were Scots so you can imagine it was like a family away from home. It was nice to meet them because we could see that they were suffering when you saw the wife going about with a revolver and a loaded weapon in one room and a loaded weapon in another room because they never knew when they were going to be pounced on.

We saw quite a lot of where the rubber tappers had been murdered by the Chinese because they hadn't the food that they were supposed to produce. They would come into the estate and if the tapper didn't have the food that they wanted they would slit his throat.

The war against the Chinese communists was an entirely different thing to say Italy. You were dealing with a people who had no compassion whatsoever. The Germans in Italy, had some good units and some not so good but then you knew them and you knew how to deal with them.

I came back from Malaya 1956 and got a staff appointment in Scotland taking command of the first intelligence unit in Scotland and became known as Scottish Command Intelligence Unit.

Bill Bain: I was living in bothy accommodation in Glentanar and had been for two years and this chap that worked at the farm, he was keen to join the army. We both had ideas about joining the police at one point. We were told that a while in the Guards wouldn't do us any harm because the police were quite keen to take ex Guardsmen: One, because their height was usually suitable and two, better discipline in the Guards. So when I volunteered to join the Scots Guards, I put his

Alan Brodie (front right pall bearer), at the funeral of a fellow Malayan Policeman, Paddy McGrarr, who had been murdered by terrorists. A long time friend of Bill Bain, they had met as gamekeepers on the Glen Tanar estate. After the Malayan campaign they ran the Aboyne Army Cadet group together

name forward as well. We joined and he arrived 10 days after me. I joined up in '48 and went out to Malaya in '49. Went down to Caterham for my training. Here things changed and we found ourselves doin' thing that we didn't like doin' and y' had t' do them to the satisfaction of others. However, if you made up your mind to get on and get the job done the less they troubled y'. This was all part and parcel of discipline. This discipline proved necessary when you went into action because you knew that you could depend on everybody.

After Caterham you were classed as a Guardsman not a recruit so then I went to Purbright. That is where y' did your weapon training and all that. The weapon trainin' and the assault courses were all designed for European warfare yet our second Battalion was in Malaya and it was all jungle warfare there which was totally different in terms of tactics. For example if you were advancin' in European warfare, before you moved you would be given covering fire so the enemy would keep their heads down so that you could move forward. In the jungle it was totally different it was more like what we did in the game-keeperin' world at fox shoots. You surrounded an area, two people here and two people there and where you could see one another. If you had a China man commin' in to the police or to your unit reporting that he was bein' pressurised to supply rice or dollars to terrorists, (a lot of them did supply them or else his family got bumped off), if he had the guts to come in, then we would get as much intelligence as we could from him. Then we would ring the village and we would allow the terrorists in and then when they tried t' get out the fun started.

David: What weapons did you have?

Bill: We would have near enough the same (in all theatres) but it was according to how many Bren guns y' had in your platoon. But again in Malaya, we didn't need Bren guns. I carried a Bren for 23 months round the back o' my neck an' I had callouses round here off the blasted strap. Not only did we have the military personnel workin' for the Malayan government but there were 'jungle squads' as well. They consisted of one European and maybe 15 to 20 Malayan people. The European would be a Sergeant or a Lieutenant but what they

> " the weapon trainin' and the assault courses were all designed for European warfare "

discovered was the white leader was bumped off and automatically the Malays threw down their weapons and walked away. They were allowed t' walk away by the terrorists because this was their means of supply of weapons and ammunition. We had Owen guns which was a better class of weapon than the Sten gun but it was the same ammo, 9mm. It had a longer barrel than the Sten and a little bit more punch. They were quite suitable because they were good up to 30 yards and that's as far as was needed.

I looked forward to going to Malaya and I remember that I came home on leave before we went but I never told my parents where I was goin'. We still had a lot of National Service men with us many of whom were to be demobbed and they had t' be replaced. We went out in the *'Empire Haladale'* which was a captured German cattle boat converted into a troop ship. It took 28 days to get from Liverpool to Singapore. I took very bad to the heat and I didn't think that I would survive it but after six weeks I was acclimatised to it.

My first introduction to Malaya was when we got on the train from Singapore and went up to Kuala-Lumpur where an army truck picked us up and we went on to Batuarang. Here there was a coal mine which was actually on fire; a fire started by the Japanese when they retreated. Part of it was opencast and part of it was underground. The open part had a lot of machinery around and these terrorists tried to do every damned thing that they could to cripple the country. Well, they used to topple the machinery into the opencast. Our task duties were to look after that. We were billeted in a huge building, which was a plywood factory. There were no doors and no windows. There was a roof but little in the way of walls. I remember goin' on guard at the mine and passin' the police station and the boys had success the day before and there were half a dozen terrorists hangin' from the trees. That was as a deterrent to others. That always sticks in my mind but it wasn't long after that we were carrying them out of the jungle tied on bamboo poles with their wrists tied together and their ankles tied together and the pole through. After six months at the coal mine we went down to Tampin and there it was all jungle patrols. Your platoon would go out into an area where reports

● Cpl. Bill Bain (right) and Cpl. Duncan Cameron (eventually Bill's 'best man') photographed in the village of Kuala Kubbu Bharu - note that they are armed for the visit

would come into intelligence that a certain group was in a certain place. You would try and locate that. It was impossible to search whole areas and we found that the easiest way to move was to walk along streams instead of hackin' y' way through dense foliage. It was dangerous, however, walkin' up streams because the enemy knew that you would use streams. You also climbed trees to see if you could see smoke or anything. You'd listen to hear for sounds of wood chopping because you would know there were no rubber planters there and so you would know that anybody there would be a terrorist. When you arrive in Malaya you weren't allowed to go into action until you had trainin' and for trainin' you had t' go into the jungle. The very first night that we went into the jungle we were ambushed. Well, we got out of it not too bad. When I had my 40th wedding anniversary my best man came with us and we relived some of our old times and I was tellin' (him about) when we were ambushed. Him and I dived behind the same tree, which he reckoned was only about four inches across. But I can only remember that I said that he wasn't much of a friend because he pushed me out of the way! There were a few anxious moments but we didn't lose anyone. The first time we were on action proper was when we had a report of terrorists puttin' pressure on several families to supply them. I think that all the headmen from each house had to produce both food and money. Our intelligence had got word of it and we went there to ring this place and wait for them to come in. We lay there for hours and hours because the terrorists didn't always come on time and some times they came early so you had to be there in plenty of time. There were five killed and

● Ablutions in the jungle

● A huge crocodile – still alive – that had been wrestled and tied up with rattan by the proudly posing Malay

three wounded who were followed up and caught eventually. We had two things we could track with. One was the E-bans from Borneo who were head-hunters. They were all tattooed on the throat. We had them as trackers and they could track things through the jungle that we couldn't. We also had RAF Corporals with Alsatians which were very, very fierce. I've seen one standing on the chest of a wounded lad with his windpipe out; they were savage. We lost one or two dogs through that because the terrorists would know they were being followed so the dogs sometimes got killed either by shooting or by grenades. We had a situation in one place where we were screening people, that is wiring off the village from the jungle. There could be no doubt that there were terrorists in that village. When y' screened the people (they) were put into this corral. The oldest or the youngest were allowed to be left in the house to be in charge to make sure that nobody stole anything or did anything. While they were all being checked out their houses were also checked for weapons. Now they were being screened at this place and some of them made a bolt for it. It was 26 in all and they all died. There was a photograph taken and published and shown in every railway station in Malaya. That was our G Company that shot them. They weren't all terrorists because there was a boy of less than 14 but he had made a bolt for it along with the rest who then got shot. The ones that didn't bolt lived to tell the tale.

I was lucky being an NCO because I got promoted out there and then I got sent down to Singapore and we trained the Malays so that they could take over from us and do the job themselves. It was only a matter of two or three years after we left that they were more or less running the show for themselves so we must have done some good.

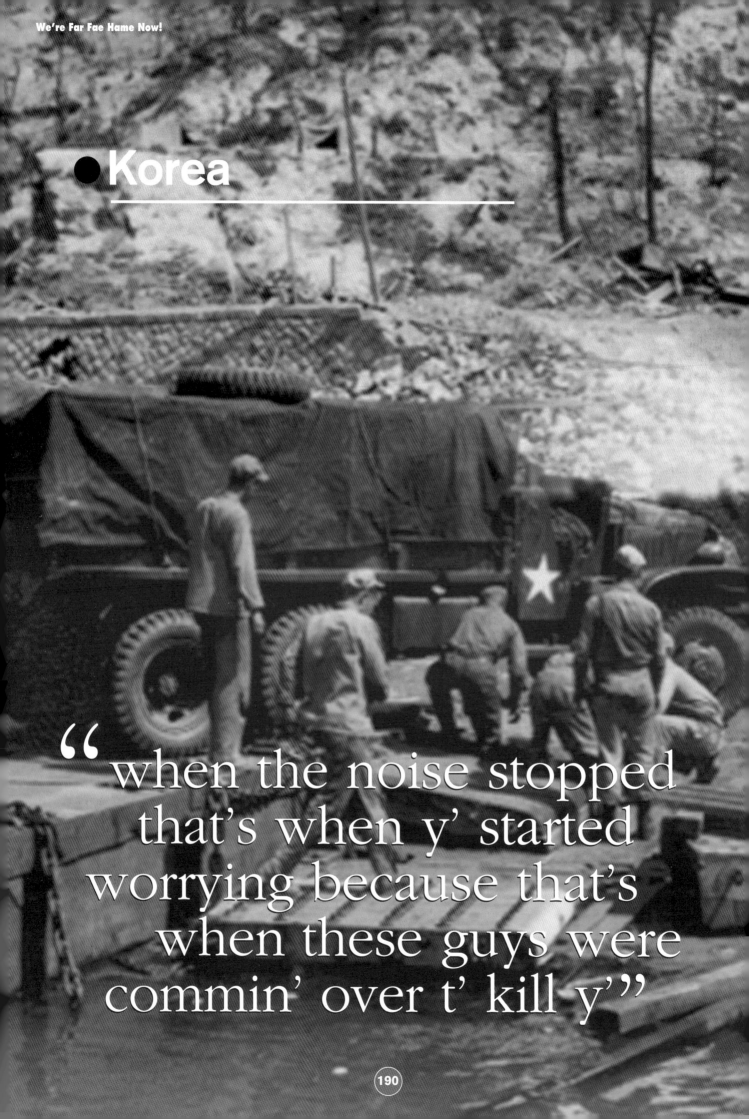

●Korea

" when the noise stopped that's when y' started worrying because that's when these guys were commin' over t' kill y' "

Korea
1950-53

*T*HE KOREAN WAR, WHICH STARTED ON THE 25TH JUNE 1950 *was a full-scale conventional war played out in the shadow of the atom bomb. The Koreans suffered over 1,000,000 casualties and the Chinese around 500,000 - 50 per cent of them being civilians. There were 142,000 U.N. service personnel killed or wounded. It has been suggested that this war achieved very little and indeed the Americans saw it as the first war that they lost. Arising out of the tension and frustration of the cold war, one interesting outcome was that the South remained loyal to the Western nations, loyal enough to send a considerable number of troops to Vietnam in support of the Americans in that later war. The hostilities ended in 1953.*

The Battle of the Hook - one of its key battles - consisted of three main phases. After relieving US Marines, the Black Watch with Canadians and Americans fought the second battle on the 18th of November 1952. Later the Gloucesters bore the brunt of the third. On its steep flanks the British sustained more casualties than in any other confrontation in the Korean War.

The Gallant Forty Twa.

(In Korea)

On the eighteenth of November
In the year of fifty Twa
The Chinks had planned an invasion
On Ronson and Warsaw

Now first they cam owra in millions
But we chased them all awar
Because in the knee deep trenches
Stood the Gallant Forty Twa.

The Vendees were on the left o' us
The Yanks were on the right
But the Watch is in the middle
Showin' them how t' fight.

Now if y' don't belive me
You shoulda been there anar
To say that you're a member
O' the Gallant Forty Twa.

Now when this battles over
And everything's gone fine,
The Yanks can tak back their tanks and guns
And put them in the line.

But if he Chinks attack again
The Yanks will all withdraw
Because they're not connected
To the Gallant Forty Twa.

● Left: The Americans landing at Inchon

● Norman Finlayson in Germany beside a somewhat rare Oxford carrier

Mr Finlayson: "So, you're lookin' for a ferret?" "Yes M' Lord." "In the hours of darkness?" "Yes M' Lord; I'll let you understand sir, when we lost the black ferret we were gettin' a couple o' rabbits for wer dinna." He said, "I don't believe you for a minute." Then I said, "Why should I poach, I've got a good job?" (I was a crane driver at that time with WC Anderson up in the creamery). Anyway we went into the chambers and he said, "I know you're guilty and you know you're guilty and if you ever come in front of me again you will get the maximum sentence." That's two years in jail or a fine of 500 pound I think it is - and this was in '56 or '57; it was all happening again.

Well t' get back to the Black Watch, when I joined them it was in 1950 and in 1951 I volunteered t' go to Korea to get away from one or two problems here.

David: So you weren't joining to do National Service?

Mr Finlayson: No, no, I'm a five year man. I joined as a professional because if I hadna joined up I woulda got two year in the jail because I'd got three outstandin' charges for poachin' so I said no, and I jined the army. I sez t' the Sergeant, - he was jist a young lad of about 17 or 18 years of age - "I want t' join the army." He said: "Name and address and where y' bide." (Then) through the medical. "When can I get away?" Within six weeks after I worked as a labourer in Donside paper mills, I (was) servin' m' time up in Fort George doin' wer trainin'. We were all nothing. We were just squaddies doin' this and doin' that. Fair enough.

After the six weeks training we had trained in unarmed combat where we learned Judo. Then we got jungle training. We did this over the 30th parallel in North Korea. The conditions were appalling to say the least but the comradeship was ideal. We were under canvas and the winter was so severe that you couldna wash or shave before midday. If you touched anything metal it stuck to your hand. We used our weapons with great difficulty 'cause we had t' wear those gloves, the ones without fingers and another glove on top o' that with a trigger finger in the forefinger. Everything was supplied by America. The Argyll and Sutherland Highlanders, they were the first Scottish regiment t' go to Korea. They came in to Korea from Hong Kong and more o' them went down wi frostbite than being shot by the Chinese! The Chinese had better winter clothing than us, what with their quilted coats an' that. The Americans copied their hooded parkas. Y' had on balaclavas wi jist y' nose and eyes showin'. How we managed t' fight I just don't know.

We got up about 6.30 but there wasn't much to do and you'd all day to do it in. Breakfast and morning parade and then lunch and still not much to do. You were told about two or three days before you were going to such and such a place and you were hyped up. You always moved up at midnight so the Chinks knew you were commin', they had more information about us than we had of ourselves!

David: What was the 'Hook'?

Mr. Finlayson: It was a line o' defence. It was jist a hill, that's all that Korea existed of, hills.

David: How did you fight with all that gear on?

> "if I hadna joined up I woulda got two year in the jail"

Mr. Finlayson: Well actually you threw them off. You were really actually sweating and the blood was pumping through your veins at some rate. We moved up to the Hook where we were going to take over from the Yanks I think it was. We had t' take up the Americans to take out their dead. We wouldna do it for them. To let y' understand, when we were up there we were livin' in what we called a 'hoochie'. You'd be maybe eight feet down in the ground. There was timber and sandbags and if a shell came over it would give a bit of protection. It came down in two layers, y' came down off the trenches then down maybe two feet and then down again. When y' came off duty the only thing you took off was your parka the rest was left on. You might be up there for one or even two months at a time and maybe you'd come down for a shower an' y' can imagine the state of us! Four of us used t' share this hooch and the four of us used t' wash and shave in a tin the size

● A collection of ephemera gathered by N. Finlayson during his Korea posting

o' a cup. It was a part of wer discipline. Y' could come outa there growin' beards but the British army didn't allow that and we respected that because of our own regiment. We always washed and shaved.

David: Did you do much active patrolling?

Mr. Finlayson: Oh yes, ha ha ha, we were terrified from the minute we left until the minute we came back. Y' knew that if you were outside and you came across the enemy , it was either him or you. We were highly trained but if you saw one of the enemy, (nine times outa ten, it was a Sergeant or a Corporal that was in charge o' y'), they would say to leave him. You could never know and these Chinese were very intelligent people, there might appear to be one o' them but there could easy be another 100 waitin' for you. They used t' let y' go past where they were so that they could find out what it was that you wanted t' find out. You'd report their positions when you got back but when the artillery started shellin' there was nobody there. They would stand either side o' the Hook and wave t' ye. Going out on patrol, we would carry the Lee Enfield rifle, the NCO would carry the Bren. We had rubber soled boots and a couple o' bands o' ammunition, our faces would be camouflaged (with Cocoa!) and then there was the tin hat. The tracks were laid out for us. It was like a rabbit warren, one patrol that way, another patrol the other way, and so on in a sort of pincer movement. You'd go maybe a quarter of a mile then stop and sit for a couple of hours and take down every minute detail. B company would do the same but our paths would (hopefully) never cross.

David: Did your poaching skills come in handy when you were on patrol?

Mr. Finlayson: Yes, I suppose so, for example, y' never walked along the top of the hill so you are in the background all the time. The Chinks used to do this regular but as I say that was just a sprat t' catch a mackerel. They knew you were watchin' them but they were watchin' you but not from up there, from a different position altogether. Another thing we used t' do at night was (this). (There were watching posts) at about 200 yards away from the trenches and there was an outer perimeter. You were inside this wi barbed wire in front o' ye but you were in a look-out post and you could see all the front line and when y' being shelled you are always on the 'phone. There'd be a flash at one o' clock, then another at three and everything that happened was noted because the Chinks were very good on mortars. If you could put down a handkerchief these guys within four or five shells would put one in the middle for y'! The wastage of life was beyond belief! They would attack in waves. They shelled us continually for about four hours then when the drums and (then) the bugles started goin' - y' didna worry about that. It was when the noise stopped that's when y' started worrying because that's when these guys were commin' over t' kill y' and I <u>meant</u> kill y'. They came over in waves. They were mostly peasants actually filled wi saki and they'd run wi bamboo canes and maybe with one knife between the first 20 or 30 of them. It was a massacre really but y'd shoot so much o' them that all yer ammunition has gone then another wave comes over and you've *really* got a fight on your hands. By Christ I'll never forget it. Experience told us to carry more ammunition (than usual) and our tanks would come up the hill and sit there with their lights on to illuminate the place. Y' saw these masses o' people and when daybreak fell they come in about. They didn't count their dead but there were very few left behind 'cause there were people t' tak back their dead.

In fact they did break through at one point but we chased them out because their idea was to come in waves either side o' ye. They did manage to take about 16 or 18 prisoners but that wasna bad for a line that was about three miles long. The Yanks were on the left of us and the Vandoos who were French Canadian were on the right. There was hand to hand fightin' although I wasna involved in it myself. I was jist shootin' in front of me and then our Pipe Major, he got wounded, and me and Bill Reynolds took him down to the first aid post. Once we were there we werna allowed back up because there was too much confusion. The Pipe Major – Major 'Daddie' Campbell -lost his feet and he recommended that I and Reynolds get a medal for saving his life. Although we got congratulated by the Company Commander no medals were forthcoming.

Gordon McRae: At the time National Service was still on so I thought that if I didn't sign up for the navy I might be called up for the army which I didn't want. I joined the Royal Navy in September 1946. I joined the HMS *Raleigh* just outside Plymouth and did my initial trainin' at Torpoint. There was a lot of square bashin', every day for quite a few weeks. We learned to use 303 rifles, did an assault course and learned seamanship and things like that. I then joined a battleship called HMS *Anson* and did my sea training.

It was very strange because all my life I'd been used to smaller vessels and to find yourself on a 32,000 ton ship, well; it was enormous! We had to scrub the wooden decks in our bare feet even in the winter time. The food was fairly basic and we always seemed to be hungry. You were out on deck at six o'clock on a winters mornin' before breakfast so we'd a good appetite anyway. I finished my sea training and went back to barracks.

From there I went to Malta.

From Malta we came home and got paid off then I went to a training school for underwater detection. I then got drafted to the Far East. In Hong Kong we took on a wartime complement because in peacetime the complement was about 150 less than what you carry in wartime, and the Korean thing had blown up. We then went to Japan because that was the naval base that we wis usin'. During that time we were rehearsing for action stations or whatever. Then we sailed up to Korea and started patrols. They were seven day patrols and we switched round the different ships, the *Belfast*, the *Jamaica* and such like.

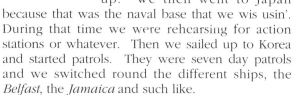

● Gordon McRae

David: What were you patrolling for?

Gordon: Anything that was goin'; we did the west coast of Korea and the Yanks did the east coast. Things started to get pretty bad then and our boys started to retreat down to Pusan right in the south. So we were standin' by off there waitin' to evacuate them off the beaches. We were quite close inshore and we could see what was going on. The smoke was goin' up and obviously there were some big battles goin' on.

There was a big Chinese junk that came near. It was filled with stuff, tins, cigarettes and goodness knows what. So we plundered it, the stuff was no good to anyone else anyway and the amount of stuff we had off that junk! Well we lay off that coast for two or three days then we cleared out there. Sometimes it was boring 'cause all we did was steam up and down what seemed to be the same bit of sea.

David: Tell us about Inchon.

Gordon: We were part of the close support group bombardin' inshore positions. I don't know how many ships there were but there were quite a lot. So we went up towards Inchon, it was quite similar to the west coast of Scotland. You go up through the islands and channels until we reached this beach which was about half a mile off and we had a grandstand view. The other ships were behind us. We were there for about two or three days and eventually the landing craft came. It was quite a busy and noisy time bombardin' the land positions. We got a bit of return fire but no one was hit. Then the troops went in, they were mainly American. We saw 15 huge American naval transports - Liberty ships - come up the channel and each one of them carries a complete detachment of marines with all of their gear so they would be independent of anything else. They had come up to land their stuff. We had our own complement of marines on our boat which numbered about 80 includin' the band, that would have been our shore party.

At Inchon, there was little fear of mines because the mine sweepers had already been up before us although there was always a chance that they had missed one.

David: Tell me about the American airmen who were rescued.

Gordon: We got through the radio that an aircraft was down, it was a Mitchell bomber I think. The plane was a good way, I can't remember how far but the weather was good so we set off to try and find it. It was a couple of hours steamin' at least. The aircraft was still floating in the water when we got there. Anyway, we picked them up, took them back and transferred them to an American ship.

● ".... we picked them up and transferred them to an American ship". (G. McRae)

Flashback to Korea.

Keith F Thomson: In 1950 I was sent off to Korea with the British contingent to the UN force. We formed the R.E.M.E. Medium Workshop and were to be based at Taigu. We had a splendid journey cruising down past the Bay of Biscay, through the Mediterranean, down the Red Sea, and then across the Indian Ocean and round passed Hong Kong to arrive at Pusan. After disembarkation we got our lorries running and drove up to Taigu.

Our billet was an old school which was not too bad but our workshop was an empty field. We erected a large tent or two and parked all our workshop wagons nearby. All very basic but workable. A fence was already there and it divided us from an American camp. Guard duty was necessary but rather boring except when the Yanks got a bit jittery and started shooting at anything that moved. We all hit the ground flat!!

One of my best chums, Willie Whitehall, was a wonderful musician. He could play almost anything. We had many a singalong on the boat but no instruments at the base. He and I hunted some of the few remaining shops and found a banjo. I still own half of it! Willie taught me to play 'Loch Lomond' on our banjo but I've lost that skill now!

When winter struck I was on a forward convoy unit just south of Seoul. It wasn't much fun lying in the snow with night temperatures falling to minus 40 deg.F. But we survived it OK. Then we were called back and sent down to Pusan to build a base workshop. We moved into an ex-American tented camp on a hillside. Then we started bulldozing and levelling off part of the slope to start building. We were all eating tinned rations until one of our gang, who was a Cockney street trader in civy street, went off down to the American base camp in one of our jeeps. He came back with a full tank of fuel and a collection of fresh turkeys, vegetables and fruit. It was a delight for us all. He never let on how he conned them into it but he went back week after week. Then disaster struck in the form of the tail end of a typhoon which wiped out the camp and all the work we had done. It was just after that that my left hip jammed up solidly and I was in severe pain. I got sent to the Swedish hospital, then to the American hospital and was finally sent to the British Base Hospital in Japan. In the end they decided to send me home and then they gave me a medical discharge.

One section of my life was over.

● Top to bottom; 1,2 and 3, courtesy KF Thomson showing conditions in Korea, his 'workshop' facilities and some friendly villagers. 4 and 5 courtesy G. McRae showing marines and officers from HMS Kenya inspecting the result of naval gunfire on North Korean defences on Wolmi Do, (a wooded island off Inchon)

●Borneo

"the things in the jungle that give you away are noise and movement"

Borneo

1963-67

Malcolm Chisholm: *THE PERIOD WE'RE TALKING ABOUT IS FROM 1963 TO 1967. The Borneo campaign happened because President Sukarno of Indonesia opposed the formation of Malasia which included the state of Sabah in Borneo and the states of Sarawak, Singapore and Malaya. He decided that he was not going to have this so he started making incursions into Sabah and Sarawak. The British army went out there in 1963 and the Marines were the first people in. The unit I was with went out shortly after 1963. What was going on in Borneo was that the Indonesians were coming over the border into the British section of Borneo. We were looking for them but we were also operating in Indonesia and finding out where their camps were, what their formations were and what their strengths were.*

Typical day; right, we would go into the jungle for about 28 days at a time on observation and intelligence gathering. We worked in four men patrols. Because we worked in small numbers we didn't make contact unless we had to. We covered a 700 mile front with less than 60 of us. Most of it was intelligence gathering for the rest of the British army. Because we worked in small numbers, operating deep penetration and cross border ops. etcetera, we had to be virtually

invisible. Nobody had to know that we were there or that we had been there. To operate like this you have to have a certain type of person and that's why we did selection courses.

The ration packs that we had were dry rations. Two well-known food companies did much of their experimentation for Pot Noodles and all the dried foods that you see in the supermarkets today. We were the guinea pigs if you like. Money was provided by the British government to develop these

● 'Oourr Hoose' a long-house in Borneo. Where the supply crates are; the canteen and ops room is just inside.
Note the five (fire) beaters in the foreground. (Lieutenant Colonel A. Cumming).

● Left: Westland Whirlwind delivering supplies in Borneo.
Courtesy Lieutenant Colonel Alistair Cumming

● November, 1965. 3 Platoon, 'A' Company, 1st Gordons at Long Banga. L to R, back row: Williams, Muckle, Ballantyne, Munro, Parry 46, Watson, McPherson, Harvey, Reid 95. Centre row: Greig, ? , O'Hara, Low 43, Sim, Gordon, McKnight, Rutherford, Sutherland, Adam, ? Front Row: Angus, Cheape, McTevendale, McCona, Cpl. Breen, Lt. Cumming, Sgt Robertson, Cpl. Raith, McErskine, Wood, Low 03.

things and these two companies benefited from this. We also had dieticians who worked out what you needed per day to keep you going in arduous conditions. These packs weighed about three pounds. There was no way that we could carry 28 times three pounds plus ammunition, radios, explosives, weapons and all the other gear. So what we used to do before we went out on patrol was to split the rations down. What it worked out to in the end was one packet of hard tack biscuits per day which was six biscuits, a small tin of processed cheese which was an ounce and a quarter, a tin of sardines and the main meal which was a block of dehydrated meat and the rice. By the time it was whittled down it was probably less than a pound per day. The main meal was a curry and because the meat blocks were like sawdust so to make it interesting we would buy dried vegetables and curry powder. This was not provided by the British army. It was then quite acceptable.

Ann Lavery: What about water?

Malcolm: The water, you collected on route. I played by the rules, some didn't but I did, we had water sterilising tablets. What you did was, you put a sterilising tablet in your water jug then after that you put in another tablet which took away the taste of the sterilising tablet so the water was ok. I always sterilised every drop of water and I never ever had any problems. I knew people who didn't and they did have problems. Some of the water looked brackish or sandy and things like that. It looked horrible but I had no trouble because I played it by the rules.

Ann: What sort of terrain was it?

Malcolm: Terrain was mountainous most of which were sharp ridge-backs. The vegetation was jungle. Borneo's jungle was lovely, it was like forest land and there was some swamp areas. I do remember one time we were in a swamp for about seven days and we were up to our waists in water for most of that time. Y' don't think about the snakes and the scorpions and everything else that was there you just carry on.

Ann: Did you see those sort of things then?

Malcolm: Yes you do but I believe that you only kill things if you have to but never for the sake of it. You have to have respect. Y' kill mosquitos because they were detrimental to your health but you never killed for the sake of it.

A typical day in the jungle - we'll start from three o'clock in the afternoon when it always rains. You could set your watch by it. You plod on and by four o'clock it had stopped raining. Then we'd make a meal, which was rice and the dehydrated meat blocks, which you turned into a curry. So you had curry and rice. You always cooked in twos.

Ann: What did you cook on?

Malcolm: Hexamine blocks which are similar to a firelighter block and we had these disposable stoves. You cooked your rice on one and the curry on the other. Full tin of rice and you split that half and half. It took about half an hour to prepare and eat the meal and then we'd be away again. We'd walk until last light, in these latitudes you had 12 hours of daylight and 12 hours of darkness and it went dark instantly. There was no twilight, it went dark at about six o'clock and it was dark in about 10 minutes. At about 5.30 you'd stop and pick a spot where you would settle for the night. If you were in a safe area then what you do is sleep in a hammock. If we were in an area which was not safe then you sleep on the ground. You would make up your hammock. Your Bergen - which is your knapsack - was always packed and ready to move, nothing was ever out. Then you would change your clothing. Take off your wet clothes and hang it up somewhere and you'd put on dry clothing. We didn't have this issued and what we'd do is, we'd get parachute material and get suits made up so you'd got a top and a bottom like a pair of pyjamas. You also carried a pair of plimsolls so you'd put these on. The idea being that if you slept then had to run during the night perhaps if you got 'bumped' by an enemy you are not running through the jungle with nothing on. It could be embarrassing! I'd like to emphasise this, you were always wet in the jungle. You are either wet from sweat or wet from the rain so your clothing was permanently wet. So, you've got your hammock up, you've got your pack all packed up and neat and tidy. You knew where everything was, including your weapon. After the light went out at about six o'clock you'd sit for an hour and just listen. Now, contrary to what you see, in those days it was virtually impossible to move through the jungle at night time. So if you sat for an hour after last light, and no one had seen you move there the chances of anybody coming after you was nil. If they did move during the night, you would be able to hear them and see the lights but this did not happen because as I say the jungle was impassable at night.

Ann: How did you move through the jungle, were there paths?

Malcolm: There were animal tracks and if you were hacking through the jungle you were going the wrong way. That's another fallacy that you see in the films. You go round you don't hack your way through. You follow animal tracks going in your direction and using a compass and a map. You have a map with ridges on but they are not necessarily accurate. You take the easiest route that you possibly can but you don't take recognised tracks because that's when you are going to meet an enemy. People use tracks, right, so you don't use them. If you're going to follow a track, then you come to the track and you loop round it then back to the track and loop round it again. The things in the jungle that give you away are noise and movement. I can remember an incident where two of us had been on a recce. We were actually in Indonesia across the border. I had to do a hop skip and a jump to stop the laddie I was with because I'd seen this (movement) in the corner of my eye and we stopped dead. We looked out of the corner of our eyes, we never moved we didn't even breathe, we counted 200 enemy troops. They were within four metres. Now if we'd have moved they'd have noticed us so we just stood there and

● An SAS patrol returns to Long Banga after a 3 week patrol

● Lunch for the Officers at Kota Belud - Dryburgh Ranges. L to R Paddy Gordon, Reggie Hunter-Blair, Malcolm Ross and David Saunders. Courtesy Lieutenant Colonel A. Cumming.

stood perfectly still frozen and although we were not in camouflage, we were in green and they did not see us because we were perfectly still. I think it's a farce where they black their faces out and things like this. I always wore long sleeves and a wide brimmed floppy hat. Anyway, night time, you're in your hammock or you are on the ground and you go to sleep. In the jungle, unlike the desert you always got a good night's sleep. Then you'd wake up before first light at about four o'clock in the morning. Pack all your gear up. Pitch black, and I mean pitch black. You've got no light from the stars or towns - literally pitch black so you do everything by touch but you know where everything is. You put your wet clothes and boots on again, that was always the horrible bit and then you wait for the first light before you move.

Ann: Is it always warm?

Malcolm: No, it can be very cold, it's according to the altitude you're at; you can be up as high as five to six thousand feet. We had a nylon sleeping bag again made out of parachutes because the standard British army sleeping bag was too heavy and bulky so we made our own out of parachute material the same as our hammocks. Without parachute material and para-cord we'd have been lost. We didn't use standard equipment, we begged borrowed and stole, or we improvised and made our own equipment. Today it's different, they tend to make the equipment that's required but in those days you had t' use your initiative.

Ann: Why was that do you think?

Malcolm: No army really catered for special type forces. They wanted them but they didn't like them, they liked their infantry and cavalry and that sort of thing. They were very traditional. Times have changed and they are ready to accept the unusual also. The Americans were very good to us. They had a lot more gear than we had so we used a lot of their equipment. With a set of British mess tins you

● A hovercraft at Tawan landing site. Much new equipment was trialed in Borneo, the hovercraft was not a great success.

could trade the Americans for anything because their mess tins were lousy and the British mess tins were brilliant. Anyway, you'd start off the next day walking at about six o'clock at eight you would stop and have breakfast which would usually consist of three hard tack biscuits and the one and a quarter ounce tin of cheese. We would sometimes toast it to make it a bit more palatable. Then you'd carry on. The other thing is that in the jungle you didn't talk much in fact you could go for 28 days in the jungle without hardly saying a word. Everything would be whispers or sign language. Because four men worked as one every one knew what they were doing.

Ann: Did you get to know them prior to going out on patrol.

Malcolm: Well, I was new and I went out there and had to prove myself. You did a selection course, right, which got you in but the chaps you were working with didn't know what you were like and I remember the first time I went out there, I had t' cook on my own and the rations were bloody horrible but nobody told me. You go and buy curry powder and onions etcetera and it's only when they get to know you and trust you that they will accept you and then you became part of the team.

Ann: Did you each have an individual role?

Malcolm: Yes, you had a lead scout who was the man who was up front. He was probably the one who would contact anybody if we met an enemy. You had a control commander who was behind him. Third man was the radio operator and the fourth man was the Tail End Charlie who kept

watch behind. I was the radio operator so I was third man. I carried more weight than anybody else. As the other's rations depleted their Bergens got lighter but I still had the radio. If you went out on a 28 day patrol, your Bergen would weigh anything between 70 and 100 pounds. The radios we were using then were quite old fashioned, they were old wartime radios but it was not the radios that weighed so much it was the batteries that you had t' take and they were quite big and heavy. You would also have to take spares.

You might have seen these radios in films where you'd see an agent would have a suitcase and he would open his suitcase and inside there would be a radio. Well, it was exactly the same radio, it was called a '128'. What we did was, we took the radio out of the case, we had plastic moulds made and we fitted it in. It came in two sections, there was a

● A basha in Borneo. Right is Sgt. Wally Joss, left is Lt. Col. Cumming's orderly, Munro.

transmitter and there was the receiver. There was also a key that you had strapped to your knee and there was a canvass headset with two little microphones. It was all as light as possible. The problem with these sets was dampness and sometimes when we got to clearings or anywhere where the sun was shining you opened up the radio to let the sun dry it out. Its main advantage was that it was a very simple radio and you could always change a valve if necessary. With today's radios they are so sophisticated you would not be able to repair them. I never had any problems, it always worked for me. For me this was good fun but today you use a mobile phone with a satellite. The satellite has changed everything.

We didn't keep a log in the sense that you wrote a book 'cause we didn't carry anything with any information. What you would do is send a situation report in morning and evening so the log was kept back in base. Everything you did was in cypher so you had to code up your messages and then send them off.

Ann: Could you throw things like batteries away when they were dead?

Malcolm: No, we never threw anything away. Anything we took out with us came back. We never left anything so that when we moved through the jungle nobody knew we'd been there, nobody knew we were there. Most of us in those days smoked and every now and then in a safe area we'd stop for a smoke break. The cigarette end, the filter tip, you would push into the earth so that it was hidden and it would not be found. You left no traces whatsoever. You watched your every footprint so that you left no tracks. You tend to get a sixth sense, you know when there is something around. It's rather like being an animal, the hairs on the back of your neck turn up and you know. I could smell a brew of tea from about 600 yards. You didn't use toothpaste, soap or anything alien like that. If you washed yourself with soap in the river the smell could carry all down the river and somebody would smell it. We didn't wash every

Evening Express Saturday July 31 1965 — 3

Smiling out of this clearing in the Borneo jungle are members of a platoon of "D" Company, 1st Bn. The Gordon Highlanders.

The picture was taken on a "chopper - pad"— helicopter landing platform — just after the platoon had returned from a week-long patrol in the jungle.

With them are their two Iban trackers, Ojan and Awa, and cradled in the arms of one of the men is the platoon mascot.

Third from the left, rear rank, is platoon commander Lieutenant Gavin Peebles, who is joining the Depot staff at Gordon Barracks in September.

Among other members of the group are:—Pte. John Gordon, Aberdeen; Pte. John Thompson, Aberdeen; Pte. Alick Howie, Bucksburn; Pte. Ian Phipps, Montrose; Pte. David Flett, Peterhead; Cpl. Alexander Stewart, Ballater; Cpl. James Forrest, Aberdeen; Pte. John Reid, Kincorth, Aberdeen; L/Cpl. James Shand, Banff; Pte. Ian Whyte, Ballater; Pte. Robert Hanratty, Aberdeen; Pte. William Neil, Culter; Pte. Norman Win-

Among RAF gymnasts

Visitors! Here is a quiz worth winning!

HOLIDAYMAKERS! Would you like the Freedom of the Granite City for a week? If you are successful your visit will be a memorable one.

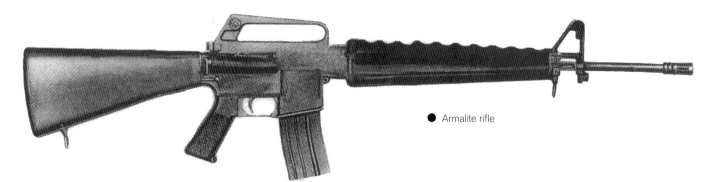

● Armalite rifle

day because we were always sweatin' so you were never really dirty and it rained every day but you smelled. It's like an animal, they are clean but they smell, so we were rather like the animals. Anyway we've had breakfast and we carry on patrolling. Every half hour or at every significant place we would decide on an RV (rendezvous point) in case of getting 'bumped'.

Getting ' bumped' means that we get a contact with an enemy. Basically you exchange fire. Because we were only four men you couldn't really stay there and have a fight because they might be 200 men. What you did if you had a contact was, you'd exchanged fire and then pull back. If the patrol got split up what we'd do is go back to the place that we decided was our last RV.

Ann: But how do you find your way back?

Malcolm: You can, it's surprising but you can. You don't mark, a lot of it is instinct; you have got your map. Your memory becomes tuned to it and you can remember actual leaves and you do find your way back. You remember the terrain.

Ann: What weapons did you use?

Malcolm: In the early days the lead scout would probably carry a Remington automatic shotgun and the rest would carry Armalites - which is the American AR16 - mainly because it was light and had the fire power. You always carried it in you hand with a round up the spout with the safety on. You tried not to have a contact because if you did, in one sense it defeated the object because you were supposed to be invisible, you are not supposed to be there. I remember one contact that we had and I was lead scout at this time. I didn't have a Remington though, I had an Armalite and we had a contact and I fired the weapon. We were going up a hill and at the same time I slipped. I'd got my gun on automatic and the bullets were going up. It was probably only a split second but it seemed an eternity and I probably only let off about two or three rounds

but it seemed as though I'd let off a whole magazine. Because of our training, I rolled over and the other three got into their positions either side of the route. They covered me with their fire as I ran back. Then the next man ran back and so on. That was a funny one, as I say, as I fired I slipped and went backwards but we got out alright.

Ann: What was the contact and how did you get away?

Malcolm: It was a patrol but I don't know how many there were. We got away from them by doubling back. What you've got to remember is that they were afraid to come looking for you. We had the advantage because after doubling back, they didn't know where we were and would be worried that they'd get shot as well. Also, they wouldn't know how many there were of you. When you run, you run fast (even) with your pack on and everything. The first time I went into the jungle I ran through the jungle and I was absolutely cut to ribbons. Eventually you get to know how to move 'cause everything in the jungle has got spikes on it. So, you do manage to run without getting caught up. The best way to explain this - and I saw this myself in Scotland - is a Red Deer running through the forest and it never catches it's antlers and it's very similar. You run through the jungle and never catch on anything. It again becomes instinctive.

So then we come up to lunch time which was probably three hard tack biscuits and the tin of sardines which were in oil. The reason for this was there was more nutritional value in the oil than there was in the sardines but we just tipped the oil away and ate the sardines.

Ann: Did you lose weight then when you were on patrol?

Malcolm: Yes, I always put on weight when I was at home. I was still very fit but I always liked a layer of fat over my body.

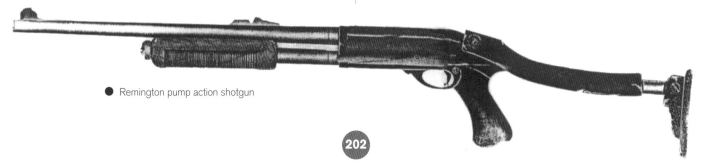

● Remington pump action shotgun

Ann: How many miles do you think you walked on an average day?

Malcolm: I think it depended on the job and how fast you were goin' and how safe the area was. You stopped, listened and looked probably every 20 minutes. You'd stop squat down and just listen and look then carry on.

We were the eyes and ears of the British Army, we were the information gatherers so they could plan their strategies. We had to report in twice a day on the radio.

Ann: Did you ever have difficulty getting through?

Malcolm: I personally never did, I had a knack for some reason I was gifted if you like!

Ann: A good knob twiddler then?

Malcolm: Ha Ha! Yes I suppose so.

I'll say this about the Borneo campaign - and a lot of people don't appreciate this - it was one of the best campaigns that the British ever handled. There was a minimum loss of life and the minimum amount of money. Unfortunately the British never praise their brilliant things they always praise things like the Charge of the Light Brigade which was a fiasco or perhaps the para. drops at Arnhem which again were a bit of a fiasco. We always seem to celebrate our failures.

Borneo could have turned into a Vietnam the difference being that the British government realised that they'd got a problem in that Sukarno wouldn't accept Malaysia. The British government sent the military out there and told the commanders to get the job done and the politicians didn't really interfere. They fought a campaign for four years and it cost the taxpayer a similar amount to that which it cost the Americans for six hours in Vietnam at it's height! It was also a good campaign in that it brought Sukano to his knees economically. They achieved all their objectives with the minimum loss of life and as I say, to the tax payer it was very economical.

Ann: Did you see any animals out there?

Malcolm: Saw quite a few snakes and I think again it comes down to respect. Man is the most feared creature on earth, right, so that most things got out of man's way. The only things that bothered us more than anything else were elephants and hornets. One was very big and the other very small. If we were on patrol and the first man saw an elephant he would shout, "Run for your lives, Gaja" and what you would do if you were on a track that an elephant was on you just had to get off the track. The elephant would not chase after you but he would keep chasing you till you got off his track. With hornets, which are nasty, nasty beasts and very aggressive, you have to run at least a 100 yards to get away from them because they would chase after you. They would sting you for no reason at all, they were very aggressive. If y come down to scorpions and snakes and things like that they didn't really bother you. If you were in a safe area and we came across a deer we would shoot it and eat it. We also killed a python once, which was about 10 to 12 feet long and we ate that as well. We weren't hungry but it was a pest to us so we ate it. Talking about snakes, when I was a lad I had a comic and I read this story, it might have been in the 'Eagle' or something like that. In this story there was a great big anaconda which bit this chaps head off or something like that. Anyway this was a childhood comic story. In 1968 I was on a plane to South America. I can't tell you what we were going there for but suddenly this comic story about the snake came back to me and I though that you get anacondas in South America. Well. It was on my mind and I actually did see an anaconda in the jungle and they were really big. Anyway, we were in the jungle and as usual there were four of us on this patrol and we did the usual thing, stop and decide an RV place. This was savannah scrub, it was not dense jungle although there was some jungle around. We made this RV on this track in case we made a contact and this time we did get bumped and so we all spread and scattered and I went back to the RV point. The anaconda crossed my mind and in those latitudes it gets dark instantly. Anyway, I was just sitting there just off this track and out of the corner of my eye I see something move. I moved my eyeballs and had a look and there was this bloody big anaconda crossin' this track. As I have said, what lets you down is movement and noise. Well, I sat there and never moved but I had to move my head to get a good look. The snake sensed the movement and turned round and went back into the jungle. I was quite worried I can tell you. I wasn't scared but I was a bit worried t' be quite honest. Anyway, the rest o' the chaps weren't comin' back by the looks of it and it was time for it to get dark. I put my hammock up and I put it as far up the tree as I possibly could and it proved a hell of a job t' climb into the bloody thing. It was only about six o'clock at night and I was in my hammock with my parang positioned plus my jackknife. I'd got my rifle with one up the spout and I was lying there half expecting a giant anaconda to come and wrap it's coils around me which would swallow and digest me but of course it didn't!

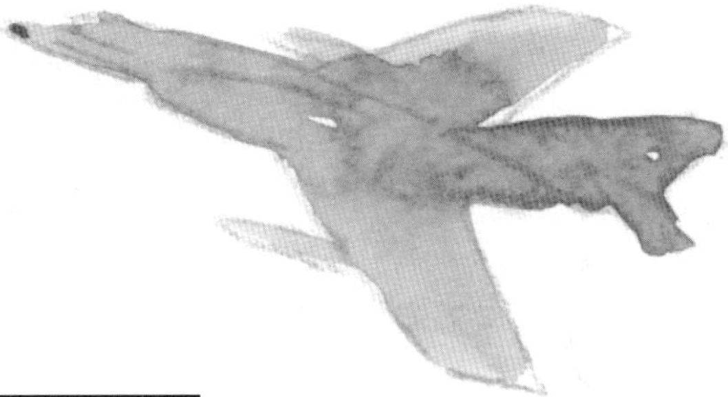

●Falklands

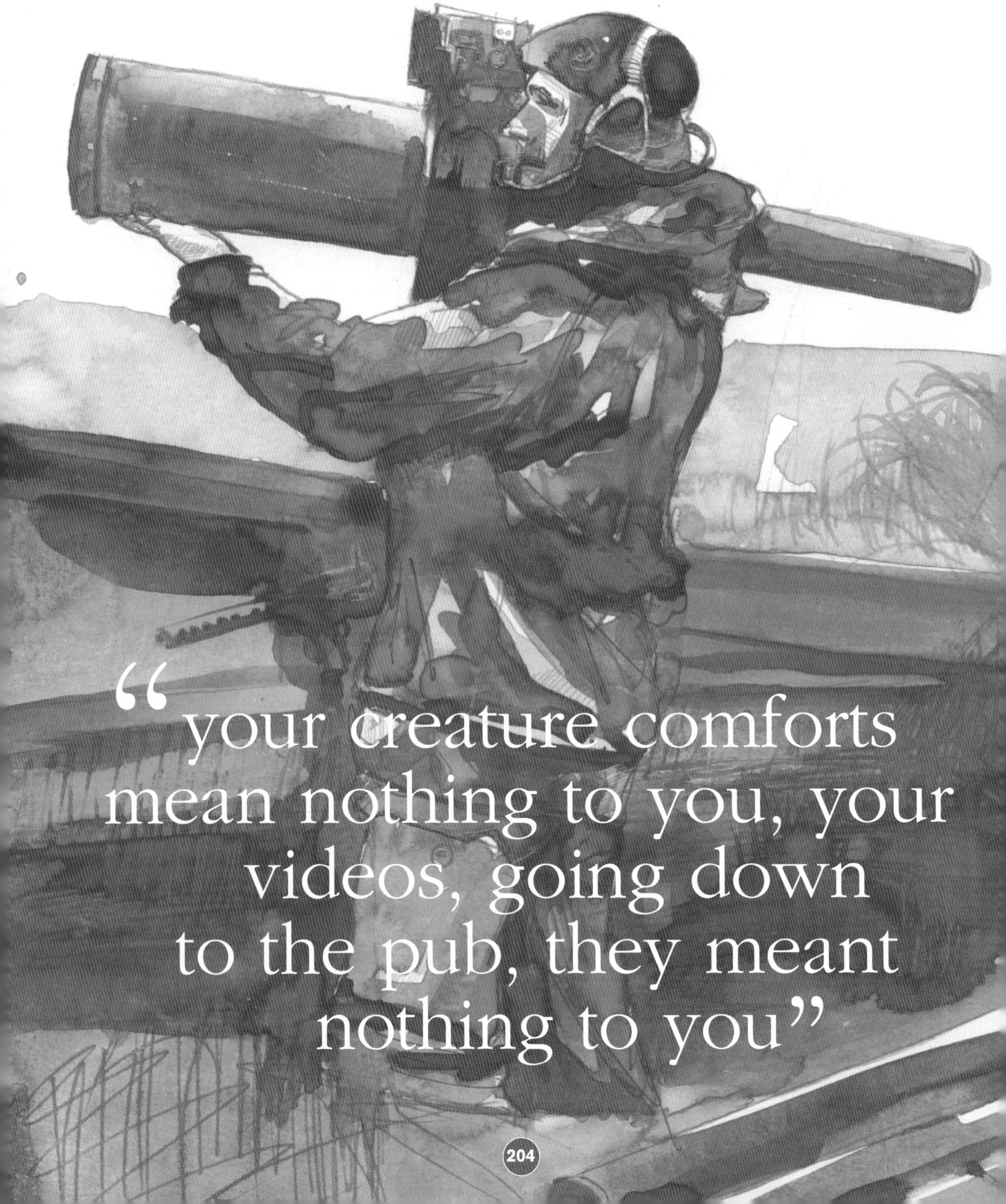

"your creature comforts
mean nothing to you, your
videos, going down
to the pub, they meant
nothing to you"

Falklands War 1990

"*THE FALKLANDS ISLANDS ARE ONCE MORE UNDER THE GOVERNMENT desired by their inhabitants. God save the Queen.*" *Major General Jeremy Moore the Land Forces Commander at the time sent these words to London shortly after the Argentine surrender on the 14th of June 1982 thus concluding the conflict which had claimed the lives of 255 British and 652 Argentine soldiers.*

This small war was hard won, the Argentine forces fought with exceptional skill and determination; they were not the push over that was expected. Furthermore, unexpected setbacks, such as the sinking of the essential supply vessel, the Atlantic Conveyor, gave the British an extremely difficult campaign.

Colin Duncan fought in the battle for Mount Longdon which proved to be perhaps the most vicious battle fought on land in that conflict. His story below is testament to that battle's intensity.

Colin Duncan: I was an anti-aircraft guided missile operator in 43 BTY, Royal Artillery, being part of a three man detachment providing close air defence support for the infantry unit which was the 3rd Battalion of the Parachute Regiment. The weapon we used was the 'Blowpipe' shoulder launched surface to air missile system. It was steered in flight by means of a joystick attached to the aiming unit. I was 19 years old and I come from Aberdeen. We provided the air defence. It was a mobile thing, you had an aiming unit and a missile canister. You split it down because it was man portable. The bigger units were fixed for example like the Rapiers.

Once you have troops on the move or going over awkward ground, that's when you need portable equipment and that's what we were doing with our missiles. So we had to hump it with the infantry

Trevor: And you took your missile with you?

Colin: If you were fighting in Europe or in NATO you would have had (wheeled) vehicles or armoured vehicles but because of the nature of the terrain in the Falklands, everything either had to be choppered or walked. The missile itself with the aiming unit was about 54 pounds. That was the missile on your shoulder with the aiming unit on it.

Split down, a detachment carried about three missiles and an aiming unit, a radio and all the rest of the equipment. The Commander, he would have the aiming unit; the other lad would have a radio and a missile and I would have two missiles. Being the junior one of the detachment I got lumbered with the two missiles plus all the standard kit - your rifle, webbing, and your pack. It was a bit like a cross because you had one missile across you and one up and down. Once you had or your equipment strapped on to you, all you could see was legs at the bottom! That's how everybody looked just stumbling about with all this equipment on so all together you were carrying about 120 pounds of equipment each.

Trevor: So when you got news that the Falklands were going to happen where were you?

Colin: I was in the barracks at the time, in Bulford on Salisbury Plain.

We first saw it on the news that the Falklands had been invaded but it wasn't till about a week later before they decided who was going and what equipment was needed. Then we were put on 72 hours notice to move. Then it was brought down to 36 hours. Then we got stood down, we weren't going, then we got stood up and we <u>were</u> going. Everybody was wanting to go 'cause it was like a

● A 'Blowpipe' in action on the Falklands.
Courtesy Jacek Kapocki

● Leaving Southampton, Colin Duncan centre

big adventure, so all the lads were excited about it and saying this is what it's all about. You were trained and you were all psyched up. No one had been to war before, if there had been some veterans there, they might have been more hesitant. We were all young lads and we were all fired up.

Initially there was only four detachments going out of the whole battery and everyone was volunteering and I was in one of the detachments that was picked to go. So we got our notice to move. Originally we were going in Land Rovers so we got all our equipment packed up in them, then we were told that we couldn't take the Rovers because the terrain wasn't suitable; we unpacked everything again. I phoned my mother up and she was tearful, she couldn't believe that I was going. She said, "Keep your head down, don't be a hero, don't do anything you are not supposed to do and remember your basic training and all the things you have been taught." We got notice to move so we went down to the rifle range to zero our rifles in. We did a lot more simulated training in missiles again just to bring us up to scratch. We did a lot of fitness training, weapons training and first aid.

At four o'clock in the morning a bus came to pick us up at the camp and we went down to the docks at Southampton and boarded a Townsend Thoresen ferry which was a cross Channel ferry which had been requisitioned by the government. There were lots of troops and ships and lots of activity. Nobody actually believed that we would be going or we'd get to the fighting stage because we thought that the diplomats and politicians would have sorted it out. Everybody was thinking that we would get as far as the Ascension Islands then be called back. We had a lot more training on the boat on the way to the

Ascensions and because we were air defence and had live missiles, while we were on the boat we were going to be the boat's defence. We set up positions around the boat so that we could defend the ship if necessary. There were paratroopers on board with us and some army air corps people so there were guns, helicopters, ourselves and various other troops. We also had to do our anti-submarine watch at night and the ship was blacked out. There were a lot of other ships joining us from other areas, warships and troop ships. We did more first aid and training, and strengths and weaknesses of the enemy, different threats and intelligence stuff. The whole task force re grouped at the Ascension Islands. That was when you had a full realisation of what you were a part of. When we arrived at the Ascension Islands at night there was a mass of warships and troop ships. It was unbelievable. We crossed decks onto the *Canberra*, because 3 Para., which was the main regiment we were attached to, was on the *Canberra*. It was good on the *Canberra* after the ferry because when the seas got rough the little ferry was tossed all over the place whilst the *Canberra* was like a solid rock. It was on the *Canberra* on the way down to the Falklands that we had to make our wills. If you had to re-write your will, this was the time to do it and maybe take the opportunity to take out more insurance. On the way down it was my birthday and I got a few cards from my Mother and others for a request to play 'Sailing' by Rod Stewart. So this request came for Colin Duncan and they played it over the ships radio but I didn't own up to it because there were thousands of troops on the ship so no one would know!

The training was getting more intense because the senior Commanders were worrying about the fitness of the troops after being so long at sea. When we hit the land there would be a lot of walking so they were worried about our physical condition. So there was a lot of running around the boats and doing weapons training and that kind of stuff. Then, we also did the air defence for the *Canberra*; we were on the *Canberra* when the *Sheffield* got hit so the whole Task Force was still at sea when the *Sheffield* was sunk. There had been attempts by the Argentine Air Force, which was trying to get in towards the task force and three aircraft had been shot down by the forward ships. There were a few air threats at the time and everybody else had to go down into the decks but the air defence crews and machine gun crews were rushed up onto the decks. We had our positions, we had missiles live and ready to use. After five weeks sailing we got nearer the exclusion zone and we transferred onto the *Intrepid* which

> " it got a bit sombre at that time because everybody realised 'this is it'. "

● 'Wasp' helicopter approaching stern of MV. Europic

was a Royal Navy landin' ship. The 3 Para. CO took us in to this big dining room. He was givin' orders out and we were realising that we were goin' in and it was going to happen now. Live ammunition was given out, radio call signs and codes were also given out. We were given our first aid equipment including morphine. They held both Catholic and Protestant services on the boat and they held communion, which I went to. Then 3 Para. CO told us which groups were landing where and what we'd be issued with and a general out line on what's happenin' and then the orders were given to the junior Commanders about what we would be specifically doin' and where we were specifically goin'. It got a bit sombre at that time because everybody realised 'this is it'. We were told that if the landings were opposed and people go down we have t' leave them, (unlike Northern Ireland where if somebody is shot the casualty comes first), because medical people would be coming up behind us and they would deal with them as they didn't want the momentum of the attack to stop. So everybody was gettin' a bit tense and nervous.

That night we moved into Falkland Sound and we had been issued with our equipment, it was dead silent and we were all sittin' there gettin' ready to go. Some people were crackin' jokes, it was quite tense. The SAS were already on the islands but our SAS group went down in a chopper and all had been drowned or maybe there were a couple of survivors. They were going to be our guides so when we went ashore they would have pointed us to where we should go. That caused a bit of a problem so they had t' call some more of these SAS troops to help us. With these SAS troops being drowned it made you realise that it was no longer a game. We had about 120 pounds of equipment,

grenades, and machine guns.

It was unrealistic because if we had been caught on the beach we wouldn't have been able to do anything because we were that encumbered. So we got in to the landing crafts and came into Falkland Sound which was right down in the middle of the islands and we'd hoped there were no sea mines. Everything was silent and very tense. By the time the door opened out on the *Intrepid* it was daylight because the landings had been held up because of some problem with another group landing on the other side of the islands. We thought we would get caught out in daylight raids as we were in the open. A risk was that all these landing ships would be caught out in the open still disgorging their troops on the islands. That was the first time I saw the islands. The doors opened and - there was news! There they were; the Islands. There it was, blue sky - it was a nice day and everything. Everybody was standing there, 'here it is' like. An air threat warning came in over the radio, air threat red came in so the guy that was driving the landing craft said he would put us down at a point where we weren't supposed to land because we had to get ready out in case of air attack. There were all these landing craft and we had to go to a location, which was convenient so that they could get us on the beach as quick as they could so that we didn't get caught. We couldn't get right in towards the land so when the door went down there was water between us and the land. When we got down into the water, it came up to our waists and it was all slimy rocks underneath and I was panicking in case I fell over. So I'm there with two missiles on my back and my machine-gun strapped on. You couldn't rush because you would just fall over. So when we landed it was a bit chaotic. There was confusion and people going in the wrong direction because we'd landed where we weren't supposed to. Landing with 3 para, we were the first giving immediate air defence for them. The landings weren't opposed, there was a small local garrison there but they had gone.

Trevor: What about the red alert from the air?

Colin: The aircraft came in and went towards ships that were out towards the sea so they never came in over the land. It seems that the Argentines didn't realise that there was a huge task force actually landing in Falkland Sound which is like the split down the middle of the two islands. So we spread and fanned out. The Sergeant Majors were shouting and screaming at people because they were going in the wrong direction. Everybody was thinking, 'What's happening, this is chaotic!' I was looking around, looking for snipers or any enemy. We all had our pre-planned locations and we had to go up towards San Carlos settlement and that was where we were going to establish the beachhead. 3 Para., who we were attached to all landed with us and obviously we were wet, then we moved up to our locations. Then an Argentine aircraft came down; a forward patrol sent a radio message saying there was a Pucara coming down the valley. It flew past them and they radioed down to us and this poor Argentine pilot came down and stumbled upon an entire British fleet of warships. We got the missile systems on to our shoulder, Bang! Bang! We fired the missiles off but he managed to get away over the side of the hill. He must have spotted us in time and he got his aircraft over the ridge as the missile screamed passed his wing - that was our first action. The ridge that the aircraft went over brought him into the view of the entire British task force so he must have wondered what he'd got himself into. I don't know whether he survived that but he just flew into a nest of nasty things that were waiting for him. The pilot then must have radioed back to his headquarters because half an hour after that there was the biggest air shoot I've ever seen. We got up to San Carlos settlement, which was a group of farm buildings. Everybody started to dig in. We got a missile system set up ready to use and then the sky erupted - just erupted - with aircraft it was unbelievable. I'd never seen anything like this. There were Mirages and Sky Hawks everywhere. Missiles and machine guns were firing on them, the planes were shooting missiles and dropping bombs, it was just a mass of missiles and rockets. You just had to snap out of it and take part because you couldn't believe it, you were just transfixed. We were firing

missiles off everywhere, even at targets we knew we could not hit, as we were told to get everything into the sky, even if we couldn't hit it as it would put the pilots off because they had such an advantage in the air compared to us. I was designated the operator because on the way down to the Falklands, on the simulator I had the best scoring rate so I was deemed the one that fired the missiles.

Trevor: What did you actually do to fire a missile?

Colin: If you imagine an old World War Two bazooka - you put it on your shoulder, you have got an aiming unit, your tracker is like a big monocular sight with times 10 magnification. You get the aircraft in the sights and you fire it. There is a joy stick and it sends a ratio control signal so when you move the joy stick left or right, that sends out a signal to the missile to move left or right. It travelled at just above the speed of sound. It was quite a fast missile but it was close air defence and had a range of about three and a half kilometres. So the aircraft were flying in from all directions. The ships were the main targets at that time but they were dropping bombs on us as well. They were those retard bombs, they come down on a parachute, explode and they send shrapnel down on you. So they were using those on the troops on the land. Well, these two Mirages came flying over the Valley from left to right and I saw this flash just above my head and a horrendous roar of the engines. I just threw the missile system to the ground and dived into a trench. I looked up to see what was coming down but they hadn't dropped anything this time. There's my mates looking down at us and I felt a right idiot but it was just instinctive. The two Mirages flew away.

There was a woman in San Carlos who had married one of the islanders and she had a baby. She would come up to trenches because her farm was right in the middle of all that was going on. She would come up in the mornings and bring rations and make pots of soup and they'd bring it up to the troops. She would bring her little baby up in amongst the trenches. Her farm was down a bit and we were all around about her farm, an entire task force dug in around about them. So this young girl would come to the trenches and tell us what was on the World Service but a couple of times she got caught in an air raid. The aircraft would scream in unawares and she wouldn't have time to get back home so she had to dive in the trench with the baby as all these missiles were being fired and bombs being dropped. Nothing ever happened to her but it always stuck in my

> " she had to dive in the trench with the baby as all these missiles were being fired "

mind, this young woman in the trenches with all this going on. She was from Edinburgh and she had married a local. She was good and she was nice looking as well, so that was OK!

We were in San Carlos for about a week. On the 22nd, these Mirages were coming in to attack, I fired a missile at the first one. It was a group of two or three I can't remember now how many. They then split up. I was aiming for the first one but by the time the missile got up to near the point, it was the last aircraft of the group and I managed to bang him just underneath at the rear. I saw the impact and then the plane went out of view almost immediately. That was my detachment's first hit. It was to be my first and only hit at that time. I had fired that many missiles in the San Carlos area just to put the aircraft off. The Argentinean pilots were very good. They came in and would drive home their attack then everything would open up. There were machine guns, missiles and everything but they just kept their course bang down the middle. Some ships would come up into the bay to try and get some protection because a lot of ships at this time were beginning to get hit and their systems weren't working right.

I remember these two Mirages come screaming down from behind the valley. I remember seeing the Rapiers and our other detachment open up and these two missiles went screaming by. The Mirages were huggin' the land and on course for a frigate in the bay and we were wondering why the frigate wasn't firing at these two jets. They were pumpin' rocket fire into the frigate, it really got hammered. The Rapier fired and it exploded to the right in front of his cockpit. I don't know how he survived it because Rapiers have a near enough 100 percent hit rate. If you were a pilot and you saw this missile exploding to your front right you would veer off but that pilot, he didn't budge and he kept straight homing in on to the ship which got a real belting. Their aircraft just kept their course, the cannon fire and the rocket fire were going into the sides of the ship and bombs went down. The bombs hit but you couldn't see any outward explosions. All you could see that showed that there was anything wrong was that smoke was coming up from the funnels,- the damage was all inside. The bombs would just go right through the skin of the ship and all you would see was smoke coming out of the portholes. That was just one of many that we saw get hit. All the violence that was happening; that quite stuck with me. I couldn't believe the level of violence and the determination that everybody had, - both the Argentines and the British - in trying to kill and destroy each other. It was unbelievable and I always used to think, 'Why

● Colin Duncan practising with 'Blowpipe' in Norway

can't people in peace time be that determined to help people, why can't we have that same urgency and determination for good in peacetime emergencies.'

Trevor: Did it change your attitude in some way?

Colin: It probably did change me to some extent but I did remember thinking how that determination could be used in peacetime. When it's peacetime, it's always so slow for things to happen but the violence that people inflicted on each other amazed me. They didn't care, they just went in.

I admired the Argentine pilots, if the Harriers didn't get them on their way in or ourselves or the ships didn't get them in San Carlos, they still had to run the gauntlet to get back home. They always seemed to attack when I was on my tea break so I always had to put down my tea and get up and do the bit. A warning would come over on the radio or people would blow whistles or bang tins. This is what worried me about our weapons system; you have to stand up to fire it, you can't be in a trench. We had to stand up and everybody else was down in their trenches and you felt very exposed. When you were waiting for an air attack to come in with the weapon on your shoulder you wouldn't know where the plane was going to come from you'd get a roar of an engine and it would be down on you instantly. Sometimes you'd see seagulls flying in the distance and sometimes a seagull would fly up and you'd pick that up and wonder if it was an aircraft or not because you were like that, y' heart rate was givin' it thump, thump, thump. When you are firin' the system and you target an aircraft and you fire, this thing just flies off your shoulder. There is a back blast. There is not a big push back but there's a huge weight loss. Then there's a bit of confusion to begin with because there's a lot of smoke and flame. The aiming unit brings the missile into your sights and then you pick it up and guide it from there. When you are targeting the aircraft you are not aware of all the chaos that's going on around you because you're so concentrated on what you're doing. It's just the aircraft and you and you're guiding the missile and you're tryin' t' get him. He's coming up, and it's just you and him but when you are waiting for an air attack to come in your heart rate is just going ballistic and it's just missiles and machine guns and tracer flying up. Our detachment had to move location to a more exposed part and we were on our own and there were Argentine commandos in the area as we were outside the defensive trenches of our paratroopers and we felt really exposed. At night, on sentry in the trenches, you had your rifle and bayonet ready in case someone crept up on us. I felt that I wouldn't have time to bear my rifle so I took my bayonet off my rifle and kept it in my hand so that if someone came near me I had got something ready at hand. As we were in the San Carlos area for about seven days and we had shot most of our

missiles off so we were left with only a limited supply. We landed with three missiles then the helicopters brought in more supplies so we had six or seven missiles but we were firing them off as fast as we were getting re-supplied. If you had to move, you could only take three with you, the rest would be brought up in helicopters. We got the order to move by the time we had lost a lot of helicopters because the *Atlantic Conveyor* had been hit so that all our helicopters and tents that we were going to use went down in the ship. We had ground sheets and had to make shelters out of that because our tents had gone. The bulk of our heavy lifting helicopters had gone down so the idea that helicopters would be moving us forward was scrapped. So we were told that we would have to yomp it everywhere.

Trevor: Were there no half-track vehicles or something like that?

Colin: There were a limited amount of helicopters which were Navy 'Sea Kings' and 'Wessexes' but not as many as we wanted and everybody vied to get the choppers for their jobs and the senior Commanders would have designated the use of the helicopters. There were some Volvo half-tracks later but they were for the artillery regiments mostly. Because we landed with the Paras we had no vehicles and it was a favour if you got one. We were lucky from the San Carlos breakout because we were a part of 3 Para. support company. Us, with the mortars, and the anti-tank, as we were heavy support weapons we got designated a helicopter for this initial move.

We got a Sea King to move us and all the other groups. It was quite impressive down at the landing zone to see all these choppers. They were seconded to us by the Royal Navy because we'd lost all our Chinooks. We were all strapped in with our equipment and there was this air crew man with the big machine gun strapped to the side of the helicopter. As we lifted off I looked out through a small window. Then I saw a big Argentine helicopter bearing down on us. They had American equipment and it was one of those Huey Iraquoys which the Americans used in Vietnam. "That's an Argentine helicopter coming in!" -with these big rocket pods coming out of the side and our chopper laden with troops and equipment. I thought we'd had it here because we were vulnerable in a helicopter because there was little you can do to defend your self apart from the guy with the helicopter machine gun. This thing was coming down and the air gunner fired and gave a quick burst at the Argentine helicopter. The next minute it seemed like we were falling out of the sky as the pilot took evasive action. We were sitting there holding on and the Argentine helicopter was coming after us but I think the Sea King was faster but there we were, sitting there strapped in and the pilot was giving it full throttle. So one minute the guy sitting opposite me would be down here then the next second he would be up in the air. I would be down here and the guy next to me, he was sick all down his combat gear with the manoeuvres the pilot was executing to get away from this Argentine helicopter. We did get away from him though. Whether he fired on us I don't know. Only the gunner at the door would have known. Anyway, we landed and got out of the helicopter. We were just glad to be out of the helicopter because you were a lot safer on the ground because you feel in more control and can deal with things better. So we got to Estancia House and got dug in. There was a time when I was a bit worried though. There was a big barn and rather than have everybody stuck out in the trenches all the time we had the minimum personnel out and then (we'd) relieve the guy in the trench from those in the barn. It was freezing and if your gear got wet it stayed wet and if you dug down, it was like peat, it was waterlogged and you couldn't dig down too much and everything was soggy and damp. The weather was ok one minute then it was snow and rain the next. One night I was in this trench with the machine gun with a night sight on it and these cattle started coming round and obstructing the view. They also tried to get into the barn where the troops were. So I'm in this trench with these big beasts moving around so I was beginning to get worried in case one of them stumbled in on top of me and of course I couldn't see. So I got out of the trench and started shooing all these cattle away running about all over the place! I thought, "What if the enemy comes down now?!" They kept coming and going all night, luckily we were doing two-hour shifts only. It was just having these huge beasts in front of you and obscuring the view!

Goose Green happened on the other side of the island from where we were. We heard through the radio and were told that Goose Green had fallen. Everybody got a bit of a boost but there was a bit of a worry because we were losing so many ships, which were getting sunk and hit and the Argentine Air Force seemed to be relentless. The attacks they pressed home seemed to make our morale to go down. Some were thinking that if we were going to lose the Navy we'd had it as there's no one to protect us because the Harriers were our air cover. This ship sank, that ship sank, we were having problems with our missile system because sometimes missiles were being fired and (then) just falling into the peat. We didn't know what was wrong, whether it was the damp. Suddenly, all this technology which we believed was invincible started to not work. You never thought a Royal Navy frigate would ever get sunk. It was coming down to the basic again; your rifle. The simple

> " we had just got dug in then the place erupted with tracer and machine gun fire "

equipment was the equipment that worked. To the next location - which was Teal Inlet - was another big move. It was a shame for the paras they would have to walk everywhere. The type of ground, it was all turfy and boggy without a straight level so you're going over on your ankles with all this equipment on. They were falling over and stumbling plus they are all wet. Us, being attached troops, we felt a bitty guilty. So rather than us walk with the system split and having to put it together quickly in case of attack, Hew Pike wanted the weapons system assembled for immediate use. (To this end) he wanted all the air defence troops on top of the tanks. So we got on the tanks with the missile system at the ready. On the top of these tanks we could see this huge line of infantry walking to the next position and you could see their faces looking at you and they could kill you for a ride on the tank! You didn't look them in the eye because you felt guilty!

Then we got to Teal Inlet, that's when we first got into their artillery range because it's not far from the high ground around Stanley. We dug in there again and that's where we started to experience artillery rounds. They were using air bursts and I'd thrown away my tin hat by this stage. The radio wasn't working very well and my Commander tried to get it changed but they wouldn't change it for him and told him to wait for the next location because we were lugging huge amounts of equipment, so he threw it away. This was a state of the art Marconi radio, a £1000 worth of equipment but he binned it and said, "I'm not carrying this any more it's dead weight." I had the batteries so I binned them. I was glad to get rid of them, they weren't big but they were heavy - so the tin hat went as well! It was the sheer weight of everything but it was to my regret: I have never experienced artillery fire before and I suddenly realised what a foolish thing I'd done and now all I had was my soft arctic warm hat. Then we moved forward to Mount Kent that's when the Argentine patrols started coming into contact with us. An Argentine helicopter landed near us - you can tell them by the different sound they make - and I got on the radio to the command post. I gave them the direction that I had heard it. They said that they were either dropping off troops or picking up casualties. I was a bit worried because we were in line of one of our machine guns arc of fire so if anything had happened we would be in front of it. We were told to move our location, which we did. We had just got dug in then the place erupted with tracer and machine gun fire. I remember being in my sleeping bag 'cause I'd just come off shift and I'm trying to open my sleeping bag. You sleep with your rifle and the lanyard around your wrist in your sleeping bag so that no one can take it away from you. The whole place erupted and there was my Scouse mate trying to get out of his sleeping bag and it was all confusion. We were bivied down in this trench and we heard all this gunfire so we thought a ground attack was coming in. Got out, didn't have time to put on my boots, so I was there in my socks. I couldn't find my boots. I got my rifle. There was a hillside, the whole place erupted with gunfire, there was an Argentine patrol but it never got as far as the hillside where we thought it was happening. The whole regiment, 3 para., was stood to, so we all thought it was coming in and I mind looking round asking myself, 'Am I in a good position here?' Because we had moved positions at night and we had not really sorted out where we were. I was annoyed with myself for not looking at a map and taking more time because if a ground attack comes in we will be vulnerable and we're not going to be able to defend ourselves. Two Pucaras came in to attack us that morning after the gun battle last night. Me and the Scouse lad was off shift again and there was this young lad Riley manning the missile system which was a bit of a way from where we were sleeping. There was all this shouting and screaming and we looked up and there was this Pucara coming in slow. They're not jets, they have propellers and are quite slow. They are quite dangerous because, unlike a jet, which just comes in and over, a Pucara can stay around an area. So there was this Pucara banking in like this and the machine guns were opening up and I was wondering why the lad wasn't firing his missile. The aircraft came round and there was another one coming in further back. Scouse opens up with his rifle and the tracer was just banging into this aircraft, how it stayed in the air I do not know. Everything, small arms fire was just belting right in to it. We assumed that they were looking for our artillery gun lines but had flown over the whole of 3 Para Battalion group instead. This plane just got everything. I started running up to the lad and I was screaming for him to fire, "Will you fire the bloody thing, will you fire!" He's dithering about and I thought, 'What's he doin'?' because there was this other Pucara coming in right behind. The first Pucara went over the hillside. He had fired rockets but probably out of panic he didn't hit anything and they went into the hillside before he flew away. Riley then fired the missile, which went screamin' over my head and fizzled out in the turf! It fell close to our mortar group and they had to dive for cover so we almost took out our own men! The Pucara that was following must have seen what was happening to the one in front of him and

he turned about. We loaded another missile and I asked our Commander if I could take him out. He decided to leave it because we were down to three missiles. The re-supply chain was getting thinner and thinner so we were only shooting at aircraft that were attacking us. Next day I think it was, we got attacked by Sky Hawks. They came screaming in - they just came down and over the valley and I fired the missile and one of the Sky Hawks went up and banked away and the missile narrowly missed him. The second Sky Hawk came straight on. I had spotted them at maximum range so I thought that we could get another missile in and have another go but we couldn't get the aiming unit off the empty canister. We were all screamin' and panickin' and others were firin' and there was all this noise! "Get that effin' thing off!" and I'm tryin' t' kick this thing off but the plane was commin' in, "Forget it!" and we just dived into this trench! It dropped retard bombs but by that time everybody flown into cover. If you're well dug in, you can protect yourselves from them but if you're caught out in the open with them they'll do y' because of all the bits of shrapnel that comes off them. To see these two planes screamin' in at y', evil nasty lookin' things and we're tryin' t' get this missile system on the go. The aimin' unit clicks on the canister then when you fired, you took the aiming unit off and put it on another canister. However, when you fire a missile the heat expands the clip and it won't come off until it has cooled down and when you've only got seconds to reload, well, that was at Mount Kent.

Anyway, everything was being moved up for the big push, the big ground attack that was on the high ground around Stanley. This was when the ground fighting started getting serious. We had to do a bit of walking distance this time because there were no vehicles. We got our equipment ready, rations etc. All our drinking water had to be boiled because it was all peaty, it looked like tea without milk. At about this time my toes were beginning to go numb at the tips. They wouldn't thaw out or anything and I tried to heat them over the fire. If I took my boots off and something touched my feet, like my sleeping bag, it was very painful. The paramedic said it was a mild form of trench foot so he gave me this powder stuff to put on it and I got a new set of boots, which were better but I had to break them in. They were brand new so I wore about three pairs of socks with them.

We got up just beyond Mount Kent into the valley of Mount Kent and this was where we prepared for the first of our land battles. Ours was to be Mount Longdon, which you could see from where our position was. So our artillery started pounding

> "the shell landed to the left and a big lump of shrapnel had gone into my ration pack"

them and they started getting hit but we came under their artillery fire as well. That was really frightening 'cause you can't do anything about it. Initially they started with ground burst shells, 155 shells - those huge monsters - and these things were screaming into your position. It was OK when they were landing miles away from your position, off target, but you could see they were bracketing and getting <u>on</u> target. There was an Argentine OP somewhere but it was like trying to find a needle in a haystack trying to locate them. You could see their artillery line of fire coming down towards your position. The noise, they make is a sort of zwish – a horrible sound - and everybody was hitting the deck. There's not really any cover, its just undulating hills and hillocks, there's no trees and you couldn't have a trench because its waterlogged so we were lying on the ground making ourselves as small as possible. I found the artillery the most frightening thing because there wasn't anything you could do against it. Once they had bracketed us, they just came screamin' in wham! bang! wham! bang! bang! Because it was peaty a lot of the heavy shells got absorbed into peat so that absorbed some of the explosions. It did get close because one morning I was cooking my own breakfast and the other two lads were manning the weapons system and the artillery started again and this shell just come screaming in and I thought this is it. It was so close, then that realisation if you've heard it, it has missed you because they travel faster than sound. You see the explosion first then you will hear a 'crump' then a 'zzzip' in reverse order, it's weird to experience that. So I hit the deck but it came and exploded to my left. That was a close one because I got right down and my breakfast went everywhere. I hit the deck rolled into a ball because you felt so vulnerable. I got up and my ration pack was lying to my right - the shell landed to the left and a big lump of shrapnel had gone into my ration pack and between me hitting the deck, this thing must have come flying, hit the ration pack and was sticking out of the other side. I was a bit shaken but I decided to keep the shrapnel as a souvenir. Then I got superstitious thinking the next one would get me so I binned it. We were getting pissed off because we wanted to move 'cause we were getting shelled all the time and getting more and more casualties and of course your morale starts to be undermined. Eventually everybody got their orders to move. We were all wet and soaking by this time but as soon as you have your breakfast your morale goes up. Your highlights of the day are your meals and mail. If you had some chocolate mixed with your porridge well, it made all the difference. It's amazing how you can adapt to the wet and that becomes your life. You sometimes think of people going to bars and supermarkets; it seems such a different world.

Once you adapted and you got into it, and roughed it, you think that you could live like it indefinitely. Your creature comforts mean nothing to you, your videos, going down to the pub, they meant nothing to you. You were just living for the moment. That was your little world, nothing else mattered. Getting through it and doing the business, that's all. It was just a case of beating them and going home, there was no question of losing now. We lost some people to trench foot because of the wet conditions. I remember one night in my sleeping bag; I was just freezing to death. Then trying to light a candle in my sleeping bag. When I thought my bag was warm I'd blow out the candle but the heat evaporated very quickly and I had to re-light the candle and when that got wet, I got really pissed off. Sometimes, when it rained, your sleeping bag used to slip out from underneath your ground sheet. You'd make mini tents out of your ground sheet and on one occasion at night, we camped down near a river bed. It was dry when we were first there but soon it rained and we felt our feet wet, we had slid down into a puddle and the sleeping bags were lying in this stream and everybody started losing their tempers with each other because we were soakin'! Your sleeping bag is your last sanctuary, it's warm and when that's wet your morale *really* sinks.

At night we heard these Canberra jets flying over us. I couldn't believe this, the Argentines had Canberras and were using them as bombers and you could hear World War Two sounds of bombs being dropped. It was quite away in the distance and I couldn't see who was being hit but you could hear the bombs come down wisssssssh! Luckily that was away in the distance, we couldn't have done very much about it anyway, because they would have been out of range. It would have been the Harriers who would have intercepted them.

We got all our equipment sorted out, a new radio and stuff like that. Then everybody moved up to the start line. Mount Longdon was going to be hit, that was our objective. So we moved upwards. 3 Para told us that because we can't use our missile

● A sangar style gun pit on the Falklands "This was our home on Mount Longdon"

system at night, they might need us when the battle begins to take ammunition up to the infantry and help with casualties. I thought, "Well, this is it, I'm not going to survive this." We moved up with the mortars and it was pitch black at night. The Moon came out occasionally it was quite eerie. I had a lot of respect for the infantry because they were away to fix bayonets and do hand to hand fighting. You saw them getting all their gear together and felt really humble. They were just young boys and you saw them fix their bayonets and everybody knew that people were going to die tonight. It's our own little world and a conscript's bullet does same as any other bullet. The violence that you do see is quite horrendous. We were given our orders, we were near the mortars and we would be used to carry equipment once the battle had started. Up until then it was all jets, aircraft, and things; it was all dangerous but more machine against machine and now this was more men against men.

First of all the Harriers went in, they and the artillery were pounding the target a few days before the start. It was going to be a silent attack, they didn't want to give them any warnin' but one of our lads stood on a land mine before they got close enough to the objective and that alerted all the troops on Mount Longdon. We were told there was an infantry regiment backed up by Marines on Longdon plus all the other troops on the hills round about. So this was the big push against the Argentine. Once all the high ground falls, that would be the finish. We got our fighting gear on; just the rifle, light food like chocolate bars, water bottle, lots of ammunition so everyone was tense when we moved up to the start line. They were just 18 or 19 year old lads, these boys were just youngsters and no one can take away from them what they were away to do. To me, they were brave because most people would want to run away from that. So in they went. We moved up with the mortars. The mortars were going Bang! Bang! Bang! We were supporting the infantry troops going forward. The battle took place at night and when the mortars opened up the whole place erupted with gunfire. From the battle's ferocity, you would have thought that there were hundreds of dead. The amount of explosions, machine gun fire and tracer, there was a crescendo of violence. Because it was at night you could see tracer bouncing off rocks, explosions, and you felt that no one was surviving that amount of violence. The mortars were breaking records for their rate of fire it was quite a thing to be there and be a part of it because this

was a land battle going into a full scale attack. 600 troops and weapons attacking its objective. These illuminated rounds were coming down on little parachutes and lit everything up and when they did, it would all go silent and stop. All you could see then was the rocky boulders and the rocky features. It was silent and very eerie. Then, as soon as the lights went out it would all start again, it was unbelievable. So we had to move nearer to the battle lines and Hew Pike's adjutant had brought in some anti-tank weapons to try and burst some enemy bunkers. When they fired them you just saw these lights streaking, streaking, and a *crump;* then it would go silent and then it would all start again! Some of them hit the target and the place - the violence was unbelievable. I thought again there must be hundreds dead up there. When the adjutant came up and told our group to get ready, I thought, "We've got to go into that and come out of it again." I got my gear, got my rifle, there were three of us getting ready to go up and three to stay back because 3 Para couldn't afford to lose all their air defence. We're moved up to a little line behind the mortars and we stayed there and watched the battle. We weren't called forward for the rest of the battle. We were more spectators than those taking part. We were never called forward to my great relief. They had problems getting the troops forward so they called in more artillery. The battle lasted about 12 hours, it doesn't sound long but when you're there seeing that level of violence it's long enough. Casualties started to filter through and by first light we started to take a lot of positions and they'd knocked the Argentines off the forward slopes. As our detachment was moving up we came under enemy mortar and artillery fire. That was a mixture between air and ground bursts and there was lots of running for cover again. 3 Para withdrew slightly because they were having problems with snipers

holding them up and were taking bad casualties with snipers 'cause a sniper can hold the whole lot down because you don't know where they are. Tracer, machine-gun fire, explosions, the anti-tank weapons were happening all over the place and there was a battle to the right of me it was either Two Sisters or Tumble Down - I can't remember now. This was the battle which we were concerned with and also there was another battle to the right so you can imagine the whole horizon at night over miles and miles with all this tracer, it was awesome to see. Eventually 3 Para started to push the Argentines off Mount Longdon and drive them on to the reverse slopes and as they were moving we moved along

> "he would occasionally tread on one of the bodies and he would be apologising to the bodies as he did so"

with them. As we got into position at the foot of Mount Longdon the carnage was horrendous. I still hadn't got my steel helmet and the artillery fire was as bad as ever. There were bodies and bits of bodies lying everywhere. We saw our lads to the right. We had to help to put them into body bags and it was horrible and impersonal because it was these silver body bags with three handles either side and a name at the front. I can't remember how many bodies there were but there were quite a few. There was one lad who was not in a body bag he was lying dead and they had put a beret over his face. He just looked like a wax dummy to me, he just looked like he was sleeping and he still had all his kit on. We started loading the body bags on to these Volvo half-tracks. I remember the first time I picked up a body bag with a lad in it. It was a strange and emotional feeling you felt the weight, there was somebody in there. Inside the bag was a young lad from Manchester, a Lance Corporal I only found out later that he was from Manchester because I remember seeing his name in the paper. When you first feel the weight of somebody in a bag it's horrible; you just saw these bags and it's only when you're lifting them that you feel the weight of the people inside and there was a big long line of them. Some people can just go about their business but with others you could see it had a big effect on them, everybody is different. So we started to load the bodies on to the back of these half track vehicles and as the boy who was inside loading them had little room he would occasionally tread on one of the bodies and he would be apologising to the bodies as he did so. Obviously, there were also Argentine dead, the place was just carnage, just carnage.

Trevor: Did you just pick up your own people?

Colin: To start with yes, the Argentine dead were left until we got our own lads sorted out. There were prisoners there, they were starting to come down and they had to be kept away from the bodies. The shelling started again and everybody had to run for cover and leave what you were doing. Eventually we got the bodies away. We went up and got dug in. Mount Longdon is like a big rocky hill, it's not a mountain, it's a huge hillside with rocky features. There's blood on the side of the stones and there's like minced meat splattered now and again and there's field dressings covered in blood and bits of flesh. Amongst all this you could see ammunition and boots. You could see that something nasty had gone on here. There was lots of ammunition, hats and equipment lying about. So we gets up on to Longdon and the shelling started in earnest and because everything is

> " **they were just young boys and you'd see photographs of their families strewn around them** "

rocky, the shells weren't being absorbed by the ground they were smashing into the rock face so you could imagine the amount of shrapnel that was coming off. The shells would scream into your position and you couldn't go anywhere, we just ducked down and this was when we started taking more casualties. There was a lad down just to my left, there was a drop down from where I was. He got hit. He was screaming for his Mom. The stretcher-bearers came in and moved him away then there was another lad who got hit and he was screaming. I remember looking, you could see his legs had gone he was just screaming and rolling about the ground. I couldn't do anything for him at that time because I was on a rocky ledge and he was about a 25ft drop below me. A lot of shells were landing on the ground and I thought I'll be a bit safer here because they will drop past me but when they started firing air bursts, I was exposed at the back. The air bursts started coming down and the shrapnel was slamming off all the rocks. So I thought, "I'll not stay here," then I got my rifle and made my way to an old Argentine bunker. The shelling came down and was smashing into the rocks so I didn't stay there and so I was bouncing over all these rocks and went in to this bunker but ten other guys had beaten me to it! So there were ten of them huddled into this bunker. The Argentines had constructed this bunker to be defended from British attacks so the entrance to it was now at the wrong end. I could only get down at the entrance 'cause they'd dug it under a big rock slab, so I'm trying to push my way down and I'm in this exposed part. There's abandoned mortar ammunition and all sorts lying around, so if a round gets hit it explodes so this was all lying around about us, it was horrendous. Every time the firing would stop we would go to our positions again but the artillery rounds I found really scary 'cause y' can't do anything about it, you're so vulnerable and helpless. You felt for a lot of the lads who took part in the hand to hand fighting and you saw the looks on their faces and you felt that you wanted to help them. There were people who you'd got to know from earlier on during the landings then later, you would hear that they had been killed or injured. I remember one lad - we always planned to go down and do this or do that we were all going to go down and have a barbecue - he was killed. One day I made myself a bit of breakfast then I looked to the right and there was a hand all by itself. It was just ripped off from the wrist. When you were searching positions you'd lift a helmet and there was a back of a head in it. Argentines were still lying about, they were just young boys and you'd see photographs of their families strewn around them.

One incident that got me a bitty was one of our own lads. All the people who'd been killed or injured were stripped of their equipment and (this) was put in a big pile. What happens is that if you have lost anything or something was damaged it was quite alright for you to take what you need. I mind going to this pack, I wanted a hat but it was full of blood so I threw that then there was a pack which had been dumped and lying outside of it was a birthday card from his family saying, 'Hello.' It was to their dad and that kinda stuff from his kiddies and you could see their innocent little writing.

● Cuttings showing Colin recieving his award on his return from the Falklands

You would know that their dad was dead. I was sick of killing by this stage. Sick of guns, sick of killin', and sick of everything but after it's finished you can't just get up and say, "Right, the wars over." because it's changed you. Then we started to take sniper fire from the four positions. Also mortars were coming in. I found them a bit more dangerous because they don't make much sound when they come in. A shell will make a big screaming noise whereas a mortar will come in almost silently and you just hear it in the last few seconds so you have no warning. With shells you seem to get more warning. I remember looking out with binoculars and you could see Port Stanley and the next thing I heard was a crack! I didn't know where it came from and I couldn't see anybody, all I heard was this swisssh and then a crack. It was a round which had pinged off a rock. Obviously someone had caught me looking through the binos. I got my head down then and decided not to stick my head up over there again. With sniper fire you can't hear it and they can zap you at say 600 metres and they are dug well in and you just can't see them. I didn't know anything about it until I heard the crack. Then these three Sky Hawks came in and I thought, "Here we go again we're going to be attacked." So we got the weapons system on but they flew right passed us. I could have banged them, they were in close enough range but we were down to two missiles and this time we had no re-supply so the Commander said, "Don't take them on. The missiles we've got need to be saved for defensive positions." If we'd have fired on them and later we'd come under attack, that would have been us finished. The whole task force was getting low on ammunition so we were told to conserve ammunition.

We were told that the next stage was that if the Argentinians did not surrender then we would have to go to Port Stanley and it would be house to house fighting. Everybody was getting geared up for that, we were consolidating our ammunition and heavy guns and sitting waiting about. Then the next day it came over the radio that the Argentines had surrendered. There had been another battle in between -Wireless Ridge - but that was done by 2 para. Anyway, it came over the radio that a white flag was flying over Port Stanley. The relief that drained out of y' was unbelievable it wasn't elation, it wasn't joy, it was relief that the killing had stopped.

We had to stay in that location in those positions because there were still some units of Argentine troops out there who wouldn't have known of the surrender, so we went into defensive positions. There was a flap after that because we got news that there were 60 to 70 Argentine troops coming in from our left flank on Mount Longdon. One of the Officers shouted, "Stand to! Stand to!" and we got prepared for attack. I couldn't believe this so the heart rate and adrenaline started to go again, bayonet fixed, got myself into a good firing position set my sights at three 100 and started looking around for blind spots. I've done it again, I've got a good arc of fire but I can't see anybody to my right. However, I worked out a way of bailing out if things got bad. Everybody is stood by their weapons, machine guns, and we saw these guys coming up in the distance and everybody is getting ready to fire but it never happened because the troops we saw coming disappeared in a different direction. Then it came over the radio some garbled message that we should stand down again.

The next thing was clearing up Mount Longdon and trying to get all the Argentine bodies together, getting all the weapons together and putting them in a pile. Even when we left there was still a lot of carnage. We were there for two more nights before we moved into Stanley. We were the rear party because a lot of people had moved off the mountain. At night, patrolling around, there were still these bodies and bits of people still lying about. We had tried to collect the Argentinian bodies but there were a lot lying everywhere. We just cleaned up where our position was and round about. We checked the bodies for booby traps. We couldn't pick up cans of Coke because many were booby traps. It was a favourite one; it was a Coke can with the bottom cut out but the top was still intact. You would look at it thinking it was a full tin of Coke but there was a grenade stuck inside it with the pin out. The can holds the handle in so when you pick up the can the grenade, being heavy, falls out, the handle springs open arming the grenade which then explodes. They booby trapped a lot of stuff so you couldn't touch anything.

Eventually, a chopper came and we got choppered into Port Stanley that's where the whole garrison of troops were moving in. There were still troops on West Falklands and they hadn't surrendered yet so we might have had to go and do that. However, they did eventually surrender so that was alright. The people who had lived in Port Stanley had either gone back to the UK or had gone to other people. So some of us were billeted in these lovely bungalows and there were all these grotty, hairy arsed British Paratroopers stomping all over their houses. The military police were called in, there were big food containers with lots of goodies but we were told just to leave it. So there were about 50 guys just squashed into one of these bungalows with a nice kitchen and garage, the guys car was still in there. It was the first time that we were sleeping in a warm dry environment.

Trevor: Were your feet still sore?

Colin: Oh yes, they were still numb even when I came back to the UK. It took us three and a half weeks to get back home and they were still numb. I mind going to see my doctor when I came home on leave to Aberdeen that was four weeks by then.

They eventually thawed out though. Anyway, we had a lot of Argentine troops who had been taken prisoner, thousands of them. We put them into work parties and then we had to guard them. This was the first time that I got to speak to them. You didn't hate them or anything like that, you felt sorry for them because they were just young boys like ourselves. Conscripts, there was a misconception about these conscripts. It was thought that they weren't doing much in the way of fighting but it took 12 hours for a Parachute Regiment to clear them off Mount Longdon so it wasn't a walk over. They stuck it out because they were backed up by Argentine marines and sniper fire. Of 3 Para, almost a third of them, 26 or 27 were killed and 50 odd wounded, now that's 70 odd casualties taken out in one action. So anyway, we were in Port Stanley and we were guarding the prisoners. We used to give them sweets but they thought we might be trying to poison them because they were a bit wary. But some of these guys were big huge chaps and I was a bit wary because sometimes you'd have maybe five or six of them or maybe more and that would be your group that you'd be responsible for and you'd just be standing there with your rifle. Some of them must have looked at me and thought, "Is this what's beaten us!" because I was a small boy compared to some o' them. These ships came in and we arranged for them, thousands of them, to be shipped away. We actually got on quite well with them and there was no animosity between us.

I couldn't wait to get home, I couldn't stand the sight of a rifle and all my pals were glad it was over. It was your job and you had to do it but you're glad when it's finished. I had another year and a half to do in the army, we had a three week journey back on the boat. The rules were relaxed and you could wear civilian clothes. The paratroopers, they got all the lime light but they deserved it, they had the hardest job and bore the brunt of the casualties as well, they got flown back from the Ascension Islands but we took three weeks on a boat but it was great commin' into Southampton. There were thousands of people lined up to greet us, tears runnin' down your eyes it was brilliant. It was elation then. For the lads that came from say Newcastle or Scotland got transport laid on and I got a Land Rover to take me all the way from Southampton to Aberdeen!

I'm glad that I had that experience and it made me appreciate all the things that I took for granted. Just goin' to a pub, such a simple delight. Going into a shop for a paper just normal simple things like that. I mind commin' home and going to the shops for messages and things and I just couldn't believe where I'd been and now it's gone and back to normality. It was strange just strange.

To me, the real unsung hero was my Mum who had lots of sleepless nights and never knowing what was happening. She was on her own just having lost my Dad the year before. She coped brilliantly!

Liberation of Kuwait

"We were going out to the Gulf knowing that we were going to a biological/chemical environment"

Liberation of Kuwait 1990

*F*INDING ITSELF IN SERIOUS DEBT AFTER ITS WAR WITH IRAN, *Iraq desperately needed to rebuild its economy. However with the OPEC countries (such as Kuwait and United Arab Emirates) holding down the price of oil, Iraq's main export opportunity was stifled. Saddam Hussein, inheriting this critical situation but with a substantial war machine at his disposal, insisted that Kuwait had been drilling for oil on land belonging to Iraq. He demanded compensation of $27 billion and the return of the disputed territory. When Kuwait refused to pay, Iraqi forces invaded, (2nd August 1990); this prompted the formation of a coalition of Arab and Western nations who were united in their opposition to his aggression. The ensuing conflict was both vicious and short, culminating in the 'Mother of all Battles' and the crushing defeat of Iraq.*

Lawrence Baldwin: We were going out to the Gulf knowing that we were going to a biological/chemical environment, which we did with considerable trepidation because we hadn't done it before in anger, as it were. We'd practised for it but we were going for real now. We had done our training and hopefully we could draw on that. We had to take with us all the suits, pills and inoculations that would give us some sort of protection. We weren't issued with any desert fatigues till the conflict started, so we were out there in green jungle fatigues due to initial logistical problems, and we didn't get desert boots until the conflict was over and we were going home! Our first day was at Al-Jubail before we were mobilised and sent off in convoy.

We were in the Gulf to repair helicopters under battle damage conditions; I was in a naval unit seconded to the army for as long as we were needed. That included fixing *any* military helicopter that required battle damage repairs. We had the experience in the Falklands to base our activities on. Our competence was such that we could, depending on the damage, rework helicopters to factory repair specifications rather than what we called battle damage repairs. We were very skilled helicopter repairers. We were given Land Rovers, we got hold of a truck eventually but initially we only had the Land Rover and the trailer behind. Before we mobilised we

manufactured formers and plates; the formers and skins we kept in the trailer. In the desert we were living in tents, which we also kept with us, in fact we were a totally self - contained unit.

David: Can you remember any specific damage that you had to repair?

Lawrence: You'll see there (referring to a photograph) that we had one damaged aeroplane but the damage to that one was so great that it had to be returned to the workshop. As you can see it was split in half. Interestingly this wasn't through battle; it was a heavy landing. In fact there *were*

● Royal Marine Westland Commando beside a ubiquitous 'bus shelter'

● An airman (Sgt. Ian Cowie of Aberdeen) in full NBC suit outside an air raid shelter in Dharan.

no incidents because the Gulf conflict was so quick and we met so little resistance that we had no battle damaged helicopters. We were there at Al-Jubail and then convoyed to KKMC (King Khalid Military Camp). Then I detached to the desert to an army unit and ended up to just below the Iraqi border. When the push came, they went up into Iraq and turned right into Kuwait; we were behind so that any repairs that had to be done were in a secure area.

What actually happened was, because there was no resistance the troops just shot off. The front line met with no resistance whatsoever and before we knew it they were in Kuwait City whilst we were still waiting for orders. We had to do a recce ahead to find out where everybody was! We then came back into a holding unit to wait for orders to advance and what happened was the cessation came. Because there was no likelihood of any action and all the skirmishes had finished, I decided to detach myself back to my unit.

David: Was your unit ever attacked?

Lawrence: No, we were always kept in a position behind the front line but we were made aware that there were skirmishes coming in towards us as well as us going towards them. What our troops were trying to do was to send in reccies to get them to

"she made us put our guns through the X-ray machine!"

fight and to find out where they were; (after this) they would just blanket the area with HE. There was also the possibility that they would do the same to us. We were always ready and waiting but the main danger was from enemy air raids for which we had to wear chemical suits. There were four occasions when the alarms went off and if you heard an air raid warning you got dressed immediately.

We were there for 'Desert Shield' as well as 'Desert Storm' so we were there as a peacetime presence and then as a military force. Because we were a special unit everybody wanted us to be attached to them but we didn't want to be attached to any body because as soon as you were attached you were another bunch of bodies to be put on a duty roster and to do what ever else. We were basically a team of Officers and Chief Petty Officers trained to be a single entity. We mobilised first of all in Britain and we flew out from Brize in a Kuwait Jumbo jet. The Land Rovers were already out there waiting.

So we were dispatched from Brize Norton and this young female, an RAF Movements Officer, had made a decision to put us all through the X-ray machine and she wasn't going to change it. We were in the departure lounge fully booted and spurred. We had our fighting webbing on, all our fighting kit; we had bags of NBC equipment and our SA 80 rifles. And this Movements Officer, this young girl, had been told that when we embark on the civil aircraft everything had to go through the X ray machine and she made us put our guns through the X-ray machine! Everybody kept saying, "It's a gun! I don't know what you're going to X-ray but it's a gun! If you find a gun inside it let me know!" Normally you prove your weapons by pulling the breach back. An inspecting Officer would say, "Clear breech and ease springs." There's no round in the chamber, you ease the spring back and you release the trigger and that is your weapon proved. It took us *two hours* because not only did we have to put the guns through he X-ray machine but every time we walked through (the screening port) we set off the metal detectors; we had webbing and all the fastenings are metal, in fact we had metal in everything! We had to strip down and put all our belongings through the X-ray machine —she was in charge and she was getting crosser and crosser and not budging at all!

So then we got out to Al-Jubail and then we went by convoy out to the desert. When we went to KKMC we went under canvas. The Land Rovers were kitted out for a communications role so we had to rip out all the bits and pieces inside so that we could get three people in plus all our kit and plus the trailers. One of the main things we had to do when we got to Al-Jubail was - as per good military practice - oil our weapons. However, unfortunately we had to spend three or four hours

● Sgt. Ian Cowie, right, in 'informal' desert dress; note the tropical style on right and desert style on left (worn by Cpl. Avon Saunders)

a day (after that) drying our weapons out because we couldn't fire them due to the accumulation of oil and sand. One of the main things we did morning and afternoon and sometimes in the evening was to strip the gun down and leave it in the sun to dry it. Gun metal absorbs oil so you had to leave it out wipe it then put it in a bag, cover it, leave it then take it to bits and dry it out again. We were given an SA80 which was an up-to-date weapon and when I dispatched to the army I took 500 rounds (of ammunition) which should have been enough for the four of us for the duration of the trip to the Regiment. The reasoning was that if we hit a problem we had ammunition after which we could use army's. So, we had SA80's which had 5. something mm. bullets. - state of the art - we got to this army aircraft workshop unit that I was attached to and they had SLR's with 7.62 mm. ammunition! My unit and I could each fire our guns 100 times then we went home because we had no bullets!

Prior to being convoyed they had managed to get some desert trousers so half of us had got kitted out and half of us didn't mostly because some of the kit didn't fit.

That was our line of tents (indicating the tents on a photograph). This shows a slit trench in case of attack and they actually did get hit the day after I left with a Scud missile. As soon as the bang went off every body dived for shelter except the sailors who came out with their cameras because the Scud had been taken out by a Patriot missile! We had early warning defence systems with electric missiles so effective that the Scud didn't detonate, instead it was hit by the Patriot missile and that put an end to it. So the sailors were taking photographs of the falling debris until the Warrant Officer of the Marines screamed at them to take cover.

David: What is happening in this picture?

Lawrence: As you can see, it was bitterly cold. It was about eight o'clock at night, we were just about ready to go to bed and it's about minus five. We woke up one morning to find everything covered with a quarter of an inch of frost.

David: So you had jungle gear and desert gear, how did you keep warm?

Lawrence: We had to get dressed at night to go to bed. We had arctic sleeping bags. As to other gear we'd got, we had glasses and that's cheese. We managed to get to a shop before we left and we took acres of food with us. There is a photo here which shows how we improved our living quarters. We actually built a table and we used to go round to KKMC and commandeer what we wanted.

● All over and Lawrence Baldwin about to rejoin Navy. Note their treasured handmade table on the roof of the Land Rover.

Building materials were what we needed, otherwise things were pretty awful.

That was after the first air raid warning at Al-Jabail which went on for two hours.

That's the NBC suit, which is impregnated with charcoal on the inside.

David: What other things did you do to make life tolerable?

Lawrence: The toilet roll was a necessity. That (pointing to photo) was what we called a 'desert rose', that's where you peed and that (pointing to another picture) was the most dehumanising piece of kit that they ever came up with; we called it the 'bus shelter'. That is where you crapped but all it consisted of was a length of wood with four holes in it, no separation, and a forty gallon drum underneath. There were people who refused to go when anybody else was in there. You had to take your weapon with you as well and if you were unlucky enough to go before the end of the day - before they had emptied out the drums - it was enough to turn you, it really was. If you were there when a helicopter was coming in to land or there was a dust storm and the back flap was open everything went back up the way - and I mean everything! If you were on your own and there was a wind there was an affectionate thing called 'getting stung by the shitty butterfly'! This was toilet paper that had blown back up again. It was a nightmare.

What you need (in these situations) is the basic comforts. As you see, there is a two man tent which was when we had just arrived so then what we did to give us a bit of protection was, we covered them to join them together. Then after we got some wood we made the table. It then became a communal area and a home from home.

This trench was for water when it rained or if anything spilled, it ran down. Also, as you can see, there is a generator in there supplying 240 volts, so we had electricity. We were the only unit with electricity and at one point we actually fed the whole of the camp city. That trench helped as an air inlet (for the generator) as well.

The most valuable bit of kit that you got was wood. When we went to fill the Land Rovers (with fuel) we detoured the on way back to see what was available. We had nothing and we made do with what we had around.

That was prior to going home as well. That's a washing line and I thought I'd get the sunset and the washing line and you could hear the bombs going off and see the B52's going over.

This one is of the oil-wells that were set on fire. If you drove through it you were left with a black film over everything.

Glossary

ADC – Aide de Camp

AGRA - Army Group Royal Artillery

ATS – Auxiliary Territorial Services

Basha – Army slang for Personal Shelter

BEF - British Expeditionary Force

B.52 – American heavy bomber

BHQ – Battalion Headquarters

BSA – Birmingham Small Arms. A British weapons manufacturer. Produced HMG's and motorcycles in WWII.

BTY - Battery

CB – Confined to Barracks

CB's – ('Sea Bees'). American Marine Corps Engineers. (Construction Battalion).

CO - Commanding Officer

DR - Dispatch Rider

DUKW – American amphibious lorry, initials taken from the manufacturers nomenclature and conveniently pronounced as 'duck'

ENSA – Entertainment National Services Association

FSMO - Full Service Marching Order

Gaja – Slang for elephant.

GOC – General Officer Commanding

HAA – Heavy Anti-Aircraft (gun regiment)

HD – Highland Division

HE - High Explosive

'Honey' – British name for the American Stuart tank in their service. The M.3. light tank

HMG – Heavy Machine Gun

HQ - Headquarters

LCI – Landing Craft, Infantry

LCT – Landing Craft, Tank

LMG – Light Machine Gun

LST – Landing Ship, Tank

KKMC – King Khalid Military Camp

MC - Military Cross

MM - Military medal

MO - Medical Officer

NAAFI – Navy, Army and Air-Force Institute (an organisation for running canteens for service personnel)

NATO - North Atlantic Treaty Organisation (A coalition of western nations including Britain and America)

NBC - Chemical warfare suit (Nuclear, Biological, Chemical)

NCO - Non-Commissioned Officer

'Nissen' (huts) – semi-cylindrical corrugated iron buildings

OP - Observation Post

Panzerbuchse 41 – German light gun with excellent armour piercing abilities at short range

Panzerfaust – German man-portable anti-tank weapon, similar to a bazooka

PIAT – Projectile Infantry Anti-Tank, a man-portable anti-tank weapon

PSM – Platoon Sergeant Major. An early WWII rank abolished end of 1940

PT – Physical Training

PU – Pick Up (truck)

RAF – Royal Air Force; the British air force

RAMC – Royal Army Medical Corps

RHQ – Regimental Headquarters

RV – Rendezvous Point

SA 80 - British army rifle

SAS - Special Air Service; (British Special Forces unit).

'Sherman' – American medium tank also used by the British, French and Russian armies

SLR - British Self Loading Rifle

SPG – Self Propelled Gun (an artillery piece on a wheeled or tracked chassis)

SS – Schutzstaffel (German WWII elite troops) – 'Protection Squad'

'Stuka' – Junkers Ju. 87; German dive-bomber

TA – Territorial Army

TAC HQ – Tactical Headquarters

'Tiger' – German heavy tank

TUC – Trades Union Council

VC – Victoria Cross; highest British award for military bravery.

VE day – Victory in Europe

VJ day – Victory in Japan

WAAF – Women's Auxiliary Air Force

Credits

We are grateful for the assistance of:

The Aberdeen Journals
The Imperial War Museum
The Tank Museum
The Highlanders Museum in Aberdeen
The Highlanders Museum in Inverness
Aberdeen Trades Council
Odhams Press Ltd
Lieutenant-Colonel Alistair Cumming OBE
Tom Cox
Cath Fleming
Graeme Fleming
Joyce Pelella
Bill Reaper
Ian Cowie

Special thanks to:

Robert Bauld, Fiona Gibson, David Kilgour, Ann Lavery,
Justine Robertson, Jim Milne, Val Plante, Brian Grassom,
Peter Rennie, W.W. Smith, George Scott and
Aberdeen Urban Studies Centre

Editor and Project leader – **David Atherton, Arts & Recreation Department, Aberdeen City Council**

Transcriber and Researcher – **Trevor Davies, Arts & Recreation Department, Aberdeen City Council**

Designer – **Bill Smith, Legal & Corporate Services Department, Aberdeen City Council**

Project assisted by **Amy Fraser, Arts & Recreation Department, Aberdeen City Council**

We're Far Fae Hame Now!

ABERDEEN
CITY COUNCIL

An Arts and Recreation Publication